PERSPECTIVES

ON THE SABBATH

BOOKS IN THIS SERIES

Perspectives on Children's Spiritual Formation: Four Views, ed. Michael Anthony; contributors: Greg Carlson, Tim Ellis, Trisha Graves, Scottie May

Perspectives on Christian Worship: Five Views, ed. J. Matthew Pinson; contributors: Ligon Duncan, Dan Kimball, Michael Lawrence and Mark Dever, Timothy Quill, Dan Wilt

Perspectives on Church Government: Five Views, ed. R. Stanton Norman and Chad Brand; contributors: Daniel Akin, James Garrett, Robert Reymond, James White, Paul Zahl

Perspectives on the Doctrine of God: Four Views, ed. Bruce A. Ware; contributors: Paul Helm, Robert E. Olson, John Sanders, Bruce A. Ware

Perspectives on Family Ministry: Three Views, ed. Timothy Paul Jones; contributors: Timothy Paul Jones, Paul Renfro, Brandon Shields, Randy Stinson, Jay Strother

Perspectives on Election: Five Views, ed. Chad Brand; contributors: Jack W. Cottrell, Clark Pinnock, Robert L. Reymond, Thomas B. Talbott, Bruce A. Ware

Perspectives on Your Child's Education: Four Views, ed. Timothy Paul Jones; contributors: Mark Eckel, G. Tyler Fischer, Timothy Paul Jones, Troy Temple, Michael S. Wilder

Perspectives on the Ending of Mark: Four Views, ed. David Alan Black; contributors: Darrell Bock, Keith Elliott, Maurice Robinson, Daniel Wallace

Perspectives on Spirit Baptism: Five Views, ed. Chad Brand; contributors: Ralph Del Colle, H. Ray Dunning, Larry Hart, Stanley Horton, Walter Kaiser Jr.

PERSPECTIVES

ON THE SABBATH

4 VIEWS

CHARLES P. ARAND · CRAIG L. BLOMBERG
SKIP MACCARTY · JOSEPH A. PIPA

EDITED BY CHRISTOPHER JOHN DONATO

B&H
ACADEMIC

NASHVILLE, TENNESSEE

Perspectives on the Sabbath: Four Views

Copyright © 2011 by Christopher John Donato

All rights reserved.

ISBN: 978-0-8054-4821-4

Published by B&H Publishing Group
Nashville, Tennessee

Dewey Decimal Classification: 263
Subject Heading: SABBATH\WORSHIP\CHURCH HISTORY

Printed in the United States of America
1 2 3 4 5 6 7 8 9 10 11 12 • 18 17 16 15 14 13 12 11
VP

Contents

For Lizzy Bee,
whose laughter fills our house

In memoriam
Samuele Bacchiocchi

Abbreviations

AB	Anchor Bible
ABD	*Anchor Bible Dictionary*, ed. D. N. Freedman. New York: Doubleday, 1992
AJT	*Asia Journal of Theology*
ANF	*The Ante-Nicene Fathers*
AUSS	Andrews University Seminary Studies
BDAG	Bauer, W., F. W. Danker, W. F. Arndt, and F. W. Gingrich, *Greek-English Lexicon of the New Testament and Other Early Christian Literature*. 3rd ed.
BDB	Brown, F., S. R. Driver, and C. A. Briggs. *A Hebrew and English Lexicon of the Old Testament*
BECNT	Baker Exegetical Commentary on the New Testament
CBQ	*Catholic Biblical Quarterly*
HALOT	Koehler, L., W. Baumgartner, and J. J. Stamm, *The Hebrew and Aramaic Lexicon of the Old Testament*, trans. M. E. J. Richardson
HBT	*Horizons in Biblical Theology*
HTR	*Harvard Theological Review*
ICC	*International Critical Commentary*
IDB	*Interpreter's Dictionary of the Bible*, ed. G. A. Buttrick et al. New York: Abingdon, 1962
Int	*Interpretation*
JBL	*Journal of Biblical Literature*
JETS	*Journal of the Evangelical Theological Society*
JSNT	*Journal for the Study of the New Testament*
JSNTSup	Journal for the Study of the Old Testament: Supplement Series
LCC	Library of Christian Classics. Philadelphia, 1953–
LQ	*The Lutheran Quarterly*
LXX	Septuagint

NAC	New American Commentary
NIB	*The New Interpreter's Bible*
NICNT	New International Commentary on the New Testament
NICOT	New International Commentary on the Old Testament
NIDOTTE	*New International Dictionary of Old Testament Theology and Exegesis*
NIGTC	New International Greek Testament Commentary
NovT	*Novum Testamentum*
NovTSup	Novum Testamentum Supplement Series
NPNF²	A Select Library of the Nicene and Post-Nicene Fathers of the Christian Church, Series 2
NTS	*New Testament Studies*
OTL	Old Testament Library
ResQ	*Restoration Quarterly*
Str-B	Strack, H. L., and P. Billerbeck, *Kommentar zum Neuen Testament aus Talmud und Midrasch*, 6 vols.
TDNT	*Theological Dictionary of the New Testament,* ed. G. Kittel and G. Friedrich, trans. G. W. Bromiley. 10 vols. Grand Rapids: Eerdmans, 1964–74
TDOT	*Theological Dictionary of the Old Testament*
TOTC	Tyndale Old Testament Commentaries
TrinJ	*Trinity Journal*
TynB	*Tyndale Bulletin*
VC	*Vigiliae christianae*
VE	*Vox evangelica*
WBC	Word Biblical Commentary
WCF	Westminster Confession of Faith
WLC	Westminster Larger Catechism
WSC	Westminster Shorter Catechism
WTJ	*Westminster Theological Journal*
ZNW	*Zeitschrift für die neutestamentliche Wissenschaft und die Kunde der älteren Kirche*

Contributors

Charles P. Arand serves as chairman of the department of systematic theology and holds the Waldemar and June Schuette Chair in systematic theology at Concordia Seminary, where he has served in various capacities since 1988. Dr. Arand earned his B.A. from Concordia College and his M.Div., S.T.M., and Th.D. from Concordia Seminary. From 1984 to 1987, he served as pastor of St. John's Lutheran–New Minden, Nashville, Illinois, and St. Luke's Lutheran, Covington, Illinois. He translated the Apology of the Augsburg Confession for the Kolb-Wengert edition of the *Book of Concord*. In addition to many articles, he is author of *That I May Be His Own: An Overview of Luther's Catechisms* and (co-authored with Robert Kolb) *The Genius of Luther's Theology: A Wittenberg Way of Thinking for the Contemporary Church*.

Craig L. Blomberg joined the faculty of Denver Seminary in 1986 and is currently distinguished professor of New Testament. He received a B.A. from Augustana College and an M.A. from Trinity Evangelical Divinity School, and he completed his Ph.D. at Aberdeen University in Scotland. Before joining the faculty of Denver Seminary, he taught at Palm Beach Atlantic College and was a research fellow in Cambridge, England, with Tyndale House. In addition to writing numerous articles in professional journals, multi-author works, and dictionaries or encyclopedias, he has authored or edited twenty books, including *The Historical Reliability of the Gospels* and *A Handbook of New Testament Exegesis*.

Christopher John Donato has served *Tabletalk* magazine in various editorial capacities over the past seven years, most recently as senior editor. He is now an editor- and writer-at-large. He received his B.A. and B.S. from John Brown University and an M.A.T.S. from Reformed Theological Seminary. He has written several articles for *Tabletalk* and was recently published in the *Harvard Theological Review* (January 2011). *Perspectives on the Sabbath: Four Views* is the first book he has edited.

Skip MacCarty has been a pastor for forty-four years, serving in Utah and Michigan. For twenty-five years he has pastored at Pioneer Memorial Church on the Andrews University campus in Berrien Springs, Michigan, organizing PMC's major public and media-based evangelistic initiatives. He holds a B.A. from La Sierra College, and an M.Div. and a D.Min. from the Seventh-day Adventist Theological Seminary at Andrews University. He is author of *In Granite or Ingrained? What the Old and New Covenants Reveal about the Gospel, the Law, and the Sabbath* and co-author with Pamela Coburn-Litvak, Ph.D., of *Stress: Beyond Coping*, a faith-based stress management seminar and e-learning course.

Joseph A. Pipa is president and professor of historical and systematic theology at Greenville Presbyterian Theological Seminary. He earned his B.A. from Belhaven College, an M.Div. from Reformed Theological Seminary, and a Ph.D. from Westminster Theological Seminary. Prior to serving at Greenville Presbyterian Theological Seminary, Dr. Pipa pastored for twenty-three years at Tchula Presbyterian Church in Tchula, Mississippi, Covenant Presbyterian Church in Houston, Texas, and, while teaching at Westminster Seminary California, planted Trinity Presbyterian Church in Escondido, California. In addition to writing a number of articles and essays, he has authored or edited ten books, including *The Lord's Day* and *Galatians: God's Proclamation of Liberty*.

Acknowledgments

There are several people whose help has been invaluable and without whom I could not have begun, much less finished, this project. Pride of place goes to my wife, Elizabeth, through whom Christ drew me to love His bride, as well as the living orthodoxy she protects. Her tireless loyalty, patience, understanding, and keen insight over the almost two decades we've known each other have sanctified me in more ways than she knows. A theologian in her own right, she has proven to be my best reader over the years, even in the midst of the persistent calling she fulfills as the mother of our two boys.

Next comes my colleague, Dr. Keith A. Mathison, with whom, over many lunches, the ideas for this project were hatched. As we've both thought through the larger issues the Sabbath question addresses, his clarifying and challenging thoughts, especially as various portions of the manuscript were turned in, have prepared me to edit this book in numerous ways. My fellow *Tabletalk* colleagues must also be mentioned—Burk Parsons, Robert Rothwell, and Scott Devor—all of whom have listened to me blather on about the intricacies of one obscure point or another as it relates to the subject matter of this work. Their willingness to engage the material and their encouragements along the way have given me much support. Also, the flexibility afforded me to work on projects such as this by Dr. R. C. Sproul and the leadership of Ligonier Ministries has been, of course, integral, and I am indebted to them for their generosity. Drs. John Frame, Frank James, and Bruce Waltke, under whose tutelages I sat intermittently during seminary in the early 2000s, provided me with the first real opportunities to wrestle with many of the foundational theological, historical, and biblical issues undergirding the discussions taking place in this volume. Like good professors ought, they didn't tell students *what* to think but instead taught them *how* to think (even at the risk of disagreement). Their positive effects are being felt to this day.

A word about the one to whom this book is offered *in memoriam*: Dr. Samuele Bacchiocchi joined us early on in this project as the representative of Seventh-day Adventist theology and practice with respect to the day of worship,[1] and the writing of his essay was well underway when in December 2008 he entered *"la gloria di colui che tutto move."*[2] A belated thank you is due for his commitment in the midst of suffering.

Finally, a hearty thanks to B&H Publishing for taking on this project and granting me the freedom to make it become everything it needed to be, Ray Clendenen's enthusiasm for it, David Stabnow's guidance and flexibility during the contractual process and the early stages of the manuscript, and Dean Richardson's adept and thorough management of this project in its final stage.

---

1. Bacchiocchi wrote *From Sabbath to Sunday: A Historical Investigation of the Rise of Sunday Observance in Early Christianity* in 1977 (Rome: Pontifical Gregorian University), which remained the standard Adventist account of Sabbatarianism for many years.
2. "The glory of the One who moves all things," Dante Alighieri, *La Divina Commedia, Paradiso*, canto I, linea 1.

Introduction

Just when the heat brings misery to Florida, the shrimp begin to run. This often results in Sunday afternoon shrimp boils, which continue to be something of a late-summer tradition, at least in what was once a small cow town protected by orange groves on the outskirts of Tampa. The smell of mustard, coriander, allspice, bay leaves, beer, and cayenne pepper permeates entire neighborhoods.

Casting a net is hard work, not least in the midday sun—unless one is night shrimping, but then it takes half the next day to recuperate. These days a shrimper's limit is five gallons with heads on. On a good day or night, then, a few shrimpers could potentially pull in 15 gallons—enough to feed everybody after the average-size church lets out on any given Sunday. Complete with corn, potatoes, and smoked sausage, the church gathers around their freezer-paper covered picnic tables (shiny side up), and the serious business of shelling and decompressing begins.

The careful reader will notice two things taken for granted by almost every Christian in the above scenario—the gathering of the church on the first day of the week and the eating of shrimp. Yet the former was not the prescribed day of worship under the Mosaic law, and the latter was expressly proscribed in old covenant times (Exod 20:8–11; Lev 11:9–12; Deut 14:9–10). Imagine you're a part of this particular community this very Sunday, peeling shrimp with fellow believers after church, seeking respite from the Florida heat under the great shade of a live oak, dodging clumps of Spanish moss. Why have you chosen to do these two things? How did you get from Leviticus to here? "Ah," you might respond, "I did not choose, for this is the way we've always done things. It's *tradition*."

— 1

On the contrary, in this modern world that's "bad faith,"[1] for one can't help but choose. The process of falsification, the creation of a false consciousness, brings about bad faith. It replaces choice with fictitious necessities: the individual, who in fact has a choice between different courses of action, posits one of these courses as necessary. Truth be told, choice is, often enough, a despicable thing. Gone are the days of unquestioned trust and subsequent action based on that trust. Nothing, it seems, is so sacred as to be beyond criticism, and thus we are forced to choose—the so-called "heretical imperative."[2] In this modern world we face a dizzying array of choices each day from what kind of milk to drink in the morning (assuming homogenized and pasteurized cow's milk, we have skim, 1 percent, 2 percent, whole, fortified with DHA, and so on) to what kind of religious tradition we want to join.

Making that latter choice, however, doesn't (unfortunately) close the deal. A whole host of idiosyncratic choices await us as we look for a place to land within the community of our choosing. One of the first and fundamental choices we Christians face is what to do with the Mosaic law. We might not think of it in such terms, as seen in the shrimp boil above, but the various traditions we entertain in making our choice all have answered this question, as evidenced in the various practices of these communities. So one of the basic measurements we can observe on our way to answering that question is how a given community understands and practices its worship of God. The related question, whether it's lawful to eat shrimp, can be left for another day. Suffice it to say that to answer one seems necessarily to affect the outcome of the other. This brings us specifically to the dilemma this *Perspectives* volume seeks to resolve: Is any particular day commanded for the regular gathering of God's assembly under the new covenant in Christ?

About 1,200 years ago people of the developed world gathered together for worship on the first day of the week and had a general consensus as to what elements worship contained, sharing as they did a single set of fundamental assumptions about the nature of such things (passed down by the various institutions in life—

---

1. See P. L. Berger, *The Sacred Canopy: Elements of a Sociological Theory of Religion* (New York: Anchor Books, 1990), 92–95, wherein he builds upon Jean-Paul Sartre's concept of "bad faith" articulated most notably in *Being and Nothingness* (1943).

2. Taken from P. L. Berger, *The Heretical Imperative: Contemporary Possibilities of Religious Affirmation* (New York: Doubleday, 1980).

e.g., church, magistrate, peers, family). There was no "choosing for one's self" (a loose translation of the Greek *hairesis*, from which the word *heresy* comes) about such matters. To choose such things for oneself surely meant some kind of uncomfortable purging by the powers that be for the sake of balance and internal consistency. Fast-forward to today and the imperative to choose about even the most mundane religious matters, not least as a result of the Protestant Reformation, has become unavoidable. Intentionally choosing anything requires that alternatives be considered, and the mere act of knowing that alternatives exist is the essence of heresy. As it pertains to Christians, in this radically pluralist world, we are faced with a heretical imperative—the opportunity and necessity of choosing our own religious community. No tradition can be taken for granted any more, and to pretend that it can is in most cases a self-delusion. Thus, paraphrasing Pius XI, Berger quips that today we are all, figuratively speaking, Protestants.[3] Life in this modern world, then, means we must live with this heretical imperative. Indeed, the series title for this book could be aptly called: *The Heretical Imperative: Four Views on the Sabbath*.

In short, the Sabbath question cannot be relegated to the shelf, for it serves as a microcosm of much larger questions fundamental to the nature of the worshipping community of Christ itself. Hermeneutical presuppositions and the covenantal (dis)continuity of God's redemptive plan, among a great many other elements, are at once exposed when discussing this question. More importantly, as Christians we take seriously God's commands; indeed, if we love Him, we will keep His commands (John 14:15; 1 John 5:3). So, then, if our motivation is to please Him, to make Him happy with us, which can only ultimately be based in love for (and not fear of) Him, what ought we to do with His Sabbath command? This book strives to answer this question, and on our way to answering it, let's first contemplate its importance as it relates to one of the primary marks of the Christian faith and destiny—worship.

If someone had it incessantly banged into his head, when it came to the practice of Christianity, that "fear is the heart of love," then we might empathize with him if he "never went back."[4] But it would still be a shame, never going back because of such a blatantly

---

3. Ibid., 65.
4. From the song "I Will Follow You into the Dark" by Death Cab for Cutie on their album, *Plans* (Atlantic, 2005).

false proposition, at least as it relates to being a follower of Jesus. Quite to the contrary, "perfect love drives out fear" (1 John 4:18). But how does love do this?

Allison argues that the answer is worship—"the means whereby we are opened to the love of God. . . . Worship is an immediate and present means of God's love, making us new creatures and giving us the ever more abundant life *now*."[5] This comes as no surprise since worship of the one true God by humans fulfills the express purpose of our creation. "To say that God made us in his image is to say that God made us for himself, and that he made us to worship him."[6]

Christian worship can, on one hand, be the most altruistic, God-centered moment in the church's common life, or, on the other hand, it can be the most viciously narcissistic. Indeed, "sometimes our worship is more a hiding from God than allowing God to find us."[7] Bishop Allison goes on to argue that the parable of the talents offers a good depiction of our propensity to hide from God, even in the midst of attempting to worship Him. In Matthew 25:24–25, the third servant, in response to his master, fearfully pleads, "Master, I know you. You're a difficult man, reaping where you haven't sown and gathering where you haven't scattered seed. So I was afraid and went off and hid your talent in the ground. Look, you have what is yours" (HCSB). Consequently, he meets his doom (vv. 26–30).

While the other two servants didn't live in such fear, which enabled them to take the talents and invest them, the third servant disbelieved in the presence of love in his master. In a sense it didn't matter what kind of person the master actually was; what mattered was what kind of person the third servant thought his master to be. And this paralyzed him. What the servant believed about him was wrong, and this affected his relationship with and service to him. So it is in Christ's church. How we relate to God in worship is inextricably bound to what we believe about Him. Is He a loveless taskmaster, a "difficult" deity?

What can keep us, as humans, from so paralyzing a thought? To be found in Christ, for the perfect love of God is shown to us in Him. "For God has not given us a spirit of fearfulness, but one of power, love, and sound judgment. . . . [and] has saved us and called us with a holy calling, not according to our works, but according to

5. C. F. Allison, *Fear, Love & Worship* (Vancouver, BC: Regent College, 1962), 17, 19.
6. E. P. Clowney, *The Church* (Downers Grove, IL: InterVarsity, 1995), 118.
7. Allison, *Fear, Love & Worship*, 14.

His own purpose and grace, which was given to us in Christ Jesus before time began" (2 Tim 1:7,9 HCSB). This holy calling, which begins now and extends into the eschaton, has a transformative goal for the called—to share in the divine nature (2 Pet 1:4), to be as fully unified with God as creatures can be (see Eph 1:3–14). A purely theocentric existence—when God is all in all (1 Cor 15:28)—remains the destiny of those in Christ Jesus, indwelt by the Holy Spirit. Indeed, as Letham notes:

> Every single aspect of salvation is seen "in Christ" or "in him."
> . . . Our proper place is to share God's glory; by sin we fell short
> and failed to participate in his glory, but in and through Christ
> we are restored to the glory of God as our ultimate destiny.
> Glory is what belongs distinctively and peculiarly to God. We
> are called to partake of what God is.[8]

Such union is the goal for all those who ingest God's Word (Matt 4:4), feed on Christ in the Supper (John 6:47–51), and have been baptized into His death and resurrection (Rom 6:3–6)—in short, for those who have been given faith by grace (Eph 2:8). And this brings us back around to worship—arguably the most human thing we can do—the very act in this time between the times that develops and disciplines our union with Christ in God by His Spirit. Through the practice of praise, supplication, confession, thanksgiving (in a word, prayer), hearing the Word, and receiving the sacraments, the final and full redemption and transformation of the church is anticipated as she gathers together in continued repentance, obedience to God's commands, and participation in a common life, caring for the needy in her midst.[9]

But one day the reconciled, yet fallen, worship of the Christic community will no longer carry the burden of Martin Luther's *simul iustus et peccator*; the way of the cross will fade (even if its marks remain), and streets of pure gold will descend from the heavens. Wendell Berry depicts this thought poetically:

---

8. R. Letham, *Through Western Eyes: Eastern Orthodoxy, A Reformed Perspective* (Fearn, Ross-Shire, UK: Christian Focus, 2007), 255, 257.

9. Ibid., 261–63. See also A. P. Ross, *Recalling the Hope of Glory: Biblical Worship from the Garden to the New Creation* (Grand Rapids: Kregel, 2006), 503–12, for a good list of "several principles that surface again and again and therefore seem . . . to be absolutely essential for developing the worship of God" (503). Noticeably absent from this list, however, is any reference to which particular day, if any, God's people ought to gather.

There is a day
when the road neither
comes nor goes, and the way
is not a way but a place.[10]

Indeed, all our work through worship (*leitourgia*) on the way
to becoming sharers in the divine nature will cease. The road ends
in the most holy place—the court of the Almighty. In the meantime we're left to choose which of the three servants we will be. We
Christians serve God directly in worship,[11] and thus it behooves us
to avoid the spiritual pride—the narcissism—to which it is always
open;[12] in brief, to engage wisely the question about which of its
elements remain in perpetuity and which of them have become obsolete in order to honor the triune Lord. It won't do to claim ignorance or hide behind tradition when seeking to resolve the Sabbath
question. If worship truly is "an immediate and present means of
God's love," then may we be zealous to keep open to its sanctifying
power, which necessarily means taking seriously the question about
on which particular day, if any, God desires His people to rest and,
in that rest, gather together as the called-out assembly, the body of
which Christ is the head.

This concern to honor the true God is, of course, paramount
for everyone involved in this volume. Despite each of us hailing
from different traditions, we nonetheless find ourselves as branches
stemming off that great trunk prior to the Protestant Reformation. In various ways and to various degrees, each of our respective
traditions has sought to accommodate and appropriate the early
church—both of the apostles and of the fathers.

Nevertheless, the irenic tone of this volume ought not be taken
for granted. The congeniality embodying the various essays and
critiques herein should not be equated with that bland tolerance
so common in public discourse today. Here is a real tolerance: a
confident display of deeply held beliefs and practices that are at

---

10. W. Berry, *A Timbered Choir: The Sabbath Poems 1979–1997* (Washington, DC:
Counterpoint, 1998), 216.

11. See Clowney, *The Church*, 117.

12. M. M. Boulton, in *God Against Religion: Rethinking Christian Theology through
Worship* (Grand Rapids: Eerdmans, 2008), argues persuasively that only through God's
entering, transforming, and, ultimately, ending (those provisional elements of) worship
can Christian worship today truly offer a foretaste of the coming vision of God's uncre-
ated glory. When worship is finally taken up into God at the time His future appears in
full, the current work of the church will cease.

once juxtaposed with, at times, the very opposite of those beliefs and practices. Some, at best, might see the other as guilty of a sin of omission or even ignorance; at worst, they might see their interlocutor as guilty of flagrant disobedience to the command of God.

The four views of the Sabbath represented in this book are by no means intended to cover all the views held throughout the centuries. Yet I don't think it is too much of a stretch to suggest that all the major views articulated throughout history can align themselves with one view or another ensconced in this *Perspectives* volume. For example, some Reformed and Anglican folks might find Arand's perspective satisfactory even if they'd take issue with the (Lutheran) way he gets there. Others in the Reformed tradition (e.g., "Klineans"[13]), some Anglicans, Baptists, and Old Order Anabaptists may resonate with Pipa's exposition, even if not in agreement with his entire argument. Throughout the West the great majority of evangelicals (as do most Anabaptists) practice what Blomberg lays out on this matter, whether or not they've given it much thought. Seventh Day Baptists, as well as a good many Messianic Jews, will no doubt find much to agree with in MacCarty's Seventh-day Adventist approach. Finally, Roman Catholics, traditional Anglicans, and the Orthodox, while maintaining a much stronger magisterial and thus "dominical" view of this matter,[14] exegetically fall somewhere in between Arand and Pipa. And, of course, all these lines were blurred during the fomenting years of the sixteenth and seventeenth centuries.

I expect many readers who pick up this book to have minds already settled. My simple hope, then, is that the representative of their particular view has done well reinforcing the matter. If a reader comes to this project undecided, then my hope is that he or she will find something to latch onto herein, so that a choice can finally be made. Others may disdain the format of such an enterprise, which presumes to speak on an important subject such as the nature and function of Christian worship without telling anyone definitively what to think in the end. Such disdain is really a pining

---

13. See M. G. Kline, *Kingdom Prologue: Genesis Foundations for a Covenantal Worldview* (Eugene, OR: Wipf & Stock, 2006).

14. See the *Catechism of the Catholic Church* (New York: Doubleday Religion, 2003), III.ii, 1.3 (also para. 1166); and *These Truths We Hold—The Holy Orthodox Church: Her Life and Teachings* (St. Tikhon's Seminary Press, 1986), http://www.stots.edu/these_truths_we_hold.html, accessed 29 June 2010 ("Orthodox Dogma and Doctrine: The Ten Commandments," no. 4), for succinct representations of this view.

after halcyon days—days in which no heretical imperative existed. The Christian church, from at least the time of the sixteenth century (and probably before the eighth century or thereabouts[15]), no longer shares a single set of fundamental assumptions with respect to the Sabbath question. Put another way, my desire is that this work will help the reader undo long-held beliefs that are untenable in light of the evidence—or instead reinforce his or her underlying suppositions regarding this issue. Either way we've got to choose.

Christopher John Donato
Lent 2011

---

15. R. J. Bauckham argues that starting in the sixth century pockets of legislative activity supporting Sunday Sabbatarianism began appearing, until finally it became assumed practice by the late Middle Ages. See his "Sabbath and Sunday in the Medieval Church in the West," *From Sabbath to Lord's Day*, ed. D. A. Carson (Grand Rapids: Zondervan, 1982), 302–4.

CHAPTER 1

The Seventh-Day Sabbath

SKIP MACCARTY

I grew up in a seventh-day Sabbath-keeping home. My only childhood memories specifically associated with a day of the week are Sabbath memories—attending Sabbath school with my friends, worshipping in church with my family, participating in church outings and ministries, taking nature walks, bike-riding with my best friend to see horses in town—the kinds of memories that established traditions that have carried into adulthood. Today, more than 15 million people worldwide in my denomination alone share similar Sabbath experiences. The Sabbath has helped God seem more real to us and nurtured our relationship with Him. The present discussion transcends a mere intellectual dialogue for us; it is a dialogue of the heart.

I appreciate the opportunity afforded me to join this valuable Sabbath conversation with Christian colleagues. Since I am more pastor than professor, this brief pastoral note: Though some of this dialogue may seem technical for some lay readers, involving original biblical languages and so on, I pray and believe that God will send His Spirit as He promised to guide all who seek to know and do His will (Luke 11:11–13; John 7:17; 16:13; Phil 3:15–16).

This chapter does not take the position that all Christians who presently worship on a different day do not love Jesus or have the assurance of salvation. Nonetheless, it argues that seventh-day

Sabbath observance is God's will for all Christians and points to the blessing they will gain when they do.

This presentation accepts the whole Bible as the authoritative Word of God and the basis of all Christian doctrine and follows this sequence: (1) the OT and NT witness for the universality and permanence of the seventh-day Sabbath; (2) objections to this universality and permanence; (3) the Sabbath in early church history; (4) the Sabbath in the old and new covenants; (5) the meaning and proper observance of the Sabbath; and (6) a brief summary and concluding statement.

Seventh-Day Sabbath—A Universal and Permanent Gift

The Old Testament Witness

A survey by the Pew Forum on Religion and Public Life and the Pew Research Center for the People and the Press asked respondents their convictions regarding the propriety of displaying the Ten Commandments in a government building. The survey found that "Americans overwhelmingly support displaying the Ten Commandments on public property, with more than seven-in-ten saying they believe such displays are proper."[1] Irrespective of one's conviction regarding the display of the Decalogue in public facilities, most agree that the Ten Commandments hold a revered place in American consciousness.

In the heart of the Ten Commandments is the focus of this book, the seventh-day Sabbath:

> Remember the Sabbath day by keeping it holy. Six days you shall labor and do all your work, but the seventh day is a Sabbath to the Lord your God. On it you shall not do any work, neither you, nor your son or daughter, nor your male or female servant, nor your animals, nor any foreigner residing in your towns. For in six days the Lord made the heavens and the earth, the sea, and all that is in them, but he rested on the seventh day. Therefore the Lord blessed the Sabbath day and made it holy. (Exod 20:8–11)[2]

---

1. "Supreme Court Rules on Ten Commandments Displays," June 25, 2005 press release, http://pewforum.org/Press-Room/Press-Releases/Supreme-Court-Rules-on-Ten-Commandments-Displays.aspx, accessed November 12, 2010.

2. In chapters 1 and 2 all Scripture references are taken from the NIV unless otherwise noted.

This fourth (third for Catholics and Lutherans) of the Ten Commandments (lit., "Ten Words"; Hb., *'aseret haddebarim*) or Decalogue has been well known and debated for millennia. Was it intended for Israel during the Old Testament period alone, or does it have a universal and permanent application? Did it begin with the Ten Commandments at Sinai or perhaps just prior to that when God gave desert-dwelling Israel manna to eat (Exod 16:13–30), or did it have an even more ancient origin?

The commandment itself points to the answers. Note its universal application to servants, animals, and "the alien within your gates," and its universal reference to the Lord who made "the heavens . . . earth . . . sea . . . and all that is in them." Buber states, "In the Sabbath Moses recognizes not merely a human law but a universal law." [3]

The Sabbath Established at Creation

When God gave the Sabbath commandment, He linked its origin to the creation week when He "rested on the seventh day," and then "blessed the Sabbath day and made it holy." [4] Note the Bible's description of the seventh day of creation week: "By the seventh day God had finished the work he had been doing; so on the seventh day he rested from all his work. And God blessed the seventh day and made it holy, because on it he rested from all the work of creating that he had done" (Gen 2:2–3).

Examining Gen 2:2–3, Cassuto concludes:

> The verb *šābbath* בתש ["finished," "ceased"] also contains an allusion to the name םוי שה בת *yōm haššabbāth* ("the Sabbath day"). This name [Sabbath day] does not occur here, and is subsequently mentioned in other books of the Pentateuch only in connection with the commandment to keep the Sabbath, which was given to Israel. Here the hallowed day is called only *the seventh day*. . . . The Torah laid here the foundation for the precept of the Sabbath; this day was already sanctified by God at the beginning of the world's history, and its greatness

---

3. M. Buber, *Moses* (New York: Harper & Brothers, 1946), 8.
4. Contrary to A. T. Lincoln's suggestion that the Sabbath commandment's reference to Gen 2:3 is an "etiological . . . play on words to make its point," in "From Sabbath to Lord's Day: A Biblical and Theological Perspective," *From Sabbath to Lord's Day: A Biblical, Historical, and Theological Investigation*, ed. D. A. Carson (Eugene, OR: Wipf & Stock, 1982), 349.

is not dependent on any other factor. . . . Scripture wishes to emphasize that the sanctity of the Sabbath is older than Israel, and rests upon all mankind.[5]

While Genesis 2:2–3 lacks an explicit Sabbath command, no command forbidding murder is recorded until Noah's day (Gen 9:9–6), and none of the other Ten Commandments is recorded until they were issued at Sinai. Yet Cain was held accountable for the murder of Abel, and Joseph knew that adultery was "sin against God" (Gen 4:6–11; 39:9). God may have included what later became the Ten Commandments when He said, "Abraham obeyed me and did everything I required of him, keeping my commands, my decrees and my instructions" (Gen 26:5). Instructively, the early chapters of the Bible do not explicitly state that God loves people, is merciful or compassionate, or will forgive sins; that was all revealed in the covenant He made and the Law He gave at Sinai (Exod 20:6; 34:6–7). Those characteristics, as well as the continued observance of the Sabbath by God's people, were all assumed in those early chapters of the Bible that cover at least 2,500 years of human history.

Furthermore, the way the Sabbath is mentioned in the manna story (Exod 16) several months before the Ten Commandments were given at Sinai (Exod 20) has led some commentators to conclude that "the existence of the sabbath is assumed by the writer."[6]

God's rest on the seventh day served "as an example to humanity upon whom devolves the duty of imitating the ways of God"[7]— six days, work; the seventh, rest. In Jesus' parable of the servant forgiven by his master of a huge debt he could not pay, the servant was held accountable for not following his master's example and forgiving his own debtors, though he had received no direct command to do so (Matt 18:23–34). Similarly, it was expected that the ways of God in ceasing from His creative work on the seventh day would be emulated by His creation—"like father, like son," as the saying goes. Indeed, humanity's creation in the image of God meant in part that they were enabled to interact with God in loving fellowship and would be eager for the opportunity. The Sabbath rest provided

5. U. Cassuto, *A Commentary on the Book of Genesis* (Jerusalem: Magnes Press—Hebrew University, 1961), 63–64.

6. B. S. Childs, *The Book of Exodus* (Philadelphia: Westminster Press, 1974), 290; cf. Buber, *Moses*, 80; U. Cassuto, *A Commentary on the Book of Exodus* (Jerusalem: Magnes Press—Hebrew University, 1967), 186.

7. Cassuto, *Genesis*, 68.

special, dedicated time for that fellowship. Theologically speaking, God's rest on the seventh day "means His ceasing the work of creation *in order to* be free for the fellowship with man, the object of his love, for the rejoicing and celebration of His completed work together with his son on earth, the *imago Dei*, 'His festive partner.'"[8]

God "blessed the seventh day and made it holy," setting it apart for special use by humankind, investing it with His own special presence.[9] This combination of the two verbs, "blessed" (Hb., *barak*) and "made holy" (Hb., *qadash*), is unique in the OT. According to J. G. Murphy:

> The solemn act of blessing and hallowing is the institution of a perpetual order of seventh-day rest: in the same manner as the blessing of the animals [Gen 1:22] denoted a perpetuity of self–multiplication, and the blessing of man [Gen 1:28] indicated further a perpetuity of dominion over the earth and its products. This present record is a sufficient proof that the original institution [of the seventh-day rest] was never forgotten by man.[10]

The creation record highlights the uniqueness of the seventh day in at least three ways: (1) The seventh day is the very first thing the Bible records being "made holy," sanctified by God. "By sanctifying the seventh day God instituted a polarity between the everyday and the solemn, between days of work and days of rest, which was to be determinative for human existence."[11] (2) In Gen 1:1–2:3, the first six days of creation are each mentioned once, while the seventh day is mentioned three times: "By the *seventh day* God had finished the work," "on the *seventh day* he rested," "God blessed *the seventh day* and made it holy." The repetition emphasizes the importance of the day in the divine economy. (3) Genesis 2:1–3 avoids the phrase "there was evening, and there was morning," which was used in

---

8. H. K. LaRondelle, *Perfection and Perfectionism* (Berrien Springs, MI: Andrews University Press, 1971), 72.

9. R. M. Davidson, *A Love Song for the Sabbath* (Washington, DC: Review and Herald, 1988), 29: "From the account of Moses at the burning bush (Ex. 3:1–6), the erection of the tabernacle (Ex. 25:8; 29:43), and other examples from Scripture, we learn that it is *God's presence* that confers holiness." Cf. J. Muilenburg, "Holiness," in *IDB*, 2:616–23.

10. J. G. Murphy, *A Critical and Exegetical Commentary on the Book of Genesis* (Andover, MA: Warren F. Draper, 1866), 71. Murphy was Professor of Hebrew at Assembly's College in Belfast.

11. C. Westermann, *Genesis*, trans. J. J. Scullion (Minneapolis: Augsburg, 1984), 143.

conjunction with the other six days of creation to conclude the activities of the day and as a transition to the creating activities of the following day. The seventh day breaks that pattern. "The divine resting concludes creation—sabbath belongs to the created order; it cannot be legislated or abrogated by human beings."[12] God sovereignly chose and sanctified the seventh day as a treasured gift and blessing He bequeathed to humankind—a sign of His covenantal protection and love.

The Role, Universality, and Permanence of the Sabbath After Adam's Fall

After the entrance of sin, God described the spiritual warfare that would ensue between Satan and humankind and revealed the grace provision embedded in His everlasting covenant of love, which promised redemption through the seed of the woman (Gen 3:15; cf. 2 Tim 1:9; 1 Pet 1:18–20). This universal, permanent gospel promise applied to all of Adam's descendants, for all have rebelled against God, His law, and His covenant: "The earth is defiled by its people; they have disobeyed the laws, violated the statutes and broken the everlasting covenant" (Isa 24:5). With humankind now engaged in a spiritual life-and-death warfare against a powerful foe, the rest that God offered on the day that He had blessed and made holy at creation became vital to His redemptive purpose to restore His image in them by making them holy as He is holy (Exod 31:13). As the need was universal, so too was the gift.

God's covenant with post-fall Adam offered grace and redemption to all his descendants. Each of His subsequent covenants (with Noah, Abraham, Israel, and others) contained the redemptive provisions of His previous covenants and had the blessing of the entire world in view. As "the everlasting covenant between God and all living creatures of every kind on the earth," God's covenant with Noah had the whole earth in view (Gen 9:16). The redemptive provision of God's covenant with Abraham, granting him a righteous standing before God based on faith, was to be shared with the entire world by Abraham's descendants who were to spread all over the earth (Gen 28:14). God designed His covenant with Israel to groom His nation into a missionary "kingdom of priests and a holy nation" so

---

12. T. E. Fretheim, "The Book of Genesis: Introduction, Commentary, and Reflections," in *NIB*, 1:346.

"that your ways may be known on earth, your salvation among all nations" (Exod 19:6; Ps 67:1–2). Through their missionary witness God intended that "the law will go out from me; my justice will become a light to the nations" (Isa 51:4). Thus foreigners, as well as God's missionary people, were invited into a share of the redemptive, spiritual blessings of God's covenants, including His gift of the seventh-day Sabbath: "foreigners who bind themselves to the Lord to minister to him, to love the name of the Lord, and to be his servant, all who keep the Sabbath without desecrating it, and who hold fast to my covenant—these I will bring to my holy mountain and give them joy in my house of prayer" (Isa 56:6–7).

God embedded the Sabbath ordinance in the heart of His universal and permanent moral law, the Ten Commandments that He wrote with His own finger (Exod 31:18) "and spoke directly to his people [Deut 4:12–13], without the mediation of Moses."[13] He chose the Sabbath as a covenant "sign" to remind His people weekly that "the Lord made the heavens and the earth," and that "I am the Lord, who makes you holy" (Exod 31:17,13). About the sign significance of the Sabbath more will be said later.

The first recorded promise of a "new heavens and new earth" was given through the prophet Isaiah:

> "See, I will create new heavens and a new earth. The former things will not be remembered, nor will they come to mind. . . . The wolf and the lamb will feed together, and the lion will eat straw like the ox. . . . As the new heavens and the new earth that I will make will endure before me," declares the Lord, "so will your name and descendants endure. From one New Moon [or better, 'month'[14]] to another and from one

---

13. R. M. Grant, "The Decalogue in Early Christianity," *HTR* 40 (1947): 1.

14. Cf. New English Translation (NET): "'From one month to the next and from one Sabbath to the next, all people will come to worship me,' says the Lord." The noun *chodesh* in the Hebrew Bible "occurs 283 times, its most common meaning being 'month.' . . . A second meaning . . . is new moon" (*NIDOTTE*, 5:38).

Although many English versions translate the Hebrew word *chodesh* in Isa 66:23 as "New Moon," the standard Hebrew lexicons agree that in connection with the special grammatical construction of this verse, the preferred translation for *chodesh* here is "month," not "New Moon." So BDB (, 191: "*as often as* month (comes) in its month"; cf. *HALOT* (, 219: "from month to month." (See also the NLT modern English version.) A virtually identical grammatical construction, using the word *shanah* "year" in the Hebrew Bible (1 Sam 7:16; 2 Chr 24:5; and Zech 14:6), clearly means "year by year" or "every year." The LXX apparently understood that Isa 66:23 referred to months, rather than to the "New Moon [festivals]" mentioned earlier in Isa (1:13,14). In Isa 1:13–14 the LXX employs the

Sabbath to another, all mankind will come and bow down before me," says the Lord. (Isa 65:17,25; 66:22–23)

The universal worship of God "from one Sabbath to another" was an implied expectation of the original creation ordinance.[15] The phrase, "new heavens and new earth" harkens back to Gen 1:1, intimating that God's re-creative activity will return the earth to Edenic conditions.[16] Note the parallels that occur even in the same chronological order:

Eden at Creation: Genesis 1–2	New Heavens and Earth: Isaiah 65–66
Humankind to "rule . . . over all the earth . . . and subdue it. . . . to work it and take care of it" (1:26,28; 2:15).	Humankind "will build houses and dwell in them; they will plant vineyards and eat their fruit" (65:21).
To "all the beasts of the earth . . . I give every green plant for food" (1:30).	"The wolf and the lamb will feed together, and the lion will eat straw like the ox" (65:25).
God "blessed the seventh day and made it holy" (2:3; cf. Exod 20:11).	"'From one Sabbath to another, all mankind will come and bow down before me,' says the Lord" (66:23).

Beaming through Isaiah 65–66, as shafts of sunlight through latticework, is the divine longing for return to Edenic conditions and God's promise to bring it about. Referring to this promise, Peter states, "In keeping with his promise we are looking forward to a new heaven and a new earth, the home of righteousness" (2 Pet 3:13).[17]

Greek term *nouménia* "new moon [festival]" (a contraction of *neoménia*), but in 66:23 it uses the Greek term *mén*—the normal Greek word for "month" (see *TDOT*, 4:229). In the NT, Col 2:16 uses the word *neoménia* "new moon [festival]," which is identified as a "shadow" pointing to Christ (see discussion later in this chapter), but Rev 22:2, in describing the monthly cycle of the Tree of Life (which, presumably, all would come to experience), uses the same word *mén* "month" as found in Isa 66:23 (LXX). It appears that Isaiah is referring to the same monthly cycle of worship for the new earth that is implied in Rev 22:2, which is not necessarily linked to any specific New Moon festival.

15. G. F. Hasel, "Sabbath," in *ABD*, 4:852: "Isa 66:23 has the context of the new creation, in which universally 'all flesh' will worship YHWH 'from sabbath to sabbath.'"

16. By linking his eschatology with a new creation, parallel to the first creation described in Genesis 1, Isaiah seems to go beyond a description of Israel's last days, viewed primarily from within history (as described by other classical prophets, as in Ezek 38–39 and Zech 12–14), to describe the final universal in-breaking of God to bring about a totally new creation (See G. K. Beale, *The Temple and the Church's Mission: A Biblical Theology of the Dwelling Place of God*, New Studies in Biblical Theology 17 [Downers Grove, IL: InterVarsity, 2004], 136).

17. *Nestle-Aland Greek Text* (Stuttgart, Germany: Württembergische Bibelanstalt, 1963), 25th ed., cross references 2 Pet 3:13 with Isa 65:17; 66:22.

John alludes to this same Isaiah passage in his own description of "a new heaven and a new earth" (Rev 21:1–5).[18] Note the parallel descriptions in the following chart:

New Heavens and New Earth Isaiah 65–66	New Heavens and New Earth Revelation 21–22
"The former things will not be remembered" (65:17).	"The old order of things has passed away" (21:4).
"The sound of weeping and of crying will be heard in it [the Holy City, Jerusalem] no more" (65:19).	God "will wipe every tear from their eyes. There will be no more . . . mourning or crying or pain" (21:3–4).
Refers to Jerusalem by name (65:18–19; 66:10,13,20).	Refers to "new Jerusalem" and "Holy City, Jerusalem" by name (21:2,10).
Refers to "a tree" and "a river" (65:22; 66:12).	Refers to the "river of the water of life" and "the tree of life" (22:1–2).
"All nations," "all mankind" are among the redeemed who will worship God (66:18,23).	"The nations . . . and the kings of the earth" are among the redeemed who will worship God (21:24–26).
God destroys the wicked by "fire" (65:14–16).	God destroys the wicked by "fire" (21:8).
The wicked slain are depicted as outside the Holy City (66:24).	The wicked slain are depicted as outside the Holy City (22:14–15).

It seems evident that John's vision of the new heavens and new earth parallels Isaiah's. When both charts above are considered, the parallels between the Edenic creation and the new heavens and new earth indicate that Sabbath observance will continue in the new earth.[19] Clearly, the eschatological message of the OT did not

---

18. *Nestle-Aland Greek Text* cross references Rev 21:1 with Isa 65:17; 66:22. The only places the term "new heavens and new earth" occurs in Scripture are Isa 65:17; 66:22; 2 Pet 3:13; and Rev 21:1, and all describe a return to Edenic conditions. The references to the wicked being slain (Isa 65:14–16; 66:24; Rev 21:8; 22:14–15) is another way of communicating that sin will no longer exist.

19. Isaiah's vision includes elements that refer to specific conditions that were not present in Eden and will not apply in the new earth—namely, death ("the one who dies at a hundred will be thought a mere child" [Isa 65:20], cf. "there will be no more death" [Rev 21:4]); and Israel's continued witness to the nations (Isa 66:19–20), cf. the new covenant promise that the time will come, presumably post-Second Coming, when no such witness will be needed (Heb 8:11). These passages are generally understood to provide evidence that Isaiah's vision of a new heaven and a new earth has primarily a post-exilic earthly environment in view. If that is the case, it would still not deny the obvious parallels in Isaiah's vision to both Edenic conditions and the new earth visions of 2 Pet 2:13 and Revelation 21–22. However, (1) regarding the reference to Israel's continued witness to the nations (Isa 66:19–20), note the parallel in Rev 21:2 and 22:14,17

anticipate eliminating the Sabbath; on the contrary it reaffirms its universality and permanence.[20]

Sabbath Reform Appeal

God's people did not always appreciate God's Sabbath gift or take advantage of its blessing potential. Apostasy in Israel focused, among other things, on desecration of the Sabbath and drew a strong response from the prophets. In Isaiah's day Sabbath observance had degenerated into a meaningless, restrictive ritual polluted by unholy living and social injustice that belied the Sabbath's intended sign significance "that I am the Lord, who makes you holy" (Exod 31:13). Through Isaiah, God appealed for spiritual revival coupled with holistic Sabbath reform: "keep your feet from breaking the Sabbath and from doing as you please on my holy day," "keep the Sabbath without desecrating it," "maintain justice and do what is right" (Isa 58:13; 56:1–2). God called Isaiah, and anyone who joined his reform movement, a "Repairer of Broken Walls" ("Repairer of the Breach," Isa 58:12 NKJV, NRSV).

---

where, in the midst of descriptions of the new earth, evangelistic appeals are still being made to unbelievers (cf. 2 Pet 3:10–14). Evidently, while describing the conditions of the final new heaven and new earth, the prophets make present-day evangelistic appeals so that none might refuse God's great gift through unbelief and disobedience. And (2), regarding reference to death occurring in the "new heavens and a new earth" (Isa 65:17) consider the comments of J. A. Motyer, *The Prophecy of Isaiah: An Introduction and Commentary* (Downers Grove, IL: InterVarsity, 1993), 530: "Throughout this passage Isaiah uses aspects of present life to create impressions of the life that is yet to come. . . . Things we have no real capacity to understand can be expressed only through things we know and experience. So it is that in this present order of things death cuts life off before it has well begun or before it has fully matured. But it will not be so then. No infant will fail to enjoy life nor an elderly person come short of total fulfillment. Indeed, one would be but a youth were one to die aged a hundred! This does not imply that death will still be present (contradicting 25:7–8) but rather affirms that over the whole of life, as we should now say from infancy to old age, the power of death will be destroyed." Isaiah 25:7–8 says: "On this mountain he will destroy the shroud that enfolds all peoples, the sheet that covers all nations; he will swallow up death forever. The Sovereign Lord will wipe away the tears from all faces; he will remove his people's disgrace from all the earth."

20. Some Jewish and early Christian writers believed that life in the new earth will be perpetual Sabbath. For example, *m. Tamid* 7:4: "On the Sabbath they sang *A Psalm: a Song for the Sabbath Day* [Ps 92]; a Psalm, a song for the time that is to come, for the day that shall be all Sabbath and rest in the life everlasting." While this does not reflect specific biblical terminology, it is natural to conceive of life in the new earth, and indeed in Eden of old, as "all Sabbath" and uninterrupted rest compared with the struggles, pain and death of the present age. However, just as life in Eden involved work and a seventh-day Sabbath rest, so will life in the new earth involve both. And both Isa 66:23 and Rev 22:1–2 refer to recurring time cycles in the heavenly city. Viewed in this light, the two concepts of "all Sabbath" and a seventh-day Sabbath are not mutually exclusive and could exist concurrently.

Jeremiah's Sabbath reform appeal decried Israel's treatment of the Sabbath as a normal workday and promised divine blessings and judgments based on how it treated the Sabbath (Jer 17:21–27). Through Amos, God lamented that while His people ceased from work on the Sabbath, they mused in their hearts, "When will the New Moon be over that we may sell grain, and the Sabbath be ended that we may market wheat?" (Amos 8:5). Ezekiel added his appeal, listing Sabbath desecration with sins of idolatry, oppressing the poor, shedding blood, gross immorality, and extortion (Ezek 22:8–11). Ezekiel reminded God's covenant people that God established the Sabbath as "a sign between us, so they would know that I the Lord made them holy" (20:12). Their desecration of the Sabbath had become a sign of its own, signifying their covenant disloyalty, which ultimately resulted in their exile to Babylon.

After the exile, Jewish captives who returned to Jerusalem almost immediately began trading on the Sabbath. When Nehemiah arrived, he instituted Sabbath reform—no more buying or selling on the Sabbath (Neh 10:30–33). Nehemiah then returned to Babylon for official business. Upon his return to Jerusalem he discovered that Jewish traders had already resumed "desecrating the Sabbath." This drew strong rebuke from Nehemiah for the "wicked thing" they were doing and necessitated another Sabbath reform, including no trading from sunset on the sixth day to sunset on the seventh (the biblical reckoning of the beginning and end of the Sabbath, Neh 13:15–21). In spite of the faithful teaching and reform ministry of the prophets, the people seemed to have lost sight of the meaning and blessing potential of the Sabbath.

During the intertestamental period, the need for Sabbath reform took another turn. To the few biblical guidelines in the OT for Sabbath observance,[21] Pharisees and rabbis added hundreds of minute restrictions in an attempt to protect the Sabbath from desecration. [22] Speaking about their own rules, the Pharisees said:

---

21. Biblical Sabbath prohibitions are few: Exod 20:8–11, working; Exod 35:3, lighting a fire (likely for cooking, a major and time-consuming task in those days); Neh 13:15–17, trading; Isa 58:13, "doing as you please" (likely secular activities that detract from the purpose of the day).

22. The Mishna tractate *Shabbath* ("the Sabbath"), abbreviated *m. Shabbath*, contains many hundreds of Sabbath rules that had been added by the Pharisees, scribes, and rabbis. The "tradition of the elders" (Mark 7:3 and parallels), known as the oral law, was passed down orally for many generations before it was codified in the Mishna and other rabbinic literature.

"The rules about the Sabbath . . . are as mountains hanging by a hair, for the [teaching of] Scripture [thereon] is scanty and the rules many[23]; "the words of the Scribes are more beloved than those of the Torah";[24] and "greater stringency applies to [the observance of] the words of the Scribes than to [the observance of] the words of the [written] law."[25] In addition, the universal application of the Sabbath was converted to a nationalistic application, teaching that the Sabbath was given only to Israel and that God raised up Israel so that there might be a people on earth to keep the Sabbath. In other words, Israel was made for the Sabbath.[26]

The need for Sabbath reform on multiple levels could not have been greater. Then Jesus stepped onto the scene.

The New Testament Witness

Jesus and the Sabbath

Jesus returned to His hometown Nazareth in order to launch His ministry on the Sabbath, in the synagogue where He had grown up (Luke 4:16). It was His "custom" to worship on the Sabbath (Luke 4:16). Young comments: "Luke's reference to Jesus' custom of worshipping on the Sabbath and healing on the Sabbath (Luke 4:16; 6:6–11; 13:10–17; 14:1–6), informs largely Gentile Christian communities some 40 or 60 years after Jesus' death *how*, not *whether*, to keep the Sabbath."[27]

Jesus' Sabbath observance was not without controversy. As Jesus walked through a grain field one Sabbath, His disciples picked some handfuls of grain and began to eat (Mark 2:23–28; cf. Matt 12:1–8; Luke 6:1–7). His critics accused them of breaking the Sabbath. When they attacked Jesus with their "you aren't keeping the Sabbath right" accusations based on their manmade regulations,

---

23. *M. Hagigah* 1.8, trans. H. Danby, *The Mishna* (London: Oxford University Press, 1954).

24. *M, Rabbah, The Song of Songs*, 1:2:2.

25. *M. Sanhedrin* 11.3, trans. Danby; cf. Danby, xvii.

26. Note especially this passage in Jubilees 2:30b–31: "The creator of all things blessed it [the seventh day], but he did not hallow all peoples and nations to keep sabbath on it, but Israel only" (translation in H. F. D. Sparks, ed., *The Apocryphal Old Testament* (Oxford: Clarendon Press, 1984).

27. N. H. Young, "'The Use of Sunday for Meetings of Believers in the New Testament': A Response," *NovT* 45 (2003): 119. "Luke refers to the Sabbath twenty-six times in his writings. . . . and not once does he provide any negative comment" (ibid).

they were accusing the architect and engineer of creation week (John 1:1–3), the one who had Himself blessed the seventh day and made it holy. He was "the spiritual rock that accompanied them" in their desert wanderings (1 Cor 10:4), and as such His was the finger that had etched the Ten Commandments, including the Sabbath, into the stone tablets (Exod 31:18), and His was the voice that spoke them directly to His people (Deut 4:12–13). He defended His disciples who had broken a Sabbath regulation established by the Pharisees but not by Scripture. He used the occasion to reiterate what had been true from the beginning: "The Sabbath was made for man, not man for the Sabbath" (Mark 2:27). Their multitudinous, minute restrictions had reversed the formula. He then announced that He was "Lord even of the Sabbath" (Mark 2:28), its very Creator, and thus its rightful Interpreter.

When Mark recorded Jesus' words, "the Sabbath was made for man" (2:27), he chose Greek terms that would communicate the universal and permanent character of the Sabbath—*egeneto*, "made" (literally, "came into existence)," and *anthrōpos*, "man." The Greek word *egeneto* linked the Sabbath with creation; it is used 20 times in the Septuagint in the Genesis 1 creation story, once in Heb 11:3 in reference to God's creation of our world out of nothing, and three times in John 1:3, which establishes Jesus as the one through whom all things were "made" (created). The Greek term *anthrōpos* is the generic term for humankind. Numerous scholars have understood Mark 2:27 as Jesus' affirmation of the creation origin and universal character of the Sabbath.[28]

Jesus' Sabbath miracles have been interpreted by some commentators as evidence that Jesus weakened, if not outright ushered out, the OT Sabbath. But nothing could be further from the truth (and one wonders what would be made of it had it been recorded

---

28. E.g., A. Y. Collins, *Mark: A Commentary* (Minneapolis: Augsburg, 2007), 203: "'The Sabbath came into being on account of man' (τό σαββατον διὰ τον ἀνθρωπον ἐγένετο) [*to sabbaton dia ton anthrōpon egeneto*], evokes the creation account of Gen 1:1–2:4a." O. P. Robertson, *The Christ of the Covenants* (Phillipsburg, NJ: Presbyterian and Reformed, 1980), 68–69: "As Jesus indicated pointedly, 'the Sabbath came into being (*egéneto*) for the sake of man (*dià tòn anthrōpon*)' (Mark 2:27). Because it was for the good of man and the whole of creation, God instituted the Sabbath." J. H. Gerstner, "Law in the NT," *ISBE*, ed. G. W. Bromiley (Grand Rapids: Eerdmans, 1986), 3:85: "In [Mark 2:27] that Christians commonly take today as liberating them from sabbatical law, Christ actually bound His followers more tightly to it." Cf. J. Marcus, *Mark 1–8*, AB (New York: Doubleday, 1999), 242; L. Williamson Jr., *Mark* (Atlanta: John Knox Press, 1983), 75.

that those same miracles had been performed on the first day of
the week). Jesus performed seven recorded healing miracles on
the Sabbath,[29] five of them strongly contested by His critics who
accused Him of breaking the Sabbath by healing people. However,
McCann rightly states, Jesus "never broke any [Sabbath] regulations found in the Torah [OT Scriptures],"[30] though the same could
not be said of the many rabbinical restrictions that had been added
to the Sabbath.[31]

The significance of Jesus' Sabbath miracles can be understood
only in light of the OT prophets' appeals for Sabbath reform. His
actions and teachings embodied their message of Sabbath reform.
Jesus liberated the Sabbath and restored it to the place that He, the
original and continuing Lord of the Sabbath, had intended for it.

Coupled with the prophets' appeal for Sabbath reform was their
appeal to "maintain justice," "to set the oppressed free," to cease
"oppress[ing] the poor and needy and mistreat[ing] the alien" (Isa
56:1–5; 58:6–14; Ezek 22:26–29; cf. Amos 8:5–6). For Jesus the Sabbath served that very purpose. By healing her He "set free on the
Sabbath day" a crippled woman "whom Satan has kept bound for
eighteen long years" (Luke 13:16). By His Sabbath-healing miracles
Jesus deliberately provoked His legalistic critics into a controversy
that would allow Him to liberate the Sabbath from the burdensome restrictions that had been placed upon it, recover its divinely
endowed blessing and sanctification potential, and restore its original purpose of rest, worship, and service to the glory of God. On
one Sabbath the Pharisees dangled a chronically ill man in front of
Jesus, hoping He would take the bait so they could further accuse
Him (Luke 14:1–6). He did. He was an incurable healer. The rabbis taught that unless it was an immediate life-and-death matter, a
medical procedure should wait until after the Sabbath. But as F. F.
Bruce points out, "Jesus argued on the contrary that the sabbath

29. (1) Mark 1:21–28; Luke 4:31–37; (2) Matt 8:14–15; Mark 1:29–31; Luke 4:38–39;
(3) Mark 3:1–6; Matt 12:9–14; Luke 6:6–11; (4) Luke 13:10–17; (5) Luke 14:1–6;
(6) John 5:1–18; (7) John 9:1–41.

30. J. C. McCann Jr., "Sabbath," *ISBE*, 4:252.

31. C. W. Dugmore, *The Influence of the Synagogue upon the Divine Office* (London: Oxford University Press, 1944), 28: "Jesus had challenged legalism at this very
point [the Rabbinical prescriptions], but he never attacked the institution of the Sabbath itself." Cf. J. Jeremias, *Neutestamentliche Theologie*, pt. 1, *Die Verkündigung Jesu*.
2nd ed. (Gütersloh: Gütersloher Verlagshaus, 1973), 201 (as cited in Hasel, *ABD*, 4:854):
"Jesus rejected the rabbinic sabbath *halakah* (law)."

was a pre-eminently suitable day for the performance of such works of mercy, whether the case was urgent or not, since such works were so completely in keeping with God's purpose in giving the day."[32] Leon Morris adds, "Deeds of mercy such as He had just done were not merely permissible but obligatory."[33]

Jesus used the Sabbath controversies as teaching moments, reminding His critics that "it is lawful to do good on the Sabbath" (Matt 12:12; Mark 3:4; Luke 6:9). In defense of one Sabbath miracle, He said, "My Father is always at his work to this very day, and I, too, am working" (John 5:17). In this response He not only claimed a divine identity like His Father's; He also characterized the Sabbath as a day for God's people to join in God's own unceasing work of liberating people from sin and its temporal and eternal consequences.

Matthew 24:20: "Pray that your flight will not take place in winter or on the Sabbath." Jesus thus instructed His followers regarding their flight from Jerusalem during its destruction by Rome that occurred in AD 70, some 40 years after He returned to heaven. Commenting on this verse, Davies and Allison conclude, "Matthew presupposed continued observance of the sabbath by Christians."[34] While various interpretations have been advanced, many scholars believe that in this text Matthew has a Sabbath-observing audience in mind.[35] Jesus' instruction safeguarding the quality of His followers' Sabbath observance would be expected of one who assumed the universal and permanent character of the Sabbath.

The Book of Acts: Five times the book of Acts records that the apostles worshipped and preached on the Sabbath (13:14,44; 16:13; 17:2; 18:4). This was their "custom" (17:2), as it had been Jesus' "custom" (Luke 4:16). Some interpreters dismiss such references, claiming

---

32. F. F. Bruce, *New Testament History* (London: Nelson, 1969), 174.

33. L. Morris, *The Gospel According to John,* NICNT (Grand Rapids: Eerdmans, 1995), 409.

34. W. D. Davies and D. C. Allison Jr., *The Gospel According to Saint Matthew*, ICC (Edinburgh: T&T Clark, 1991), 2:328, cf. 3:349–50.

35. E. Lohse, "σάββατον," in *TDNT*, 7:29; W. Carter, *Matthew: Storyteller, Interpreter, Evangelist* (Peabody, MA: Hendrickson, 2004), 82; D. A. Hagner, *Matthew 14–28*, WBC (Dallas: Word, 1995), 701–2; J. A. Overman, *Church and Community in Crisis: The Gospel According to Matthew* (Valley Forge, PA: Trinity Press International, 1996), 177; F. V. Filson, *A Commentary on the Gospel According to St. Matthew* (London: A. and C. Black, 1960), 255; A. W. Argyle, *The Gospel According to Matthew* (Cambridge: Cambridge University Press, 1963), 183; A. Plummer, *An Exegetical Commentary on the Gospel According to S. Matthew*, 2nd ed. (London: J. Clarke, [1910]), 333; Str-B, 1:952–53.

that because Jesus and the apostles also observed the annual feast days on occasion, and those days are no longer observed by almost all Christians, the record that Jesus and the disciples worshipped on the Sabbath does not suggest that they were endorsing its continued observance by the Christian community, especially by Gentile Christians. While their point is acknowledged, it is also true that had Jesus and the apostles believed in the universal and permanent character of the Sabbath, as attested throughout the OT Scriptures (their own Bible), their practice of worshipping every Sabbath as the NT records is exactly what would have been expected. And if they had intended to change it, we would expect them to have done so explicitly.

The apostles hardly limited their preaching on the Sabbath to Jews or to the synagogue. During Paul's extended stay in Corinth, "every Sabbath he reasoned in the synagogue, trying to persuade Jews and Greeks" (Acts 18:4). In Pisidian Antioch, Paul was invited back to speak at the synagogue "the next Sabbath," and "on the next Sabbath almost the whole city gathered to hear the word of the Lord" (13:42,44). "Almost the whole city" certainly included Gentiles in the audience. When they went to Philippi there was no synagogue, so on the Sabbath they found a riverbank to worship where other worshippers gathered for prayer (16:13).

Hebrews 4:9: "There remains, then, a Sabbath-rest (Gk., *sabbatismos*) for the people of God." The majority interpretation of this text, viewed in its wider context of 3:7–4:13, presents the Sabbath as an old-covenant type of a new-covenant spiritual rest in Christ and/or a type of an eschatological rest in the yet-to-come kingdom of God. Thus, now that Christ and the new covenant era have come, the old-covenant type (the seventh-day Sabbath) has met its antitype and no longer applies to new covenant Christians. What the Sabbath pointed forward to in the old covenant has been fulfilled and superseded by a present and continuous rest in the salvation and eternal hope assured by the death and resurrection of Christ, making the old, typical Sabbath of physical rest one day a week obsolete. Thus Moo writes, "The content of all but one of the Ten Commandments is taken up into 'the law of Christ,' for which we are responsible. The exception is the Sabbath commandment, one that Hebrews 3–4 suggests is fulfilled in the new age as a whole."[36] In our view this position seriously misinterprets Hebrews 3–4, and specifically Hebrews 4:9, a text that we believe affirms the universality and permanence of the seventh-day Sabbath. Consider the following points:

First, Gane rightly points out: "If God instituted the Sabbath for human beings before the Fall (Gen 2:2–3), the function/applicability of the Sabbath cannot be dependent upon its belonging to the system of temporary types which God set up after the Fall in order to lead human beings back to belief in him."[37]

Second, an historical type exists only until the historical antitype comes and replaces it. Thus, if the OT Sabbath were a mere historical type of the divine, antitypical "rest" experience—an assured present salvation and heavenly hope—offered to NT believers in Hebrews 4, then that "rest" experience should not have been available to the OT believers who had the seventh-day Sabbath type, because "the type and the antitype do not function at the same time."[38] But the message of Hebrews 3:17–4:13 belies that conclusion.

Hebrews 3:17–4:13 builds on David's appeal in Psalm 95 for the people in his generation not to harden their hearts in unbelief and disobedience as their ancestors did when they disobeyed God's command to cross the Jordan and take Canaan (a reference to the rebellion recorded in Numbers 14). Joshua later gave the post-Numbers 14 generation "rest" from their enemies and appealed to them to be faithful to God (Josh 22:4–5), but because of their continued unbelief and disobedience, they failed to obtain the spiritual rest in God that was offered to them (Heb 3:17–19; 4:8). In Psalm 95 David appealed to his own generation not to "harden your hearts as you did in the rebellion," and thus fail again to enter the spiritual rest God offered them (Heb 3:7–11). The clear and forceful message of Heb 3:17–4:13 is that Moses' generation failed to enter God's rest not because it was not available to them but because of their unbelief and disobedience (3:18–19).

Through His covenants with Adam, Noah, Abraham, Israel, and in the historical new covenant era, God had made His "rest"

---

36. D. Moo, "The Law of Christ as the Fulfillment of the Law of Moses," in *Five Views on Law and Gospel*, ed. S. N. Gundry (Grand Rapids: Zondervan, 1996), 376. Moo footnotes Carson (ed.), *From Sabbath to Lord's Day* in support.

37. R. Gane, "Sabbath and the New Covenant," *Journal of the Adventist Theological Society*, 10 (1999): 318.

38. Ibid.

universally available to all who would believe (Heb 4:2; 11:13–16). Throughout the OT period the proclamation of the gospel inviting people to enter God's rest, by trusting His promise of present salvation and ultimate eternal rest, existed side by side with the observance of the seventh-day Sabbath, as it does yet today. Throughout salvation history the seventh-day Sabbath has functioned not as a temporary *type* of that rest but as a permanent *sign* of it—"so you may know that I am the Lord, who makes you holy" (Exod 31:13).

Third, all eight previous and subsequent uses of the word *rest* in Hebrews 3–4 are a translation of the Greek word *katapausis*. But in Hebrews 4:9 the author deliberately used the Greek word *sabbatismos*, a word not used elsewhere in the NT but used in the Septuagint and extrabiblical sources to mean observance of the seventh-day Sabbath.[39] In Heb 4:9 the author left no doubt as to what he intended to say, that in the NT/new-covenant historical era a *sabbatismos* (Sabbath observance) remains for the people of God. And he left no doubt what he meant by "Sabbath observance," for in verse 4 he referenced it to the original Sabbath rest experienced and provided by God at creation: "For somewhere he has spoken about the seventh day in these words: 'And on the seventh day God rested from all his work.'" Justin Martyr (ca. AD 150) asserted that if Sabbath observance (*sabbatismos*) was not needed before Moses, there is no need for it now (in the NT era).[40] The very seventh-day Sabbath observance that Justin claimed did not remain, and that many modern expositors claim does not remain, the author of Hebrews maintains does: "There remains, then, a Sabbath-rest [*sabbatismos*, Sabbath observance] for the people of God" (4:9).[41]

---

39. A. T. Lincoln, "Sabbath, Rest, and Eschatology in the New Testament," in *From Sabbath to the Lord's Day*, ed. Carson, 213: "The term [σαββατισμός (*sabbatismos*)] denotes the observance or celebration of the Sabbath. This usage corresponds to the Septuagint usage of the cognate verb σαββατίζω [*sabbatizō*] (cf. Exod 16:30; Lev 23:32; 26:34f.; 2 Chron 36:21) which also has reference to Sabbath observance." Cf. S. Bacchiocchi, *The Sabbath Under Crossfire* (Berrien Springs, MI: Biblical Perspectives, 1998), 124: "*Sabbatismos* . . . was used by pagans and Christians as a technical term for Sabbath-keeping. Examples can be found in the writings of Plutarch, Justin, Epiphanius, the Apostolic Constitutions, and the Martyrdom of Peter and Paul." Bacchiocchi references Plutarch, *De Superstitione* 3 (Moralia 1660); Justin Martyr, *Dialogue with Trypho* 23, 3; Epiphanius, *Adversus Haereses* 30, 2, 2; *Apostolic Constitutions* 2, 36.

40. *Dialogue with Trypho*, 23.

41. W. G. Johnsson, *Hebrews* (Boise, ID: Pacific Press, 1994), 96: "In my judgment, Heb 4:1–11 gives us the strongest evidence in favor of the seventh-day Sabbath in the entire New Testament. . . . Our rest in Christ, says the author, has the *quality* of the Sabbath. It is *like* the Sabbath. . . . Two conclusions seem inescapable. First, for him and

Fourth, in Hebrews 7–10 the author went to great lengths to explain that the OT priesthood and animal sacrifices, those functions associated directly with the earthly temple, functioned as types, and that they met their antitype in the heavenly priesthood and once-for-all sacrifice of Jesus and are thus "obsolete" (Heb 8:13). In Hebrews 3–4 he went to equal lengths to affirm that "there remains, then, a Sabbath-rest [*sabbatismos*, Sabbath observance] for the people of God" (4:9). In other words, the seventh-day Sabbath as observed by OT believers (as represented, for example, by those honored in Hebrews 11) "remains . . . for the people of God" in the NT era.

Fifth, note the following parallels between the way the NT treats the creation ordinances of the Sabbath and marriage as permanent:

Hebrews 4:4–9	Ephesians 5:31–33
Reference to the creation ordinance of the Sabbath: "On the seventh day God rested from all his work" (v. 4, quoting Gen 2:2).	Reference to creation ordinance of marriage: "A man will leave his father and mother and be united to his wife" (v. 31, quoting Gen 2:24).
Deeper spiritual meaning and application of the Sabbath as gospel rest: "Some [will] enter that rest . . . the good news proclaimed to them" (v. 6).	Deeper spiritual meaning and application of marriage: "I am talking about Christ and the church" (v. 32).
Reaffirmation of the permanence of the creation ordinance of the Sabbath: "There remains, then, a Sabbath-rest [Sabbath observance] for the people of God" (v. 9).	Reaffirmation of the permanence of the creation ordinance of marriage: "Each one of you also must love his wife . . . , and the wife must respect her husband" (v. 33).

While the NT gives the creation ordinance of marriage an even deeper meaning now that Christ has come, it does not thereby consider the marriage institution as a type to be replaced by Christ and the church. If anything, it invests the marriage institution with an even greater significance. The same is true of the Sabbath.

Sixth, the Lord's Supper signifies both the death of Jesus for our sins and His return in glory (1 Cor 11:26). When a believer experiences a spiritual death and resurrection with Christ, signified by baptism (Rom 6:2–3; Col 2:12), and begins eagerly to "wait for the

---

his readers, the Sabbath had a positive connotation. If they had considered it a burden, the last remains of a religion of bondage, the author would have lost his audience at this critical moment. Second, both he and his audience were keeping the Sabbath. They had no thought about any other day. Certainly they weren't debating the merits of Sabbath versus Sunday. Only in such a context could he call rest in Christ a *sabbatismos*."

blessed hope—the glorious appearing of our great God and Savior, Jesus Christ" (Titus 2:13), that does not make participation in the Lord's Supper obsolete. The Lord's Supper, like the Sabbath, does not function as a *type* of that experience but as a divine institution designed to *enhance* that experience. Similarly, to experience a present gospel rest in Jesus and eagerly expect the eschatological rest in His kingdom when He returns does not make Sabbath observance obsolete but *enhances* it. In fact, only true gospel believers who trust the Lord as their righteousness and rest in Him, not in their own works, can truly observe the Sabbath as a holy people.

Seventh, note the logic of the author's continuing message in Heb 4:8–16: Just as Joshua provided Israel with *physical* rest from their enemies but could not provide them with *spiritual* rest because of their unbelief and disobedience (Heb 4:8), in the same way one may cease from *physical* labor on the Sabbath and not enter the deeper *spiritual* rest it signifies. Thus, while a Sabbath observance remains for the people of God (Heb 4:9), only a holy people can observe a holy day. "Anyone who enters God's rest [resting in the gospel promise of righteousness by faith rather than works, and in the promise of the new earth to come—both themes of Heb 11] also rests from their works, just as God did from his" (Heb 4:10). Then the author of Hebrews appeals, in the classical tradition of the Sabbath reform prophets: "Let us, therefore, make every effort to enter that [deeper spiritual, gospel] rest, so that no one will perish by following their example of disobedience" (Heb 4:11). And finally, verses 12–13 remind the reader that the "word of God," and indeed God Himself, are "alive and active" and judge "the thoughts and attitudes of the heart" (Heb 4:12–13). In other words, God will reveal the true "thoughts and attitudes" of one's heart with regard to the quality of their Sabbath observance, which serves as an indicator to the quality of one's spiritual condition generally. If God were to convict someone of ignoring the Sabbath for financial gain or to pursue their own pleasures, that would be a warning signal regarding the un-ideal state of their spiritual health generally. The same would be true if God revealed that one's Sabbath observance was legalistically tainted, robbed of spiritual significance or delight. However, that very divine judgment would also be a "living and active" word of grace and promise—a promise to all who draw near to His throne of grace to receive His mercy and grace to make them holy as He is holy (Heb 4:14–16). And of just such an assurance the Sabbath was appointed as a sign (Exod 31:12; Ezek 20:12).

Objections to the Universal and Permanent Seventh-Day Sabbath Position

Many objections have been made to the universal and permanent character of the seventh-day Sabbath. This section briefly considers the major ones.

Texts Related to the Sabbath's Perpetuity

Colossians 2:16–17: "Therefore do not let anyone judge you by what you eat or drink, or with regard to a religious festival, a New Moon celebration or a Sabbath day. These are a shadow of the things that were to come; the reality, however, is found in Christ." The majority view holds that Paul here proclaims that the seventh-day Sabbath was a mere shadow of things to come, and now that Christ has come, Sabbath observance is no longer applicable.

Against this interpretation is Isaiah's revelation that in the new earth yet to come, "'from one New Moon [or "month"[42]] to another and from one Sabbath to another, all mankind will come and bow down before me,' says the Lord" (Isa 66:22–23). Paul does not nullify in Col 2:16 what God through Isaiah declared will remain universal and permanent.

Although the question of the heresy that the apostle is attacking is hotly debated, it is clear that it has to do with a "hollow and deceptive philosophy, which depends on human tradition and the elemental spiritual forces of this world" (Col 2:8). It is based on "human commands and teachings" (2:22). That description cannot be applied to the Sabbath commandment of the law of God. Even when the apostle refers to the regulations of the heresy as being "a shadow of the things that were to come" (v. 17), the Sabbath is excluded because, as we indicated already, it was instituted before the fall. Any interpretation of the passage that finds in it the proper observance of the Sabbath commandment goes against the context.

---

42. In Isa 66:23 the LXX employs the Greek term *mēn*—the normal Greek word for "month" (see *TDOT*, 4:229), whereas Col 2:16 uses the word *neomēnia* "new moon [festival]," which is identified as a "shadow" pointing to Christ. See n. 14.

Numerous scholars, for differing reasons, believe that Paul never intended his Col 2:16–17 statement as an abolishment of the Sabbath as a sacred day of worship.[43]

---

43. E.g., T. Martin, "Pagan and Judeo-Christian Time-Keeping Schemes in Gal 4:10 and Col 2:16," *NTS* 42 (1996): 105–19, suggests that Paul was admonishing Colossian believers not to be deterred from their observances of these days by critics. Representative of scholars who believe that Col 2:16 warns against legalistic observance of sacred days is R. P. Martin, *Colossians and Philemon* (Grand Rapids: Eerdmans, 1973), 90. Representative of the view that the New Moon and Sabbath celebrations mentioned in Col 2:16 referred exclusively to the ceremonial sacrifices offered at these special celebrations, which sacrifices were indeed "a shadow of the things that were to come" and that had now found their "reality in Christ," is P. Giem, "*Sabbatōn* in Col 2:16," *AUSS*, 19 (1981): 195–210. Representative of the view that the Sabbaths in Col 2:16 are ceremonial Sabbaths rather than the seventh-day Sabbath is G. H. Clark, *Colossians: Another Commentary on an Inexhaustible Message* (Phillipsburg, NJ: Presbyterian and Reformed, 1979), 94–97. Especially promising, representing this latter view, is R. du Preez, *Judging the Sabbath: Discovering What Can't Be Found in Colossians 2:16* (Berrien Springs, MI: Andrews University Press, 2008), which in private correspondence he summarized for this chapter as follows.

"Examination of all 180 occurrences of sabbath terminology in Scripture (i.e., *šabbt*, *sabbaton* and *sabbata*) reveals that the writers consistently surrounded these terms with definitive, reliable syntactical and linguistic markers that enable the reader to quickly recognize which type of sabbath is being indicated. In both Hebrew and Greek, about 85% of the cases deal with the weekly Sabbath, while the rest refer to something else, such as ritual sabbaths, or weeks. Thus, linguistic links and context are vital in interpreting the *sabbata* of Colossians 2:16.

"Several passages from Numbers, 1 and 2 Chronicles, Nehemiah, and Ezekiel are alleged to contain a three-part *yearly, monthly, weekly* sequence (or its reverse), supposedly similar to that located in Colossians 2:16. However, serious exegetical scrutiny of each passage reveals that they have a different focus, and are rather distinct from the Colossian text.

"Interestingly, Hosea 2:11 and Colossians 2:16 have several similarities: both make no mention of any daily ritual activity, both consist of essentially three main terms given in the singular number and stated in the same sequence, both focus on the appointed times rather than the sacrifices, and both lack linguistic markers that identify the weekly Sabbath. The linguistic evidence reveals that the Hebrew word *ag* of Hosea 2:11 refers to the three annual pilgrim festivals of Passover, Pentecost, and Tabernacles. *ōdeš* refers to the new moon, which played a vital role in determining dates for other appointed sacred seasons. The term *šabbatth* (her sabbath) identifies this as Israel's ritual sabbath(s), rather than the weekly seventh-day Sabbath, which is never spoken of in this way.

"Similarly, linguistic study of the crucial terms of Colossians 2:16 reveals that in the New Testament *heortē* is limited to the three annual festivals (i.e., Passover, Pentecost, and Tabernacles), *neomēnia* indicates the lunar new year celebrations, while *sabbata* includes the three ritual rest times (i.e., Trumpets, Atonement, and Sabbatical years). In short, the lexicographical evidence, the linguistic markers, and the context together show that this three–part phrase in Hosea 2:11 (i.e., feast, new moon, sabbath) synchronizes well with the similar phrase in Colossians 2:16, and seems to show evidence of a characteristic of Semitic communication—a semantic inverted parallelism, in which the writer moves from annual to monthly and then on to augmented annual festivals, as follows:

A	*festivals*	=	*3 annual pilgrimage feasts*
B	new moons	=	monthly celebrations
A+	*sabbaths*	=	*2 annual & 1 septennial rest*

Galatians 4:10–11: "You are observing special days and months and seasons and years! I fear for you, that somehow I have wasted my efforts on you." Many have interpreted this as an anti–sabbatarian text. But even if Paul did have the seventh-day Sabbath in view here, numerous scholars have suggested that Paul is not arguing against the observance of sacred days but against a legalistic observance of them.[44]

In Gal 4:10–11 Paul addresses those who "did not know God" (v. 8), most likely former pagans whose worship practices followed a pagan religious calendar. Martin's research reveals that Paul's reference to "days and months and seasons and years" was "most characteristic of a pagan time-keeping system" and suggests that Paul's warning in this passage is addressed to Christian converts from paganism who were in danger of reverting to their former pagan sacred times and rituals.[45]

Romans 14:5: "One person considers one day more sacred than another; another considers every day alike. Each of them should be fully convinced in their own mind." This is a key text for those who believe there are no divinely ordained sacred days in the NT era.

Paul begins this chapter by admonishing Christians against "passing judgment on *disputable matters*" (v. 1, emphasis added). It is highly unlikely that Paul was suggesting that the Sabbath, which God embedded in the Ten Commandments, which Jesus said "was made for man," and on which God said that "all mankind will come and bow down before me" in the "new earth," was a "disputable matter."

"The above finding is further reinforced by Colossians 2:17, which provides an immediate context. The *skia* is here understood as a foreshadowing, since it is directly linked with the *tōn mellontōn*, that is, things to come—a recognized phrase used for the messianic age and kingdom that had arrived with Jesus Christ. The ancient Israelite ritual system—with its pilgrim feasts, new moon celebrations, and various ceremonial sabbaths—included symbols pointing forward to the work of the Messiah. In Christ, the reality has come, of which the sacred observances were the prefigurement.

"In brief, the compelling weight of inter-textual, comparative, linguistic, semantic, syntactical, grammatical, structural, and contextual evidence synchronizes to demonstrate that the *sabbata* of Colossians 2:16 refers to ancient Hebrew ritual sabbaths, and not the weekly Sabbath of the decalogue."

44. E.g., K. S. Wuest, *Galatians in the Greek New Testament* (Grand Rapids: Eerdmans, 1946), 122; W. Hendriksen, *New Testament Commentary: Exposition of Galatians* (Grand Rapids: Baker, 1968) 166.

45. T. Martin, "Pagan and Judeo-Christian Time-Keeping Schemes," 112. Another scholar who agrees with Martin's conclusion of a pagan calendar scheme in Gal 4:10 is M. D. Nanos, *The Irony of Galatians: Paul's Letter in First-Century Context* (Minneapolis: Fortress Press, 2002), 267, 270.

The NIV translation of Rom 14:5, "considers one day more sacred than another," adds "sacred" to the Greek text, which literally says, "judges a day above a day" (*krina hēmeran par hēmeran*). Some scholars believe that Paul had in mind fast days rather than sacred days, a conclusion supported by the wider context of Romans 14.[46] A number of scholars add that the dispute within the Jewish Christian community included whether Christians could or should observe certain ceremonial days, such as Passover, which had been fulfilled by Christ's sacrifice, as distinguished from the Sabbath that Christ had instituted at creation.[47]

Paul's message in Romans 14 is: In *disputable* matters of whether to observe ceremonies and days not specifically prescribed in Scripture, let each decide for himself. Such observances are neither prohibited nor required. Let each be convinced in his own mind about such things.

The First Day of the Week Texts

Many Christians believe that the practice of worship on Sunday is based on an explicit New Testament command that clearly states that the observance of the seventh-day Sabbath should be replaced with worship on the first day of the week in honor of Jesus' resurrection. Scholars know this not to be the case. This section briefly examines the eight NT passages that mention "the first day of the week" and one that mentions "after eight days," in light of the controversy over which day should be observed, if any.

The Resurrection Texts

In a matter-of-fact statement, Matthew specifies the time of Jesus' resurrection in these words: "After the Sabbath, at dawn on the first day of the week" (28:1). Similar language is used in Mark 16:1–2, Luke 24:1, and John 20:1 for the timing of His resurrection. Mark 16:9–14 adds that He appeared later that same day to Mary Magdalene, to two others (cf. Luke 24:13–35), and to "the Eleven" disciples. John adds that Jesus' visit to the disciples that day included His breathing on them that they might receive the Holy Spirit (20:19–23). John also

---

46. E.g., R. J. Karris, "Romans 14:1–15:13 and the Occasion of Romans," in *The Romans Debate*, ed. K. P. Donfried (Minneapolis: Augsburg, 1977), 89–90.

47. E.g., C. R. Erdman, *The Epistle of Paul to the Romans* (Philadelphia: Westminster Press, 1966), 143: "So, too, one man regards certain days as particularly holy, while another regards all days alike, excepting of course the Sabbath Day."

records a visit Jesus made to the disciples "a week later" (lit., "after eight days," *meth' hēmeras oktō*) to show Himself to Thomas who had not been present at Jesus' first visit with the disciples and who doubted that He had been resurrected (20:26–29).

There is no hint in any of these accounts of any expectation that "the first day of the week" might have significance as a continuing worship day, replacing the Sabbath commandment. The Gospel writers mention the Sabbath as many times (6) in the resurrection narrative as they do the first day of the week. While most were matter-of-fact references, one was not. Luke, writing years after the fact, pointed out that as Jesus rested in the tomb, a group of His close followers "rested on the Sabbath in obedience to the commandment" (Luke 23:56; cf. Mark 16:1). Davies and Allison comment: "These texts imply that the women in Jesus' entourage kept the sabbath. Would they have done so if they had learned from Jesus not to observe it?"[48]

Acts 20:7: "On the first day of the week we came together to break bread. Paul spoke to the people and, because he intended to leave the next day, kept on talking until midnight." Many interpreters consider this to be evidence of a Communion service on the first day of the week, Sunday, thus indicating that the early church considered Sunday a holy day.

Does "break bread" refer to the Lord's Supper or to a fellowship meal on the eve of Paul's departure the next morning, which would fit the context? Note that Acts 2:46 uses the term "broke bread" in reference to daily gatherings in their homes. If Acts 20:7 does record a Lord's Supper observance on this particular occasion, it would not establish Sunday as a weekly worship day in the early church. Participating in the Lord's Supper on any given day does not establish that day as a universal and permanent sacred day. In 1 Corinthians 11 Paul gives instructions for the observance of the Lord's Supper. Rather than directing that the Lord's Supper be celebrated

---

48. Davies and Allison, *Matthew*, 2:312, n. 33. Cf. M. D. Goulder, *Luke: A New Paradigm* (Sheffield, England: Sheffield Academic Press, 1989), 2:772; I. H. Marshall, *The Gospel of Luke* (Grand Rapids: Eerdmans, 1978), 883; F. Godet, *A Commentary on the Gospel of Saint Luke* (Edinburgh: T & T Clark, 1870), 2:343. This position harmonizes with the findings of G. W. Klingsporn's Baylor University Ph.D. dissertation, *The Law in the Gospel of Luke* (1985), 431, 434–35: "Throughout his gospel, Luke presents the law in a favorable light. . . . He makes no attempt to 'Christianize the law,' that is, to reinterpret it with a view to the Christian church. As the law was a sign of Israel's identity as God's people, so it is also a sign of the identity of Jesus and the church as people of God who stand in continuity with God's people and God's promises of the past."

on a specific day, he designates the appropriate timing as "when you come together as a church" (vv. 18–19,33). Over the years I have participated in the Lord's Supper on each of the seven days of the week as my church has come together for many different occasions. But that doesn't establish any of those days as universal and permanent sacred days. Only the sovereign God Himself has the authority to establish a day holy as a continuing worship day.

1 Corinthians 16:1–2: "Now about the collection for the Lord's people: Do what I told the Galatian churches to do. On the first day of every week, each one of you should set aside a sum of money in keeping with your income, saving it up, so that when I come no collections will have to be made." Many interpreters cite this text as evidence that Corinthian believers were already meeting on Sunday as their weekly worship day.

Acts 18 records Paul's extended visit to Corinth during his second missionary journey. While there, "every Sabbath he reasoned in the synagogue, trying to persuade Jews and Greeks" (v. 4). The church he established there was undoubtedly a mixture of the Gentile and Jewish audience he had been reasoning with "every Sabbath." It was only a few years after he planted the church in Corinth that he wrote 1 Corinthians, around AD 55. It seems to us highly unlikely that this entire congregation of Jewish and Gentile converts would have been worshipping every Sunday in honor of the resurrection of Jesus so soon after their conversion. There is no corroborating evidence for such a precedent in the NT. This unlikelihood is strengthened further by the fact that many in the Corinthian congregation had already lost faith in a resurrection, as the entire fifteenth chapter of 1 Corinthians, which addresses this problem, attests. Would these worshippers be worshipping weekly on a day that honors a resurrection they didn't believe happened?

F. F. Bruce finds: "It is doubtful whether there is any liturgical significance in this mention of the first day of every week, except that the week was plainly introduced to the Gentile churches from the earliest days. Nor were the individual sums to be taken to church and handed over to the community treasurer: each member is to put something aside *par' heautō,* 'at home,' and store it up there" (emphasis original).[49] Once Paul arrived back in Corinth, he would collect it from them to distribute it to the needy in Jerusalem (1 Cor 16:3).

Why Paul's admonition to set the money aside on the "first day of the week"? Paul could simply have had in mind the beginning of the week. McKnight suggests that Paul was simply "encouraging others among his churches to set aside funds weekly in an orderly fashion so when he arrived there would be a full allotment for the saints."[50]

It seems to us that God would hardly have chosen such an oblique vehicle as an offering appeal to announce the annulment of the sanctity of the day He sovereignly chose to bless and sanctify at creation, and embedded in the heart of the Ten Commandments.

The "Lord's Day" Text

Revelation 1:10: "On the Lord's Day [Gk., *kuriakē hēmera*] I was in the Spirit, and I heard behind me a loud voice like a trumpet." John proceeds to describe a vision given to him by Jesus, possibly containing the entire book of Revelation. Scholars generally consider the "Lord's Day" in this text as a reference to Sunday, indicating that Sunday was considered a sacred day in John's time. But even if John's phrase "Lord's Day" in this text meant Sunday, that would not establish Sunday as a weekly day of worship replacing the Sabbath of creation and the Sabbath commandment.

However, biblical evidence that the "Lord's Day" meant Sunday is entirely lacking. As does the rest of the NT, John in his own Gospel twice refers to Sunday as "the first day of the week," not the "Lord's Day."

There is no evidence that the term "Lord's Day" was ever used as an appellation for Sunday until decades after John used it in Revelation 1:10.[51] Barnabas of Alexandria (c. AD 130) and Justin Martyr in

49. F. F. Bruce, *1 and 2 Corinthians* (London: Oliphants, 1971), 158; cf. D. R. de Lacey, "The Sabbath/Sunday Question and the Law in the Pauline Corpus," in *From Sabbath to Lord's Day*, 185: "Our text [1 Cor 16:2] gives no support for the positing of any particular practice or belief relating to Sunday on the part of Paul or the church."

50. S. McKnight, "Collection for the Saints," in *Dictionary of Paul and His Letters*, ed. G. F. Hawthorne, R. P. Martin, and D. G. Reid (Downers Grove, IL: InterVarsity, 1993), 143.

51. For expanded sabbatarian analyses of the use of this term in early Christian literature see K. A. Strand, "The 'Lord's Day' in the Second Century," in *The Sabbath in Scripture and History*, ed. K. A. Strand (Washington, DC: Review and Herald, 1982),

Rome (c. AD 150), whose writings give the earliest evidence of weekly Christian worship on Sunday, never use the term "Lord's Day."

The *Didache*, an early[52] church polity manual, uses the phrase (*kuriakēn kuriou*), literally, "the Lord's of the Lord," but does not supply a noun for the adjective "Lord's" (*kuriakēn*), leaving the missing noun to be supplied by the translators. While many interpreters supply the word *day* and suggest it refers to weekly Sunday worship, others interpret "the Lord's of the Lord" to mean an annual Easter celebration,[53] and still others have supplied the word *doctrine* ("the Lord's doctrine").[54] The latter interpretation, in our view, more closely favors the internal evidence.

Ignatius, Bishop of Antioch, writing to the Magnesians around AD 115, used the phrase, "No longer sabbatizing [Gk., *sabbatizontes*], but living according to the Lord's [*kuriakēn*]." Again, as with the *Didache*, "the Greek word for 'day' [*hēmeran*, in the accusative case] is *not* in the text," and has to be supplied by translators,[55] a choice which, in our view, is suspect. In context Ignatius refers to the *OT prophets* as the ones who were "no longer sabbatizing [*maketi sabbatizontes*], but living according to the Lord's."[56] Ignatius surely did not mean the OT prophets had given up the Sabbath and were worshipping on Sunday.[57] The oldest remaining Greek copy

---

346–51; A. M. Rodríguez, "The Biblical Sabbath: The Adventist Perspective," unpublished paper available at adventistbiblicalresearch.org, 19–20.

52. *Oxford Dictionary of the Christian Church*, ed. E. A. Livingstone (Oxford University Press, 1997), 479: The earliest manuscript available, 1056, is from a composition scholars date variously from AD 60 to the late second century, but "author, date and place of origin are unknown."

53. C. W. Dugmore, "Lord's Day and Easter," *Neotestamentica et Patristica* (festschrift for Oscar Cullmann), NovTSup 6 (Leiden, 1962): 272–81, cited in Strand, "The 'Lord's Day' in the Second Century," 351.

54. E.g., J. B. Thibaut, *La Liturgie Romaine*, 1924, 33–34, this and other references cited in S. Bacchiocchi, *From Sabbath to Sunday: A Historical Investigation of the Rise of Sunday Observance in Early Christianity* (Rome: Pontifical Gregorian University Press, 1977; reprint, Berrien Springs, MI: Biblical Perspectives, 2000), 114.

55. Strand, "The 'Lord's Day' in the Second Century," 349.

56. Ibid.

57. R. J. Bauckham in "The Lord's Day," in *From Sabbath to Lord's Day*, ed. Carson, 229, suggests that Ignatius may have meant that the OT prophets "abandoned the practice of Judaism and lived in hope of the new life, which would become available on the day of Christ's resurrection (cf. the whole context in chapters 8 and 9)." We find that highly unlikely, especially if Bauckham means Ignatius taught that the OT prophets abandoned the Sinaitic covenant to which they continually admonished Israel and Judah to be faithful. In "the whole context of chapters 8 and 9" (four verses total) to which Bauckham refers, we find insufficient support for his suggestion. He also claims (240) that in this disputed verse (Ignatius, *To the Magnesians* 9:1) "the association of Sunday

of Ignatius's letter[58] supplies the word "life" (*zōēn*), rendering the phrase, "living according to the Lord's life."[59] Thus, Ignatius argues against living a legalistic lifestyle (*sabbatizontes*) but instead "living according to the Lord's life."[60] In our view this better fits the context, for the next phrase in the sentence reads, "on which [i.e., on Christ's life] our life as well as theirs [the OT prophets] shone forth."[61]

The first unambiguous use of "Lord's" (*kuriakē*) with the noun "day" in reference to Sunday occurs somewhere between AD 150 and 190 in the apocryphal *Gospel of Peter*, but it refers to the actual day of Christ's resurrection and not to a weekly day of worship.[62] The apocryphal *Acts of Peter*, "perhaps in the decade 180–190," appears to use the term "Lord's Day" (*kuriakē hēmera*) for a Christian weekly Sunday, but it also refers to the Sabbath as a day people brought their sick to be healed.[63]

The historical records reveal that the first unambiguous connection between "Lord's Day" and Sunday does not show up in Christian literature until the second half of the second century, many decades after John used the term. Therefore, it is clear that those who interpret the "Lord's Day" in Rev 1:10 as Sunday do this on the basis of extrabiblical evidence that is much later than the time when John wrote Revelation. This is an unsound methodology of biblical interpretation.

[worship] with the Resurrection" is clear. However, *Magn*. 9:1 makes no explicit or even implied reference to the resurrection.

58. There are three recensions of Ignatius's letters: long, middle, and abbreviated. Modern scholars generally agree that the authentic version of Ignatius's letters is that known as the middle recension. The only surviving manuscript of Magnesians in the middle recension in Greek is the eleventh-century Mediceo-Laurentianus, which reads *kuriakēn zōēn*. The two manuscripts of the Latin version of the middle recension lack this.

59. *Patrologue*, ed. J. P. Migne (Paris: Apud Garnier Fratres, 1894), 5:670b.

60. R. K. McIver, *Beyond the Da Vinci Code* (Nampa, ID: Pacific Press, 2006), 123–24: "While 'Lord's day' might balance the reference to 'sabbatizing,' it is not the only possibility. Indeed, as the Greek manuscript says 'Lord's life,' this has to be the preferable translation. If that is the case, 'Sabbatizing' might be a reference to living too rigidly according to the Jewish laws, rather as Paul asks 'If you, though a Jew, live like a Gentile, and not like a Jew, how can you compel the Gentiles to live like Jews' (literally: how can you compel Gentiles to 'Judaize'?—Greek, *Ioudaïzein* [Gal 2:14])."

61. *Early Christian Fathers*, ed., trans. C. C. Richardson (Philadelphia: Westminster Press, 1953), 96. For further analysis from a sabbatarian perspective, see Strand, "The 'Lord's Day' in the Second Century," 349; cf. Rodríguez, "Biblical Sabbath," 19–20.

62. *The Gospel of Peter* 9:35, 12:50; *New Testament Apocrypha*, ed. W. Schneemelcher (Cambridge: J. Clarke, 1991), 1:221, 224–25.

63. *Acts of Peter*, 1, 29–31; *New Testament Apocrypha*, 2:283, 285, 311–12.

Bauckham claims that the context of the Apocalypse suggests that the "Lord's Day" in 1:10 refers to Sunday as the day on which the churches to which John was writing worshipped.[64] Bauckham argues that a major theme in Revelation is the sovereignty of God exercised through Christ versus Satan's claim to sovereignty and suggests that Christian worship on the Lord's Day, Sunday, acknowledged the sovereign lordship of Christ that had been established by His resurrection (Rev 1:5,18; 2:8) on the first day of the week. He rightly suggests another major theme as that of "worship," mentioned eight times in Revelation 13–14 alone. However, in Revelation the appeal to worship God is linked to the Sabbath commandment rather than the first day of the week. Compare the italicized phrase in Rev 14:7, "Worship him, who *made the heavens, the earth, the sea and* the springs of water," with the italicized phrase in Exod 20:11, "in six days the Lord *made the heavens* and *the earth, the sea, and* all that is in them, but he rested on the seventh day . . . blessed the Sabbath day and made it holy" (Exod 20:11).[65] Furthermore, the larger context of Rev 14:7 contains references to "God's commandments," which certainly include the Decalogue, and describes God's people just prior to the Second Coming as those who "keep his command and remain faithful to Jesus" (14:12,14–20; cf. 11:19; 12:17).[66]

---

64. Bauckham, "The Lord's Day," 240–45.

65. Note the matching Greek words from Rev 14:7 and the LXX Greek translation of Exod 20:11:

| Lev 14:7: | *poiēsanti ton ouranon kai tēn gēn kai tēn thalassan kai* |
| Exod 20:11: | *epoiēse ton ouranon kai tēn gēn kai thalassan kai* |

(*Poiēsanti* and *epoiēse* are different forms of the same verb—make/made.) The missing *tēn* ("the") in Exod 20:11 is found in several ancient Greek manuscripts. Nestle-Aland Greek Text cross references Rev 14:7 with Exod 20:11. Cf. J. Paulien, "Revisiting the Sabbath in the Book of Revelation," *Journal of the Adventist Theological Society* 9/1–2 (1998): 185: When the verbal and thematic connections and structural parallels of Rev 14:7 are matched with Exod 20:11, "the cumulative evidence is so strong that an interpreter could conclude that there is no direct allusion to the Old Testament in Revelation that is more certain than the allusion to the [Sabbath] commandment in Rev 14:7."

66. Revelation 11:19 records John's vision of the heavenly temple containing "the ark of his covenant" accompanied by physical manifestations associated with the giving of the Ten Commandments on Mount Sinai. Numerous commentators on Rev 11:19 have reminded their readers that the ark of the covenant in the OT temple contained the Ten Commandments (Exod 25:10–22; Deut 10:1–5) and that the dramatic physical manifestations associated with this vision recall the giving of the Ten Commandments on Mount Sinai (Exod 19:16–19). Nestle-Aland Greek Text cross references Rev 11:19 with Exod 19:18. See also J. M. Ford, *Revelation*, Anchor Bible Commentary (Garden

If one bases the interpretation of Rev 1:10 on the Bible itself instead of extrabiblical sources, the result is quite different. Scripture describes the seventh day of creation and the day referenced in the Sabbath commandment as "a sabbath to the Lord your God" (Exod 20:10), a day that God Himself calls "my Sabbaths" (Lev 19:3,30) and "my holy day" (Isa 58:13). Jesus claimed this day exclusively as His: "The Son of Man is Lord of the Sabbath" (Matt 12:8; Mark 2:28; Luke 6:5). Jesus never proclaimed, "The Son of Man is Lord of the first day." Had He in fact made such a claim, would it not be the key to establish the "Lord's day" in Rev 1:10 as a reference to Sunday? Why then would His proclamation, "The Son of Man is Lord of the Sabbath" not be the key to establish the "Lord's day" in Rev 1:10 as a reference to the seventh-day Sabbath? Based on Scripture alone, John's use of the term "the Lord's Day" more likely supports the perpetuity of the seventh-day Sabbath than the substitution of Sunday for Sabbath.

The texts discussed in this section lack any clear command from God that the sanctity of the seventh day—the day He sovereignly established at creation to be blessed and sanctified, included in the Ten Commandments, and honored as a perpetual day of worship in the new earth—was ever withdrawn and another day of worship substituted in its place. This section also reveals the paucity of texts that can be summoned to support Sunday observance. Most of them contain no hint that such a change was even contemplated, let alone initiated. The three texts that could be even remotely interpreted as anti-Sabbath (Rom 14:5; Gal 4:10; Col 2:16), or the four texts possibly suggesting a Sunday meeting of some kind (John 20:26; Acts 20:7; 1 Cor 16:2; Rev 1:10), are all circumstantial at best and do not alter the universality or permanence of the seventh-day Sabbath. All of the texts above presented opportunities to the biblical authors to state explicitly that God was withdrawing His sovereign blessing and sanctification of the seventh day and transferring it to another. But no such revelation was forthcoming. Given the substantial unanimity of the sacred record regarding the seventh-day Sabbath in OT Scripture, God could hardly hold it against a NT believer for expecting an explicit announcement annulling it had He intended such. Such announcements were explicitly and

City, NY: Doubleday, 1975), 182; H. B. Swete, *The Apocalypse of St. John* (Grand Rapids: Eerdmans, 1951), 145.

strongly provided regarding circumcision (e.g., Acts 15; Gal 5:2), which had been neither blessed and sanctified at creation nor embedded in the Ten Commandments. But the sacred record lacks any such announcement with regard to the Sabbath. To the contrary, Paul taught: "Circumcision is nothing and uncircumcision is nothing. Keeping God's commands is what counts" (1 Cor 7:19).

The Record of Church History

Many scholars cite documents from early church history as evidence that Christians from NT times worshipped almost unanimously on Sunday instead of Sabbath in honor of Jesus' resurrection. Even were that the case, we would still take our cue from Scripture, not from church history.[67] But a careful study of the historical documents raises serious questions about such a conclusion. For example, note the following testimony of two fifth-century church historians: "For although almost all churches throughout the world celebrate the sacred mysteries [the Lord's Supper] on the Sabbath [Saturday] of every week, yet the Christians of Alexandria and at Rome, on account of some ancient tradition, have ceased to do this."[68] "Assemblies are not held in all churches on the same time or manner. The people of Constantinople, and almost everywhere, assemble together on the Sabbath, as well as on the first day of the week, which custom is never observed at Rome or at Alexandria."[69]

Clearly, as late as the fifth century, many Christian churches were still worshipping on the seventh-day Sabbath, albeit with religious services also increasingly being held on Sunday.[70] While an examination of all the evidence for such a conclusion and its implications would take volumes, I attempt a brief summary here.[71]

67. Paul warned the Ephesians that from among them some "will arise and distort the truth" (Acts 20:30), and he warned the Thessalonians that "the secret power of lawlessness is already at work" in the church (2 Thess 2:7). It would not be surprising or unexpected to find errors in theology and practice developing early in church history.

68. Socrates Scholasticus, *Ecclesiastical History* 5.22 (*NPNF²*, 2:132).

69. Sozomen, *Ecclesiastical History* 7.19 (*NPNF²*, 2:390).

70. So Dugmore, *The Influence of the Synagogue upon the Divine Office* (London: Oxford University Press, 1944), 36, traces the beginning of the decline of Sabbath observance to the middle of the fourth century and notes, "The two days were still regarded with almost equal veneration in the fourth century in Asia Minor."

71. Not discussed here, for instance, is the evidence that the earliest Christian services held on Sunday were likely not weekly worship services but annual Easter services corresponding to the OT First Fruits festival held two days after the Passover. For a thorough discussion of the history and factors involved in the change of the day of

The first clear references to a weekly "eighth day"[72] (Sunday) Christian celebration is found in Barnabas of Alexandria (ca. AD 135). The reason given is that literal Sabbath keeping is impossible because humans are sinful and are unable to keep the Sabbath holy. Therefore Christians should celebrate "the eighth day," which symbolizes "another world" Jesus will make at His Second Coming, and because it is "the day also on which Jesus rose again from the dead."[73] The second clear reference is Justin Martyr in Rome (ca. AD 150)[74] who wrote:

> Sunday, [lit., 'the day of the sun,' *tē tou hēlion legomenē hēmera*] is the day on which we all hold our common assembly, because it was the first day on which God, having wrought a change in the darkness and matter, made the world: and Jesus Christ our Savior on the same day rose from the dead.[75]

Justin taught that the Sabbath was given to the Jews because of their transgressions and the hardness of their hearts.[76]

Over the next several centuries the resurrection emerged, understandably, as the dominant justification given for weekly Sunday worship. The practice grew in part due to pressure applied by church leaders at Rome who imposed fasting on the Sabbath, something neither God nor the Bible writers ever did, which helped "to wean Christians away from the veneration of the Sabbath, and, on the other hand, to enhance Sunday worship exclusively."[77]

---

worship from Sabbath (Saturday) to Sunday from a sabbatarian perspective, see S. Bacchiocchi, *From Sabbath to Sunday;* cf. *The Sabbath in Scripture and History*, ed. K. Strand, 131–263, 323–32.

72. "Eighth day" is not a NT term. It first appears in Christian sources in the second century.

73. Barnabas, *Epistle* 15, *ANF* 1:147.

74. But see W. H. Shea, "Justin Martyr's Sunday Worship Statement: A Forged Appendix," *Journal of the Adventist Theological Society* 12/2 (Autumn 2001): 1–15.

75. Justin, *First Apology*, 67, ANF 1:186. Interestingly, while Justin opposed the seventh-day Sabbath, in *Dialogue with Trypho*, 47 he acknowledges seventh-day Sabbath-keeping Christians and is personally willing to accept them as brethren.

76. Justin, *Dialogue with Trypho*, 18. For a discussion of the theology of Sunday as developed in the early Christian literature, see Bacchiocchi, *From Sabbath to Sunday*, 270–302.

77. Bacchiocchi, *From Sabbath to Sunday*, 197; pp. 187–97 present abundant historical documentation of Rome's imposition of the Sabbath fast, a fact few scholars dispute. The only fast required in the Bible was on the annual OT Day of Atonement (Lev 16:29,31; 23:27–32; Num 29:7). To this day Sabbaths in Jewish tradition have always been days of feasting and celebration, not fasting and glum solemnity.

In the second century a mixture of political, social/cultural, pagan, missiological, and religious influences contributed to the rise of Sunday observance. Emperor Hadrian (AD 132–135) outlawed the Jewish religion, including Sabbath worship, after losing many thousands of soldiers in the Jewish Bar Kochba rebellion of AD 135.[78] Anti-Jewish sentiment led some church leaders to disparage keeping the Sabbath of the Ten Commandments, to help separate Christianity from Judaism.[79]

In the fourth century the influence of the pagan practice of feasting on Sunday ("the venerable day of the sun") in honor of the sun god influenced church leaders at Rome in their choice of sacred days. The church adopted the pagan birthday of the sun (December 25) as the day to celebrate Christ's birthday. Church leaders at Rome unashamedly acknowledged a similar influence in their choice of Sunday as the day for weekly worship.[80]

It appears that Sunday observance began at the intellectual centers of Rome and Alexandria not as a replacement day for the Sabbath but as an ordinary workday to which a worship service had been added.[81] That changed on March 7, 321, when the "Christianized" Emperor Constantine issued the following decree to be observed throughout the empire:

On the venerable Day of the Sun [note: not "the day of Christ's resurrection," but the pagan "venerable Day of the Sun"] let the magistrates and people residing in cities rest, and let all workshops be closed. In the country, however, persons engaged in agriculture may freely and lawfully continue their pursuits.[82]

---

78. S. Krauss, "Bar Kokba," *Jewish Encyclopedia* (New York: Funk and Wagnalls, 1902), 2:509.

79. Bacchiocchi, *From Sabbath to Sunday*, 169–85; cf. S. Schaeffer, "The 'Gospel of Peter,' the Canonical Gospels, and Oral Tradition," Ph.D. thesis, Union Theological Seminary, 1991, 242–43: "Anti-Judaism was . . . a generalized antagonism that is an unfortunate characteristic of Christian literature in the early centuries."

80. E.g., Jerome on Christian Sunday worship: "If it is called the day of the Sun by the pagans, we most willingly acknowledge it as such, since it is on this day that the light of the world [a reference to the first day of creation] had appeared and on this day the Sun of Justice has risen." See *In die dominica Paschae homilia corpus Christianorum, Series Latin* (Turnholti: Typographi Brepols Editores Pontificii, 1953–) 78.550.1.52., quoted in Bacchiocchi, "The Rise of Sunday Observance in Early Christianity," 141; see pp. 139–42 of Bacchiocchi's chapter for further documentation.

81. Strand, "The Sabbath and Sunday from the Second Through Fifth Centuries," 330.

82. Codex Justinianus 3.12.3., trans. P. Schaff, *History of the Christian Church*, 5th ed. (New York, 1902), 3:380n1.

Now Sunday became a state-legislated day of rest throughout the Roman Empire. Constantine's decree would be broadened by later emperors and church councils. In about AD 364 a regional church council at Laodicea stipulated: "Christians shall not Judaize and be idle on Saturday but shall work on that day; but the Lord's day they shall especially honour, and, as being Christians, shall, if possible, do no work on that day. If, however, they are found Judaizing, they shall be shut out from Christ."[83] Pope Innocent I, in an early fifth-century decretal attempting further to discourage seventh-day Sabbath observance, declared, "In these two days [Friday and Saturday] one should not celebrate the sacraments."[84] Leo I issued another Sunday law in 469. In 534 Emperor Justinian revised the Roman law code, incorporating the previous official Sunday laws of Constantine and Leo I. The Council of Orleans in 538 prohibited labor, even for farmers, so they could attend worship services on Sunday. With these decrees the Sabbath commandment had been completely reversed, turning the Sabbath into a common workday and Sunday into a day of rest. And on whose authority? Political decrees and church councils!

A breach had been made in God's law.

All this happened during the same time that an unbiblical priesthood system was being established and elevated to absolve sins and when a theological process was underway that would raise Mary[85] to a venerated and near coequal position to Christ and establish other unbiblical doctrines such as purgatory.

One wonders how this could possibly have happened. Why wouldn't Christians who were willing to die for their faith on other issues object to such unbiblical developments within the church? But realize that for centuries the Scriptures had to be copied by hand and were available only to the wealthy. Furthermore, during the Dark or Middle Ages church leaders resisted the translation of Scripture into common languages and considered it a crime punishable by death for lay members personally to possess any portion

---

83. Quoted in Strand, "The Sabbath and Sunday from the Second Through Fifth Centuries," 329.

84. *Ad Decentium*, Epist. 25, 4, 7, *Patrologia Latina* 20, 550, cited in Bacchiocchi, "Sunday Sacredness," 38, 48.

85. *Oxford Dictionary of the Christian Church*, 1048: Prayers to Mary have been found from the third and fourth centuries. "After the Council of Ephesus [AD 431] . . . her name was even substituted in the official service books in place of that of the Lord at the end of some of the liturgical prayers."

of Scripture. Thus the laity were kept at the mercy of the clergy as to what the Scriptures taught. Eventually, however, among the monks and priests who did have access to the Scriptures, a reformation was ignited. We view return to the seventh-day Sabbath as a continuation of that reform movement.

Bauckham suggests that "the primary *reason* for [the origin of Sunday worship] must be the Christian need for a time of distinctively Christian worship."[86] But we ask, why would those who had worshipped on the Sabbath with Jesus have believed it necessary to choose another day in order to experience "distinctively Christian worship"? My own community of faith believes we experience "distinctly Christian worship" when on the Sabbath of the Ten Commandments, the day on which Jesus worshipped, we celebrate God's creation and redemption through Christ (see pp. 64–65 below, numbers 3 and 4). If the choice of another day of worship from what God gave us in the Ten Commandments was necessary for Christians to experience "distinctively Christian worship," what argument can be used against the claim that images of Christ, the apostles, and Mary were necessary, despite the Second Commandment (Exod 20:4–5), to make their worship more "distinctively Christian"?

This is not to deny that Jesus' resurrection was a cataclysmic event in the history of salvation and that some form of at least annual celebration in remembrance of it would be natural for Christ's followers, even though Jesus did not institute it as He did the Lord's Supper. But to establish weekly worship on the first day of the week, even for such worthy motives as celebrating the resurrection, to the abandonment of observing the seventh-day Sabbath commanded in Exod 20:8–11, is in our opinion unscriptural in both doctrine and practice.

In our understanding, coincident with whatever pure motives may have been involved among those who ultimately influenced the change of the day of worship, another power was also at work with a different objective. In one of his apocalyptic visions, Daniel saw the emergence of a "little horn" power that "will speak against the Most High and oppress his saints and try to change the set times and the laws" (Dan 7:25, cf. vv. 8,21). Based on the "historicist school of [prophetic] interpretation"[87] accepted nearly unanimously by all leading

---

86. Bauckham, "The Lord's Day," 238.
87. The three dominant schools of interpretation for the apocalyptic books of Daniel and Revelation are: "historicist" (the prophecies reveal God's workings through history

pre-Reformation, Reformation, post-Reformation, and Protestant American expositors of Daniel and Revelation from the thirteenth to the nineteenth centuries, this vast crowd of interpreters identified the prophesied "little horn" persecuting power of Daniel 7 as the Roman Catholic Church.[88] In our own ecumenical age, few modern Protestants are even aware of this prophetic viewpoint, but it was one of the most important contributing factors in the origin and growth of the Protestant Reformation. The Reformers first tried to reform the Catholic Church. When that failed, they either seceded from it or were excommunicated. Many in the Reformation movement were martyred at the hands of the church. Although the Reformers had differences on many issues, they were nearly all united in the belief that the theological and ecclesiastical abuses of the church were the fulfillment of Daniel's prophecy of the "little horn . . . try[ing] to change the set times and the laws" of God.[89] They identified many of the errors that had come into the church that needed to be reformed—departure from righteousness by faith in Christ alone, the introduction of images explicitly forbidden in Exod 20:4–5, and so on. But in our view they failed to identify one of the most obvious errors—the change of the Sabbath commandment.

The Aramaic phrase "set times" (*zimmin*, plural) and the word *law* (*dat*, singular), functioning in Daniel 7:25 as a hendiadys (two words taken together to express a single idea), indicates repeated points in time connected to the law of God, pointing to the Sabbath commandment. "The little horn seeks to prevent worship practices ordained by God in his Word."[90] While many Catholic theologians, and many Protestants, have defended Sunday worship by appealing

---

as it impacts His people); "preterist" (the prophecies are symbolic depictions of events that took place in the prophet's day); and "futurist" (the prophecies, for the most part, depict events yet to take place, at the very end of time, beyond even our own day). The preterist and futurist schools were advanced, respectively, by the counter-Reformation Jesuit priests Luis de Alcazar and Francisco Ribera. They tried to divert attention away from the identification of the papacy with the persecuting "little horn" power. Thus they assigned the fulfillment of the little horn power to the remote past or the distant future. See: L. E. Froom, *The Prophetic Faith of Our Fathers* (Washington, DC: Review and Herald, 1946), 2:486–93, 507–13.

88. Ibid., vols. 2–3; see esp. 2:462–63, 486–521, charts on 2: 528–31, 784–87, 3:252–53, 746. Those same charts show that the Reformers and prophetic interpreters before and after them also identified the antichrist "man of lawlessness" prophesied in 2 Thess 2:3–10 as the papacy.

89. Ibid.

90. A. E. Steinmann, *Daniel*, Concordia Commentary (St. Louis, MO: Concordia, 2008), 363; see also 373–74.

to the NT, numerous Catholic apologists of stature, and with the approval of the Church, have claimed that the change resulted solely from the decrees of the Catholic Church, which was purportedly given divine authority that supersedes the authority of Scripture. Furthermore, they have flaunted this purported authority, challenging Protestants thus: If you believe in *sola Scriptura*, then why do you not worship on Saturday, as the Bible instructs, rather than on Sunday, a day established solely on the authority of the Catholic Church?[91] Our reading of Scripture and church history on this issue is in agreement with the claims of those apologists, namely, that the change of the day of worship was indeed a product of Catholic Church influence over a period of centuries and not something introduced in Scripture. We believe that whatever the motives of the church leaders involved may have been, they were fulfilling the prophecy of Daniel 7:25 regarding the attempt to change "the set times and the laws" of God. In our view any discussion of the change of the day of worship from Sabbath to Sunday without this prophetic perspective is incomplete. While the earlier Reformers had other battles to fight with the Church of Rome, once the Reformation began, it was inevitable that there would be a controversy over the identity of the true Sabbath. We believe that time is well past due.

---

91. E.g., J. Cardinal Gibbons, *The Faith of Our Fathers* (London: John Murphy, 1917), 110th ed., 89, (repub., Rockfield, IL: Tan Books, 1980): "The Scriptures alone do not contain all the truths which a Christian is bound to believe, nor do they explicitly enjoin all the duties which he is obliged to practice. Not to mention other examples, is not every Christian obliged to sanctify Sunday and to abstain on that day from unnecessary servile work? . . . You may read the Bible from Genesis to Revelation, and you will not find a single line authorizing the sanctification of Sunday. The Scriptures enforce the religious observance of Saturday, a day which we never sanctify." The *Catholic Mirror* was the official organ of Cardinal Gibbons and the Papacy in the United States. In September 1893 it ran four consecutive editorials to prove from Scripture that Saturday, not Sunday, is the day of worship upheld throughout the Bible, and to challenge Protestants to worship on Saturday or return to the mother Church on whose sole authority the day of worship had been changed. Those articles were compiled into a pamphlet entitled *Rome's Challenge*, which is still available today through ABC bookstores. On December 23, 1893, the *Catholic Mirror* ran a follow-up editorial, also now included in the pamphlet (pp. 31–32). It concludes: "The arguments contained in this pamphlet are firmly grounded on the word of God, and having been closely studied with the Bible in hand, leave no escape for the conscientious Protestant except the abandonment of Sunday worship and the return to Saturday, commanded by their teacher, the Bible, or, unwilling to abandon the tradition of the Catholic Church, which enjoins the keeping of Sunday, and which they have accepted in direct opposition to their teacher, the Bible, consistently accept her in all her teachings. Reason and common sense demand the acceptance of one or the other of these alternatives: either Protestantism and the keeping holy of Saturday, or Catholicity and the keeping of Sunday. Compromise is impossible."

This does not suggest that there have not been many saved Catholics through whom God has touched the world with His love and grace. Nor would the Reformers have denied such, even as they decried the errors of the church. But our present discussion asks, "What is true doctrine, God's will for His Church?"

The Sabbath in Context of the Old and New Covenants

Some may think that the discussion thus far has ignored the most important issue—the old and new covenants. They see the seventh-day Sabbath as an exclusively old covenant institution, specifically limited to the covenant God made with Israel at Sinai, and a covenant "sign" between God and Israel alone (Exod 31:13). The New Testament, in their view, emphatically declares the old covenant, including the Sabbath, as obsolete (Heb 8:13), that which produces slave children (Gal 4:24–25), a law engraved on stone rather than in the heart (2 Cor 3:7), a letter that kills (2 Cor 3:6) and a "ministry that brought death" (2 Cor 3:7), in contrast to the new covenant. They consider promoting seventh-day Sabbath observance in the new covenant era as seriously misguided at best and a regression into old covenant bondage and salvation-threatening legalism at worst.

Space will allow only a brief discussion of this issue.

The Everlasting Covenant and the Covenant of Redemption/Grace

The Everlasting Covenant: Both God and His covenant are declared to be everlasting (Ps 90:2; Heb 13:20). This must be understood in light of the uniquely biblical revelation that by nature God "is love" (1 John 4:8). The love bond of wholehearted, selfless, sacrificial commitment to the best interests of the other that exists within the Trinity is surely the origin and essence of the everlasting covenant.[92] As He brought it into existence, God enfolded the whole of His created order, including Adam, into the everlasting covenant of His love (Hos 6:7; cf. Jer 33:20). God would always treat Adam and his descendants as He would want to be treated Himself, and He

---

92. Cf. Luke 22:29: "I confer on you a kingdom, just as my Father conferred one on me." The Greek term for "confer" in this text is the verb form of the Greek word for "covenant," which Jesus used to refer directly to the covenant between Himself and the Father.

expected a loving, trusting, obedient response from Adam in return (Gen 2:15–17; Luke 6:31; Matt 7:12).

The Covenant of Redemption and Grace: Through disobedience Adam broke God's covenant with him. Adam's descendants have universally followed Adam's lead: "The earth is defiled by its people; they have disobeyed the laws, violated the statutes, and broken the everlasting covenant" (Isa 24:5). God immediately renewed His covenant commitment by promising to send a Redeemer who would crush the head of the serpent, humanity's powerful spiritual foe (Gen 3:15; Rev 12:9). God adapted His everlasting covenant into a covenant of redemption and grace designed to meet Adam and his descendants in their now fallen and spiritually bankrupt state and restore them to the original destiny He had intended for them, namely, "the hope of eternal life, which God, who does not lie, promised before the beginning of time" (Titus 1:2).

In the history of God's covenant of redemption/grace, God has entered into numerous covenants with different individuals and groups, principally with Noah (Gen 9:8–17), Abraham (Gen 15:18; 17:3–21), Israel at Sinai (Exod 20:1–17; 24:7; Deut 4:13), David (Isa 55:3), and the Israel of faith in the new covenant (Jer 31:31–34; Heb 8:8–12). Each of these covenants is called "an everlasting covenant" because it expressed the primordial everlasting covenant of divine love perfectly adapted to the need of the people to whom it was addressed.[93] Each successive covenant retained the eternal truths revealed in previous covenants and progressively revealed further details of His plan to redeem humanity and restore to them the eternal inheritance that had been lost through Adam's sin. The unifying thread running through these covenants was God's love for His people, intent upon awakening a corresponding love for Him in return: "You God, you are my God, earnestly I seek you; I thirst for you, my body longs for you . . . because your love is better than life, my lips will glorify you" (Ps 63:1–3).

> The longing of these verses is not the groping of a stranger, feeling his way toward God, but the eagerness of a friend, almost of a lover, to be in touch with the one he holds dear. . . . This

---

93. Noah (Gen 9:16); Abraham (Gen 17:3–7,13,19); Israel at Sinai (Exod 31:16; Lev 24:8; 1 Chr 16:14–18; Ps 105:8–10); David (2 Sam 23:5); and spiritual Israel (Heb 13:20).

relationship is the heart of the covenant, from the patriarchs to the present day (Gen 17:8c; Heb 8:10c).[94]

The Old and New Covenants

Now to the old and new covenants—the ones all the controversy is about. Israel had repeatedly broken the covenant God made with them at Sinai (generally referred to as the "old covenant"[95]), had repeatedly rejected His appeals to repent of their unfaithfulness, and thus had forfeited God's protection and faced defeat and deportation by the Babylonians (a redemptive disciplinary measure provided for in the covenant, Lev 26:27–45). God promised to make a new covenant with Israel, one that would be different in some ways from the one they had repeatedly broken. To grasp the true meaning of the old and new covenants, it is crucial first to discover the similarities and contrasts, continuity and discontinuity between them.

Continuity Between the Old and New Covenants—New Covenant "DNA"

To discover the continuity between the two covenants, we must first examine the definition God Himself gave of the new covenant as recorded almost identically in Jeremiah and Hebrews. Note God's four promises/provisions (identified by bracketed numbers) that constitute the DNA markers, so to speak, of the new covenant:

> "The time is coming," declares the Lord, "when I will make a new covenant with the house of Israel and with the people of Judah. It will not be like the covenant I made with their ancestors when I took them by the hand to lead them out of Egypt, because they broke my covenant, though I was a husband to them," declares the Lord. "This is the covenant I will make with the people of Israel after that time," declares the Lord. "[1] I will put my law in their minds and write it on their hearts. [2] I will be their God, and they will be my people. [3] No longer will they teach their neighbor, or say to one another, 'Know the

---

94. D. Kidner, *Psalms 1–72: An Introduction and Commentary on Books I and II of the Psalms*, TOTC (Downers Grove, IL: InterVarsity Press, 1975), 224.

95. In 2 Cor 3:14 the term "old covenant" appears to refer to the entire OT. In the NT the terms *covenant* and *testament* are both translations of the same Greek word, *diathēkē*.

Lord,' because they will all know me, from the least of them to the greatest," declares the Lord. "[4] For I will forgive their wickedness and will remember their sins no more." (Jer 31:31–34; cf. Heb 8:8–12)

Theologically speaking, the first promise regards God's *sanctification* of believers. The second represents *reconciliation, redemption, restoration* of lost sinners to a saved fellowship with God. The third anticipates conditions in the new earth when evangelism won't be necessary anymore, but until then it represents the *mission* of the church to make God known until the day that all will know Him in the kingdom to come (cf. 2 Cor 2:14–16). The fourth promise represents the *justification* of repentant sinners. Viewed thus, the new covenant contains the core elements of the gospel (justification, sanctification, reconciliation, and mission). Indeed, it is not theologically overreaching to equate the grace-based, gospel-bearing, mission-directed, faith-inducing new covenant with "the everlasting gospel" (Rev 14:6)—the same gospel Paul said that anyone who deviated from would "be eternally condemned" (Gal 1:6–9).

Highly significant for this study is the discovery that these very same four gospel promises, the DNA markers of the new covenant, were embedded in every major covenant God made with humans! (See the "New Covenant DNA" chart, p. 51.) In the covenants with Adam and Noah, the evidence is strongly implied. With all the others it is explicitly evident. Moreover, the OT is saturated with clusters of the four new-covenant-DNA-marker promises grouped within a few verses or chapters of each other or within thematically related passages. This means that every major covenant God initiated with humans must be characterized as grace-based, gospel-bearing, mission-directed, and faith-inducing, including God's covenant at Sinai, the old covenant.[96] Thus the author of Hebrews could write: "We also [who live in the NT era] have had the gospel

---

96. E.g., Matt 23:23, where Jesus listed "faith" (*pistis*) among the weightier, "more important matters of the law." Cf. F. C. Holmgren. *The Old Testament and the Significance of Jesus: Embracing Change—Maintaining Christian Identity* (Grand Rapids: Eerdmans, 1999), 91: Jeremiah "speaks to them of a 'new' covenant with God, but, as most scholars admit, this 'new' covenant has the same character as the mosaic covenant"; cf. Holmgren, 79–95. For a more in-depth analysis of the new covenant promises in the Sinaitic covenant, see S. MacCarty, *In Granite or Ingrained? What the Old and New Covenants Reveal About the Gospel, the Law and the Sabbath* (Berrien Springs, MI: Andrews University Press, 2007), 37–56.

New Covenant DNA

Covenant	Everlasting	Humanity at Creation	Adam after His Fall	Noah	Abraham	Sinai	David	Covenant Consciousness at Temple Dedication	Covenant Consciousness in Isaiah 51-54 (54:10 "Covenant of Peace")	Covenant Language in Ezekiel 36-37	Messiah Jesus Isa. 42:6-7; Isa. 49:4-6; Mal. 3:1	New Covenant	Eden Restored
Made by God with	Earth and universe Gen. 9:16 Isa. 24:5 Eph. 3:10 Col. 1:19-20	Adam/ humanity Gen. 1:26-27 Gen. 2:15-22 Hos. 6:6-7	Adam/ humanity Gen. 3:15	All life through Noah Gen. 9:8-17 Isa. 54:9-10 2 Pet. 3:3-9	Abraham and his promised seed Gen. 15:18 Gen. 17:1-22	Israel and foreign converts Exod. 19-23 Deut. Isa. 56	David and his descendants 2 Sam. 23:5 Isa. 55:3	Israel and foreign converts 1 Kings 8:41-43 Isa. 56	Israel and foreign converts Isa. 56	Post-exilic Israel and converts	Israel, Gentiles, "The ends of the earth" Isa. 42:6-7; 49:6	Israel and Judah Jer. 31:31 Heb. 8:8	Overcomers
"I will write My laws in your hearts": Sanctification	Heb. 13:20-21 Rom. 2:14-16	Gen. 1:26-27,31 implied	Gen. 3:15 implied	Ezek. 14:14,20 Heb. 11:7 implied	Gen. 26:5 with John 15:5 implied	Exod. 31:12-13 Lev. 20:7-8 Deut. 30:6, 11-14	Ps. 40:8	1 Kings 8:61,58	Isa. 51:7,15-16 with Deut. 30:6, 11-14 and Rom. 10:6-16	Ezek. 36:26-27	Heb. 10:7 with Ps. 40:8	Jer. 31:33 Heb. 8:10	Rev. 22:11 implied
"I will be your God and you will be My people": Reconciliation	Ps. 103:17-22 Isa. 19:25 Col. 1:19-20	Gen. 1:26-27,31 implied	Gen. 3:15, 21 implied	Ezek. 14:14,20 Heb. 11:7 implied	Gen. 17:7 Deut. 29:12-13	Exod. 6:7 Lev. 26:12	2 Sam. 7:5-16 Ps. 89:3-4,20-29	1 Kings 8:59 (cf. vv. 16, 30,33-36)	Isa. 51:15-16	Ezek. 36:28 Ezek. 37:23,27	Matt. 1:23 Matt. 3:17 Heb. 11:5	Jer. 31:33 Heb. 8:10	Rev. 21:2-3,7
"All will know Me": Mission	Isa. 19:25 Isa. 45:22 Ps. 19:1-4 Rom. 1:20 John 17:3 Col. 1:19-20	Hos. 6:6-7 Gen. 1:26-27 Gen. 2:15-22 implied	Gen. 3:15 implied	1 Kings 8:46 Ezek. 14:14,20 Heb. 11:7 implied	Gen. 12:3 Gen. 28:14	Exod. 19:5-6 with 1 Pet. 2:9 Ps. 67:1-2 Ezek. 36:22-23	2 Sam. 23:5 with 1 Chron. 16:7-33 Isa. 55:3-5	1 Kings 8:41-43	Isa. 52:7-15	Ezek. 36:23 Ezek. 37:28	Matt. 1:21 John 17:25 John 14:7,9 John 10:30	Jer. 31:34 Heb. 8:11 2 Cor. 2:14-16	Rev. 21:2-3 Hab. 2:14 John 17:3 1 Cor. 13:12
"I will forgive your sins": Justification	Heb. 13:20 Matt. 26:26-28 Mark 14:24	Not needed but provided for 1 Cor. 1:23-24 1 Cor. 2:2,7 2 Tim. 1:8-9 1 Pet. 1:18-20 Rev. 13:8 Heb. 13:20	Gen. 3:21 implied		Gen. 15:6 Rom. 4:1-4	Exod. 34:6-10 Ps. 103:2-14	Ps. 32:1-5 with Rom. 4:6-8 Isa. 55:3-7	1 Kings 8:30, 33-34 1 Kings 8:46-51	Isa. 53:5-12	Ezek. 36:25 Ezek. 37:23	Eph. 1:3-8 Rom. 2:9,14-17 Heb. 9:15 1 Pet. 2:22-24 1 Pet. 1:18-20 Rev. 1:5 Rev. 13:8	Jer. 31:34 Heb. 8:12	Rev. 7:9,13-14 with Zech. 3:1-5

Covenant / Gospel Provisions

preached to us, just as they [with whom God made His covenant at Sinai] did" (Heb 4:2). [97]

Discontinuity Between the Old and New Covenants

If the old and new covenants contained the same gospel, why then did God say that the new covenant "will not be like the covenant I made with their ancestors when I took them by the hand to lead them out of Egypt" (Jer 31:32; Heb 8:9)? God Himself answered in the part of the sentence that I left out: "*because they broke my covenant*, though I was a husband to them,' declares the Lord" (Jer 31:32, emphasis added); "*because they did not remain faithful to my covenant*, and I turned away from them,' declares the Lord" (Heb 8:9, emphasis added). What God Himself said He expected to be different about the new covenant was the *response* of the people to His covenant promises, to the gospel. The OT recipients had by and large rejected those gospel promises, and He expected a different *response* from people living in the historical era after Jesus came.

The master of the vineyard in Jesus' parable, after his servants were beaten and killed by the tenants of his property, finally "sent his son to them. 'They will respect my son,' he said" (Matt 21:33–37). So also in the new covenant, God effectively says, "Having rejected My prophets' appeals for repentance and offers of a new heart and spirit by My grace, surely My people will not reject My Son whom I will send to ratify my covenant with them by His own blood. Surely," He says, "this covenant will be new in the positive way My people will *respond* to it. How could they reject My Son?"

---

97. In Heb 4:2,6 the expression "had the gospel preached" translates *euangelizesthai*, a passive form of the Greek verb *euangelizō*, which means "receiving a message . . . of the gospel" (BDAG, 402). Cf. A. T. Hanson, *Jesus Christ in the Old Testament* (London: SPCK, 1965), 94, 168: "The direct oracles of Christ which Moses was privileged to hear . . . was probably the gospel as far as it could be apprehended before the incarnation (Heb 4:2). . . . The message was the message of Christ." Cf. P. Ellingworth, *The Epistle to the Hebrews* (Grand Rapids: Eerdmans, 1993), 241. "In Hb. 4:2,6 εὐαγγελίζεσθαι [*euangelizesthai,* having the good news/gospel preached] is used of OT as well of NT proclamation" (*TDNT*, 720). "Jews have received an εὐαγγέλιον [*euangelion,* gospel] as well as Christians. For Jews the ἐπαγγελίαι [*epangeliai,* promises] now fulfilled in Christ are the Gospel, and the NT Gospel is simply a proclamation of the old promises. There is no substance in the usual distinction which refers ἐπαγγελίαι [{OT} *epangeliai,* promises] to salvation still to come and εὐαγγέλιον [*euangelion,* gospel] to salvation already come" (*TDNT*, 585n67).

Paul's Treatment of the Old and New
Covenants—an Experiential Focus

For Paul old covenant and new covenant were defined not by the terms of the covenant itself, which have proved in every case to be grace-based and gospel-bearing, but by how the recipients of the covenant *responded* to it! For Paul rejecting the gospel invitation extended in any of God's covenants was an *old covenant response,* while accepting it in faith was a *new covenant response.* Again for Paul *responding to God's covenant invitation by rejecting it or legalistically responding to it was old covenant; responding to it by accepting it in faith and "the obedience of faith" (Rom 1:5) was new covenant.* In Paul's treatment of the subject, the old and new covenants are not defined by the historical era in which the participants lived but by how they *respond* to the gospel invitation conveyed in God's covenant with them. With respect to Paul's treatment of the covenants, we agree with Rayburn:

> The distinction between the new covenant and the old covenant has nothing to do with the distinction between the situation before Christ came and the situation after or between the religion and revelation before Christ and that after. It is rather the distinction between flesh and Spirit, between the old man and the new man, between death and life, between condemnation and righteousness, and between guilt and the forgiveness of sin. . . . In a proper sense, all salvation is the new covenant.[98]

Consider, for example, Paul's description of the "two covenants" in Gal 4:21–5:1 (NIV), the only place he uses that exact term:

---

98. R. Rayburn, "The Contrasts Between the Old and New Covenants in the New Testament" (Ph.D. diss., University of Aberdeen, 1978), 166. Cf. J. O. Buswell, *A Systematic Theology of the Christian Religion* (Grand Rapids: Zondervan, 1962), 1:307: "The Scriptures themselves used the term 'old testament' [read 'old covenant' as the Greek term *diathēkē* is the same for both translations] to refer, not to the thirty-nine books that preceded the earthly life of Christ, nor to the revealed system of worship that the thirty-nine books contained, but to refer to a legalistic, self-righteous attitude in the contemplation of those books and their provisions. Similarly the words 'new testament' [read "new covenant"] in Scripture refer not to the twenty-seven books given since the time of Christ on earth, but to that renewed relationship into which God's elect, in every age since the fall of man, have entered by faith." Cf. also Robertson, *Christ of the Covenants,* 57–58, 60–61, 180–82. Many have caught glimpses of this interpretative principle; few have realized its far-reaching implications.

Tell me, you who want to be under the law, are you not aware of what the law says? For it is written that Abraham had two sons, one by the slave woman and the other by the free woman. His son by the slave woman was born according to flesh; but his son by the free woman was born as the result of a divine promise.

These things are being taken figuratively: The women represent two covenants. One covenant is from Mount Sinai and bears children who are to be slaves: This is Hagar. Now Hagar stands for Mount Sinai in Arabia and corresponds to the present city of Jerusalem, because she is in slavery with her children. But the Jerusalem that is above is free, and she is our mother. . . .

Now you, brothers and sisters, like Isaac, are children of promise. At that time the son born according to flesh persecuted the son born by the power of the Spirit. It is the same now. But what does the Scripture say? "Get rid of the slave woman and her son, for the slave woman's son will never share in the inheritance with the free woman's son" [quoting Gen 21:10]. Therefore, brothers and sisters, we are not children of the slave woman, but of the free woman.

It is for freedom that Christ has set us free. Stand firm, then, and do not let yourselves be burdened again by a yoke of slavery.

Note the following table that lists the distinctive characteristics of the old and new covenants as described in this passage:

The First or Old Covenant	The Second or New Covenant
Abraham's experience with Hagar, the slave woman (4:22)	Abraham's experience with Sarah, the free woman (4:22)
Mount Sinai, corresponding to the "present" city of Jerusalem (4:24–25)	Corresponds to Jerusalem above which is "free" (4:26)
"Born according to the flesh" (4:23,29)	"Born as the result of a divine promise," "born by the power of the Spirit" (4:23,29)
The persecutor (4:29)	The persecuted (4:29)
"Will never share in the inheritance" (4:30)	Receives "the inheritance" (4:30)
"Burdened . . . by a yoke of slavery" (5:1)	Free in Christ (5:1)

If Paul means the left–column characterization above to describe the Mosaic covenant that God Himself designed in every detail and commanded His people to obey, then for 1,500 years between Sinai and the Last Supper, God bound His people to "a yoke of slavery" designed to produce "persecutors" who "will never share in the inheritance" of His eternal kingdom.

Galatians 4:23 and 29 characterize old covenant people as born "according to the flesh" and new covenant people as "born by the power of the Spirit." Did God design the Mosaic covenant to produce children "according to the flesh" and another covenant for the NT era to produce children "of the spirit?" Consider the staggering implications of such a conclusion in light of the NT's descriptions of the contrasting lives and destinies of those who are of "the flesh" or of "the Spirit:"[99]

The Flesh	The Spirit
"That which is born of flesh is flesh" (John 3:6).	"That which is born of the Spirit is spirit" (John 3:6).
"The righteous requirement of the law might be fulfilled in us who do not walk according to the flesh" (Rom 8:4).	"The righteous requirement of the law might be fulfilled in us who . . . walk . . . according to the Spirit" (Rom 8:4).
"To be carnally [lit., 'fleshly'] minded is death" (Rom 8:6).	"To be spiritually minded is life and peace" (Rom 8:6).
"Those who are in the flesh cannot please God" (Rom 8:8).	"You are not in the flesh but in the Spirit, if indeed the Spirit of God dwells in you" (Rom 8:9).
"If you live according to the flesh, you will die" (Rom 8:13).	"If by the Spirit you put to death the deeds of the body, you will live" (Rom 8:13).
"The flesh lusts [i.e., wars] against the Spirit" (Gal 5:17).	"The Spirit [wars] against the flesh" (Gal 5:17).
"The works of the flesh are . . . adultery, fornication, uncleanness, lewdness, idolatry. . . . Those who practice such things will not inherit the kingdom of God" Gal 5:19–21).	"The fruit of the Spirit is love, joy, peace, longsuffering. . . . Those who are Christ's have crucified the flesh with its passions and desires" (Gal 5:22–24).
"If anyone thinks he may have confidence in the flesh, I more so . . . concerning the righteousness which is in the law, blameless" (Phil 3:4–6).	". . . not having my own righteousness, which is from the law, but that which is through faith in Christ, the righteousness which is from God by faith" (Phil 3:9).

99. The NKJV is used in this table as it renders the Greek term *sarx* more consistently as "flesh" than does the NIV.

The Hebrews 11 list of representative OT believers, most of whom were nurtured by the Mosaic covenant, cannot possibly be described by the left column characterizations in the two tables above. They were new covenant people. Upon conversion these believers were not delivered from the covenant, as from a yoke of slavery, but were set free by the indwelling Spirit of God to love and obey God and His covenant, which was designed to groom them into a heaven–bound, holy people through whom He would manifest His own holiness to the nations.

But does not Gal 4:25 specifically identify the covenant described by the left column above as the covenant God made at "Mount Sinai"? Actually not. Paul uses "Mount Sinai" (v. 25) and "the present city of Jerusalem" (v. 25) "*figuratively*" (v. 24), as an illustration, to represent a *faithless, rebellious national response* to God's gracious gospel invitation (cf. Exod 32; Rom 9:30–31). Similarly, he used Abraham's faithless experience with Hagar to represent a *faulty personal response* to God's covenant promise (Gal 4:22–25; Gen 16). They are both *old covenant responses*. In Gal 4:21–5:1, Paul has an old covenant *experience* in view and uses historical references only as examples to drive his point home.

Paul's exclusive use of the term "two covenants" in Gal 4:24 identifies Gal 4:21–5:1 as the interpretative key to his old and new covenant polemic, pitting one against the other, and is often the key to understanding his polemical presentations on Mosaic law.

In 2 Corinthians 3, Paul characterizes the old covenant as "written in stone" only, "the letter that kills," "the ministry that brought death [and] condemns men," in contrast to the new covenant that is written "on tablets of human hearts" by "the Spirit [that] gives life," as "the ministry that brings righteousness" and "freedom." This characterization does not portray a covenant God made with His people at Sinai that will only "kill" them by bringing "death" and "condemnation," in contrast to an entirely different covenant that Jesus or the apostles instituted in the NT period that under the tutelage of "the Spirit . . . brings righteousness" and "freedom." Rather, Paul was contrasting two vastly different human *responses* to God's gospel invitation extended in His covenants in every historical period. "Whenever [in every historical period] anyone turns to the Lord, the veil [of unbelief and resistance to the gospel] is taken away" (2 Cor 3:16; 4:3–4).

Unfortunately, space precludes further application of this interpretative principle to other challenging passages (e.g., Gal

3:21–25).[100] For Paul, the threatening issue involved with the two covenants had little or nothing to do with how God related differently to people in two historical eras, one characterized as a "yoke of slavery," the other as "freedom." It had everything to do with the profound contrast between faith and the obedience of faith versus unbelief, rebellion, and legalism; between life in the Spirit versus life in the flesh—with opposite destinies attending each. To interpret Paul as warning against what God offered and taught His people at Sinai is to miss Paul's point entirely.

Paul's treatment of the old covenant has been used by many to deny the universal and permanent applicability of the Ten Commandments. However, it has not been so considered by a major wing of Reformation scholars.[101] Indeed, the law is an integral part of "the holy Scriptures" Paul referred to that "are able to make you wise for salvation through faith in Christ Jesus," and "is useful for teaching, rebuking, correcting and training in righteousness, so that the servant of God may be thoroughly equipped for every good work" (2 Tim 3:15–17). "So then, the law is holy, and the commandment is holy, righteous and good"; "the law is spiritual" (Rom 7:12,14). "By this faith" in Jesus, our righteousness, we "uphold the law" (Rom 3:31).

Hebrews' Treatment of the Old and New Covenants—a Historical Focus

In contrast to Paul's *experiential* focus on the covenants viewed from the perspective of people's *responses* to the gospel, Hebrews

---

100. See MacCarty, *In Granite or Ingrained*, 77–142, where all NT polemical passages related to the Mosaic law and covenants are examined in light of this interpretative principle. Cf. Rayburn, "The Contrasts Between the Old and New Covenants."

101. C. E. B. Cranfield, *On Romans: and Other New Testament Essays* (Edinburgh: T&T Clark, 1998), 123: "The importance attached to the Decalogue in Christian education by such Reformed catechisms as the Geneva of 1541, the Heidelberg of 1563, the Westminster Larger and Shorter of 1648, is well known. . . . And in this matter of the place of the law in the life of Christians the Church of England has stood alongside the Reformed churches, as may be seen from the fact that in the 1662 Book of Common Prayer (as also in the 1552 Prayer Book) the rehearsing of the Ten Commandments has its place in the order of the Lord's Supper (note the repeated response, 'Lord, have mercy upon us, and incline our hearts to keep this law'), while both in Rite A and in Rite B of the Alternative Service book of 1980 provision is made for either the Summary of the Law (itself, of course, including two quotations from the law) or the Ten Commandments to be read." Cf. Grant, "The Decalogue in Early Christianity," who explores evidence for the NT's high regard for the Decalogue as a continuing divine standard of holiness for the believer.

7–10 focuses on specifically identified *historical* components of the covenants—namely, the priesthood and sacrificial systems. The OT priesthood and animal sacrifices associated with the OT sanctuary of the "first covenant," "the old one," are set in a type/antitype schema to the heavenly priesthood and once-for-all sacrifice of Christ, which fulfilled the former and made them obsolete (7:24–25; 8:6,13; 9:1–5,23–10:12). Jesus' atoning death is salvation's center of gravity, making effective forgiveness for sins committed not only in the present era but also "committed under the first covenant" (9:16). Hebrews 8:8–12 affirms that the same gospel, framed as the four universal and permanent new covenant promises, overarched both covenantal dispensations, providing redemptive continuity rooted in "the eternal covenant" (cf. 4:2,6; 13:20).

Instructively, immediately following Hebrews 7–10's discussion of the covenants, Hebrews 11 provides a representative list of OT witnesses who were as surely new covenant believers, internalizing the four new covenant promises, as any living in the NT historical era.[102] Just as instructively, Paul warned those living in the NT historical era that if they returned to an old covenant life of the flesh they would become old covenant people whose share in the inheritance with the saints would be in jeopardy (Gal 4:21–30).

Relationship of the Historical and Experiential Perspectives on the Covenants in Hebrews and Paul

The chart on p. 59 depicts the relationship between the historical and experiential perspectives of the covenants in Hebrews 7–10 and the writings of Paul respectively.[103]

The "Everlasting Covenant" illustration on p. 60 diagrams the relationship of the historical and experiential perspectives of the old and new covenants to each other and to the primeval everlasting covenant.

The Sabbath as the Covenant Sign

Meredith Kline notes that the Sinaitic covenant was structured much like an "international treaty found in the ancient Near East" of

---

102. Based on Jeremiah's description of Josiah in Jer 22:15–16, Holmgren comments that *"Josiah, in his faithfulness to the Sinai teaching, is a new covenant person!"* (emphasis original); *Old Testament and the Significance of Jesus,* 80. In our view, all devout OT believers were "new covenant persons."

103. For a more thorough discussion, with accompanying charts, see MacCarty, *In Granite or Ingrained,* 77–89, 251–66, 294–300.

	Old Covenant	New Covenant
History (primary focus of Hebrews 7–10)	**God's Provision** • God's four new covenant promises • Old Testament era human priesthood and animal sacrifices; a sanctuary on earth • Grace-based, gospel-bearing, faith-inducing, mission-directed • Before Jesus came	**God's Provision** • God's four new covenant promises • New Testament era high priesthood of Jesus and His sacrifice; a sanctuary in heaven • Grace-based, gospel-bearing, faith-inducing, mission-directed • After Jesus came
Experience (primary focus of Pauline writings)	**God's Provision Rejected** • God's four new covenant promises rejected, perverted, and externalized by the sinful nature into lawlessness or legalism • The experience of unbelievers of every historical era • Before faith is exercised • Unconverted—Lost	**God's Provision Accepted** • God's four new covenant promises received, internalized, and fulfilled through the agency of the Holy Spirit • The experience of believers of every historical era • After faith is exercised • Converted—Saved

Moses' day.[104] One significant feature of such treaty/covenant structures was the placement of the seal of the initiator of the covenant in the middle of the covenant documents. Based on Deut 4:13—"[God] declared to you his covenant, the Ten Commandments"—Kline notes that where we would expect the covenant initiator's "dynastic seal," we find the Sabbath.[105] Then citing Exod 31:13,17, Kline comments: "The Creator has stamped on world history the sign of the sabbath as his seal of ownership and authority."[106] God appears to have specifically positioned His creation ordinance in the heart of the Decalogue to represent its unique role as the sign of His covenant (see Exod 31:12–13; cf. Ezek 20:12,20). Rightly understood and observed, the Sabbath would be a divine antidote to legalism, for it would constantly remind God's people that they had no holiness of their own, that their Maker was their Redeemer–Sanctifier, the only One who could make them holy as He is holy—the great purpose of the covenant of redemption.

---

104. M. G. Kline, *Treaty of the Great King: The Covenant Structure of Deuteronomy, Studies and Commentary* (Grand Rapids: Eerdmans, 1963), 13–15.
105. Ibid., 18.
106. Ibid., 19.

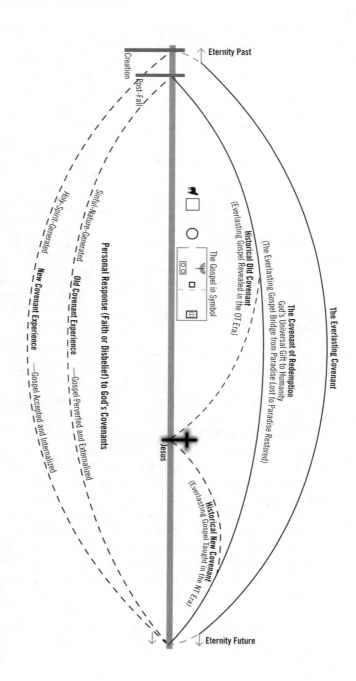

Kline adds:

> If the Sabbath ordinance serves as a symbolic *sign* of God's covenantal lordship in the holy kingdom of Israel, it is surely because *the original divine Sabbath represented the Creator's covenantal lordship over the world.* . . . The meaning of the original Sabbath (Gen 2:2) is mirrored in the Sabbath ordinance (Gen 2:3), the record of which emphasizes that the Sabbath is set apart as sacred to the Creator.[107]

A common objection raised at this point is that God specifically designated the Sabbath as a sign between Him and the nation of Israel exclusively, not between Him and His new covenant people.[108] But that's just the point. *The Sabbath* was *the covenant sign between God and Israel. And it was precisely* with **Israel** *that He made His new covenant!* "'This is the covenant I will make *with the house of Israel* after that time,' declares the Lord" (identical wording in Jer 31:33 and Heb 8:10, emphasis added), followed by God's description of the new covenant (Jer 31:33–34; Heb 8:10–12).

The new covenant, like the old, was not made with the nations at large. It had application to the world of unbelievers only through the faithful witness of God's covenant people—namely, spiritual Israel, "those who believe" (Gal 3:7).[109] "If you belong to Christ, then you

---

107. M. G. Kline, *Kingdom Prologue* (Overland Park, KS: Two Age Press, 2000), 19.

108. E.g., H. H. P. Dressler, "The Sabbath in the Old Testament," in *From Sabbath to Lord's Day*, 30: "As a sign of the covenant the Sabbath can only be meant for Israel, with whom the covenant was made."

109. The definitive work on the NT's view of Israel as the believing, worshipping, covenant people, the true messianic community, is H. K. LaRondelle, *The Israel of God in Prophecy* (Berrien Springs, MI: Andrews University Press, 1983). Cf. Holmgren, *Old Testament and the Significance of Jesus*, 57: "Earlier Paul had declared that Christians through Christ, who is the seed of Abraham (Gal 3:16), have Abraham as their ancestor. Now in Gal 4:21–31 he asserts that Christians are the children of Sarah. In these passages Paul is claiming that the Christian movement is the 'true' Israel." T. Crosby ("Did the Apostolic Council Set Aside the Sabbath? [part 1]," *Ministry* 77, 2 [Feb. 2005], 25n6) cites evidence of recent scholarship's emphasis on the New Testament's presentation of a nonethnic, spiritual Israel: "According to B. Kinman, 'Lucan Eschatology and the Missing Fig Tree,' *JBL*, 113, no. 4 (1994); 675n23, in recent scholarship on Luke/Acts the essential unity of Israel and the church has been emphasized by defining Israel as an entity consisting of those Jews and Gentiles who believed Jesus to be the Messiah. Israel has been redefined so as both to incorporate believing Gentiles and to exclude ethnic Jews who do not believe. See J. Jervell, *Luke and the People of God: A New Look at Luke/Acts* (Minneapolis: Augsburg, 1972) 41–74; E. Franklin, *Christ the Lord: A Study in the Purpose and Theology of Luke-Acts* (London: SPCK, 1975) 77–115; D. L. Tiede, *Prophecy and History in Luke-Acts* (Philadelphia: Fortress, 1980), 9–11; idem, 'The Exaltation of Jesus and the Restoration of Israel in Acts 1,' *HTR* 79 (1986); 278–86;

are Abraham's seed, and heirs according to the promise" (Gal 3:29). All unbelievers who respond to the witness of God's new covenant "Israel" by putting faith in God and His Son Jesus, allowing His Spirit to make them a holy people manifesting an "obedience that comes from faith," will be incorporated into the covenant people, the true Israel of God. This brings new significance to God's statement that the Sabbath "will be a sign between me and the Israelites forever" (Exod 31:17). *If the Sabbath applied exclusively to the ethnic nation of Israel, then so does the new covenant.* However, just as the new covenant, which was specifically "for the house of Israel," applies to all "those who believe," then the Sabbath—which was God's chosen "sign" between Himself and Israel—should likewise apply, universally and permanently, to all "those who believe."

Unless God Himself revoked the Sabbath commandment with the same or greater clarity and force as He revoked circumcision, which was not part of the Decalogue, the Sabbath must continue as a sign between God and new covenant Israel, the church, throughout the new covenant historical era.

The Meaning and Proper Observance of the Sabbath

What, then, is the nature of this "Sabbath-rest" (*sabbatismos*, "Sabbath observance") that "remains . . . for the people of God" (Heb 4:9) as a continuing covenant sign that their Creator-Redeemer is the one who will make them holy? The Bible provides a sevenfold answer.

1. The Sabbath Is "Blessed"

At the end of creation week, "God blessed [Hb., *bârak*] the seventh day" (Gen 2:3). The Sabbath commandment reiterated: "Therefore the Lord blessed the Sabbath day" (Exod 20:11). God's blessing of the day was meant even more as a blessing on those who observed the day. "If you call the Sabbath a delight . . . and if you honor it . . . then you will find your joy in the Lord, and I will cause you to ride in triumph on the heights of the land" (Isa 58:13–14). The devout in Israel sought this blessing not for themselves alone but that it might enhance their witness to the nations—their mis-

Fitzmyer, 59; J. T. Carroll, *Response to the End of History: Eschatology and Situation in Luke-Acts*, Society of Biblical Literature Dissertation Series 92 (Atlanta: Scholars Press, 1988)."

sion as new covenant people: "May God be gracious to us and bless us . . . that your ways may be known on earth, your salvation among all nations" (Ps 67:1–2). True Sabbath observers place themselves in the path of divine blessing that they might both receive the blessing and share it.

2. The Sabbath Is "Holy"

At creation, "God blessed the seventh day and made it holy [Hb., *qadash*]" (Gen 2:3). The Sabbath commandment echoes, "The Lord blessed the Sabbath day and made it holy" (Exod 20:11). Boice comments on Gen 2:3, "God sets the Sabbath day apart to teach that we are to enter not only into rest but also into holiness."[110]

Quoting the Sinai covenant, Peter reiterated God's highest ideal for His children: "Just as he who called you is holy, so be holy in all you do; for it is written: 'Be holy, because I am holy'" (1 Pet 1:15–16, quoting Lev 11:44–45; 19:2; 20:7). God chose the Sabbath as His "sign" that "I am the Lord, who makes you holy" (Exod 31:13). True Sabbath observance constantly reminds God's people that they have no holiness of their own apart from their relationship to God. They have nothing, and need nothing, that recommends them to Him. His grace is enough. Sin incapacitated humanity's ability to seek God apart from God's saving initiative (Rom 3:10–19). The Sabbath is a sign that God takes the initiative, always and continually. "I will put my laws in their minds and write them on their hearts" (Heb 8:10). The fulfillment of this new covenant promise empowers God's people for their mission as His witnesses: "The nations will know that I am the Lord, declares the Sovereign Lord, when I am proved holy through you before their eyes" (Ezek 36:23).

The holiness of God, His sanctification of believers, the ability to represent God rightly to others—these things hold no attraction for unbelievers. But for believers, in whose hearts the Spirit has created a longing for God, for His salvation, and for an effective witness for Him, the Sabbath is a gift supreme.

Because God "blessed" the Sabbath day and "made it holy," faith accepts that on the Sabbath,

> we meet God on a plane not possible on any other day of the week. . . . While it is true that we do not automatically realize this Sabbath quality by merely resting on the Sabbath day,

---

110. J. M. Boice. *Genesis* (Grand Rapids: Zondervan, 1982), 87.

there is a quality of Sabbath observance that cannot be found on any other day than God's own day, the day He "blessed."[111]

3. The Sabbath Links Us with Our Creator

In the Exod 20:8–11 version of the Sabbath commandment, God rooted the motivation for Sabbath observance in creation: "for in six days the Lord made the heavens and the earth, the sea, and all that is in them, but he rested on the seventh day." His covenant sign would continually remind His people where they came from and to whom they belong. Rightly understood and observed, the Sabbath serves as an antidote to pride and racism, reminding that all nations, races, social classes, and genders come from the hand of God and are of one blood, made in His image, brothers and sisters, equal and precious in His sight.

Similarly, the Sabbath's testimony to creation serves as an antidote to an evolutionary view of naturalistic origins. Sabbath observance reminds us that we are not the result of impersonal natural processes in a universe devoid of morality but are moral beings created in the image of an almighty God of love who wanted us. God sovereignly chose the Sabbath to make Himself available to us in a unique intimacy, to remind us of the extreme value He places on us as His created children and covenant partners. "It is this unfathomable intimacy of Creator and creature, Father and son, that gives this day the fullness of its significance."[112] The Sabbath reminds us that "God created us with a purpose in life—a purpose fulfilled in relationships, companionship, and love."[113]

As Sabbath observance directs one's mind back to creation, it also nurtures an eager anticipation of the new creation with its return to the peaceful, pristine, robust environment of Eden. There "the wolf and the lamb will feed together," "there will be no more death or mourning or crying or pain," and "the dwelling of God is with men . . . they will be his people, and God himself will be with them and be their God" (completely fulfilling the second new covenant promise, Heb 8:10; see Isa 65:17,25; Rev 21:3–4). There "'from one Sabbath to another, all mankind will come and bow down before

---

111. R. Dederen, "Reflections on a Theology of the Sabbath," in *The Sabbath in Scripture and History*, ed. Strand, 301–2.
112. Ibid., 297.
113. Davidson, *Love Song for the Sabbath*, 47.

me,' says the Lord" (Isa 66:23); imagine what celebrations those will be!

4. The Sabbath Links Us with Our Redeemer

In the Deut 5:12–15 version of the Sabbath commandment, God rooted the motivation for Sabbath observance in Israel's deliverance and redemption from slavery: "Remember that you were slaves in Egypt and that the Lord your God brought you out of there with a mighty hand and an outstretched arm."[114] The imagery of redemption from Egyptian slavery conveys a message that reaches far beyond the historical deliverance to the even greater deliverance and redemption from slavery to sin (Rom 3:10–19; 6:16–23).

The two versions of the Sabbath commandment join creation and redemption as motivators for Sabbath observance. "The original creation brought man forth unto God out of that which was nonexistent; redemption brought man forth unto God out of that which was lost."[115] True Sabbath observance never forgets either and celebrates both. It has the potential to keep alive the wonder of the "I once was lost but now am found" experience, the wonder of "my sins have been forgiven" (the fourth new covenant promise, Heb 8:12) and "in Christ" I am "a new creation" "created to be like God in true righteousness and holiness" (2 Cor 5:17; Eph 4:24). "'Tis mercy all, immense and free; For, O my God, it found out me."[116] Redemption!

Jesus' Sabbath miracles were acts of redemption, setting people free from their physical infirmities with an eye on releasing them from spiritual bondage. True Sabbath observance joins God in the work of redemption, relieving the burdens of the oppressed, in which He is always engaged (John 5:16–17). "It is lawful to do good on the Sabbath" (Matt 12:12).

Jesus' dying announcement, "It is finished" (John 19:30), and His subsequent Sabbath rest in the tomb, infused the Sabbath with the added significance of a *completed redemption*. He who as Lord of the Sabbath rested from a finished creation on the seventh day

---

114. For a discussion on the "complementary" nature of the Creation and redemption themes in the two versions of the Fourth Commandment, pointing to "the rich theological meaning of the Sabbath," see E. Mueller, "The Sabbath in Deuteronomy 5:12–15," *Journal of the Adventist Theological Society,* 14/2 (Fall 2003): 141–49.

115. G. Cohen, "The Doctrine of the Sabbath in the Old and New Testaments," *Grace Journal* 6 (1965): 10.

116. From Charles Wesley's hymn, "And Can It Be?"

now rested as Lord of salvation from a finished redemption on the Sabbath day. Sabbath observance, therefore, celebrates His completed work in grateful, loving response.

5. The Sabbath Provides Rest

Divine "rest" marked the original Sabbath (Gen 2:2; Exod 20:11; Exod 31:17; Heb 4:4). "Sabbath" (Hb., *shabbâth*) means "to cease." God provided Sabbath rest even before sin entered the picture. He knew we needed it even more afterward. He even *commanded* it, which was needful for type-A people such as me; had He not, I would feel guilty for *not* working seven days a week. True Sabbath observance reminds us that we do not belong to our work and are not defined by our work; we belong to God and are defined by our relationship to Him. As important as our work can sometimes be, the Sabbath releases us from the tyranny of work and puts it in proper perspective, bringing back into view the very things that make our lives meaningful—God, family, friends, people who need us.

Ceasing from work every Sabbath is a test of faith for some of us. What will happen if I stop work on that project for a whole day or don't get the lawn mowed while the weather is good? How will I support my family if I do not accept that job offer that requires work on the Sabbath? (There is at times a cost to discipleship.) To those fears Jesus quietly answers, "Seek first [God's] kingdom and his righteousness, and all these things will be given to you as well" (Matt 6:33).

On a deeper level Sabbath rest invites us to let our many fears be quieted by His sheer presence. The OT assurance, "My Presence will go with you, and I will give you rest" (Exod 33:14), was echoed in Jesus' invitation, "Come to me, all you who are weary and burdened, and I will give you rest" (Matt 11:28).[117] True Sabbath observance enters that rest (Heb 4:9) and its residual effects extend through the week. Those effects may be an unnatural calmness in difficult situations, an increased efficiency in our work or studies so that we accomplish more in six days than we would have in seven

---

117. Matt 11:28–30 appears as an introduction to the Sabbath incidents in Matt 12:1–14. Jesus' invitation to come to Him for rest does for the Sabbath what His statements in the Sermon on the Mount do for the commandments regarding killing and adultery (Matt 5:21–30). As the Sermon on the Mount statements enriched, but did not annul, the commandments against murdering and adultery, so the "rest" Jesus offers in Matt 11:28 enriches, but does not annul, the Sabbath.

had we not honored God on the Sabbath, or a trust that God will yet provide employment adequate to meet our needs.

As designed by God, the Sabbath meets a deep human need. I have in my library a stack of recently published books on the Sabbath. None of them recommend the observance of the Seventh-day Sabbath, and some of them are not even particularly religious. However, all of them note societal and personal damage that has resulted from the loss of Sabbath as practiced by the ancients and urge a return to some weekly respite to renew energy resources and regain perspective. This problem was created in part by the church itself. However well-intentioned the motivation may have been for abandoning the seventh-day Sabbath, once done it was only a matter of time before whatever was substituted in its place would no longer involve an entire day of rest as God intended, but would at best degenerate into a few hours of worship and then back to life in the fast lane.[118] Physically, emotionally, socially, psychologically, and spiritually, the creational Sabbath of the Ten Commandments is health-promoting when properly observed. Truly, "the Sabbath was made for man" (Mark 2:27).

6. The Sabbath Invites Worship

"The seventh day is a day of Sabbath of rest, a day of sacred assembly" (Lev 23:3). Derek Kidner asserts that Psalm 92, "A psalm. A song. For the Sabbath day," "is proof enough if such were needed, that the Old Testament sabbath was a day not only for rest but for corporate worship ('a holy convocation,' Lev 23:3), and intended to be a delight rather than a burden."[119] In his discussion of Genesis 2:1–3, Gibson comments, "The chief association of the Sabbath, both in Judaism and in Christianity, is with worship."[120] So Dederen: "To keep the Lord's day holy is also to gather together to hear and to study God's Word, to confess and to share the Christian faith, to offer prayer and praise to God."[121]

---

118. Those who appeal for a 24-hour Sabbath observance on Sunday based on the Decalogue have a huge task. By abandoning the seventh-day identity of the Sabbath specified by the commandment, they have lost the moral high ground and the ability to argue their case by appealing to Scripture.

119. D. Kidner, *Psalms 73–150: An Introduction and Commentary on Books III–V of the Psalms*, TOTC (Downers Grove, IL: InterVarsity Press, 1975), 334.

120. J. C. L. Gibson, *Genesis* (Edinburgh: Saint Andrews Press, 1981), 1:92.

121. Dederen, "Reflections on a Theology of the Sabbath," 301.

Some reject the Sabbath commandment, claiming that as part of their new covenant experience, "every day has become a Sabbath for me." While respecting that such a sentiment may represent a sincere desire for a wholehearted, constant walk with the Lord, on evaluation it fails in three respects as a defense for not observing the Sabbath commandment. (1) It is not practical, even in retirement, to refrain from work every day, including ordinary house and yard work, to the extent that the commandment enjoins. (2) Treating every day as a Sabbath free from work is not even biblical, for the commandment also states, "Six days you shall labor and do all your work." (3) It implies that OT believers who observed the Sabbath related to God and worshipped God only one day a week. The opposite was the case: it was their "delight" to meditate on spiritual things "day and night," "when you sit at home and when you walk along the road, when you lie down and when you get up" (Ps 1:2; Deut 6:7). God gave the Sabbath not to limit our communication with Him and worship of Him but to enhance it in the same way that being with one you love for a special time does not put them out of mind in the days that follow, but even more in mind. Observing the seventh-day Sabbath in the full biblical sense casts a Sabbath glow over the rest of the week, which may be filled with activities and be fraught with difficulties. You do not have to abandon seventh-day Sabbath observance in order to sense God's presence the rest of the week; rather, Sabbath observance enhances it.

7. The Sabbath Offers Delight

'If you keep your feet from breaking the Sabbath ["cease to tread the sabbath underfoot," New English Bible], and from doing as you please on my holy day, if you call the Sabbath a delight and the Lord's holy day honorable, and if you honor it by not going your own way and not doing as you please or speaking idle words, then you will find your joy in the Lord, and I will cause you to ride on the heights of the land and to feast on the inheritance of your father Jacob.' The mouth of the Lord has spoken. (Isa 58:13–14)

What a far cry the Sabbath experience Isaiah describes is from the experience of those Amos described who, while complying with the requirement to cease working, impatiently counted down the hours till "the Sabbath be ended that we may market wheat" (Amos 8:5).

God invites us to find "delight"[122] in the Sabbath. That is not always an instant experience for someone newly come to the Sabbath. How can you find delight in the Sabbath when you're told that it involves "not going your own way and not doing as you please"? Some of this instruction applies to business-related activity and some, to make a modern-day application, probably to activities such as watching sports and other secular media, playing video games, surfing the Internet, and so on. We don't have checklists these days, for good reason. The principle is to eliminate from our lives those things that distract us from focusing on God and our relationship with Him, free us to worship Him in a Christian gathering, get some healthful rest, get out in nature, become involved in ministry activities that will bless others and show them God's love, and share wholesome time with family and friends who have similar goals. God never intended the Sabbath to be a burden but to be a delight.[123]

The understanding of the Sabbath presented above requires a faith that exceeds sensory confirmation. Scientists have not discovered any empirical differences between Saturday and any other day of the week. We have no laboratory evidence confirming that Saturday has been blessed and made holy by a Creator/Redeemer God who invests that day with His special presence, making Himself available on that day as on no other, thus making it a holy day. That must all be taken by faith, which becomes its own evidence of things not seen. "Christians will never understand what it really means to keep *the Sabbath* until they try it—and try it not merely as a day of rest, but on the level of its full God-centered potential for divine-human fellowship."[124]

For us Sabbath observance is more than mere obedience to a command; it is seizing a wonderful opportunity. The Sabbath is a multidimensional blessings package God has placed under the tree, with our name on it.

---

122. Davidson, *Love Song for the Sabbath*, 16: "The Hebrew root (*'ng*) behind this special word in Isaiah 58 (*'oneg*) occurs as a noun only one other time, where it describes the palaces of royalty. As a verb it appears in the Bible only 10 times. This rich Hebrew word denotes not just that which brings delight, but in particular that which delights because of its surpassing quality, that which satisfies and pleases because it has a delicate beauty or regal charm. In short, 'exquisite delight.'" Davidson cites BDB, 772.

123. For helpful suggestions on making the Sabbath a delight, see Davidson, *Love Song for the Sabbath*, 92–106; J. C. Brunt, *A Day for Healing: The Meaning of Jesus' Sabbath Miracles* (Washington, DC: Review and Herald, 1981), 55–63.

124. Dederen, "Reflections on a Theology of the Sabbath," 302.

Ultimately, the rich, sevenfold meaning of the Sabbath points to Jesus as the Sabbath's ultimate fulfillment. Not fulfillment as is sometimes unfortunately presented by interpreters as a synonym for annulment or abrogation but a fulfillment in which Jesus embodies for us everything the Sabbath signifies. Jesus is the one who (1) blesses us (Matt 5:3–11) and (2) sanctifies us (John 17:19). Jesus is our (3) Creator (John 1:1–3), our hope (John 14:1–3) and (4) our Redeemer (Rev 5:9). In Jesus we (5) rest (Matt 11:28). Jesus is (6) worthy of our highest worship (John 20:28–29). In Jesus we find our (7) joy and delight (John 15:11). For us, Jesus' fulfillment of the Sabbath doesn't make Sabbath observance obsolete; rather, it infuses it with even richer meaning than the most devout OT believer had the privilege of understanding or experiencing. Rightly observed, the Sabbath does not divert our attention away from Jesus but focuses it on Jesus, bonding us to Him ever more strongly in covenant love.

Summary

- At creation God blessed and sanctified the seventh day for universal and permanent application for humankind (Gen 2:1–3).
- The Sabbath ordinance was assumed in the manna story, prior to Sinai (Exod 16).
- God embedded the Sabbath in the heart of the Decalogue, which He wrote with His finger and spoke audibly to the people (Exod 20:8–11; 31:18; Deut 4:12–13). There God linked the Sabbath to creation and admonished, "Remember the Sabbath day to keep it holy."
- Foreigners were included in the universal application and blessing of the Sabbath (Isa 56:6–7).
- God's first promise and description of a "new heavens and new earth" include all humankind worshipping Him "from one Sabbath to another" (Isa 66:22–23).
- It was the "custom" of Jesus and the apostles to observe the Sabbath in a manner that would be expected of those who believed in its universality and permanence (Luke 4:16; Acts 17:2).
- Jesus' ministry included the holistic Sabbath reform for which the prophets had appealed (Isa 56:1–5; 58:6–14; Ezek

22:26–29; cf. Amos 8:5–6). With His Sabbath miracles, Jesus disclosed His divine identity as equal to the Father and Lord of the Sabbath, affirmed the Sabbath's universal application, released the Sabbath from many burdensome regulations the scribes and Pharisees had attached to it, and reestablished the Sabbath as a day to do good and join in the Father's redemptive mission (Matt 12:8; Mark 2:27–28; John 5:16–18). To preserve the Sabbath's sanctity among His followers, He told them to pray that they would not have to flee from invading armies on the Sabbath, an event that occurred 40 years after he ascended to heaven (Matt 24:20).

- Referencing the Sabbath ordinance of creation, Hebrews affirms, "There remains, then, a Sabbath-rest [*sabbatismos*, Sabbath observance] for the people of God," and appeals for NT believers to "make every effort to enter that rest" as a holy people who believe and obey (Heb 4:4,9,11).

- John received his Revelation vision on "the Lord's Day," the seventh-day Sabbath, the day of which Jesus said He is Lord (Rev 1:10; Mark 2:28).

- John in Revelation describes God's people just prior to the Second Coming as those who "obey God's commandments [including the Decalogue] and remain faithful to Jesus" (14:12,14–20; 11:19; 12:17). Revelation's end-time appeal to worship God contains an allusion to the Sabbath commandment (Rev 14:7; Exod 20:11).

- Paul's treatment of the old and new covenants was dominantly experiential, not historical, with the new covenant including both OT and NT believers.

- God made the new covenant specifically with "the house of Israel," not with Gentiles (Heb 8:8,10). In the NT era "the house of Israel" is the church (Gal 3:7,29). Therefore, the Sabbath continues as His covenant sign between Himself and Israel (Exod 31:12–13).

- Daniel 7:25 prophesied that an ungodly power would "try to change the set times and the laws" of God, including the Sabbath. In our view, this, rather than a biblical teaching, accounts for the widespread abandonment of the observance of the seventh-day Sabbath.

Concluding Statement

Modern seventh-day Sabbath observers perceive that a breach has been made in God's holy law. We see ourselves, much as did the Sabbath reformers that preceded us, as "repairers of the breach." Sabbath reform is only one part of that mission, but it is an important part. It is set in the wider context of the everlasting gospel of salvation by grace through faith that manifests itself in the obedience of faith, coupled with a humanitarian commitment to the sick, the poor, and the oppressed (physically and spiritually)— the companion reform appeal and practice of the prophets and Jesus, doing the one without leaving the other undone. We do not consider ourselves better than people who do not worship on the seventh day. We do not judge them; God has not left such weighty matters in our hands. He has simply asked us to be faithful to the teachings of Scripture as we understand them and to our mission as "repairers of the breach" in light of the great gospel commission to make disciples of all nations, baptizing them and teaching them to observe everything Jesus taught us (Matt 28:19–20). In that context, and for all the reasons cited in this chapter, we believe that the seventh-day Sabbath still remains for the people of God, universally and permanently, as a covenant sign between God and new covenant "Israel," the church, that He is our Maker, our true rest and hope, our Redeemer-Sanctifier—"the Lord who makes you holy."

CHAPTER 2

Responses to Skip MacCarty

Response by Joseph A. Pipa

I thank Skip MacCarty for his challenging study. I enjoyed his article and often found his exegesis helpful. In terms of the continued obligation of the Sabbath commandment, obviously we are in agreement. I, however, would challenge his conclusion stated in the quotation from J. G. Murphy: "The solemn act of blessing and hallowing is the institution of a perpetual order of seventh-day rest" (p. 13). I would say God revealed a perpetual order of *a* seventh-day rest. As I seek to show in my chapter, which day of the week is not part of the moral requirement; one day in seven, however, is required.

I concur as well that "God embedded the Sabbath ordinance in the heart of His universal and permanent moral law, the Ten Commandments that He wrote with His own finger (Exod 31:38)" (p. 15).

I also appreciate his work on the relation of the Sabbath to the promise of the "new heavens and new earth" in Isa 65:17,25; 66:22–23 (pp. 15–16) and his comparison of Isaiah 65–66 with Revelation 21–22. I believe, however, he fails to take fully into account the principle he enunciates in footnote 19 (p. 17). In that footnote he explains that reference to living to an advanced age and the continued witness to the nation are God's accommodating his language to that which the people could grasp. He quotes with approval Motyer: "Throughout this passage Isaiah uses aspects of present life to create impressions of the life that is yet to come. . . . Things we have no real capacity to understand can be expressed only through things we know and experience" (p. 18, n. 19). The principle is that God uses Old Testament terminology to prophesy New Testament reality. For example, the Messiah is called David; the church, Zion; and the work of Christ, sacrifices. Therefore, there is nothing inherent in the prophecy that the seventh-day Sabbath will continue, but only a Sabbath will continue.

I also appreciate the way he relates Christ's teaching on the Sabbath to the prophetic work of Sabbath reform (p. 23). His exegesis of Mark 2:27–28 rightly connects Jesus' language to the creation and the creation ordinance of the Sabbath (p. 22).

But I think his interpretation of Matt 24:20 is wrong: "Pray that your flight will not take place in winter or on the Sabbath." He concurs with a quotation from Davies and Allison: "Matthew presupposed continued observance of the sabbath by Christians" (p. 23). In fact, the more consistent interpretation is that Jesus was referring to the Jewish Sabbath, since flight on that day would entail hardship in getting supplies and the like.

I also think he misses the mark when he takes the five passages in the book of Acts to maintain that the "apostles worshipped and preached on the Sabbath (13:14,44; 16:13; 17:2; 18:4)" (p. 23). The context of these passages suggests that it was Paul's missionary strategy to go to the synagogue first and preach that Jesus of Nazareth is the Messiah. His strategy was to take the gospel first to the Jews and then the Gentiles (Rom 1:16). As long as he was allowed to preach in the synagogues, he would, but when the Jews refused Christ, the apostle moved his evangelistic activity to other sites (Acts 13:46; 18:7). This interpretation seems to be confirmed by Luke's frequently referring to the synagogue as the "synagogue of the Jews" (Acts 13:5; 14:1; and 17:1). Moreover, in Acts 18:7 and 19:9, he left the synagogue when they refused to hear him any longer.

I find myself, for the most part, in agreement with MacCarty's treatment of Heb 4:9. His comparison of Paul's treatment of the creation ordinance of marriage in Eph 5:31–33 to the treatment of the creation Sabbath ordinance in Heb 4:4–9 is very instructive: creation ordinance (Sabbath and creation, Heb 4:4, quoting Gen 2:2; marriage and creation, Eph 5:31, quoting Gen 2:24); deeper spiritual meaning and application (Sabbath as gospel rest, Heb 4:46; marriage, Christ and the church, Eph 5:32); reaffirmation of permanence of the ordinance (Sabbath, Heb 4:9; marriage, Eph 5:33).

Although I agree with MacCarty's exegesis up to this point, I disagree with his conclusion. In commenting on verse 9, he asserts that since the epistle to the Hebrews demonstrates how the priesthood and sacrifices were fulfilled in Christ, one would expect the same to be said of the Sabbath if it were to be abrogated. He writes, "In Hebrews 3–4 he went to equal lengths to affirm that 'there remains, then, a Sabbath-rest [*sabbatismos*, Sabbath observance] for the people of God' (4:9). In other words, the seventh-day Sabbath as observed by OT believers (as represented, for example, by those honored in Heb 11) 'remains . . . for the people of God' in the NT era" (p. 27). My problem with MacCarty's conclusion is his failure to note the absence of a definite article. The writer does not say *the* Sabbath observance remains, but *a* Sabbath observance remains.

Moreover, he fails to note the grammatical connection between verses 9 and 10. Verse 9 is connected to verse 10 with the word "for." In other words, verse 10 gives the basis for an ongoing New Testament Sabbath, and, as I point out in my chapter (see pp. 158–61), the writer to the Hebrews establishes the change from the seventh-day observance to the first-day observance. So a Sabbath-keeping remains, but it is on the day of Christ's resurrection.

My interpretation of Heb 4:9–10 leads us to consider the texts MacCarty refers to as objections to his interpretation. The primary text is Col 2:16–17: "Therefore do not let anyone judge you by what you eat or drink, or with regard to a religious festival, a New Moon celebration or a Sabbath day. These are a shadow of the things that were to come; the reality, however, is found in Christ." MacCarty asserts that Paul is not abrogating the seventh-day Sabbath in this passage. He suggests in footnote 43 a number of alternative interpretations, although he does not offer a specific interpretation.

The various interpretations offered in footnote 43 fail to take into account that the three phrases—festival, new moon, Sabbath—are used to describe the holy days of the old covenant era, including the weekly, seventh-day Sabbath. These three terms are often used together to describe the special holy days of Jewish worship (2 Chron 8:13; 31:3 and Lev 23:1–25). Paul was addressing the problem that some Jewish Christians sought to require the observance of these days in addition to the Lord's Day. Paul countered that Jewish Christians were free to observe these days (for a brief period of time), but they could not obligate others to observe them.

Paul clearly abrogates the observance of the seventh-day Sabbath, along with the festival Sabbaths, because those days pointed to Christ and were fulfilled in Him. MacCarty refutes this interpretation by comparing this text with Isa 66:22–23: "'From one New Moon [or "month"] to another and from one Sabbath to another, all mankind will come and bow down before me,' says the Lord" (p. 29). He concludes: "Paul does not nullify in Col 2:16 what God through Isaiah declared will remain universal and permanent." The problem with this interpretation is the NT should always interpret the Old and not vice versa. The key to understanding Isaiah 66, as I wrote above, is that Old Testament prophecies often used OT language to depict NT reality. The reference in Isaiah to new moons confirms this interpretation, since MacCarty does not argue that the other ceremonial observances apply in the new covenant. I will omit discussing Gal 4:10–11 and Rom 14:5, since I think they are explained by Col 2:16–17.

Moving on to the resurrection appearances of Christ, MacCarty admits that they were all on the first day of the week but sees no importance in this fact (p. 32). The argument, however, is that not only did Jesus rise on the first day of the week but also the only recorded appearances to His disciples during the 40-day interval (with the exception of His ascension) were on the first day of the week. The argument is that by these meetings Jesus was teaching His followers that the day for special communion with Him would be the first day of the week. This argument ties into Heb 4:10, which I interpret that Christ rested on the first day of the week from His work of redemption as God rested from the work of creation on the seventh day of creation week. Hence, the day was changed by the resurrection.

MacCarty's reference to the women observing the Sabbath in obedience to the commandment (Luke 23:56; cf. Mark 16:1) demonstrates that the Sabbath remained in effect: "These texts imply that the women in Jesus' entourage kept the Sabbath. Would they have done so if they had learned from Jesus not to observe it?" (p. 33, quoting Davies and Allison). The answer is obvious: Until the resurrection the seventh-day Sabbath was to be observed by the followers of Christ. Only after the resurrection did Christ and the apostles change the day of observance.

Closely connected to this interpretation is the theological reality that Jesus' death and remaining in the tomb for three days were part of His humiliation. His burial was not a rest from His labors but part of His humiliation prophesied in Isa 53:8–9.

Of course, the reasoning based on Heb 4:10 and the resurrection appearances is strengthened by the fact that the NT teaches the early church worshipped on the first day (Acts 20:7; 1 Cor 16:1; Rev 1:9). MacCarty labors to prove that these texts do not describe first-day worship.

With respect to Acts 20:7, notice in the first place that Mac-Carty uses the NIV, which truncates the quotation: "On the first day of the week we came together to break bread. Paul spoke to the people and, because he intended to leave the next day, kept talking until midnight." Luke actually writes, "And on the first day of the week, when we were gathered together to break bread, Paul began talking to them, intending to depart the next day, and he prolonged his message until midnight" (NASB). The purpose of his using this translation seems to be to support his assertion that this was simply a "good-bye get-together," and, if breaking bread refers to the Lord's Supper, it was simply observed on this special occasion.

Luke's language, however, notes that they met on the first day as was their custom. He does not say, "On the first day of the week, when they gathered to say good-bye to Paul," but, "On the first day of the week when we were gathered together to break bread, Paul began talking to them." It was the custom of the early church to meet for worship on the first day of the week.

This interpretation is confirmed by the fact that although Paul was racing to be in Jerusalem for the feast, he remained in Troas seven days in order to join with the church in worship on the first day of the week. He repeated this pattern in Tyre (Acts 21:4). If Paul wanted to have a special meeting with the church, he could have arranged it earlier in the week. No, Paul remained for weekly worship.

The second text that posits first-day worship is 1 Corinthians 16:1–2: "Now about the collection for the Lord's people: Do what I told the Galatian churches to do. On the first day of every week, each one of you should set aside a sum of money in keeping with your income, saving it up, so that when I come no collections will have to be made." MacCarty offers two arguments against this being stated weekly worship. First, "It was only a few years after he planted the church in Corinth that he wrote 1 Corinthians, around AD 55. It seems to us highly unlikely that this entire congregation of Jewish and Gentile converts would have been worshipping every Sunday in honor of the resurrection of Jesus so soon after their conversion. There is no corroborating evidence for such a precedent in the NT" (p. 34).

MacCarty's argument is circular. He assumes that Paul did not instate first-day worship as he established the churches. If Paul did so, then there would be no difficulty with Jewish converts. As to corroborating evidence, Acts 20:7 and the reference to the Galatian congregations surely is sufficient.

Second, he argues that many had lost faith in the Resurrection, and so it would not make sense to meet to celebrate the resurrection. In response to this argument, I would say two things. First, there is no evidence that many had lost faith in the resurrection, and second, the false teachers were not denying the resurrection of Jesus Christ, only that of believers.

The argument that Paul is referring to the stated meeting of the church is confirmed by the statement that it was the practice of the Galatian churches. The church met on the first day of the week, and a collection was taken for the poor.

Contrary to F. F. Bruce's interpretation, the money was not collected at home. No, Paul was instructing people to bring the money to the church since he wanted to avoid having to make a collection when he arrived. He wanted the church to take a collection on the first day of each week, which is evidence that the apostolic church was committed to first-day worship.

MacCarty's last exegetical argument is that John's reference to the Lord's Day in Revelation 1:10 is not to Sunday. He claims that it was not until the second half of the second century that the term is used for Sunday. To fortify his argument, he seeks to explain away the early references in the *Didache* and Ignatius to the Magnesians.

In the *Didache* (early second century) the term "Lord's Day" is used to describe the day of worship: "And on the Lord's own day gather yourselves together and break bread." (notice the similarity to Acts 20:7).[1] And Ignatius related the Lord's Day to the completed work of Christ: "If then they who walked in ancient customs came to a new hope, no longer living for the Sabbath, but for the Lord's Day, on which also our life sprang up through him and his death."[2]

---

1. *Didache* 14. For discussion of the textual variants see N. Lee, *The Covenantal Sabbath* (London: The Lord's Day Observance Society, 1966) 298–99.
2. Ignatius, *Magnesians* 9.

MacCarty argues that the phrase in the *Didache* (*kuriakēn de kuriou*), on the Lord's of the Lord, does not refer to a day, since the word *day* is missing. He prefers the translation: "the Lord's doctrine." The context, however, clearly points to a day of worship: "come together, break bread and hold Eucharist, after confessing your transgressions that your offering may be pure; but let none who has a quarrel with his fellow join in our meeting until they be reconciled, that your sacrifice be not defiled." Obviously, they were gathered for worship, therefore, the weight of evidence lies with the traditional adding of the word *day*.

According to MacCarty, "Ignatius argues against living a legalistic lifestyle (*sabbatizontes*) but instead 'living according to the Lord's life'" (p. 37). He argues that the clause "they who walked in ancient customs came to a new hope" referred to the Old Testament prophets and that they would not have repudiated the Sabbath day. The clause, however, appears to apply to those who had been brought up in the ancient order but changed to keep the Lord's Day.[3] Further evidence for the word *day* being supplied is the more full reference to the Lord's Day as the first day of the week in the longer version of the passage: "And after the observance of the Sabbath, let every friend of Christ keep the Lord's Day as a festival, the resurrection-day, the queen and chief of all the days [of the week]."[4]

Moreover, in considering the use of the phrase in Revelation 1:10, we must note that the term John uses means a day that belongs peculiarly to the Lord Jesus Christ (as argued in my essay, pp. 165–67).

MacCarty concludes: "The four texts possibly suggesting a Sunday meeting of some kind (John 20:26; Acts 20:7; 1 Cor 16:2; Rev 1:10), are all circumstantial at best and do not alter the universality or permanence of the seventh-day Sabbath. All of the texts above presented opportunities to the biblical authors to state explicitly that God was withdrawing His sovereign blessing and sanctification of the seventh day and transferring it to another. But no such revelation was forthcoming" (p. 39).

I respond that the Acts 20 and 1 Corinthians 16 texts are much more than circumstantial, particularly in view of the abrogation of the seventh-day Sabbath in Col 2:16–17. In fact, the argument for the change of day is cumulative: all the recorded resurrection

---

3. *ANF*, 1:63.
4. Ibid.

appearances were on the first day; Paul abrogates the seventh day; the church meets for worship on the first day; Hebrews 4:9–10 gives the rationale for the first day. The New Testament records the church meeting on the first day of the week for worship.

As to MacCarty's historical material, he admits that the early church worshipped on the first day of the week: from Barnabas's *Epistle* 15 we see it written, "The present Sabbaths are not acceptable to Me [God], but that is which I have made, [namely this,] when, giving rest to all things, I shall make a beginning of the eighth day, that is, a beginning of another world. Wherefore, also, we keep the eighth day with joyfulness, the day also on which Jesus rose again from the dead. And when He had manifested Himself, He ascended into the heavens."[5] MacCarty also admits that Justin uses the term *Sunday* (p. 41). But he goes on to say that in the fourth century the church adopted Sunday as a pagan accommodation and so quotes Constantine's decree. As Schaff pointed out, Constantine's Sunday law "must not be overrated."[6] Whatever Constantine's motives, the church was not accommodating herself to a pagan concept as may be seen from Jerome's quotation in which he changes the meaning of the term: "It is called the day of the sun by the pagans we most willingly acknowledge it as such, since it is on this day that the light of the world [a reference to the first day of creation] had appeared and on this day the Sun of Justice has risen."[7] The church had been consistently observing Sunday as the day of corporate worship.

Admittedly, the church for the most part did not base its observance on the Sabbath commandment. Schaff quotes Hessey: "In no clearly genuine passage that I can discern in any writer of these two [the fourth and fifth] centuries, or in any public document, ecclesiastical or civil, is the fourth [Sabbath] commandment referred to as the ground of the obligation to observe the Lord's Day."[8] True, and it would be the Puritans who clearly worked out the theological relation of the first day of the week to the Sabbath commandment; nevertheless, as I point out in my chapter, some of the early fathers saw the link.

---

5. *Epistle of Barnabas* 15, *ANF* 1:147.
6. P. Schaff, *History of the Christian Church,* 5th ed. (Grand Rapids: Eerdmans, 1985), 3:380.
7. *Catechism of the Catholic Church*, 2nd ed., 1166 (New York City: Doubleday Religion, 2003), 330–31. Quoting Jerome, *Pasch.* from Corpus Christianorum, Series Latina, 78, 550. See p. 42, n. 80 for full title.
8. Ibid., 385 n1.

Although the term *Sabbath* would not be regularly used for the Lord's Day until after Constantine, this usage began earlier. As I pointed out in my chapter (p. 151), Origen used the term in this way, as did Eusebius (a contemporary of Constantine).

MacCarty's final argument in this section is that the Roman Catholic Church changed observance to the first day of the week. He said that the Roman Catholic Church did this in fulfillment of the prophecy of Daniel 7:25 (p. 45). Daniel prophesied that one will arise in the fourth kingdom that "will speak out against the Most High and wear down the saints of the Highest One, and he will intend to make alterations in times and in law" (NASB). He interprets this prophecy to be about the pope and the Roman Catholic Church changing the observance of the Sabbath from the seventh day to the first. In response I would note a number of things.

First, there is no majority opinion that the little horn is the pope or the Roman Catholic Church. Matthew Henry gives a good summary of the Reformation views:

> Some will have the fourth kingdom to be that of the Seleucidae, and the little horn to be Antiochus, and show the accomplishment of all this in the history of the Maccabees; so Junius, Piscator, Polanus, Broughton, and many others: but others will have the fourth kingdom to be that of the Romans, and the *little horn* to be Julius Caesar, and the succeeding emperors (says Calvin), the antichrist, the papal kingdom (says Mr. Joseph Mede), that *wicked one*, which, as this little horn, is to be consumed by the *brightness of Christ's second coming.* The pope assumes a power to *change times, and laws, potestas*. . . . Others make the *little horn* to be the Turkish *empire*; so Luther, Vatablus, and others.[9]

Moreover, even if the little horn were the pope, the changing of times could not refer to the change of day, which the church had been observing from its inception and clearly long before the Middle Ages.

I do not have the space to deal with MacCarty's development of covenant continuity. Obviously, I am committed to covenant continuity, but covenant continuity does not rule out the change of day. The principle is well established by the language of Westminster Confession of Faith:

---

9. M. Henry, *Commentary on the Whole Bible*, vol. 4, *Isaiah to Malachi* (McLean, VA: MacDonald Publishing, 1985) 1075.

As it is the law of nature, that, in general, a due proportion of time to be set apart for the worship of God; so, in his Word, by a positive, moral, and perpetual commandment binding all men in all ages, he hath particularly appointed one day in seven, for a Sabbath, to be kept holy unto him: which, from the beginning of the world to the resurrection of Christ, as the last day of the week; and, from the resurrection of Christ, was changed into the first day of the week, which, in Scripture, is called the Lord's Day, and is to be continued to the end of the world, as the Christian Sabbath.[10]

As I stated at the beginning of my response, there is much I appreciate about MacCarty's view. Our primary difference is with respect to the day of the observance. Therefore, I concur with his positive statements in the section "The Meaning and Proper Observance of the Sabbath" (pp. 62–70). May God the Holy Spirit guide us into all truth.

Response by Craig L. Blomberg

Skip MacCarty has produced a fine study of the Sabbath from his Seventh-day Adventist perspective. He also preserves a respectful tone and a positive outlook toward Christians who hold other views than his. He disarms potentially hostile readers by stating that he does *not* think that those who worship on a different day don't love Jesus or aren't saved. He also acknowledges his presupposition that the entire Scripture is God's authoritative word; thus we can continue our conversation not merely as Christian brothers but as fellow evangelicals, for which I am grateful. I will make my comments on his chapter more or less in the order in which the issues appear in it.

A majority of my demurrals concerning MacCarty's positions are hermeneutical rather than exegetical. Does one uniquely privilege the Ten Commandments as somehow more universally binding than all other biblical legislation? Many Christians, not limited to those who worship on Saturday, do, but I find nothing in Scripture itself, particularly in the New Testament, that does so. Does the distinction between commands first given in the Mosaic covenant and practices that preceded the law prove decisive for what is incumbent on Christians? Sometimes this is a helpful distinction, one the New

10. WCF 21.7.

Testament itself exploits, such as Abraham's salvation by faith prior to the giving of the law (see esp. Romans 4 and Galatians 3). But other times the New Testament supersedes even that which preceded Sinai, as with the circumcision legislation. What about creation ordinances? Surely anything instituted before the fall must be timelessly mandatory for all of God's people, right? Again, there are occasions when New Testament writers appeal to this kind of argument (e.g., Matt 19:1–9 and 2 Tim 2:8–15). But Jesus declares *all* the Law and Prophets fulfilled in Him (Matt 5:17). To put it in modern terms, and following the order of English translations of the Bible, everything from the beginning of Genesis to the end of Malachi must be interpreted and applied by the Christian in the light of Jesus' message and ministry, including as interpreted by the inspired New Testament authors.

Ultimately, then, no text of the Old Testament nor any combination of texts, taken by themselves, can settle the Sabbath debate. It will have to be New Testament teaching that is finally decisive. If one had only the Old Testament, one could readily assume, with Orthodox Judaism past and present, that all 613 commandments of the law are timelessly binding. One would then agonize over the loss of the temple in Jerusalem and, as some ultraorthodox Jews are in fact currently doing, plan for how to rebuild it, should the opportunity ever arise, and to reinstitute animal sacrifices in accordance with Mosaic legislation. Christians, especially in light of the book of Hebrews, should *not* support such plans because we understand Jesus to have been our once-for-all sacrifice that does away with the need for the temple (and all other forms of worship could occur in synagogues/churches).

Still, it is not at all clear that Genesis 1–2 institutes Sabbath-keeping at any point. It is one thing to say that God's resting on the seventh day of creation was the basis for the later institution of Sabbath-keeping; it is entirely something else to argue that God established it for Adam and Eve and their descendants to observe from the beginning of the human race. The first claim is undeniable; the second, highly unlikely. It seems equally unlikely that we will practice one-day-in-seven Sabbath-keeping in the eternal state, if we will even follow current rhythms of time at all. Yes, Isaiah 65–66, which first introduces the language of "new heavens and new earth" into Scripture, does refer to the Sabbath but in the context of conditions that, however idyllic, fall clearly short of the perfections of eternity.

MacCarty's extended footnote (pp. 17–18, n. 19) quotes amillennialist scholar Alec Motyer, but Seventh-day Adventists are historically premillennial, as I am. Texts like these in the Old Testament provide good support for understanding a temporary, millennial kingdom after Christ's return, which in many ways resembles the eternal state so that sometimes the identical language of the eternal state can be used of it but which still stops short of perfection and which temporally precedes the eternal state. Perhaps because the millennium is the time of the fulfillment of all as-yet-unfulfilled prophecies given to Israel, there will be Sabbath-keeping during that thousand-year period, at least by ethnically Jewish people; no one knows for sure one way or the other. But there is certainly no hint of Sabbath-keeping in Revelation's new heavens and new earth in the last two chapters of the Bible. Indeed, John explicitly notes that there will be no temple in the new Jerusalem (Rev 21:22), despite the elaborate prophecy of Ezekiel 40–48 (which may well also be fulfilled during the millennium), as if to stress the difference from an earlier era that may have highlighted central Old Testament institutions.

Turning to the teaching of Jesus, I fully agree with MacCarty that Jesus nowhere transgressed any of the written laws of the Hebrew Scriptures, nor did He ever teach anyone else to do so, *during the period of time in which the law was still in force.* Had he done so, He could not have been sinless. Had he not been sinless, He could not have been our perfect, divine, and eternal sacrifice. But the key hermeneutical question here is whether He spoke in any way, implicitly or explicitly, to suggest that, *after* His death, resurrection, ascension, and sending of the Holy Spirit at Pentecost to indwell believers permanently and to inaugurate the new covenant, some of the Old Testament laws might apply in different ways to His followers than they did previously. Unless one is prepared to affirm that affirmations like Mark 10:45 and 14:24 do not at all represent what Jesus ever spoke or intended, then He indeed did understand that He was giving up His life as a ransom for others in a fashion that would mean they did not need to continue bringing bulls, sheep, and goats to the temple for the forgiveness of their sins. But if something so central to Israelite religion as commandments about how one's sins were (at least temporarily) forgiven need no longer be followed literally by Jesus' disciples, there is no reason *in principle* the same might not be true of Sabbath-keeping as well. We cannot presuppose that any of the Ten Commandments is so unvarying that New Testament teaching could not modify the way it is applied.

Here is where Jesus' teaching becomes so suggestive. What does it mean that it is lawful to do good on the Sabbath (Mark 3:4)? I discuss this and related texts in my chapter. Here my point is simply that if one does not come to Jesus' teachings already assuming that He could not possibly be suggesting a new way of keeping the Sabbath, this is a sweeping statement indeed. Doing good on the Sabbath can hardly be limited to urgent care, necessary services for society, and the like. Jesus' Sabbath healings never once treat individuals in danger of dying or even in danger of having their conditions deteriorate had he waited one more day before performing His miracles. He is deliberately confronting the Jewish authorities, explicitly over their Sabbath *halakah*, but implicitly even over their time-honored cessation from work as prescribed in the Ten Commandments.

What about Acts? If one focuses solely on individual texts that describe (rather than prescribe) the first generation of Jewish-Christian behavior, one can start a good debate over whether they were more law-keeping than not. But if one pays attention to Luke's larger narrative and literary structure, all the evidence points to his showing how "the Way" (as Jesus' followers were first called) increasingly *broke* from Judaism. Of course, to the extent that they wanted to engage in mission "to the Jew first" and then "also to the Greek" (Rom 1:16), they worshiped in the synagogues in hopes of having the chance to preach Christ there. But that strategy hardly proves that they understood seventh-day worship to be a timeless mandate for Jewish and Gentile believers alike.

Does not Hebrews 3–4 clearly teach that one's entire life in Christ fulfills the Old Testament commands for Sabbath rest? Mac-Carty makes much of the switch from *katapausis* to *sabbatismos*, and rightly so. It is not just some general concept of rest that is fulfilled when a person trusts in Jesus; it is the very Sabbath command itself that is so fulfilled. But as with every other blessing of the Christian life in this age, it is only partial. We live with the tension between the "already" and the "not yet." "There yet remains a Sabbath-rest for the people of God" (Heb 4:9) can scarcely mean we will cease work one day in seven in the eternal state. Just exactly what work would we be ceasing from? Hebrews 4:9 means that the complete fulfillment of the Sabbath, in the perfect rest we can experience in Christ "24–7," as it were, still awaits the new heavens and new earth. And if it were really true that types and antitypes cannot overlap, then all of New Testament eschatology is rendered nonsensical. The very "already but not yet" framework that pervades the New Testament is predicated on the conviction that the old age remains even as the new age has broken in.

As we turn to Paul, Col 2:16 does indeed prove pivotal. I have discussed the text in my chapter, including the strained proposal of du Preez on which MacCarty relies. Here it is worth repeating simply the heart of the argument. It is hard to imagine any reader of Colossians in any time or culture, aware of the fact that Paul was a Jew writing to Christians confronting a heresy that had at least some significant Jewish elements to it, and aware of the Israelite triad of annual, monthly, and weekly holy days, with the Sabbath as the last of these, coming to 2:16 and concluding that this verse had nothing to do with the standard Jewish Sabbath. One basically has to presuppose on some other grounds that Paul could not possibly have been treating the Sabbath as akin to other festivals or ritual laws and then look for the best remaining option for interpreting the passage, however improbable it may be. But of course that is to presuppose one's conclusion. If one cannot imagine that the New Testament could ever change the application of the Sabbath law, then obviously one will never find the New Testament doing so. But if one allowed Jesus and the inspired writers of the New Testament to speak for themselves, without presupposing what would or would not change from old to new covenants, one would never come up with solutions like du Preez's.

As for Galatians, Troy Martin's views are in a minority concerning the historical background. Yet irrespective of the background from which the Galatian Christians came, the challenge they are facing is from Judaizing Jewish Christians from Jerusalem, not from paganism. With respect to Rom 14:5, MacCarty again assumes what he needs to demonstrate. "Surely the Sabbath could not be a 'disputable matter'" is, in essence, the gist of his argument (pp. 31–32). Therefore, the disputable matters about which Paul gives latitude can't include the Sabbath. But that is not exegesis. The way to determine if Paul thinks the Sabbath is a disputable matter is to determine if it is a likely meaning for one of the ways some in Rome were celebrating special days. If it is, then it comes under the category of a disputable matter. We know there was a significant Jewish-Christian minority in Rome. MacCarty's own evidence for the slowness of the change in practice in early Christianity with respect to Sabbath-keeping makes it highly probable that some in the Roman church were practicing seventh-day rest and worship. And that makes it highly likely that the days that are *adiaphora* for Paul included, even if they were not limited to, the regular Jewish Sabbath.

Unlike MacCarty, I *do* think that the "first-day" and "Lord's day" references in the New Testament refer to early Christian worship on Sunday, as my chapter spells out. But I agree with him that whatever the texts are referring to, there is no *commandment* in them to worship on Sunday. That is one of the reasons I do not accept the "Sunday as Christian Sabbath" perspective. I am *not* as impressed as MacCarty with the lack of earlier unambiguous references to Sunday worship practice in the first half of the second century simply because we have a small "database" of texts from that period on topics where we might expect some reference to appear anyway. Nor am I equally convinced about all of the texts in which one has to supply words in English translation. For MacCarty's hypothesis concerning the "lateness" of Sunday-worship references in the patristic literature to stand, he has to be right about his different translations of every single passage traditionally seen as referring to first-day worship. If he is wrong even once, then we do have earlier attestation for Sunday worship.

First Corinthians 7:19 is a significant text that would appear to support my position more than the Seventh-day Adventist one, even though it is not talking about the Sabbath at all. Linger with me on Paul's remarkable words there, which don't strike modern Gentile readers anything like they would have ancient Jewish ones: "Circumcision is nothing and uncircumcision is nothing. Keeping God's commands is what counts" (TNIV). Imagine the outraged reaction of a law-abiding first-century Jew: "How can that apostate Saul say circumcision and uncircumcision are nothing and then stress keeping God's commands? Circumcision *is* God's command. It is as central as any command He ever gave the Israelites, to mark them out as His uniquely elect people, as the sign of covenant membership. Saul of Tarsus has lost his mind. He makes no sense." But of course, what Paul means is that we must keep God's commands as we now understand them in light of new covenant revelation.

Circumcision was arguably even more central to Israelite religion than Sabbath-keeping. Yet God could lead Christians to understand that it was an *adiaphoron*. We dare not presume that He couldn't do something similar with the Sabbath.

I doubt one can explain the shift from Saturday to Sunday worship as simply as MacCarty does or blame pagan influences to the same degree. Even his account of the early Christian testimony makes clear that Sunday worship began and proliferated well before Constantine legalized it. Celebrating the "Day of the Sun" allowed Christians to worship and rest, in part when their non-Christian contemporaries were also doing so, and created the least amount of conflict between Christianity and paganism, at least until post-Constantinian developments put more pressure on pagans to conform to Christian norms. The likelihood of the prophet Daniel referring to anything post-first-century is virtually nil, as almost all commentators today will acknowledge, even as they puzzle over the specific pre-Christian historical referents intended. About the only place in MacCarty's essay where the last half-century or more of scholarship was ignored was in his trying to make Daniel predict the "horrors" of Roman Catholicism. Historically, it is not ecumenism that made people reinterpret Daniel nearly so much as a recognition of what Daniel did and did not mean (and a lot of other biblical passages as well) that began to open the door for ecumenism.

Discussion of the purposes of the law, especially in Galatians 4, has to be kept in the context of Paul's larger treatment of the topic, beginning in 3:19. Galatians 3:19–4:6 makes plain that Paul did in fact believe that two of the central purposes of the law were to highlight humanity's sin and point them to their need for a Savior. He did not, of course, imagine that no one was "saved" in Old Testament times, just that God temporarily overlooked the fact that a full provision for the forgiveness of their sins had not yet been made (Rom 3:25). Chapters 5–6, however, balance this out by pointing out the abiding significance of the moral law as an ethical guide for Christians but only once it is understood how that law is fulfilled in the command to love one's neighbor (Gal 5:14) or in "the law of Christ" (6:2). One hardly has to take "fulfill" as a synonym of "abrogate" to recognize that one cannot take it as a synonym of "preserve unchanged" either. The term, as in its frequent prophetic contexts, means to bring to completion the full meaning of some earlier teaching or event. One cannot postulate *a priori* how much continuity or discontinuity with the Old Testament this will involve; one has to take each New Testament context as it emerges.

Thus one can exegete Jer 31:31–34 in minute detail and become convinced that the new covenant will not change a single one of the 613 prescriptions of the Torah and not apply to anyone outside Israel. But when Jesus and the apostles clearly go beyond this exegesis, we need to have the flexibility to seek to understand what they are doing. Intriguingly, the fullest reference to this passage from Jeremiah, which is also the longest uninterrupted quotation of the Old Testament anywhere in the New (Heb 8:8–12), is followed immediately by the strongest statement anywhere in the NT about the *discontinuity* between the new covenant and previous covenants: "By calling this covenant 'new,' [God] has made the first one obsolete, and what is obsolete and outdated will soon disappear" (v. 13 TNIV). This verse hardly inspires confidence that *any* command anywhere in the Old Testament can be assumed to carry over into the new covenant unchanged. We have to turn to the New Testament and find out what actually happens. Nine of the Ten Commandments are reaffirmed, and they clearly functions as "moral laws." One, at the very least *potentially* more akin to other more clearly ritual laws, is never unambiguously reaffirmed, and a strong case can be made that it is taught that the nature of its observance will profoundly change.

In other words, it confuses matters to speak of Old Testament believers as new-covenant saints. If the point is that they were truly saved, and that this salvation was by God's grace through their faith in His promises, then yes, fine, absolutely. But whereas the old age continues even as the new age begins, the new covenant was only foreshadowed and prophesied in the old. It was not yet inaugurated. This is why MacCarty's schematic that links both OT and NT together as one "everlasting covenant" is also unhelpful and potentially misleading, introducing terminology used in a way that Scripture never does. There *are* new contents to the new covenant, which we must allow to remain new and not try to read back into the old. God's Word is not threatened, and His authority in no way diminished if He sovereignly chooses to have His people obey His commands in different ways in different ages. Here is where the classic Lutheran law-gospel distinction, even if occasionally overdone, is so helpful.

Having said all this, I am grateful that MacCarty reminds us that he does not "judge" his Christian brothers and sisters. Not all of his Seventh-day Adventist (or Seventh Day Baptist) predecessors have been this discerning. In turn, neither should we judge those whose beliefs, practices, and attitudes match MacCarty's. I have worshipped in more than one Christian church in my life on Saturday, even if not frequently. I have on a few more occasions worshipped in a Messianic Jewish context on Friday evenings, the beginning of the Jewish Sabbath, and found something compelling about going immediately from the workweek to worship without having even Friday night to start any weekend "relax and play" routine that might be on tap. It was as if I were giving God the greater priority by worshipping before beginning to "enjoy the weekend." (Christians who consciously think about Sunday as the *first* day of the week can have the same experience, putting worship before the workweek.) I can appreciate why some Christians, including those who were not brought up as MacCarty was, have switched to Friday or Saturday worship and seventh-day rest and found it personally meaningful. The last thing I would ever want to do is to try to talk any such person out of their practice, given how few people in our society practice *any* kind of true Sabbath rest. But neither could I say that "seventh-day Sabbath observance is God's will for all Christians," as MacCarty does (p. 9).

Response by Charles P. Arand

Pastor MacCarty's essay offers a profitable and insightful look into the Seventh-day Adventist way of thinking and provides a helpful basis for dialogue. I always regard it a good day when I've learned something new, and in the case of this paper, I learned a great deal! Prior to this project, I must confess that I knew little of Adventist views on a range of topics, much less the various arguments for the contention that Christians should continue to observe Saturday as the Sabbath. So in this regard MacCarty's paper was helpful and enlightening.

Responding to this paper is a bit more difficult than simply absorbing what MacCarty has to offer. The paper covers an enormous amount of ground. And so I'm not sure where to begin or what items I should focus on that might constitute a helpful exchange of ideas that could take place between Lutherans and Adventists. Instead of focusing on the details of all the biblical texts and historical instances cited by MacCarty, I think I will try to focus on several fairly broad, yet crucial, areas on which Lutherans and Adventists might begin and focus their exchange.

Hermeneutical Framework

The first area that invites further discussion is the various hermeneutical issues related to the Sabbath. I was delighted to see that Lutherans and Adventists share a strong commitment to the Scriptures as the Word of God and desire to remain faithful to God's Word in Scripture. For example, MacCarty's use of Gen 3:15 as the first gospel promise in Scripture—though it is rarely identified as such today among many biblical scholars—is one point with which many Lutherans would agree.

I also commend MacCarty for laying out the biblical data that Adventists bring to the table in support of their Sabbath observance. In this connection I do wonder how Adventists would treat the other Sabbath laws regarding the seventh year and the seventieth year, as these seem to be expositions and applications of the Sabbath command much as the material in Deuteronomy 12–26 provides detailed applications of the Decalogue as a whole. How one relates these various texts together deal with some crucial theological frameworks (like creation and redemption) within which to interpret the Sabbath.

Having said that, there are several areas about which I need to understand how the Adventists approach the Scriptures. At times I felt that the essay strung together Bible passages in ways that made it difficult to identify how the texts were being related. In other words, the absence of some explicit hermeneutical assumptions within the paper made it difficult to see where common ground might be found for a discussion between Lutherans and Adventists. This is not to say that they were absent altogether. A number of intriguing hints in the paper would be beneficial to pursue in further conversations. That having been said, I'd like to single out a couple areas that, from a hermeneutical perspective, need further discussion.

Creation and the Sabbath. Perhaps one of the most important hermeneutical questions, at least from a Lutheran perspective, has to do with the way in which Adventists understand the Ten

Commandments in general and the relationship of the Decalogue to natural law in particular. Lutherans affirm, as it seems MacCarty does also, that God has woven His will into the fabric of creation and written it on to the hearts of His human creatures. Natural law describes how God created the world to function. It describes the grain of the universe. In some ways one might even liken it to instructions for the proper use of creation. Thus, things go better when we cherish our spouse as opposed to ignoring or abusing our spouse. Things run more smoothly when we speak well of our neighbor and seek to enhance or protect all that belongs to our neighbor. I have the sense that MacCarty would probably agree with this so far.

In some respects it is precisely because God's will is woven into the fabric of creation that all people, whether or not they hold to the Bible as the Word of God, can have some access to it. Most people will still acknowledge that murder is wrong. For example, people on both sides of the volatile abortion debate will admit that murder is wrong. C. S. Lewis (in the *Abolition of Man*) noted that even New Guinea headhunters acknowledged that murder is wrong. They just didn't acknowledge other tribes to be human. The simple point I'm trying to make is that natural law, or God's design for creation, remains evident in creation (J. Budziszewski has done some helpful work in this area[11]).

To be sure, the natural knowledge of God's will is minimal. Sin has obscured God's will and has prompted us to evade His will. Like an Etch A Sketch that we shake in order to erase the picture, we seek to erase God's will from our hearts. But even then, if one looks closely at the Etch A Sketch, we can still see the faint hints of the drawing we made. The same is true for God's law in creation. To some extent the Decalogue given in Exodus 20 brings that natural law into bold relief. Here is what life looks like as God intended it in creation and now is restoring it in redemption.

I like the point that MacCarty made about the commandments being found in Genesis prior to their being given on Mount Sinai. It would not be hard to show how nearly all of the Ten Commandments are found scattered throughout Genesis. Cain kills Abel and knows it was wrong. But where does the command exist that murder is wrong? Joseph flees Potiphar's wife. But where is it written

---

11. See, for example, J. Budziszewski, *What We Can't Not Know: A Guide* (Dallas, TX: Spence, 2004); and *Written on the Heart: The Case for Natural Law* (Downers Grove, IL: IVP Academic, 1997).

prior to that event that adultery was wrong? And yet there appears throughout an awareness, however dimmed it may be, of how God designed life to function. That brings us to the Sabbath command.

MacCarty's paper repeatedly affirms that the Sabbath command is rooted in creation, that is, in God's design for creation. With that I would agree. And, frankly, I think this is potentially his strongest argument. But now the question arises, What is it about the Sabbath that is rooted in creation? First, there is the problematic meaning and function of the Sabbath. Does it mean "rest" or "cease from work"? Add to this the fact that in Genesis 2 the word is used as a verb rather than a noun. Derived from that is the application to the seventh day. But is the specific 24 period at the end of the week itself the point, or is it the fact that we need to take time out for restful delight that characterized God's own Sabbath? I would argue for the latter. Both observation and experience show that God did not design His creatures (human or nonhuman) to work 24–7–365. He wove the importance of rest into the life patterns of all His living creatures (those that are *nephesh*, that is, animated creatures).

It is much less obvious when observing God's design for creation that for either the nonhuman creation or the human creation a specific day is better for rest than other days. Some African societies organize the week on a four-, five-, six-, or nine-day cycle, depending on the movement of the market from village to village, although the seven-day week is also widespread. In addition, while Hindus and Buddhists insist on the necessity of individual worship, they do not have weekly assemblies; they gather chiefly for festivals. Interestingly, in the wake of growing Christian influence in the global South, Southeast, and East Asia, some groups within Hinduism and Buddhism are moving toward the weekly assembling of themselves together.

The explicit command to observe Saturday as a Sabbath is found in Exodus and Deuteronomy. God gives this command specifically to the Israelites as a follow-up to their Sabbath observances in the wilderness wanderings. Had the observance of a specific day (as opposed to rest itself) belonged in some way to natural law, one might expect to find some remnants of its practice among the surrounding nations. But there is no indication in the Old Testament that any other nation observed this particular day for worship other than the

Israelites. This is unlike the prohibitions of theft and murder, which did find expression among the surrounding nations.

Having said that, there is no doubt that in Gen 2:2 God rested on the seventh day. In the preceding narrative that describes the first six days of creation, the seventh marks the culmination of God's work. A number of scholars (e.g., Walter Brueggemann, Ellen Davis, Terence Fretheim[12]) make a good point that the creation of humans does not mark the culmination and pinnacle of creation; the Sabbath does. In other words, God creates His earth, carves out spaces (first three days), fills those spaces (second three days), and then on the seventh day expresses His sheer delight with what He had made and how it all worked harmoniously by means of His desisting from work or resting. It seems to me that the flow of the narrative moves toward the goal of God's work (and with it, our work) as a restful delight in all He has made for His beloved creatures.

In this connection, I wouldn't like to see work and rest (Sabbath) contrasted or pitted against each other. Only with the fall into sin did labor became exasperating. And only in that context does rest provide relief from the exhaustive character of work that wears one down. Such a view does not fit with either the reason for God's rest on the seventh day (He was not tired from His creative work) or with God's commission for Adam and Eve to cultivate and protect creation. Their work was part of God's creative design. In other words, activity was not antithetical to rest. More likely, rest marked the culminating joy and delight in result of one's work and activity.

Old and New Covenant. Another hermeneutical issue that stands out for me concerns the relationship between the old covenant and the new covenant as described in MacCarty's essay. Here I found his discussion of continuity and discontinuity both interesting and helpful. It seemed, however, that he took up the issue less because it's important for Adventists than it is important for others. In any case, I do appreciate his emphasis on the continuity between the two covenants. It is important not to view the old covenant exclusively in terms of law and the new covenant exclusively in terms of grace and the gospel. Admittedly, there have been tendencies within

---

12. See E. F. Davis, *Scripture, Culture, and Agriculture: An Agrarian Reading of the Bible* (Cambridge: Cambridge University Press, 2009); T. E. Fretheim, *God and World in the Old Testament: A Relational Theology of Creation* (Nashville: Abingdon Press, 2005); W. Brueggemann, *Genesis*, Interpretation, A Bible Commentary for Teaching and Preaching (Atlanta: John Knox, 1982).

the Lutheran tradition to talk that way. When viewed this way, one might ask, why even bother with the OT since the new covenant has fulfilled and even replaced the old covenant? For Melanchthon, Martin Luther's "lieutenant" and right-hand man, nothing could be further from the truth. In his Apology of the Augsburg Confession (Article IV), Melanchthon makes the point that the same gospel promise runs through both testaments. The OT promises forgiveness on account of the Christ who was to come, the New Testament promises forgiveness on account of the Christ who has come. So I think there is some room for agreement regarding the continuity of the two covenants.

When it comes to the discontinuity between the two covenants, we need to ask what's "new" about the new covenant? Is the difference only one of degree, or is it qualitatively different? Here I read MacCarty's essay with a great deal of interest, if not always with agreement. His essay argues that the fundamental difference between the two covenants lies in the response of the people. For him the distinction between the two covenants seemed to lie primarily in how people responded to God's covenant invitation. The old covenant response involved a rejection of the covenant—or a legalistic response to it. The new covenant response entailed an acceptance of it, in faith. Two things troubled me with respect to that suggestion. First, it meant that the primary or fundamental difference between the two covenants finds its origin in what humans do or don't do. Second, and more importantly, it did not seem Christ played a significant or decisive role in the new covenant.

I agree with MacCarty's paper that we must affirm continuity between the two covenants. But the key difference between them lies in the difference between promise and fulfillment. The old covenant promises find their decisive and final fulfillment in the person and work of Jesus Christ. This applies to the three major covenants of the Old Testament (Abrahamic, Sinaitic, and Davidic).

The Abrahamic covenant, in particular ways, is the easiest to recognize. The promise God made to Abraham—that He would bless all the nations through the seed of Abraham—finds fulfillment in Jesus Christ. In this regard MacCarty's focus in the subsection "Discontinuity Between the Old and New Covenants" (pp. 52–57) on the response to the covenant from the human side in God's direction differs from Luther's focus on God's promise in the covenant and the faith in Jesus Christ this promise establishes in the human heart. Paul's point in Galatians 4 is explicitly that Hagar's children are bound in slavery to the observance of God's commands for human performance, whereas those who are free as Abraham's true heirs live in the freedom to be human, that is, to love (Gal 5:13–14).

The Sinai covenant contains two elements. It affirms God's complete dedication to Israel, and it details Israel's responsibility to dedicate itself completely to God. Jeremiah 31:31–34 becomes key for understanding Israel's future in the new covenant. God promises to make a new covenant *with Israel*. The new covenant will not be like the old covenant, which was breakable. This is not to say that the old covenant was bad. But it was breakable from the nation of Israel's side. The new covenant will not be breakable. Why? Because Jesus is the new Israel. In Him we see the complete dedication of God to humans, and we see in Him, as the new Israel, the complete dedication to God in the keeping of the First Commandment. Through Him the new covenant will be written into our hearts in the eschaton, the messianic age that has already dawned, as the Spirit conforms us to Christ. Luther's concept of the assurance of a promise from God, who does not go back on His promises, is important here. At the same time Luther took seriously the mystery of the continuation of sin and evil in the lives of the baptized and with it the mystery of our ability to run away from God's protection and promise and even to elude the Good Shepherd whom He sends after us, and then to die far from home in the gutters of the streets of a foreign city.

Finally, in the Davidic covenant, God promises that a descendant of David will sit on His throne forever. Again, this promise finds its complete and decisive fulfillment in Jesus Christ. After His resurrection and ascension, He now sits at the right hand of God ruling over all creation.

In the wake of this fulfillment of God's covenant promises, several other things change from the old covenant to the new covenant. First, Israel is no longer a theocracy. It is no longer a church-state with defined geographical boundaries, and it is no longer governed by distinctive civil-political laws of a nation. Second, the new Israel has been expanded to include Gentiles from all over the world. The new Israel, the people of God spread out to the ends of the earth, as Christians take the gospel to all peoples. Where the Word goes, there we find the new Israel.

Historical-Theological Issues

In addition to the hermeneutical issues revolving around the relationship of natural law to the Decalogue and the relationship of the two covenants, several theological and historical issues surfaced that might be worth considering.

The first and perhaps the most important issue with which the Reformation dealt has to do with the way in which God relates to human beings. How do we interact with God? Does He deal with us primarily through conversation or through ritual? Luther's critique of medieval practices of Christianity presumed a sharp difference between what he viewed as God's way of dealing with human beings, relating to them through His Word, and what he viewed as ritualistic ways of approaching God through human effort by the exercise or performance of sacred rituals that please God and merit His favor. He and his colleagues rejected the mandated devotional activities that were designed to be expressions of one's love for God and by which one merited justification, with, of course, the assistance of grace.

In this medieval context Luther rephrased the Sabbath commandment in the Small Catechism in order to make clear that God was a God of conversation. From the beginning God created human beings to be a conversational community. And so from Genesis 1 on through the entire Bible, God makes clear that He wanted to continue the conversation begun in Eden. He anticipated renewing that conversation with the first gospel promise on the day that Adam and Eve sinned. Luther focuses on the Word. God's word of blessing makes the day holy, and His Word that we hear proclaimed makes us holy.

A practice of Christianity that focuses on fulfillment of specific ritual rules, such as adherence to Saturday as the Sabbath, does not necessarily void the conception of Christian faith and the true relationship with God as one that God initiates. In his paper MacCarty makes clear that God takes the initiative out of His love for us. But when the Reformation is considered historically in its context, it is clear why it never would have occurred to Luther to insist on some sort of ritual observance as a source of the blessing—as MacCarty seems to affirm immediately on the first page of his essay.

MacCarty's comments in his first paragraph reveal how deeply the ritual aspects of religion do inform the faith of all Christians. That is seen again on pages 62–70, where MacCarty speaks of the blessings that a Sabbath observance brings. But the blessings Mac-Carty contends come through such ritual observance, Luther saw as stemming from hearing the Word of God and treasuring it. Luther would have found it unacceptable to believe that "faith accepts that on the Sabbath, 'we meet God on a plane not possible on any other day of the week'" (p. 63). Luther reserved such blessings for God's coming to us in the oral, written, and sacramental forms of His Word, not in our keeping a specific ritual command. Perhaps for this reason MacCarty finds the argument of Cardinal Gibbons helpful. It may be that Adventists and Roman Catholics share, at least to that extent, an understanding of the necessity of ritual observance as a vital part of the Christian faith.

This is not to say that Lutherans believe ritual has no place within the Christian life (although we may give that impression at times). The issue for Lutherans has to do with the nature and purpose of ritual. Rather than saying that the observing of rituals establishes, maintains, or strengthens our relationship with God, we would say that ritual serves the purpose of providing the context and setting in which we can hear the Word of God. In this regard ritual plays an important role. The discipline of developing a regular devotional life of prayer keeps our hearts and minds turned to God throughout the day.

Luther shifted the daily devotional life of the Christian away from the somewhat artificial canonical hours of the day, which had become prominent in the Middle Ages, and instead keyed them to their creaturely, daily activities. One must get up in the morning, eat meals, and go to bed at night. These rhythms provide opportune moments for prayer and devotion. And so Luther provides a pattern for such practices in the Small Catechism.

The habit of reading the Scriptures and attending church regularly places us in a setting whereby we hear the Word through which the Spirit can bring the gifts of Christ to us. Without such rituals or habits, our prayers will be far and few between, and our attending to the Word of God will wane. But as rituals or practices, they do not directly bring those blessings to us. They provide the context in which God can converse with us through His Word.

Summary

Overall MacCarty's article provided me with a better understanding of the Adventist position and arguments. I also think that Adventists have something to contribute with regard to the value of Sabbath rest as part of God's design in an age when constantly being "on the go" is given greater value. As a result, we've become more and more distanced from God's purposes for creation. Having said that, a number of issues merit further discussion. For the most part I have not chosen to respond in detail to individual passages, which is something that needs to be done as the conversation continues. Instead, I have focused on larger interpretive and theological themes that provide the framework for considering those passages. Hopefully, it is a good beginning.

Final Remarks
Skip MacCarty

It has been a humbling honor to be involved in this Sabbath dialogue with such eminent scholars as Drs. Arand, Blomberg, and Pipa. I have learned from their essays and been sharpened by their critiques of my own. We have discussed with passion a point of difference, but in Christ we agree more than we differ.

Most objections raised in the critiques of my essay have been addressed sufficiently in my essay and further in my own critiques of theirs. A few warrant further comment or reiteration; several deserve expanded treatment.

Specific Texts

Genesis 2:2–3: Pipa and I agree that the Sabbath institution is established at creation. Arand and Blomberg grant that the Sabbath commandment was *rooted* in creation but not *established* until Exodus (pp. 83, 93). But the seventh day was divinely blessed and sanctified at creation, not Sinai (Gen 2:3; Exod 20:11). As the institution of the Sabbath culminated the first creation account

(Gen 1:1–2:3), the institution of marriage culminated the second (Gen 2:4–25); both were established for cultivating relationships— the Sabbath for God/human, marriage for husband/wife. Jesus' statement that "the Sabbath *was made* for man" uses a term repeated 20 times in Genesis 1, further tying the seventh-day Sabbath to creation (see p. 21).

Isaiah 66:22–23: Pipa understands Isaiah's reference to weekly Sabbath worship in the new earth to refer to Sunday, rather than the seventh day of creation, based on the text's reference to "new moon," which he concludes will not be observed in the new earth (pp. 75–76). But he ignores the scholarly evidence that the "new moon" (better, "month") reference in this text is the term Rev 22:2 uses in connection with the new earth (p. 15, n. 14).

Blomberg objects on the basis that conditions in Isaiah 65–66 "fall clearly short of the perfections of eternity" and elsewhere asks, "Just exactly what work would we be ceasing from [in the new earth]?" (pp. 83, 85). But my essay establishes Isaiah's vision as a return to Edenic conditions, which parallel the description of the new earth in Revelation 21–22 (pp. 16–17). Adam and Eve were not idle in Eden (Gen 1:26,28; 2:15), nor will we be idle in the new earth (Isa 65:21) from labor that invites a Sabbath. Blomberg is willing to grant that the seventh-day Sabbath may be observed during the millennium but not in the new earth (p. 84), yet Isaiah specifically says the Sabbath will be observed in "the new heavens and the new earth," the very terms used by both Peter and John describing the eternal state (2 Pet 3:13; Rev 21:1–5).[13]

Acts 20:7: Pipa suggests that I chose the NIV translation of this verse because it better supports our interpretation (p. 77). However, the NIV was my default translation; I would happily use his choice of translation here. Observing the Lord's Supper, if that is what "break bread" means in this text, does not sanctify a day; indeed, the early believers "broke bread" from home to home daily (Acts 2:46; see also

---

13. "It is fully in character with Revelation's allusions to mention a mere fragment of a text and yet to intend the entire Old Testament passage to come into view. For this reason the Sabbath of Isaiah's vision [66:22–23], as in the Genesis creation account, belongs undiminished within Revelation's view of the new earth [Rev 15:4]." S. Tonstad, *The Lost Meaning of the Seventh Day* (Berrien Springs, MI: Andrews University Press, 2009), 406. Tonstad's book, published since I wrote my essay and critiques, may be the most significant book written on the Sabbath from a seventh-day perspective within the last century.

27:35). Pipa's assertion that Luke's language in Acts 20:7 indicates "it was their custom" to celebrate the Lord's Supper every Sunday (p. 77) overshoots. The only such language in Acts references Sabbath observance, not Sunday: *"As his custom was,* Paul went into the synagogue, and on three *Sabbath days* he reasoned with them from the Scriptures" (17:2, emphasis added).

Romans 14:5: The probability that some Christians at Rome worshipped on Sabbath, some on Sunday, Blomberg contends makes it likely that the "disputable matters" Paul discusses in Romans 14 include the day of worship (p. 87). If so, then the entirety of Romans could have "disputable matters" in view since it is likely that some Roman Christians could have been found questioning any specific teaching in Paul's letter. Yet not until Romans 14 does Paul announce that he is now addressing "disputable matters," which fact supports the view presented in my essay (pp. 29–32). In our understanding the NT never presents any part of the Decalogue as a "disputable matter."

1 Corinthians 7:19: Blomberg writes: "Imagine the outraged reaction of a law-abiding first-century Jew: 'How can that apostate Saul say circumcision and uncircumcision are nothing and then stress keeping God's commands? Circumcision *is* God's command'" (p. 87). But 1 Corinthians was not written to "law-abiding first-century Jew[s]," but to Christians in Corinth whom he had already visited since the Jerusalem Council that rescinded circumcision as a ceremonial rite having continuing spiritual value; they undoubtedly would have already been thoroughly instructed on that point. In this text Paul affirms that keeping God's moral law of Ten Commandments did have such value. Not saving value, but value as the Reformers later affirmed as the "third use" of the law (see pp. 271–72)—a guide to Christian living—something that the morally struggling Corinthian church still desperately needed to hear (e.g., 5:1–3).

1 Corinthians 16:2: Pipa's arguments (p. 78) downplay the Corinthians' disbelief in the resurrection. And yet 1 Corinthians 15 is dedicated to countering their remarkable disbelief regarding the resurrection of both believers and Christ. Pipa also argues that Jewish Christians would have had "no difficulty" changing their day of worship from the seventh day to Sunday had Paul taught it. But the NT is completely silent on any controversy that would have erupted among the Judaizers over a purported change in the day of worship, even surpassing the challenge they mounted, as attested in the NT, to the change regarding circumcision.

Galatians 4:10: Though Blomberg objects (p. 86), the immediate context (4:8) suggests that, just as Paul elsewhere in Galatians warns Christian Jews against returning to their ceremonial ritual, so in 4:8–11 he warns converted pagans not to return to their formal pagan ritual. The scholarly evidence favors that verse 10 references a *pagan calendar*, not a Jewish one.

Colossians 2:16–17: Blomberg believes this passage abrogates the Sabbath commandment *in toto*. Pipa believes it abrogates only the seventh-day provision but otherwise leaves the commandment intact. We hold the sabbaths referred to here are ceremonial sabbaths, not the seventh-day Sabbath of the Decalogue. While ours may not be the majority view, we believe that both Scripture and the best scholarship favor our understanding (pp. 29–30; pp. 372–74). Hebrews 8:5 and 10:1 make clear that the ceremonial law dealing with the sacrificial system, not the Decalogue, was the "shadow" whose "reality . . . is found in Christ" (Col 2:17). The least that could be said is that the precise meaning of this text is as uncertain as is the understanding of "the precise nature of the false teaching afflicting the Colossian church" (p. 341) that Paul sought to correct. This should hardly be considered as pivotal a text for our discussion of the Sabbath as both Blomberg and Pipa have made it for their conflicting views (pp. 341–45; pp. 86–87; pp. 128,146; pp. 75–76, 78).

Hebrews 4:9: Blomberg, Pipa, and I have considered this verse key to our positions (pp. 348–52; p. 86; pp. 151, 153–60; pp. 75–76; pp. 25–29; pp. 368–69; pp. 176–79). Blomberg and Pipa both reinterpret *sabbatismos* (Sabbath-keeping) to mean something other than it does in both Scripture and early church historical sources. Pipa cites Origen of Alexandria (AD 185–254) on Heb 4:9 to establish that *sabbatismos* meant *Sunday* for third-century Christians. But Origen's statement nowhere uses "Lord's day" or "first day" but only "the Christian Sabbath," which some scholars believe indicates a continuing observance of the seventh-day Sabbath in Origen's day.[14]

Pipa further argues that Hebrews 4:10 refers to the resurrection and thus redefines *sabbatismos* to mean Sunday worship. But if Heb 4:10 did refer to the resurrection, which is uncertain, it would not redefine *sabbatismos*. Hebrews 4:4's quotation of Gen 2:2, "And on the seventh day God rested from all his work," establishes that *sabbatismos* in Heb 4:9 refers specifically to the observance of the seventh-day Sabbath that "remains . . . for God's people."

Pipa claims that "God the Son rested from His work of redemption on the first day of the week," the day of His resurrection, thus making Sunday a Sabbath. But this is not a NT teaching. More accurately, the same Jesus who as Creator rested on the seventh day at the end of creation week, rested on the seventh day in the tomb at the completion of His earthly ministry of redemption (Luke 23:52–24:2).

Against Pipa's assertion that his interpretation of Heb 4:9 is supported by the fact that all the resurrection appearances of Jesus to His disciples after His resurrection occurred on Sunday (which he qualified slightly in his critique), see pp. 181–82 that establishes that most of such appearances occurred on unspecified days.

Blomberg's objection that "if it were really true that types and antitypes cannot overlap, then all of New Testament eschatology is rendered nonsensical," mistakes type-antitype for promise-fulfillment. The ritual types were the ceremonial laws that pointed forward to Jesus' death. Daniel 9:27 specifically indicates that Christ's death would bring to an end the sacrifices and offerings (and their attendant ceremonies). So does Psalm 40 as explained in Hebrews 10. When Christ died, this system of types and shadows came to an end in the antitype. There was no overlapping in which the sacrifices somehow continued after Christ's death and resurrection.

Revelation 1:10: Pipa views the reference to the Lord's Supper in 1 Cor 11:20 as evidence that "the Lord's day" reference in Rev 1:10 means Sunday (p. 78). However, seventh-day Sabbatarians could just as easily reference it in support of their position. It proves neither. Pipa quotes "the longer version" of the Ignatius letter (p. 79)

---

14. E.g., C. W. Dugmore, *The Influence of the Synagogue upon the Divine Office* (London: Oxford University Press, 1944), 30–31.

to prove what "the shorter version" he had cited in his essay failed to prove namely, that "the Lord's day" was a term used for Sunday early in the second century. However, that "longer version" is actually from a corrupted, fourth-century source, not a second-century source as he implies, and thus cannot prove what he claims for it.[15]

Had Jesus declared that He was Lord of the first day, would this not have become the key text for interpreting "the Lord's day" in Rev 1:10 as a reference to Sunday? Why would His statement, "The Son of Man is Lord even of the Sabbath" (Mark 2:28) not establish the seventh-day Sabbath of the Decalogue as the biblical "Lord's day"?

Old and New Covenant Issues

My essay's all-too-brief discussion of the covenants (pp. 47–62) gave rise to thoughtful questions for clarification and several objections by Arand (pp. 94–97) and Blomberg (pp. 89–90). Arand is understandably troubled that my presentation appeared to focus the primary distinction between the old and new covenants on "how people responded to God's covenant invitation" and "what humans do and don't do" rather than on the "decisive role [Christ played] in the new covenant."

Arand differentiates the old covenant from the new on the basis of the old being "breakable," whereas he believes the new is not. It seems to me that Arand thereby gives significant weight to the "human response" dimension of the covenants. Furthermore, it seems clear that the NT teaches that the new covenant is also breakable. Bracketing Hebrews 7–10's extensive discussion of the covenants are two of the most severe warnings the NT gives against apostasy (6:1–8; 10:26–31).[16] Nevertheless, I welcome Arand's invitation to affirm the central role of Christ in the new covenant.

Paul's emphasis on the covenants does indeed focus on the *human response* to the gospel; it is an *experiential* orientation. For Paul, a response of faith is new covenant; a rebellious or legalistic response is old covenant. The emphasis in Hebrews, however, is on the *historic* shift that took place when Jesus died; the sacrifi-

---

15. J. Quasten, *Patrology* (Utrecht-Antwerp: Spectrum Press, 1966) 1:74: "In the fourth century the original collection [of the Ignatius letters] was tampered with and interpolated." See also *ANF* 1:46–48, 62–63.

16. See also the words of Jesus: "The one who stands firm to the end will be saved" (Matt 24:13).

cial, priestly, and festival types that were a shadow of the Messiah's atoning sacrifice and priesthood became obsolete when His once-for-all atoning sacrifice occurred. But in both cases, whether the covenants are viewed from their *historical* or *experiential* perspectives, Christ played and plays the decisive role.

Without the atoning sacrifice of Christ made in history, there would be no *historical* new covenant/NT. What makes the one covenant "old" and the other "new" is precisely that Jesus came in the middle. The same can be said of the OT and NT. A parallel is the divine command to "love one another," which John described as an "old command" that humanity "had from the beginning" (1 John 2:7–8; 2 John 5–6); yet in the same breath John described it as a "new command," even though the command itself had not changed. What, then, made it a "new" command? Once it had been seen lived out in Jesus' life, the understanding of what it means progressed exponentially so that subsequently it could adequately be described only as breathtakingly "new." Similarly, the *historical* old covenant could be seen and understood in exponentially brighter light once Jesus came in the middle and we saw God's moral law and covenant promises lived out in His life.[17]

At the same time, however, Jesus' central and decisive role in the historical old covenant's becoming new should not eclipse His central and decisive role in the historical old covenant itself; the covenant originated in Him, and He unceasingly embraced His covenant people with an everlasting covenant love as their compassionate Father and faithful Husband (Hos 11:1–4; Jer 31:32).

Experientially, the difference between a person's response of damning unbelief or saving faith to the covenant's gospel promises also depends entirely on Jesus' coming in the middle of their personal experience, at the point of their conversion and new birth under the supervision of the Holy Spirit—"whenever anyone turns to the Lord, the veil is taken away" (2 Cor 3:16). So in either case, whether viewed from a *historical* or *experiential* perspective, the presence of Jesus in both history and personal experience is what makes His covenant new.

Commenting on Paul's contrast of the old and new covenants, Arand writes: "Paul's point in Galatians 4 is explicitly that Hagar's

---

17. This agrees with Arand's citation of Melanchthon that "the same gospel promise runs through both testaments."

children are bound in slavery to the observance of God's commands for human performance, whereas those who are free as Abraham's true heirs live in the freedom to be human, that is, to love (Gal 5:13–14)." Interpreting this historically (Hagar's children representing the OT era; Abraham's children, the NT) would mean that Hagar represents a covenant God made with Israel at Sinai that would have kept OT believers "bound in slavery" to "human performance," and that only after Jesus came in history could believers become "true heirs" and be free "to love." But this cannot be, or who in the OT era could have been saved? In Galatians 4 Paul has an *experiential*, not historical, perspective in view.

Blomberg writes: "It confuses matters to speak of Old Testament believers as new-covenant saints." But this would seem to suggest that OT believers were neither "born again" nor engaged in the same spiritual warfare between "flesh and spirit" that NT believers are, since such terminology was first introduced in the NT. We contend that all believers in both historical eras were "saved by grace through faith," based on the atoning sacrifice of Jesus. These are universal and timeless truths.

If OT believers fought the same spiritual battles as NT believers and were saved by the same gospel promises God crafted into the new covenant, why should they not be called new covenant believers? That is who they were—*experientially* new covenant believers living in the *historical* old covenant era. Immediately following Hebrews 7–10's discussion of the covenants, Hebrews 11 lists representatives from this very faith community—OT but new covenant.

In this context Blomberg also writes: "The new covenant was only foreshadowed and prophesied in the old. It was not yet inaugurated then. . . . There *are* new contents to the new covenant, which we must allow to remain new and not try to read back into the old." We agree that the new covenant was officially "inaugurated" with Jesus' atoning sacrifice, providing forgiveness of sins not for our own era only but also for the "sins committed under the first covenant" (Heb 9:16). But the new covenant, by God's own definition—the four gospel promises (Jer 31:33–34; Heb 8:10–12)—preexisted the death of Jesus. None of the authors in this book questioned this definition of the new covenant or the chart I provided establishing that the four gospel promises of the new covenant were embedded throughout the OT, including in the Sinai covenant (see pp. 56–57). Thus Lohfink: "From the standpoint of this actual content, it is clearly a question of the same 'covenant.'"[18]

Blomberg continues: "This is why MacCarty's schematic that links both Old and New Testaments together as one 'everlasting covenant' is also unhelpful and potentially misleading, introducing terminology used in a way that Scripture never does." And yet this is precisely the terminology used by Scripture and precisely the message Scripture conveys. It describes "the everlasting covenant" as incorporating "all life on the earth" (Gen 9:16–17) and being "broken" universally in that all people of the earth have "disobeyed the laws" of God (Isa 24:5); yet for this very sin Jesus made atonement "though the blood of the eternal covenant" (Heb 13:20). God's everlasting covenant of love expressed in the creation and redemption of humanity is the unifying thread woven throughout both testaments. The biblical story of redemption is not chopped up into segmented covenantal periods with God's working differently with mankind in each period but is a unified story, progressively unfolding, with each new chapter of salvation history linked with the previous ones by the four gospel promises.

After citing Jer 31:31–34 and Heb 8:8–12, which identify the four gospel promises of the new covenant, Blomberg quotes Heb 8:13: "By calling this covenant "new," [God] has made the first one obsolete; and what is obsolete and outdated will soon disappear." Blomberg then comments: "This verse hardly inspires confidence that *any* command anywhere in the Old Testament can be assumed to carry over into the new covenant unchanged." In its wider context, however, verse 13 conveys a different meaning than Blomberg supplies. The primary focus of Hebrews 7–10 is the revelation that the OT sacrificial and priestly types have met their antitype now that Christ has made sacrifice for sin and become our continuing high priest—the distinguishing characteristic of the historical new covenant. This made the ceremonial types, not the moral law and gospel promises of the Sinai covenant, obsolete.[19] The only reference to the moral law of God, including the Decalogue, in Hebrews 7–10 occurs in Hebrews 8:10 where God reiterates His OT promise to "put

---

18. N. Lohfink, *The Covenant Never Revoked* (New York: Paulist Press, 1991), 47.

19. This historical development was prophesied in Ps 40:6–8, which Heb 10:5–14 quotes and interprets in exactly this way.

my laws in their minds and write them on their hearts."[20] Lohfink correctly observes: "If one asks whether this [new covenant] is a 'covenant' other than the first, broken one, then one learns with amazement at least one thing: this 'new covenant' too is concerned with God's torah. It is not said that God will give a new torah. It is therefore the same torah."[21]

Why so much emphasis on the covenants in a book discussing the Sabbath? This subject is important to dispensationalists because they believe that the NT teaching on the historical old and new covenants creates a sharp demarcation between them and requires that no law in the OT can be considered applicable in the NT era unless it has been explicitly restated there. And since they do not accept Heb 4:4,9 as a NT reaffirmation of the observance of the seventh-day Sabbath for the NT people of God, they consider the Sabbath commandment no longer binding. However, we believe that the NT builds on the continuity of the covenants, incorporating God's eternal moral law and gospel promises as the continuing foundation of His covenant, seen as new in Christ and inaugurated by Christ. This would make the default position that any moral law of the OT not specifically rescinded by Jesus or the apostles still applies in the NT era, especially including the commands to love God and others as expressly specified in the Ten Commandments.

What the other authors failed to address in their essays or critiques, but I expect each will yet do so in their final responses, is this question: If God made the new covenant specifically with Israel (Heb 8:8,10), and made the seventh-day Sabbath the sign of His covenant with Israel (Exod 31:12–13; Ezek 20:12,20), why would the seventh-day Sabbath not remain as the sign between God and His new covenant people? Arand agrees with us that "the new Israel has been expanded to include Gentiles . . . the people of God spread out to the ends of the earth, as Christians take the gospel to all peoples." New covenant people are the "new Israel." Many theologians agree

---

20. Parenthetically nested into Hebrews 7–10's discussion of the obsoleteness of the ceremonial types in the presence of the antitype, is Heb 8:8–12. Strategically located just prior to verse 13's announcement of the first covenant's obsolete status, this passage highlights the continuity of the old and new covenants based on God's moral law and the four gospel promises (vv. 10–12). Hebrews 8:7,9's reminder that Israel broke the covenant by disobedience and lack of faith reinforces the warnings issued elsewhere in Hebrews that in the presence of rebellious disobedience and apart from persistent faith, the gospel cannot save—a universal and timeless truth.

21. Lohfink, *Covenant Never Revoked*, 46.

on this latter point,[22] without appreciating its implications for the continuing applicability of the seventh-day Sabbath.

Church History

Blomberg is not convinced by my essay's arguments for "the lack of earlier unambiguous references to Sunday worship practice in the first half of the second century" or "the 'lateness' of Sunday worship references in the Patristic literature" (p. 87). But rather than discuss the sources I cited, his defense is that "we have a very small 'database' of texts from that period on topics where we might expect some reference to appear." We agree and suggest *that* as another reason the few early church historical sources available are not a safe source for interpreting the practice of the entire early church. We acknowledge that Barnabas of Alexandria (AD 135) and Justin Martyr in Rome (AD 150) do unambiguously refer to Sunday worship in those localities but believe it is not sound biblical hermeneutics to read Sunday worship back into NT practice from such later references.

Blomberg further states, "[MacCarty] has to be right about his different translations of every single passage traditionally seen as referring to first-day worship. If he is wrong even once, then we do have earlier attestation for Sunday worship." But if I was wrong in both instances to which he must be referring (the *Didache* and Ignatius[23]), it would not prove that Sunday worship was the accepted practice in the NT. Our authority is Scripture, not church history. Paul warned the Ephesians that from among them some "will arise and distort the truth" (Acts 20:30); he warned the Thessalonians that "the secret power of lawlessness is already at work" in the church (2 Thess 2:7). It would not be surprising or unexpected to find errors in theology and practice developing early in church history.

In our view the historical evidence suggests that Sunday worship likely began in Rome and Alexandria sometime during the second century and spread in later centuries. Rather than being based on NT teaching, the process was governed more by legislation (not merely suggested or encouraged but *mandated*) by church council edicts and imperial decrees—legislation that denigrated the seventh-day Sabbath as it promoted Sunday sacredness. Yet in spite

---

22. See n. 109 on pp. 60, 62.
23. See discussion on pp. 36–37.

of the ecclesiastical and political pressure to do otherwise, many believers continued to observe the seventh-day Sabbath as specified in the commandment. None of the critiques of my essay disputed the historical reports I cited from two fifth-century church historians, Socrates Scholasticus and Sozomen, that in their day "almost all churches throughout the world," except at Rome and Alexandria, were still worshipping on the seventh-day Sabbath (p. 40). The fourth-century *Apostolic Constitutions* likewise conveys a "positive attitude toward the [seventh-day] Sabbath"; it includes a prayer for the Sabbath and, along with advocating Sunday observance, calls on Christians to observe the Sabbath "as the day on which the creation of the world is commemorated."[24] The least that can be said on this subject is as Rouwhorst concluded after reviewing the scholarly literature: "Every attempt to find an explanation for the origins of Christian Sunday necessarily remains speculative."[25]

Blomberg (p. 88) and Pipa (p. 81) challenge my use of Dan 7:25 as a prophecy that papal Rome would be instrumental in changing the Sabbath commandment of the Decalogue. Blomberg thinks "the likelihood of Daniel referring to anything 'post-first-century' is virtually nil." And yet Dan 7:9–10 graphically describes the clearly "post-first-century" final judgment, bracketed by his introduction (7:8) and description (7:11) of the "the little horn" with persecuting and law-changing power (7:25). It appears as though Daniel wanted to *assure* that his reader *would not miss* the "post-first-century" application of the little horn's powerful and doleful effect upon God's people.

Blomberg says that I purposely ignored "the last half century or more of scholarship" in an effort to "make [Dan 7:25] predict the 'horrors' of Roman Catholicism." First, while we greatly respect modern scholarship and seek to be scholars ourselves, we are not slavishly beholden to the latest opinion; Jesus did not always consider the modern scholarship of His day to be the last word in biblical interpretation. And second, my discussion of Dan 7:25 mentioned nothing about "the 'horrors' of Roman Catholicism." But does

---

24. G. Rouwhorst, "Jewish Liturgical Traditions in Early Syriac Christianity," *VC* 51 (1997): 81.

25. G. Rouwhorst, "The Reception of the Jewish Sabbath in Early Christianity," in *Christian Feast and Festival*, ed. P. Post, G. Rouwhorst, L. van Tongeren, and A. Scheer (Louvain: Peeters, 2001), 253, cited in Tonstad, *The Lost Meaning of the Seventh Day*, 301.

Blomberg propose to rewrite church history? Catholic historians do not deny the church's practice of persecuting dissenters for centuries. While speaking in Lima, Peru, I visited a house of torture used for that purpose during the inquisition, now a sobering museum owned and operated by the Roman Catholic Church. This historical reality does not make modern Catholics any more suspect than admitting the Holocaust makes modern Germans, or even many innocent German people during the Holocaust, suspect. But we do modern civilization no service by denying the atrocities of persecution produced by both.

Pipa cites Matthew Henry's list of Reformation interpretations of Daniel 7:25 in an attempt to portray that there was no dominant Reformation position on the identity of "the little horn." But Henry's list includes more than the Reformers; and Henry himself presents "papal [activities] against the Christian religion" as one of the primary fulfillments of both Daniel's little-horn prophecy and similar prophecies in Revelation.[26]

The most systematic and extensive study of its kind that I am aware of showed that of the pre-Reformation, Reformation, and post-Reformation scholars (1300–1700) who interpreted Daniel 7:25, 80 percent (39 of 49) interpreted the little-horn persecuting power that would try to change God's law as the Roman Catholic Church.[27] Ninety-four percent (63 of 67) of eighteenth- and mid-nineteenth-century American commentators on prophecy concurred.[28] While there may have been other, more diverse views on this text, the facts show the identification of the little horn with the medieval church was a dominant influence in Protestant thought from its beginning through most of the nineteenth century. Nor is modern scholarship completely voiceless on this position.[29] Sabbatarians may be right-

---

26. *Matthew Henry's Commentary* (Wilmington, DE: Sovereign Grace Publishers, 1972), 1:271.

27. Le R. E. Froom, *The Prophetic Faith of Our Fathers* (Washington, DC: Review and Herald, 1946), vols. 2–3; see esp. 2:462–63, 486–521, charts on 2:528–31, 784–87, 3:252–53, 746. Those same charts show that those same interpreters also identified the antichrist "man of lawlessness" prophesied in 2 Thess 2:3–10 as the papacy.

28. Ibid., 3:252, 744.

29. E.g., Lutheran scholar, A. Steinmann, discusses his conclusion, and that of his denomination, in the context of Dan 7:25 and other passages in Daniel and elsewhere in Scripture: "The judgment of the Lutheran Confessions that the office of the papacy is the Antichrist is a historical one. That is, no passage in Scripture explicitly equates the papal office and system in the Roman Catholic Church with the Antichrist. Instead, this equation remains a judgment that the portrait of the Antichrist in Scripture fits the events of history subsequent to the writing of the book of the Bible involving the teach-

ly accused of unapologetically continuing this historic Protestant position that has been almost completely lost to the understanding of most modern Protestants.

As noted in my essay, some Catholic apologists have not only acknowledged the Catholic Church's authoritative role in changing the day of worship but have challenged Protestants for inconsistently claiming to follow the Bible while worshipping on Sunday instead of Saturday. My essay (p. 46, n. 91) cited Cardinal Gibbons's challenge. Another example, among many, is J. O'Brien, Catholic apologist and professor for over 30 years at Notre Dame University, from which he received the Laetare Medal in 1973:

> Since Saturday, not Sunday, is specified in the Bible, isn't it curious that non-Catholics who profess to take their religion directly from the Bible and not from the Church, observe Sunday instead of Saturday? Yes, of course, it is inconsistent; but this change was made about fifteen centuries before Protestantism was born, and by that time the custom was universally observed. They have continued the custom, even though it rests upon the authority of the Catholic Church and not upon an explicit text in the Bible. That observance remains as a reminder of the Mother church from which the non-Catholic sects broke away—like a boy running away from home but still carrying in his pocket a picture of his mother or a lock of her hair.[30]

The Ten Commandments

The critical point on which this entire Sabbath discussion turns is on how each of us and the faith communities we each represent regard the Ten Commandments. Arand believes the Ten Commandments to the extent that they can be validated by nature and because the observance of the seventh-day Sabbath has not been verified outside the OT and early Christian community, it must apply more generally to taking time to hear the Word of God. Blomberg believes

---

ing of the pontiff of the Roman Catholic Church. Thus this identification is not the unassailable and explicit teaching of Scripture. Rather, it is a conclusion based on Scripture and subsequent history. This commentary concurs with that conclusion which is based in part on the book of Daniel." A. Steinmann. *Daniel,* Concordia Commentary (St. Louis, MO: Concordia, 2008), 554.

30. J. A. O'Brien, *The Faith of Millions: The Credentials of the Catholic Religion* (Huntington, IN: Our Sunday Visitor, 1938), 473. This best-selling book has been reprinted in 27 editions and published in 10 languages.

that the Ten Commandments have no privileged status in the OT and apply in the NT only if reinstituted there, which he believes all but the Sabbath Commandment were; he then reinterprets the Sabbath commandment to mean, for the NT era, remaining faithful to Jesus and experiencing rest in Him 24–7. Pipa believes the Ten Commandments are equally authoritative in both OT and NT eras but that the Sabbath commandment was always intended as a one-day-in-seven principle, to be observed on the seventh day in the OT as a temporary/ceremonial provision of the commandment but on the first day in the NT era. I believe the Ten Commandments, the only part of the Bible God wrote with His own finger and spoke audibly to the people, the seventh-day Sabbath included, are God's permanent moral guide for all humanity.

Blomberg suggests that in the new covenant, which he defines exclusively in historical, dispensational terms, authoritative revelation regarding divine law essentially started over. He repeatedly says that no OT command can be assumed to be applicable in the NT era simply because it was given in the OT; it needed to be explicitly reinstituted in the NT. But we believe that is contrary to the NT's own teaching that "all Scripture [primarily the OT in Paul's day] is God-breathed," "able to make you wise for salvation through faith in Christ Jesus," and "useful for teaching ['doctrine,' NKJV], rebuking, correcting and training in righteousness" (2 Tim 3:15–16). Luke commended NT believers who "examined the [OT] Scriptures every day to see if what Paul said was true" (Acts 17:11). This pattern of testing later revelation by its correspondence with earlier revelation had already been scripturally established: "To the law [the Pentateuch] and to the testimony [the remainder of the OT]! If they do not speak according to this word, they have no light of dawn ['no light in them,' NKJV]" (Isa 8:20). Thus when Paul and Hebrews announced that Jesus had fulfilled the symbolic foreshadowing of the ceremonial types—animal sacrifices and temple festivals—Jesus was accepted by NT believers as the antitype that made the former types obsolete. The moral law, however, remained unchanged, useful for "teaching, rebuking, correcting and training in righteousness" (the law's third use).

Circumcision appears to have represented the entire ceremonial law, as the Sabbath represented the moral.[31] When the Jerusalem

---

31. See my essay (pp. 59–62) on my discussion of the significance of the location of the Sabbath commandment in the Decalogue.

Council (Acts 15), under the guidance of the Holy Spirit, declared circumcision to be no longer required, it affirmed the abrogation of the ceremonial system as had been prophesied in Dan 9:27 and had been signaled by God's rending of the temple veil as Jesus was being crucified (Matt 27:50–51). The ensuing controversy over this action rages throughout the NT as the Judaizers, realizing that the entire ceremonial system was at stake, fought to maintain the requirement of circumcision. But again, no such controversy is evident over the Sabbath. Had a change of the Sabbath been instituted during the NT period, the Judaizers would surely have fought such a change with even greater intensity than they had the change regarding circumcision: circumcision had neither been instituted at creation nor embedded in the Ten Commandments.

The early Christians recognized the distinction between the ceremonial laws and the Ten Commandments. C. Seitz attests:

> No one reading very long in the literature of the early church will miss the signal importance of Israel's law retained for the Christian assembly. . . . The *Didascalia Apostolorum* [a third-century Christian document] assumed a distinction between the commandments God spoke to all the people (that is, the Decalogue) and those Moses subsequently delivered. The "first legislation," it was argued, is to be maintained, while the latter, the "second legislation," is not.[32]

Wilken concurs that the understanding of the Decalogue's applicability in the NT era "can be traced back to the New Testament and the early church."[33]

My critique of Blomberg (pp. 359–72) made a scriptural case for the unique and privileged place of the Ten Commandments as permanent and practical expressions of the great commandments to love God and others. Seitz concurs: "The Ten Commandments are unique in their context. Unlike the more than six hundred laws

---

32. C. Seitz, "The Ten Commandments: Positive and Natural Law and the Covenants Old and New—Christian Use of the Decalogue and Moral Law," in *I Am the Lord Your God: Christian Reflections on the Ten Commandments*, ed. C. Braaten and C. Seitz (Grand Rapids: Eerdmans, 2005), 23, 19. See also W. Horbury, "Old Testament Interpretation in the Early Church," *Mikra*, ed. J. Mulder (Peabody, MA: Hendrickson, 2004), 746: "In the *Didascalia Apostolorum* . . . a distinction is drawn within the Pentateuch between the true and moral law, including at least the Decalogue, and the (ceremonial) 'second legislation' (*deuterosis*)," citing *Didascalia* 6:17; 2:5.

33. R. Wilken, "Keeping the Commandments," in *I Am the Lord Your God*, 245.

mediated by Moses, these ten are given directly by God."[34] They were the only commandments God wrote with His own finger (Exod 31:18), spoken directly to the people (Deut 4:12–13) at Sinai, and were kept *inside* the ark of the covenant (Deut 10:4–5); in contrast, the other 600-plus laws were written by Moses and kept *beside* the ark (Deut 31:24–26). Jesus, Paul, and James all cited the Decalogue directly (Matt 19:18,19; Rom 7:7; 13:9; Eph 6:1–3; James 2:10–12).

When John described God's last-day people as those "who obey God's commandments" (Rev 12:17; 14:12), his contemporaries would certainly have thought this included the Decalogue; the wider context in 11:18–19 mentions the ark of the covenant complete with characterizations of Sinai and the final judgment. Even more significantly for the present discussion, the immediate context, 14:7, borrows language directly from the Sabbath commandment: "Worship him who made the heavens, the earth, the sea and the springs of water" (see also Exod 20:11).

Why the Seventh Day Matters

While partaking of the Lord's Supper on a recent Sabbath, I felt an immense emotional and spiritual bond with Christians through the ages who had participated in its observance since Jesus instituted it two millennia ago. Simultaneously, I felt a similar bond with believers who for even more millennia had worshipped on the seventh-day Sabbath ever since God rested on the seventh day of creation, blessing it and declaring it holy.

What makes these ancient traditions so profoundly significant is the fact that God Himself instituted them and assigned them specific meanings that are neither discerned nor confirmed by science or natural law but by faith. When associated with the Lord's Supper, the bread and the cup become more than everyday dinner fare; they represent Jesus' broken body and shed blood for our redemption. When observed in loving obedience to the Sabbath commandment, the seventh day of each week becomes more than another 24 hours for work and recreation; it becomes a day of rest and reflection on our Creator-Redeemer God who, solely by His grace, saves us and restores us into a holy people who reflect His image.

Arand insightfully discusses ritual versus conversation (pp. 97–99). But these are not either/or propositions. Divinely ordained

---

34. Seitz, "The Ten Commandments," 29.

rituals such as the Lord's Supper, baptism, and the Sabbath *invite* us into conversation—facilitating, informing, and deepening it when they are observed as intended.

No one is saved by observing the Lord's Supper. But were it to be lost to the church, the portfolio of meanings it carries and the purpose for which Jesus instituted it would be seriously compromised, to say nothing of the outright disobedience involved in discarding it or substituting another institution in its place. No substitute for a divinely ordained ritual or institution can carry the same meaning or achieve the same purpose God assigned to the original. By tampering with the Sabbath commandment, the post-NT early church opened the door for a confusing proliferation of views regarding the Sabbath and for the eventual, stealthy entry into the church of the theory of evolution to explain human origins with its profoundly attendant implications and theological erosions on multiple levels.

My essay presents seven meanings and purposes scripturally assigned to the Sabbath that cannot be represented in the same way by a substitute (pp. 62–70). No such portfolio of meanings has been scripturally ascribed to any other day of the week. In our view the demise of the seventh-day Sabbath has resulted in enormous loss both to the church and to society.

Christmas, Good Friday, and Easter are Christian holidays that some Sabbatarians also observe, though not on the same level with the Lord's Supper, baptism, and the seventh-day Sabbath, for none of the former was instituted by God. Corporate worship on Sunday is understandable as a weekly extension of the annual Easter celebration, but there is no text in the Bible where God blesses Sunday, sanctifies it, assigns a meaning to it, or calls for its observance as a day of rest or worship. The divinely specified institution symbolizing the believer's spiritual participation in the death, burial, and *resurrection* of Jesus is *baptism* (Rom 6:3–5; see Col 2:11–12), not worship on Sunday, not even Easter Sunday. However, it is not wrong to worship God on Sunday or any other day. What is wrong is the substitution of such worship in place of the divine institution of the seventh-day Sabbath specified in the commandment, for with any substitute comes an attendant compromise of scriptural meanings assigned to the Sabbath.

Rome's Council of Trent in the sixteenth century appealed to "natural law" as the basis for the change it had made with respect to the Sabbath: "The other [nine] Commandments of the Decalogue are precepts of the natural law, obligatory at all times and unalterable. . . . [In] this [Sabbath] commandment, we are not instructed by nature to give external worship to God on [the seventh] day, rather than any other."[35] By such reasoning, rooted in ancient "natural law" philosophy, the Roman Church could declare the seventh-day provision of the Sabbath ceremonial, arbitrary and subject to change.

The sophistry of this philosophical reasoning was more ancient than the church realized. It was first whispered by the serpent in the garden of Eden when it essentially asked the woman, "Why would God arbitrarily forbid eating the fruit from *this* particular tree?" The argument made sense. She could see no basis in nature for such an arbitrary command. The marriage command seemed rooted in nature. But by natural appearances, the arbitrarily forbidden fruit appeared "good for food and pleasing to the eye . . . [so] she took some and ate it" (Gen 3:6).

Many today are suspicious of the Sabbath commandment's seemingly arbitrary specification of the seventh day as the day of worship. But could such "arbitrariness," as an expression of divine sovereignty, possibly hold the key to its potential for expressing loving obedience?

R. Dederen observes: "In an arbitrary manner God appointed that on the seventh day we should come to rest with His creation in a particular way. He filled this day with a content that is 'uncontaminated' by anything related to the cyclical changes of nature or the movements of the heavenly bodies. That content is the idea of the absolute sovereignty of God. . . . As the Christian takes heed of the Sabbath day and keeps it holy, he does so purely in answer to God's command, and simply because God is his Creator."[36]

Must there be any other reason needed for the observance of the seventh-day Sabbath than that God has commanded it?

In his novel *Perelandra*, C. S. Lewis describes a scene where Weston (the Satan figure) tempts the Lady (an Eve-type figure) of the new, mostly ocean planet to disobey a command Maledil (the God figure) had given her. She could visit the "Fixed Island" during daylight,

---

35. *Catechism of the Council of Trent*, trans. J. McHugh and C. Callan (New York: Joseph F. Wagner, 1934), 399–400.

36. R. Dederen, "Reflections on a Theology of the Sabbath," in *The Sabbath in Scripture and History*, ed. K. A. Strand (Washington, DC: Review and Herald, 1982), 302.

but Maledil had specified that before sunset each evening she must return to her floating-island home that pliably molded itself to each sea swell. Weston's argument rested on the fact that every other command Maledil had given her had a basis in nature except this solitary command. He reasoned that the arbitrariness of the command indicated that it was meant to be temporary—Maledil surely would not expect continual obedience to such purely arbitrary specificity. Enamored by Weston's argument, the Lady appealed to Ransom (the Christ-type figure) for counsel. Ransom responded: "I think [Maledil] made one law of that kind in order that there might be obedience. In all these other matters what you call obeying Him is but doing what seems good in your own eyes also. Is love content with that? You do them, indeed, because they are His will, but not only because they are His will. Where can you taste the joy of obeying unless He bids you do something for which His bidding is the *only* reason?"[37]

What if, indeed, the *only* defense for the observance of the seventh-day Sabbath is that it is His bidding?

H. Dressler describes the meaning and blessing of the Sabbath for the faithful in Israel: "After [the Sinai] encounter with God, the glory of the Sabbath permeated Israel's working days and enabled her to see all her labors, anxieties, and shortcomings in the light of His grace. Trained by the regular recurrence of this gracious gift of the Sabbath, Israel was to be able to stand before the Creator in freedom, responsibility, trust, and gratitude; she worshiped Him, the Lord of the Sabbath, and looked forward with joy and anticipation to the coming of the final Rest."[38] This "Sabbath-rest" blessing, more brilliant and radiant as seen in Christ, "remains . . . for the people of God" (Heb 4:4,9), "the new Israel," and ever more as the day of His return draws nearer.

When you, fellow traveler in His way, finish sifting through all the arguments of this Sabbath discussion, I invite you to experiment with God's invitation to meet Him in the seventh-day Sabbath. See if the attendant portfolio of meanings He assigned to it, and the blessings of the communion with Him that He offers in its observance, do not enrich your life and deepen your walk with Jesus—your Creator and Redeemer and Lord.

---

37. C. S. Lewis, *Perelandra* (New York: Scribner, 1972), 101.

38. H. Dressler, "The Sabbath in the Old Testament," in *From Sabbath to Lord's Day: A Biblical, Historical, and Theological Investigation*, ed. D. A. Carson (Eugene, OR: Wipf and Stock, 1982), 35.

CHAPTER 3

The Christian Sabbath
Joseph A. Pipa

From the time of the Reformation until the mid-twentieth century, the great majority of Protestant Christians held fairly strict views regarding the use of Sunday. Most in practice would have fallen into the category this book calls the "Christian Sabbath" view. With the encroachments of liberalism, the rise of dispensationalism, and the ubiquitous presence of the television, this practice has so declined that today only a small minority of Christians in the West hold to this position.[1] Who is correct? Does the Bible require Christians to observe one day in seven, or are all days equal? Is Sunday the required day, or may the church select any day she chooses? My thesis in this chapter is that we should restore the Sabbath to its purpose and uses as described in the Westminster Standards, and to that end we will examine a number of passages that support the position of that Confession.[2]

The Sabbath as Creation Ordinance

We begin seeking to discover God's intention for the Sabbath by turning to its institution in Gen 2:1–3. Along with work (Gen 1:28;

---

1. For contemporary works against sabbatarianism, see D. A. Carson, ed., *From Sabbath to Lord's Day: A Biblical, Historical and Theological Investigation* (Grand Rapids: Zondervan, 1982) and P. K. Jewett, *The Lord's Day* (Grand Rapids: Eerdmans, 1972). For support of the position of this chapter, see R. L. Dabney, *Lectures in Systematic Theology* (Grand Rapids: Zondervan, 1972), 366–97; C. Hodge. *Systematic Theology,* 3 vols. (Grand Rapids: Eerdmans, 1982) 3:321–48; J. Owen, *An Exposition of the Epistle to the Hebrews,* 4 vols. (Marshallton, DE: National Foundation for Christian Education, 1960, 7 volumes in 4), 1:263–460; and J. Pipa, *The Lord's Day* (Fern, Ross–shire, UK: Christian Focus, 1997).
2. Some of the material in this chapter is adapted from my book *The Lord's Day.*

2:15) and marriage (Gen 2:18–25), God instituted the Sabbath to govern the lives of all mankind. Just as the ordinances of work and marriage are permanent, so is the ordinance of the Sabbath.[3]

God instituted the celebration of the Sabbath both by His example and by His words of institution. To begin with, He established the principle of Sabbath-keeping by resting on the seventh day: "By the seventh day God completed His work which He had done, and He rested on the seventh day from all His work which He had done" (Gen 2:2).[4] The term *sabbath* is derived from the word rendered *rested*.[5] By resting on the seventh day, God Himself established the principle and practice of Sabbath observance. In order to understand the Sabbath ordinance, we first must consider why God rested.

First, by resting, God declared that His work as Creator was completed, as we observe in Gen 2:1 where God pronounced that He had completed His work as Creator: "Thus the heavens and the earth were completed, and all their hosts." The words *heavens*, *earth*, and *hosts* encompass all the results of God's creative work on days one through six.

God's rest, however, was not a cessation from all work, for He continues to work in providence,[6] governing the processes of life and all aspects of His created order; He also worked in accomplishing redemption and continues to work by calling His people unto Himself and sanctifying them. Hence, God did not rest from all His work but only from the work of creation (John 5:17).

Since He continues to work, why this emphasis on rest? When God rested from the work of creation, He declared that it was completed exactly as He intended. Never again would there be need for this work. It is finished! He bids us to worship Him as Creator of heaven and earth.

Second, God's rest expressed His delight in creation. Moses amplifies this concept in Exod 31:17: "It [the Sabbath] is a sign between Me and the sons of Israel forever; for in six days the Lord

---

3. For a discussion of these "creation ordinances" see J. Murray, *Principles of Conduct* (Grand Rapids: Eerdmans, 1964), 27–106.

4. All Scripture references are taken from the New American Standard Bible unless otherwise indicated.

5. D. Kidner, *Genesis: An Introduction and Commentary* (Downers Grove, IL: InterVarsity Press, 1972), 53: "literally 'ceased'; from *sabat*, the root of 'Sabbath.'" Cf. F. Delitzsch, *A New Commentary on Genesis*, 2 vols. (Minneapolis: Klock & Klock, 1978), 1:108–9.

6. Westminster Shorter Catechism, Q. 11 (hereafter WSC).

made heaven and earth, but on the seventh day He ceased from labor, and was refreshed."

What a delightful statement: "God ceased from labor, and was refreshed." But what does it mean? Certainly God did not require rest because His creative work had wearied Him. The refreshment of God on the seventh day was through joy as He contemplated the beauty and perfection of all the creation: at the conclusion of the sixth day, "God saw all that He had made, and behold, it was very good" (Gen 1:31). Just as one steps back to contemplate with pleasure something built or accomplished, God stepped back to contemplate His work with pleasure. By resting on the Sabbath, God reflected on the beauty and glory of His completed work, taking joy in it.

Third, by resting on the seventh day, God pictured the rest that He would provide for His people. He offered Adam and his descendants life (eternal rest), so had Adam not fallen into sin, he would have entered into that rest without passing through death. God, by resting on the seventh day, pictured the promised rest, which was a type of our eternal rest.

The Creator's example of rest is a reason for His not recording the end of the seventh day. The first six days were concluded by the cycle of evening and morning, but the ending of the seventh day is not recorded. For Adam and Eve the seventh day ended as had the previous six days; the cessation of the day, however, is left unspecified to picture the eternal rest that God would provide for His people.

God graciously did not cancel the offer of rest after the fall; rather, He renewed the promise of life, not through Adam's obedience but through a Redeemer. According to God's eternal purpose, the day of rest became a weekly promise and reminder to sinners that He would provide redemption and rest.

By resting, therefore, God declared that He had finished His creative activity, reminding us that He is the all-powerful Creator who completed His work and has authority and power to govern it. He contemplated with joy the finished work of creation; He calls us to seek our rest in Him as we contemplate His goodness in the beauty of creation and His mercy in the gracious offer of redemption. He gave us a picture of the eternal rest that belongs to His people; He promises the reality of entering into His eternal rest. In our Sabbath-keeping, we celebrate that God's works of creation and redemption are finished; we contemplate the complex beauty of His works and are refreshed in communion with Him; and we anticipate our eternal life with Him.

Having demonstrated these truths by His own rest, God explicitly consecrated the seventh day for man to keep the Sabbath. For in addition to giving us the example of His rest, "God blessed the seventh day and sanctified it, because in it He rested from all His work which God had created and made" (Gen 2:3). In this dual action of blessing and sanctifying the day, God instituted the pattern of six days of work and a seventh day of rest.

Some suggest that God blesses His eternal rest, not the seventh day. In the Sabbath commandment, however, God bases our responsibility to sanctify the seventh day on His blessing of the Sabbath day: "Therefore the Lord blessed the sabbath day and made it holy" (Exod 20:11b). We conclude that God specifically blessed the seventh day in the weekly cycle.[7]

By blessing the day, God assigned it special purpose. In the creation account, when God blessed something, He established its purpose and endowed the thing created with the ability to fulfill that purpose. For example, when God blessed the animals in Gen 1:22, He established their purpose of multiplying and filling the earth and endowed them with the inclination and ability to procreate so that they might accomplish that purpose (see also Gen 1:28). In like manner, when God blessed the seventh day, He gave it purpose and the ability to fulfill that purpose.

Furthermore, He promised those who would follow His example of rest every seventh day that He would bless them. So by blessing the day, He made the day a blessing for man. Surely Christ had this blessing in mind when He said, "The Sabbath was made for man, and not man for the Sabbath" (Mark 2:27).

God's purpose in blessing the day is made clearer when we understand what is meant by His "sanctifying" the day, by declaring it to be holy. When God sanctified something, He removed it from its common use and set it apart for a special religious use connected with His worship and service. For example, He declared to be holy or sanctified the garments of the priest, the altar, the sanctuary, and all the furnishings and utensils used in the tabernacle and, later,

---

7. Murray, *Principles of Conduct*, 32.

the temple. On account of this sanctification, these things were to be used only for the holy purposes of worship (e.g., Exod 30:37–38).

How, then, do we apply this sanctification to the seventh day? We may reasonably assume that in the same way God has set aside certain things for His special use and service, He also set aside the seventh day for the special purpose of worship and service. This is not to deny that the other six days are holy and are to be used for God's glory. Christians are to glorify God in all of life; everything we do is to be a holy service unto the Lord. However, He established the seventh day as a holy day, set apart for special purposes.

By blessing and sanctifying the day, God communicated to Adam and Eve, and through the Scriptures to us, the principle of Sabbath-keeping. We are to treat as holy what God declares to be holy, concluding that the observation of one day out of seven is a perpetually binding moral obligation because of this creation ordinance.

The Moral Ground for Keeping the Sabbath

In the Sabbath commandment (Exod 20:8–11), God reinforced man's moral responsibility for keeping holy one day in seven and also instructed us how to keep the day holy. The Sabbath commandment, building on the creation Sabbath ordinance (v. 11), legislates how the day is to be structured in the same way that the commandment forbidding adultery structures the creation ordinance of marriage. Furthermore, the Sabbath commandment and the commandment not to steal jointly structure the creation ordinance of work.

Some attempt to counter this moral ground for keeping the Sabbath by suggesting that the Sabbath commandment is merely ceremonial because God declared it to be a sign of the Mosaic covenant only (Exod 31:16–17); therefore, when that covenant was fulfilled in Christ and the new covenant, the covenant sign of the Sabbath was abrogated.[8] For a number of reasons, however, we must regard the Sabbath commandment as a perpetual moral law rather than merely ceremonial. First, the nature and unity of the Decalogue teach that the Sabbath commandment is an expression of God's universal moral will for all people. The unity of the Decalogue is seen in the manner in which God gave the Law at Mount Sinai, described in

---

8. For an exposition of this position see G. D. Long, *The Christian Sabbath—Lord's Day Controversy* (Stirling, VA: Grace Abounding Ministry, 1980).

Exod 31:18: "When He had finished speaking with him upon Mount Sinai, He gave Moses the two tablets of the testimony, tablets of stone, written by the finger of God" (cf. Deut 10:4). The Ten Words, which were given in such an awesome manner at Mount Sinai and engraved by the finger of God in stone, stand together as a unit. They served as the foundation of Israel's covenant relationship to God because they are the timeless expression of God's moral will. Therefore, it is contrary to all sound reason to wrench out one commandment, claiming that it was ceremonial and consequently no longer binding.

We also see the unity of the Decalogue in its role as a summary of God's moral law. The Westminster Larger Catechism (Q. 93, hereafter WLC) defines "moral law" as "the declaration of the will of God to mankind, directing and binding everyone to personal, perfect, and perpetual conformity and obedience thereunto, in the frame and disposition of the whole man, soul and body, and in performance of all those duties of holiness and righteousness which he oweth to God and man: promising life upon the fulfilling, and threatening death upon the breach of it." In answer to question 98 "Where is the moral law summarily comprehended?" the Catechism responds, "The moral law is summarily comprehended in the Ten Commandments, which were delivered by the voice of God upon Mount Sinai, and written by him in two tables of stone; and are recorded in the twentieth chapter of Exodus. The first four commandments containing our duty to God, and the other six our duty to man."[9]

Although advocates of the position that the Sabbath commandment serves only as a ceremonial sign for Israel assert that the Ten Commandments are not a summary of moral law but rather a summary of covenant law,[10] the New Testament, to the contrary, treats the Ten Commandments as a summary of God's moral law. For example, when asked what the greatest commandment is, Christ responded, "'You shall love the Lord your God with all your heart, and with all your soul, and with all your mind.' This is the great

---

9. Ezekiel 22:1–16 offers another good example of the unity of the Law. The violation of the Sabbath is placed alongside violations of the other Commandments as reason for God's judgment on Judah. Note that the Westminster Standards enumerate the Ten Commandments differently from Lutherans and Roman Catholics (who consider the Third Commandment to be the Sabbath commandment), which enumeration is shared by the majority of Protestants (as well as Eastern Orthodox).

10. Long, *Christian Sabbath*, 16–19.

and foremost commandment. The second is like it, 'You shall love your neighbor as yourself.' On these two commandments depend the whole Law and the Prophets" (Matt 22:37–40). Jesus based His answer on two Old Testament passages (Deut 6:5 and Lev 19:18) that summarize the Ten Commandments. In Matthew 19:18–19, Jesus taught the clear relationship of the second summary ("Love your neighbor as yourself") to the Ten Commandments. In answering the rich young ruler's question about which commandments he should keep, Jesus said, "You shall not commit murder; You shall not commit adultery; You shall not steal; You shall not bear false witness; Honor your father and mother; and You shall love your neighbor as yourself" (cf. Jas 2:8–11). Here we see that Jesus considered the second greatest commandment to be a summary of the last six commandments. Should we not reason that if the summary is morally binding, that which it summarizes is morally binding as well?

Some respond that the last six Commandments still have moral standing because they are repeated in the New Testament. Jesus, however, in quoting the last six commandments, recognizes the Ten Commandments as a summary of God's moral law. And while none of the first four commandments are quoted in the New Testament, all four are alluded to and applied in the New Testament.[11]

As a summary of God's moral law, the Ten Commandments are a unified expression of God's will. The first four deal with our duty to God and the last six our duty to our neighbor. The Sabbath (fourth) commandment, therefore, is necessary to teach us the entirety of the duty we owe to God. The First Commandment tells us that God alone is to be worshipped; the second instructs us how He is to be worshipped; the third teaches the proper attitude of the worshipper; while the fourth specifies that there is to be a day of each week devoted to that worship.

A second argument demonstrating that the Sabbath commandment is a moral law binding on all people rather than a ceremonial law is the theological basis God gives for the Commandment. As

---

11. Some claim that an Old Testament commandment must be repeated in the NT in order to have a binding moral character on the Christian. They say the other nine commandments are repeated in the NT while it remains silent about the Sabbath commandment. As we shall see, the NT is not silent about this commandment. But even if it were, since the Decalogue is a summary of the moral law, its moral principles are binding whether or not repeated, since each commandment is an unchangeable expression of God's moral will for mankind.

already noted, God declares that the ground for Sabbath observance is the creation ordinance: "For in six days the Lord made the heavens and the earth, the sea and all that is in them, and rested on the seventh day; therefore, the Lord blessed the sabbath day and made it holy" (Exod 20:11; cf. 31:17). God hereby bases the Sabbath commandment on the prefall Sabbath ordinance. Some suggest that, since in Deuteronomy 5 the deliverance of Israel from Egypt is given as the ground of the Sabbath commandment (Deut 5:15), the creation ordinance cannot be reason for the commandment. They claim that if two different reasons were given, Scripture would contradict itself.[12]

The fact that the Bible gives more than one reason for a law or an act of God in no way suggests confusion or contradiction. God often adduced more than one reason for His acts. For example, Jude 7 states that God destroyed Sodom and Gomorrah for their gross immorality, while Ezekiel emphasizes their arrogance and oppression of the poor (Ezek 16:49–50). Is there any conflict in the two different reasons? Of course not; clearly, God destroyed them for both types of wickedness. Jude emphasized one reason and Ezekiel the other.

Surely no difficulty is involved in God's giving two reasons for Israel to keep the Sabbath. The Ten Commandments served a special function for Israel as God's covenant people because the Commandments are a summary of His moral law. Therefore, God commands Israel to keep the Sabbath because Sabbath-keeping is part of the moral duty of all people. When they were about to enter the promised land, He gave a second reason: they were God's redeemed people.

A third argument for the perpetual character of the Sabbath commandment is that the deliberate desecration of the Sabbath day brought the death penalty (Exod 31:14–15). As Hodge points out, only the violation of moral laws required the death penalty:

> Another argument is derived from the penalty attached to the violation of this commandment. . . . The violation of no merely ceremonial or positive law was visited with this penalty. Even the neglect of circumcision, although it involved the rejection of both the Abrahamic and the Mosaic covenant, and necessarily worked the forfeiture of all the benefits of the theocra-

---

12. Long, *Christian Sabbath*, 15–16.

cy, was not made a capital offence. The law of the Sabbath by being thus distinguished was raised far above the level of mere positive enactments. A character was given to it, not only of primary importance, but also of special sanctity.[13]

A fourth reason for regarding the Sabbath commandment as a moral law binding on all people and not the Israelites alone is the scope of the commandment: "You shall not do any work, you or your son or your daughter, your male or your female servant or your cattle or your sojourner who stays with you" (Exod 20:10). Within the covenant context of Israel, the stranger was the unconverted, or in some instances the converted but uncircumcised Gentile, who lived among God's people in the land. God obligated the unconverted Gentiles to observe the structure of the Sabbath, even though they could not take part in the feasts or in temple worship. We see an application of this prohibition in Neh 13:15–21: traders and merchants (at least some of whom were Gentiles, v. 16) were forbidden to conduct business on the Sabbath. Nehemiah threatened them with force if they persisted (v. 21). I chose this example because Israel, though still in covenant, was no longer an independent nation but a vassal state under foreign rulers. Nevertheless, Nehemiah applied the Sabbath commandment to Gentiles as well as Jews. This example leads to the conclusion that the Sabbath commandment was more far-reaching than a sign of God's covenant with Israel.

I do not contend that there are no ceremonial aspects in the Sabbath commandment. Rather, all the ceremonial and judicial laws of Israel are based on the Ten Commandments.[14] The Ten Words summarized man's moral responsibility to God. The judicial laws applied the moral law to the civic life of Israel, while the ceremonial laws applied the moral law to her worship. All of the Ten Commandments, therefore, have both civil and ceremonial ramifications. For example, the Commandment forbidding idolatry (Exod 20:4–6) is applied to the entire system of tabernacle/temple worship, sacrifices, and religious festivals.[15] All of these things and practices were types of Christ and His work and thus would pass away, but the moral requirement of this specific Commandment would remain.

---

13. Hodge, *Systematic Theology*, 3:324.

14. Westminster Confession of Faith, 19.3–4 (hereafter WCF). I recognize that the distinction of moral, ceremonial, and judicial is not clear-cut in the Old Testament. This distinction, however, is valid as it notes the various ways the moral law was applied.

15. See Deuteronomy 12.

Another example is the commandment to honor one's father and mother, which promises prosperity and long life in the land (Deut 5:16). In Eph 6:3, when the apostle Paul repeats the promise he changes the wording to "that it may be well with you, and that you may live long on the earth." He alters the promise by taking away the theocratic element as it applied to Israel in the land and adjusts the promise to New Testament covenant children. In fact, each of the Ten Commandments had ceremonial and judicial applications. Because the ceremonial and judicial laws were but the application of the moral law, we find all three types of commandments mixed together, as in Leviticus 19.

The Sabbath commandment, therefore, contained ceremonial aspects—seventh-day worship, special Sabbaths (new moon, seventh year, and jubilee), and religious feasts. These aspects applied exclusively to Israel, and Christ fulfilled them (Col 2:16–17). The principle, however, that God would have human beings devote a whole day of each week to worship and religious service is part of the moral fabric of the universe.

There is, therefore, no tension between the permanent, moral obligation of the Sabbath commandment and the fact that it was appointed as a sign of the Mosaic economy (Exod 31:16–17). The moral obligation in its seven-day cycle distinguished the old covenant people from all the other nations of the earth. For this reason redemption from Egypt was given as the ground for the Sabbath in Deut 5:15. God was not annulling the basis of the creation ordinance, which was stated when the Commandment was first given at Mount Sinai. Rather, He added a second reason for His covenant people, who were also to keep the Sabbath because they had been redeemed. As such, Sabbath-keeping had a distinctly covenantal role, but this role never exhausted the purposes of the Sabbath. God gave the Jews the seventh-day Sabbath as a memorial of redemption, and since the redemption from Egypt pictured the greater redemption accomplished by Christ, the memorial day of the former promised the latter. As Paul says in Col 2:16–17, the seventh-day Sabbath pointed to the Savior to come. Therefore, the evidence is clear that the Sabbath commandment, though containing a ceremonial element, is a perpetually binding moral obligation for all people.

With these things in mind, we turn to investigating the role of the Sabbath commandment in regulating the observance of the

Sabbath. By referring to the Sabbath as "the market day of the soul," the Puritans reminded us that God gave us this day above all other days to conduct spiritual commerce.[16] The purpose of the commandment is to free us from our daily business so that we may do business with Him on "the market day of the soul."

The Sabbath commandment states the purpose of the Sabbath by saying, "Remember the sabbath day, to keep it holy." The word *remember* has a twofold significance. In the first place God is commanding, "Do not forget or neglect it," as the Old Testament writers often used the term. For example, in Exod 13:3 Moses reminds the people not to forget the historical act of their redemption, the exodus: "Moses said to the people, 'Remember this day in which you went out from Egypt, from the house of slavery; for by a powerful hand the Lord brought you out from this place. And nothing leavened shall be eaten.'" Christ uses a similar term, *remembrance*, this way in the institution of the Lord's Supper: "Do this in remembrance of Me" (Luke 22:19).

The call to remember the Sabbath teaches that the Sabbath as an institution had already been established—building on His having established the sanctity of the Sabbath day by a creation ordinance. Hence, in the Sabbath commandment He exhorts us to remember that fact.

In the Bible, however, the term *remember* means more than not forgetting. It also means to observe and celebrate. If asked, did you remember your anniversary? You are not simply asked whether you remembered the date but whether you observed the occasion. We "remember" special occasions by, for example, giving gifts, going out to dinner, or gathering friends together. When God calls us to "remember the sabbath day," He summons us to observe it in a unique way, to commemorate it.

This concept of remembering is illustrated in Exod 12:14: "Now this day [referring to the day of the Passover] will be a memorial to you." The noun "memorial" comes from the same root as the verb *remember*. How was it a memorial? "You shall celebrate it as a feast to the Lord; throughout your generations you are to celebrate it as a permanent ordinance." Not only were they to remember the

---

16. The Puritans applied this terminology to the Sabbath to picture the idea that the day was for special transactions, like the English "market day."

historical occasion, but also they were to celebrate the historical occasion by observing the Passover feast (cf. Exod 13:3).

One "remembers" the Sabbath by observing it according to God's regulation. For this reason, when God repeated the Ten Commandments 40 years later, He used the word *observe* instead of *remember*: "Observe the sabbath day to keep it holy . . . therefore the Lord your God commanded you to observe the sabbath day" (Deut 5:12,15).

When one rightly understands the significance of remembering, one recognizes that the day was never merely a day of idleness. Some suggest that the sole purpose of the Sabbath commandment was to provide physical rest for Israel. As God's rest, however, was not a rest of inactivity, the rest commanded by the Sabbath commandment is not a rest of inactivity but of holy commemoration. According to Lev 23:2–3, Sabbath rest entailed corporate worship:

> Speak to the sons of Israel and say to them, "The Lord's appointed times which you shall proclaim as holy convocations— My appointed times are these: For six days work may be done, but on the seventh day there is a sabbath of complete rest, a holy convocation. You shall not do any work; it is a sabbath to the Lord in all your dwellings."

A holy convocation was a time of corporate worship. Therefore, at least part of the purpose of the Sabbath rest was to observe the day by participating in public worship. In this we also see the term *remember* teaching that the Sabbath is a day for holy transactions, a "market day of the soul." God based this commandment on the special claim He has on the day: "Six days shall you labor and do all your work, but the seventh day is a sabbath of the Lord your God."

Because the day belongs to God in a special sense, we are to remember it by keeping it holy. Properly used, the day enables us to remember God and His saving work. We are to sanctify it, as the Shorter Catechism teaches:

> The Sabbath is to be sanctified by holy resting all that day, even from such worldly employment and recreation as are lawful on other days, and spending the whole time in the public and

private exercises of God's worship, except so much as is to be taken up in the works of necessity and mercy.[17]

Some wrongly interpret the Heidelberg Catechism Q. 103:

First, that the ministry of the gospel and the schools be maintained; and that I, especially on the sabbath, that is, on the day of rest, diligently frequent the church of God, to hear his word, to use the sacraments, publicly to call upon the Lord, and contribute to the relief of the poor. Secondly, that all the days of my life I cease from my evil works, and yield myself to the Lord, to work by his Holy Spirit in me: and thus begin in this life the eternal sabbath.

Some therefore claim that in the New Testament the Sabbath commandment requires only public worship. They assert that Christ in the resurrection fulfilled the requirement of rest, so now we rest by forsaking our sinful ways and looking forward to the eternal Sabbath.

The Sabbath commandment, however, teaches that we rest, setting aside our usual occupations in order to worship. The cessation from work and recreation prescribed by the Sabbath commandment frees us to worship. This position is precisely that of Ursinus (one of the framers of the Heidelberg Catechism). He wrote that "all those other works which men ordinarily perform on the other days of the week might on the Sabbath give place to the private and public worship of God."[18] With respect to the ceremonial aspect of the Sabbath commandment he wrote that the commandment has two parts: "the one moral and perpetual, as that the Sabbath be kept holy; the other ceremonial and temporary, as that the seventh day be kept holy."[19]

Others argue that cessation from regular work is not part of the continuing moral requirement of the Sabbath commandment because Christ occasionally violated the Jewish Sabbath. We know, however, that Christ could not have broken the Sabbath commandment and still fulfilled His role as the Messiah who came to do the will of God (Ps 40:6–8; Matt 5:1–20). He violated only Jewish traditions.[20]

---

17. WSC 60.

18. Z. Ursinus, *Commentary of Dr. Zacharias Ursinus on the Heidelberg Catechism* (Phillipsburg, NJ: Presbyterian and Reformed), 558.

19. Ibid., 557. For a more detailed discussion of the teaching of the church fathers and the Reformers see Pipa, *Lord's Day*, 130–55.

20. See Pipa, *Lord's Day*, 68–94.

The prohibitions of the Sabbath commandment teach us how to structure the day in order to derive the most benefit from it (Exod 20:9–10), showing us how to structure our lives personally, domestically, and socially.

Personally, the Lord frees us from our ordinary work: "The seventh day is a sabbath of the Lord your God; in it you shall not do any work." The term *work* includes all types of work. Verse 9 uses the word *labor*, which refers to manual labor—agricultural and other forms of labor that are performed by the hands. The term *work* is a more comprehensive word that embraces the work described by *labor* but also includes all business, trading and commerce, and domestic chores. By using both terms, God makes clear that He prohibits all our regular work and activity.

We observe, though, that this prohibition is set against the backdrop of His giving us six days to accomplish every kind of work: "Six days you shall labor and do all your work." We often focus on the deprivation perceived in the Ten Commandments and fail to notice their wonderful blessings. God focuses on the twofold privilege—six entire days to tend to all our labor and business and one entire day to devote ourselves to Him and His business. God gives us over 85 percent of the week for our work and recreation, and blesses us with one whole day to devote to enjoying Him. In effect, He is saying, "I have given you six days; I require you to give me one."

God not only structures our occupational life for the market day, but He also commands us to structure our domestic lives: speaking to us in our roles as parents and guardians, He includes, "you or your son or your daughter" (v. 10). We are to structure the lives of our covenant children so that they as well may be freed from work in order to devote themselves to the special transactions of the day.

We set an example of Sabbath-keeping for them. Moreover, we are to teach them what they should be doing, helping them to order their lives and schoolwork, and giving them only truly essential chores around the house on the Sabbath. We use the day as well to teach them that there is greater enjoyment in life than playing. Furthermore, we are to create for them a day they will enjoy, a day they will anticipate, not a day that hangs over the week like an ominous cloud.

In addition to being a family responsibility, structuring of the Sabbath day requires a social responsibility. You are to structure the day for others in society for whom you are responsible. First, you have a responsibility to your servants. Few of us have servants in our homes, but if we do, we are to release and protect them from unnecessary work in the same way we protect ourselves and our children.

Some of us, however, are employers, and economically our employees are equivalent to our servants. As an employer you have the responsibility of not requiring your employees to break the Sabbath by doing work that should be done during the other six days.

In a sense all of us are indirectly responsible for some employees, specifically those working in service industries and businesses. In our economy these people serve the consumer, and we are to protect their Sabbaths as well as our own. To do so, we should avoid shopping, unnecessary dining out,[21] and recreational activities that cause others to work on the Lord's Day (this would include those events mediated by television, which necessitates hundreds of employees being at work). It is a lame excuse to say, "They are going to be there anyway, so it really doesn't matter what I do." Really? You are commanded not to cause others to do unnecessary work, and if you use a person's services, you are partly responsible for that person's working on the Lord's Day.

Furthermore, as part of our social responsibility, God commands us to rest our animals because they need rest just as people do. Because Israel was an agrarian society, a portion of their work was performed with animals. God reminds us that He built into the fabric of creation the need for all living things to rest. Even the land was to rest (see Lev 25). The necessity of the land's resting is illustrated by the importance of crop rotation that allows a portion of the land to lie fallow.

Furthermore, it is a reasonable inference to apply this principle of rest to anything that can wear out. Just as employees have replaced domestic servants, machines have replaced animals. And like the living things they replace, machines wear out in proportion to

---

21. I recognize that those who are on trips may have to eat in a public facility on the Lord's Day, even as they may have to stay in a hotel. Interestingly, the Puritans recognized this need as well. The Puritan-controlled Parliament in 1644 in a bill to regulate the Sabbath added: "Provided, and be it Declared, That nothing in this Ordinance shall extend to the prohibiting or dressing of Meat in Private Families, or the dressing and sale of Victuals in a moderate way in Inns or Victualling–Houses, for the use of such as otherwise cannot be provided for." Quoted in J. Dennison, *The Market Day of the Soul: The Puritan Doctrine of the Sabbath in England 1532–1700* (New York: University Press of America, 1983), 94.

use. Take for an example your automobile: the fewer miles, the better resale value, because cars wear out with usage. There may be a necessity for certain types of industry to operate seven days a week; however, a greater portion of industrial activities could shut down on the Lord's Day. What might be the economic and environmental benefits if they did?[22] Perhaps the extended life span for an expensive piece of machinery, fewer repairs, and less pollution in the air and water could be realized.

Finally, as God teaches us how to structure His day socially, He includes those outside the church: "your sojourner who stays with you" (v. 10). In Israel the sojourner or stranger was the Gentile who chose to live in the midst of God's people. God commanded that they, as well as the covenant people, cease from their labor on the Sabbath day, even though they could not participate in the feasts or in temple worship. Although one may not legislate that people go to church, may not one legislate that businesses and shops be closed on the Lord's Day? Such laws, once prevalent in the United States and Britain, created an environment that was not only spiritually healthy, but also mentally and physically beneficial.[23]

Christ and the Sabbath

In spite of what we have said thus far, many continue to object to the principle that the Lord's Day is the Christian Sabbath. Objectors claim not only that the New Testament never repeats the Sabbath commandment but also that Jesus repeals strict Sabbath-keeping. We will examine Matt 12:1–14 to evaluate this claim.

In Matt 12:1–8, Jesus asserted His authority over the Sabbath and established some principles that regulate its observance. As Jesus and His disciples were walking through a grain field one Sab-

---

22. Some suggest that we ought not to promote the rest of the Sabbath on the basis of pragmatic or humanitarian benefits (e.g., Jewett, *Lord's Day*, 148). I would agree that such things ought not to be the basis of our argument, but God does call us to think of our animals. Moreover, just as the laws concerning marriage, work, and property have social benefits, the Sabbath also has social benefits.

23. Some raise the question, "What about those whose religion demands they observe a different day?" I recognize the tension here and do not claim to have all the answers. But if we believe that God structures the day for the unconverted person as well as the Christian, we need to wrestle with this. The difficulty for adherents of other religions is not only with Sunday closing laws. The laws of our land demand monogamous marriage, while Muslims and certain Mormons believe in polygamy. They are required to conform to our laws if they want to live in this nation.

bath morning, His disciples became hungry and began to pick and eat some grain. Observing this action, the Pharisees accused them of breaking the Sabbath: "Look, Your disciples do what is not lawful to do on a Sabbath" (Matt 12:2).

Many mistakenly assume with the Pharisees that the disciples were breaking the Sabbath commandment. The disciples, however, were not breaking any Old Testament Sabbath laws; they were violating only Jewish manmade laws. The Pharisees and scribes had a commendable zeal for the law of God. They loved the law and desired to help people not violate it; therefore, they "built fences" around God's law to prevent people from coming near any transgression of it. Just as men place fences at dangerous places like the Grand Canyon to keep people from walking too close to the edge and falling over, the Jews devised laws to keep people back from the dangerous precipice of breaking God's law.

Because of their zeal, they devised hundreds of laws to keep people away from the cliff of violation. In the book of these laws (compiled centuries after the time of Jesus) called the Talmud, 24 chapters itemize some 39 occupations, with multiple subdivisions, that might not be done on the Sabbath. For example, on the basis of the prohibition of work on the Sabbath day during planting and harvest time (Exod 34:21), the Talmud forbids picking grain (harvesting) and rubbing it between your fingers (threshing). Hence, the law the disciples broke was Jewish tradition, not God's law.

Jesus, therefore, did not defend Sabbath-breaking but the violation of the Jewish tradition, and when He defended His disciples, He asserted His authority as the lawgiver and law interpreter: "For the Son of Man is Lord of the Sabbath" (Matt 12:8). By this claim He asserted His unique relationship to the law, claiming absolute authority to interpret what is or is not to be done on the Sabbath. Because of the Jewish misconceptions about the nature of the messianic king, Jesus adopted the title "Son of Man" from Dan 7:13 to portray Himself as the Messiah. The title indicates His humiliation as well as His exaltation as God's appointed Savior-King.

His assertion, "but I say to you" (Matt 12:6) is reminiscent of His earlier claims in Matthew 5, where He repudiated other manmade interpretations of God's law:

> Do not think that I came to abolish the Law or the Prophets; I did not come to abolish but to fulfill. For truly I say to you,

until heaven and earth pass away, not the smallest letter or stroke shall pass away from the Law until all is accomplished. Whoever then annuls one of the least of these commandments, and teaches others to do the same, shall be called least in the kingdom of heaven; but whoever keeps and teaches them, he shall be called great in the kingdom of heaven. (Matt 5:17–19)

Jesus asserted the perpetuity of God's moral law. Consider that if Jesus Christ in His earthly ministry had contradicted the law of God, He would have been discredited as the Messiah, for according to Ps 40:6–8, the Messiah would come to do the will of God. "Sacrifice and meal offering You have not desired; my ears You have opened; burnt offering and sin offering You have not required. Then I said, 'Behold, I come; in the scroll of the book it is written of me. I delight to do Your will, O my God; Your Law is within my heart.'"

Consequently, in Matt 12:1–8, Jesus was repudiating the false interpretations of the Jews and asserting the true interpretation of the Law. He defended His disciples by asserting that He is the Lord of the Sabbath, the only authoritative interpreter of the Holy Sabbath and its proper observance. Therefore, He did not abolish the careful observance of the Sabbath day, but reestablished the day as the time to celebrate the spiritual rest of God's people. Having proclaimed Himself as the promised restgiver (Matt 11:28), He began to free the day of rest for its God-appointed purposes.

Before we leave this point of Jesus' authority, note how often He dealt with Sabbath observance. In the three years of Christ's ministry recorded in the Gospels, on six different occasions He crossed swords with the Jews over the proper observance of the Sabbath. Furthermore, two of the occasions are recorded in three of the Gospels: the two accounts in Matt 12:1–14 are repeated in Mark 2:23–3:6 and Luke 6:1–11. Some continue to insist that the NT does not reassert the Sabbath commandment. Christ taught about murder on only one occasion and three times on marriage, but six times He taught about the Sabbath. If this commandment were destined for the dustbin of ceremonial law, why do the Gospel writers devote so much attention to it? Is there any ceremonial law regarding which Jesus spent so much time correcting misunderstandings? No, but on six occasions He cleared away the accretions to the Sabbath commandment in order to establish the proper use of the Sabbath.

Having asserted His authority over Sabbath law, Jesus, the chief justice of the supreme court, examined the laws of the Jews and threw out as unconstitutional (unbiblical) every law that contradicted God's purposes for the Sabbath commandment. In the defense of His disciples, applying three OT passages, He specified the principles for the proper observance of the Sabbath.[24]

Jesus drew His first argument from the history of God's covenant people (1 Sam 21:1–6): "Have you not read what David did when he became hungry, he and his companions, how he entered the house of God, and they ate the consecrated bread, which was not lawful for him to eat nor for those with him, but for the priests alone?" (Matt 12:3–4). Jesus chose this account because of the parallels between David and his followers and Christ and His disciples: both events occurred on the Sabbath, both involved the Lord's anointed who was about the Lord's business and neither was a life-or-death matter—the followers were hungry, so they strengthened themselves that they might continue in the Lord's business.

In this instance Jesus argued from the greater to the lesser, implying that if it was proper for the Lord's anointed to violate a ceremonial law while on the Lord's business on the Sabbath, then surely the Anointed and His followers may break a man-made law while they were doing the Lord's business on the Sabbath. From this first argument, Jesus taught the principle that on the Sabbath we are to do those things that strengthen us for the Lord's work.

Jesus drew His second argument from the Law itself. Alluding to Num 28:9–10, He said, "Have you not read in the Law, that on the Sabbath the priests in the temple break [or profane] the Sabbath and are innocent? But I say to you that something greater than the temple is here" (Matt 12:5–6). The priests not only had to work on the Sabbath, but in fact their work was intensified. They offered double sacrifices on the Sabbaths, while continuing all the other labor connected with running the temple: trimming the sacred lamps, changing the shewbread, and performing all the other daily temple rituals. Nevertheless, they were not guilty of Sabbath breaking because their work was necessary so God's people could worship.

---

24. For a discussion of Christ's arguments see Pipa, *Lord's Day*, chap. 5 and 6, and J.-B. Kim, "An Exegetical and Theological Study of Jesus' Argument in the Sabbath Controversy in Matthew 12:1–14," Th.D. diss., Greenville Presbyterian Theological Seminary, 2007.

By this comparison Jesus argued from the lesser to the greater because He was the fulfillment of the temple: "But I say to you that something greater that the temple is here" (v. 6). That which the temple pictured and pointed to was the Lord Jesus Christ, the temple of God who was tabernacling among men (John 1:14). Therefore, those who labored with Him in His Sabbath work were not violating the Sabbath when they ignored a humanly invented law. To the contrary, they were doing the true work of the Sabbath as they labored with Jesus in the service of preaching, evangelizing, and worshipping. They were the true Sabbath-keepers, while the Pharisees who followed them seeking to entrap the Savior were breaking the Sabbath. On the basis of this argument, Jesus taught the principle that one may do those things necessary to promote the purposes of the day.

Jesus drew His last argument from Hosea 6:6: "But if you had known what this means, 'I desire compassion, and not a sacrifice,' you would not have condemned the innocent'" (Matt 12:7). He claimed the innocence of His followers by reminding the Jews that God is not looking for heartless ritual on the Sabbath but heartfelt worship—true devotion that loves God and one's neighbor. The third principle is that the Sabbath is to be a day for the exercise of mercy.

This third principle is a bridge to the second confrontation, recorded in Matt 12:9–14. Although all three Gospel writers group this occurrence with the preceding one, they occurred on different Sabbaths.[25] The writers combined them in order to paint a comprehensive picture of Jesus' teaching concerning the Sabbath.

On this second occasion Jesus expanded on the principle of the Sabbath as a day of mercy by teaching the principle that the Sabbath is a day for doing good to one's neighbor. The event recorded in these verses is one of the classic spiritual confrontations between Jesus and the Jewish religious rulers. Knowing that He would come to the synagogue to worship since He faithfully kept the Sabbath, they set their trap there.

Furthermore, foundational to their plan was the assumption that Jesus was able to heal. What an amazing insight into the wickedness of their hearts and the depth of their depravity! Their hearts were so hard that they never stopped to ask, "Who is this who can

---

25. Luke 6:6 records that the second incident occurred on another Sabbath.

heal the sick, cast out demons, and raise the dead?" The Pharisees elaborately set the scene. They positioned the man with the twisted, paralyzed arm in a prominent place in the synagogue so that it would have been impossible for Jesus not to see the man or his tragic condition. As Jesus entered, they asked Him, "Is it lawful to heal on the Sabbath?" In reality they cared nothing about Jesus' opinion other than as grounds to discredit Him. Again the issue was not God's law but their laws. According to their traditions, one could heal only if life were in danger. On another occasion a ruler of the synagogue said, "There are six days in which work should be done; so come during them and get healed, and not on the Sabbath day" (Luke 13:14).

The trap also depended on Jesus' character. They tacitly acknowledged not only His power but also His compassion. He regularly acted to alleviate the suffering of the needy.

Jesus' response is astonishing. Normally He avoided confrontation like this; He did not usually initiate controversy with the Pharisees. Nevertheless, on this occasion He stepped forward and provoked the Jews: "He said to the man with the withered hand, 'Get up and come forward!'" (Luke 6:8). Placing the poor man in the middle of the congregation, He asked, "Is it lawful to do good or to do harm on the Sabbath, to save a life or to kill?" (Mark 3:4).

Why does the Savior who is gentle and meek, who often avoided confrontation, rise to their bait? He could have healed the man later, so why let Himself be ensnared? This question is all the more pertinent when we realize that in the majority of the Sabbath confrontations, Jesus took the initiative by deliberately healing on the Sabbath.[26] Why did He provoke His enemies on this issue?

Obviously the correct observance and use of the Sabbath was so important to Him that He aggressively sought occasions to free the day from the laws of men by scraping away centuries of accretions. On the basis of this observation, we ask, "Why do so many teachers assert that the NT is silent regarding the Sabbath commandment?"

Jesus provoked the confrontation by asking the Pharisees challenging questions; Mark and Luke record one question while Matthew records two other questions. According to Mark and Luke, Jesus asked, "Is it lawful to do good or to do harm on the Sabbath, to save a life or to kill?" (Mark 3:4; "or to destroy it," Luke 6:9). Jesus'

---

26. John 5:1–18; 9:1–14; Luke 13:10–17; 14:1–6.

question drives them back to the foundational, moral principle. Suddenly, they were caught in their own snare because the answer to His question was obvious; since it never was lawful to do harm or to destroy, they would have to say, "It is lawful to do good and to save a life." This answer is necessary because to fail to do good is to do harm, and the failure to save a life, when in one's power, is to destroy. This conclusion is based on a proper understanding of how to interpret biblical law, namely, the opposite of whatever is commanded is forbidden, and the opposite of what is forbidden is commanded.[27] For example, when God forbids adultery, He is requiring faithful, monogamous marriage.

Jesus rightly implied on the basis of the (Sixth) Commandment not to kill that, if one has the opportunity within one's calling and circumstances to save a life and refuses, one is sinning. Since He could heal by the exercise of His will, when faced with proper circumstances, it would be wrong for Him not to do so.[28]

His question silenced them since to do that which is morally required cannot be a violation of God's Sabbath law. No wonder the Bible tells us they were silent and refused to answer Him.

Matthew records Jesus asking them another question that was aimed at their pocketbooks: "What man is there among you who has a sheep, and if it falls into a pit on the Sabbath, will he not take hold of it and lift it out?" (Matt 12:11). According to their man-made laws, although it was unlawful to heal on the Sabbath, if one's livestock fell into a ditch, one could lower food and water to it. Moreover, they provided, under some circumstances, for getting an animal out of a ditch on the Sabbath. Why were they more concerned for their livestock on the Sabbath than for a man? Were they more concerned about their material well-being than with people?

With His last question Jesus challenged them, "How much more valuable then is a man than a sheep!" (Matt 12:12). He implied, "Your law allows you to feed or save one dumb animal on the Sabbath but forbids one who has the divine power to heal a man." On another occasion He phrased the question even more forcibly. In Luke 13:15–16, after healing the woman who had been

---

27. WLC 99: "That as, where a duty is commanded, the contrary sin is forbidden; and, where a sin is forbidden, the contrary duty is commanded."

28. This statement applies to Jesus Christ who alone is sovereign in His ministry. The apostles and perhaps others during the apostolic age could heal when Christ was willing. This special gift of healing ceased with the apostolic age.

bent double for 18 years, He answered the indignant synagogue official who rebuked the people for seeking healing on the Sabbath:

> You hypocrites, does not each of you on the Sabbath untie his ox or his donkey from the stall and lead him away to water him? And this woman, a daughter of Abraham as she is, whom Satan has bound for eighteen long years, should she not have been released from this bond on the Sabbath day?

The Savior's spiritual logic was irrefutable—a person made in the image of God, a member of the covenant people, is infinitely more valuable than an animal. Again by their silence, the Pharisees conceded the truth of His argument and the conclusion was obvious: "So then, it is lawful to do good on the Sabbath" (Matt 12:12).

Matthew's conclusion to the confrontation establishes the principle that the Sabbath is an appropriate day to do good. In fact, this is part of the purpose of the day: What day is more appropriate for doing good than the day appointed by God to picture eternal life? Jesus, therefore, did not do away with the Sabbath but with the human additions that made the Sabbath a burden. As Mark reports Jesus saying: "The Sabbath was made for man, and not man for the Sabbath" (Mark 2:27).

From Matt 12:1–14 and the parallel accounts, theologians have derived the principle that on the Lord's Day we are to do deeds of necessity and mercy, as the Shorter Catechism says, "Spending the whole time in the public and private exercises of God's worship, except so much as is to be taken up in the works of necessity and mercy" (Q. 60). John Murray specifies these works as deeds of piety, necessity, and mercy. Integral to the exercise of mercy are works necessary for preservation of life.[29]

In Matt 12:1–8, Jesus teaches that on the Lord's Day we may do those works of piety and necessity that promote the purposes of the day. We have learned that we devote ourselves to public and private worship, Christian fellowship, and service, in order to strengthen ourselves, advance His kingdom, and anticipate our heavenly rest with Him. Everything we do should be examined in light of these purposes. Does it promote the purposes of the day?

---

29. This fourth category comes from the editor of a tract who published John Murray's address given at Golspie, Sutherland, August 12, 1953, reprinted in *Collected Writings of John Murray* (Edinburgh: Banner of Truth, 1976), 1:205–16.

Many of us will be required to do deeds of piety that are necessary to accomplish the purposes of the day. As the priests ministered in the temple, ministers must preach and Sunday school teachers must teach; someone might need to come early to turn on the heat or the cooling system, or perhaps to shovel snow from the driveway and sidewalk. So anything necessary to enable the congregation to gather for corporate worship, edification, and fellowship is permissible.

This principle gives us criterion for evaluating Lord's Day activities. All that we do may be measured by the question, Does this activity promote the purpose of the day? We have a perverted legalism that is willing to live by the letter of the law but does no more in obedience than is absolutely necessary. Often we approach the Lord's Day like children who push the rules of their parents as far as possible. Rather than asking, "What may we do to please God and enjoy Him?" we ask, "How much can I do for my own pleasure? How far can I go without actually sinning?" This attitude does not honor God. We should be asking whether an activity will enable us to keep the Sabbath better or detract from the purposes of the day.

A proper grasp of the principle of necessity will help us to examine the various issues. For example, some say that the Shorter Catechism forbids physical rest when it requires "spending the whole time in the public and private exercises of God's worship" (Q. 60). Does this mean it is wrong to take a nap on Sunday afternoon? To answer the question you must determine the purpose of the nap. Is it to refresh you so that you can pursue with renewed vigor the purposes of the day and your calling, or is it a choice of idleness because you do not want to do anything else? Some people need a nap to stay awake for the evening service or to be able to read later without drowsiness, while others might need to go for a vigorous walk in order to be alert. Our children often need some kind of physical activity so that the day will not be a burden on them.

In addition to deeds of piety and necessity, we learn from Matt 12:9–14 that deeds of mercy and preservation are appropriate as well. We rightly infer that the work of those professions and deeds necessary for protection of life and the promotion of the well-being of our neighbors are appropriate on the Sabbath. Those who do good, who protect and save life, such as soldiers, firefighters, police officers, physicians, nurses, and pharmacists are not violating the

Sabbath. A doctor ought not to schedule nonemergency surgery on Sunday, but in the case of a crisis, he will operate in order to save a life or protect someone from more serious danger or illness.

Emergency repair work also may be considered as an act of mercy. Once when I had preached a sermon on the Christian Sabbath, a young man who was a plumber expressed concern for what he should do when someone had a serious plumbing emergency on the Lord's Day. If it were something that would cause no damage to the property, the work usually could wait until Monday, but if a pipe is broken or a sewage line is backing up, it is an act of compassion to repair the damage on the Lord's Day since the physical well-being of the people with the problem depends on his work. Furthermore, they could hardly enjoy the Sabbath undistracted while a water leak was ruining their home or sewage backed up in their bathroom.

And so the Sabbath is a day for doing those things that preserve life and promote the well-being of your neighbor. This exception does not apply only to human life; the Jews were correct to make provisions for their livestock. Farmers need to feed their herds; dairy workers must milk their cows; and the veterinarian will have to tend to sick animals.

The Sabbath is also a day for doing spiritual good to our neighbors. Therefore, in addition to corporate worship and times of private and family reading and fellowship, it is a day for Christian service by doing good, for example, through ministering in nursing homes, visiting those who live alone or cannot get out of their homes, and evangelism. Both the early church fathers and the Puritans made provision for distributing food and money to the poor on the Lord's Day, recognizing that God designed this day for doing good.

Another application is that we may do those things necessary for the preservation of society at large. Some postulate that since ours is a technological society and the Sabbath was for an agrarian culture, it cannot be observed today. Pointing to factories with large furnaces that cannot be shut down on Sunday, they claim it is impossible to apply Sabbath principles to our society. In effect, those who raise such objections are denying the sufficiency of Scripture. Part of the work of theology is to discern the principles in the biblical account or narrative and to apply them to modern circumstances.

An example is the command to build a parapet around one's roof (Deut 22:8); the parapet was a wall built around a flat roof that served as an outdoor living space. Though most of us do not have flat-roof houses, the principle still applies that we are to take the necessary precautions so that no one is injured on our property— for example, keeping a dangerous animal confined or fencing in a swimming pool.

We, therefore, look for the principles of Scripture regarding the Sabbath that we must apply to our culture. One principle is that when by nature an activity cannot cease without affecting the work and livelihood of the other six days, it may continue. We derive this principle from the life of a crew on a ship at sea. For example, both Solomon and Jehoshaphat had fleets of ships (2 Chron 8:17–18; 20:35–36). A ship at sea could not sit idle on the Sabbath. A number of necessary duties had to be performed for the well-being of the crew: sails had to be trimmed, the course charted, general maintenance performed, and provision made for the physical needs of the crew. In applying the principle we ask, "Is the work necessary for the good or well-being of our neighbor and the continuance of his or our lawful calling?" Therefore, the operation of a factory that cannot shut down without affecting its work the remainder of the week is a deed of necessity, falling in the same category as an electrical generating plant, a hospital furnace room, or a college cafeteria.

Jesus, therefore, does not abrogate the careful observance of the Sabbath but lays down principles by which we may properly keep the Lord's Day holy. We may lawfully perform those acts that promote the purposes of the day.

The New Testament Sabbath Day

Because the creation ordinance and the Sabbath commandment specify the seventh day, are we not compelled either to observe the seventh day or to admit that the Sabbath commandment's requirement for cessation from work is dated and no longer binding? The answer to this question lies in understanding the difference between positive law and moral law.

Most Christians concede that the Sabbath commandment required a careful observance of the Sabbath, and I have sought to establish that its moral requirements are in effect today. But if the Sabbath commandment remains in effect today, why do we not worship on the seventh day? We have already noted that God's commandments have temporary ceremonial and judicial aspects, in addition to their permanent moral requirements. Theologians distinguish between that which is permanent in God's law and that which is temporary by the terms *positive law* and *moral law*.

A positive law is a commandment of God that is not morally necessary (i.e., is not inherently right or wrong). God requires or forbids certain things at different times in the history of redemption to regulate His relation to His people and their relation to one another. Such laws are binding only on the person or nation to whom they were given. For example, the prohibition given to Adam and Eve not to eat of the Tree of the Knowledge of Good and Evil was a positive law. There was nothing inherently moral about eating or not eating the fruit of the tree; rather, the prohibition was the means by which God chose to test their willingness to obey Him (Gen 2:16–17). The laws of consanguinity in marriage or the ceremonial laws of the Mosaic covenant were also positive laws.

A moral law, on the other hand, is a commandment that reflects the moral nature of God, as well as our relation to Him and one another. These laws are absolutely necessary for our spiritual well-being as image bearers of God and are permanently binding on all people. Murder is wrong not only because God's Word prohibits it but also because it is inherently evil. Thus, "You shall not murder" is a permanently binding obligation on all people in all ages.

The Westminster Confession refers to the Sabbath law as a positive and moral law.[30] As noted above, this means that the moral law of Sabbath-keeping had positive elements, among them "which day?" Because the particular day is positive law, the day can be changed without affecting the moral nature of the law.[31] The Westminster Confession states that the day

> from the beginning of the world to the resurrection of Christ, was the last day of the week; and, from the resurrection of Christ, was changed into the first day of the week, which in

---

30. WCF 21.7.
31. Some argue that the Sabbath commandment requires only one day in seven and not the chronological seventh day. Exegetically I prefer the interpretation that refers to the seventh day as the seventh chronologically. Either way, the moral nature of the commandment remains.

Scripture is called the Lord's Day, and is to be continued to the end of the world, as the Christian Sabbath.[32]

In Col 2:16–17, Paul abrogated the seventh-day Sabbath: "Therefore no one is to act as your judge in regard to food or drink or in respect to a festival or a new moon or a Sabbath day—things which are a mere shadow of what is to come; but the substance belongs to Christ." I recognize that some use this passage, along with Rom 14:5–6 and Gal 4:9–10, to teach that the NT does away with the principle of a required holy day. Such an interpretation, however, fails to take into account the context of these passages. Paul was dealing with Jewish practices about food and religious observances, not requirements of the moral law. He made this distinction clear by the terms he used in Col 2:16—"a festival or a new moon or a Sabbath day." These three terms are often used together to describe the special holy days of Jewish worship (2 Chron 8:13; 31:3; Lev 23:1–25). Paul was addressing the problem that some Jewish Christians required the observance of these days in addition to the New Testament Sabbath. Paul countered that Jewish Christians were free to observe these days (for a brief period of time), but they could not obligate others to observe them.

The Sabbath in the Early Church

Paul, however, abrogated the observance of the seventh-day Sabbath, along with the festival Sabbaths, because those days pointed to Christ and were fulfilled in Him. The church was not free to continue the observance of the seventh day, nor was she permitted to set whatever day she preferred. The New Testament church immediately began to worship on the first day of the week (Acts 20:7; 1 Cor 16:1–2). As we shall see below, she did so by divine warrant.

At this point we need to note that the observance of the first day of the week was not a practice begun under Constantine in the fourth century, as argued by some Seventh-day Adventists. Others argue that, although the church met on the first day of the week, it was only for the purpose of worship, and there was no commitment to spending the whole day in the worship and service of the Lord.

It is difficult to determine the attitude or practice of the early church on a number of issues because those who lived closest to

32. WCF 21.7.

the time of the apostles had the greatest difficultly in grasping the truth in a systematic fashion. They were, after all, pioneers—the first surveyors of the terrain, seeking to understand what Christ and the apostles taught, and their task was enormous. The Bible is not a theological textbook but a collection of history, poetry, prophecies, and letters. The church has the responsibility of searching the Scripture and systematizing its truth. Like a toddler her earliest steps often were faltering.

For example, early writers like Origen were unclear regarding the relationship of God the Son to God the Father. Not until the Council of Nicaea in AD 325 did the church clearly formulate an orthodox statement of the deity of God the Son, and decades passed before the issue was settled throughout the churches.

Clearly such confusion was also the case with respect to the doctrine of the Sabbath. I believe, however, that a careful reading of the early church writers demonstrates that many of them were committed not only to worshipping on the first day of the week but also to ceasing from work and spending the whole day in worship and service. Admittedly a considerable number of early Christians were slaves who would not have been free in a pagan culture to do much more than worship; nevertheless, there seems to have been commitment to keep the entire day holy.

Part of the disagreement arises because of the remarks of early Christian writers against Sabbath-keeping. These statements were made in the context of a perverted Judaism. To the early church Judaism was a Christ-denying, superstitious, legalistic religion. The early Christians mistakenly thought the Jews of their day derived their practices from the OT. In their polemic against the Jews, the Christians repudiated the Jewish seventh-day Sabbath because they viewed it as part of the ceremonial system of the old covenant. Therefore, they often spoke disparagingly about the Sabbath as part of their polemic against the Jews. The historian Philip Schaff, who edited an English edition of the church fathers, commented, "There was a disposition to disparage the Jewish law in the zeal to prove independent originality of Christian institutions."[33] Wilfrid Stott wrote of their attitude to the Sabbath, "It was one of the signs of the Old Covenant with Israel. . . . The attitude of the Fathers is that with the passing of the whole system, temple, sacrifice, circumcision, clean

33. P. Schaff, *History of the Christian Church* (Grand Rapids: Eerdmans, 1985), 2:202–3.

and unclean, went the Sabbath as a sign."[34] For example, consider Ignatius (ca. 110):

> Be not led astray by strange doctrines or by old fables which are profitless. For if we are living until now according to Judaism, we confess that we have not received grace. . . . If then they who walked in ancient customs came to a new hope, no longer living for the Sabbath, but for the Lord's Day, on which also our life sprang up through him and his death.[35]

Some early church fathers viewed the Jewish Sabbath as part of the Mosaic bondage. Justin Martyr (ca. 100–165), in dialogue with a Jew, maintained that before Moses the patriarchs did not keep a Sabbath and that Christianity does not require one particular Sabbath but a perpetual Sabbath: "Moreover, all those righteous men, already mentioned, though they kept no Sabbaths, were pleasing to God."[36] He goes on to say that God gave them Sabbaths because of their hardness of heart.[37] Irenaeus (115–ca. 200) wrote of Abraham, "And that man was not justified by these things, but that they were given as a sign to the people, this fact shows—that Abraham himself without circumcision and without observance of Sabbaths, 'believed God, and it was imputed unto him for righteousness.' "[38]

Tertullian (ca. 160–230) in *An Answer to the Jews* argues that the Sabbath was temporary and fulfilled with the coming of Christ:

> Therefore, since it is manifest that a sabbath temporal was shown, and a sabbath eternal foretold; a circumcision carnal foretold, and a circumcision spiritual pre-indicated. . . . And, indeed, first we must inquire whether there be expected a giver of the new law, and an heir of the new testament, and a priest of the new sacrifices, and a purger of the new circumcision, and an observer of the eternal sabbath, to suppress the old law, and institute the new testament, and offer the new sacrifices, and repress the ancient ceremonies, and suppress the old circumcision together with its own sabbath.[39]

34. R. T. Beckwith and W. Stott, *The Christian Sunday: a Biblical and Historical Study* (Grand Rapids: Baker, 1980), 52.
35. Ignatius, *To the Magnesians* 9.1.
36. Justin Martyr, *Dialogue with Trypho* 19.
37. Ibid., 19.
38. Irenaeus, *Against Heresies* 4.16.2.
39. Tertullian, *An Answer to the Jews* 6.

Furthermore, the Jews' misuse of the Sabbath was a recurring theme: "The Jews are accused of spending the day in 'inactivity' (*argia*). Instead of using the day as it was intended by God in a study of the Scriptures and gaining knowledge, they spent it in idleness, in dancing and in the pleasures of debauchery."[40]

On the other hand, the early fathers believed that the Lord's Day replaced the Sabbath. Schaff wrote,

> The fathers did not regard the Christian Sunday as a continuation of, but as a substitute for, the Jewish Sabbath, and based it not so much on the Sabbath commandment, and the primitive rest of God in creation, to which the commandment expressly refers, as upon the resurrection of Christ and apostolic tradition.[41]

Following the example of the apostles, the early church replaced the seventh-day worship with worship on the first day of the week. Schaff wrote that undoubtedly this change was of apostolic origin.[42] They referred to it as the "first day," the "Lord's Day," and the "eighth day." Justin Martyr said the church met for worship on Sunday, the first day of the week:

> And on the day called Sunday, all who live in cities or in the country gather together to one place, and the memoirs of the apostles or the writings of the prophets are read. . . . But Sunday is the day on which we all hold our common assembly, because it is the first day on which God, having wrought a change in the darkness and matter, made the world; and Jesus Christ our Saviour on the same day rose from the dead.[43]

Understanding that the day belonged in a special way to the Lord, the church immediately adopted the phrase of the apostle John, "Lord's day" (Rev 1:10).[44] In the *Didache* (early second century) the term *Lord's Day* is used to describe the day of worship: "And on the Lord's own day gather yourselves together and break

---

40. Beckwith and Stott, *Christian Sunday*, 51–52.
41. Schaff, *History of the Christian Church*, 2:202.
42. Ibid., 201.
43. Justin Martyr, *Apology* 1.67.
44. See Pipa, *Lord's Day*, chap. 8.

bread."[45] Ignatius related the Lord's Day to the completed work of Christ, "on which also our life sprang up through him and his death."[46]

The third term used to highlight the importance of the first day is *eighth day*. The Epistle of Barnabas (ca. late first century) referred to Sunday by this designation. Speaking to express the attitude of the Lord, the writer said, "The present sabbaths are not acceptable to me, but that which I have made, in which I will give rest to all things and make the beginning of an eighth day, that is the beginning of another world." He continued, "Wherefore we also celebrate with gladness the eighth day in which Jesus also rose from the dead."[47] The early church derived this title from John 20:26. Nigel Lee observed on this section of Barnabas:

> Apart from the rest of this Epistle, ch. 15 is striking evidence that "the eighth day" (i.e., Sunday—cf. John 20:1,19 & 26) was already being "kept" (*agomen*), that the day already had strong soteriological and eschatological significance, and that it was even then regarded as a memorial of the Lord's resurrection (cf. John 20:1), and possibly of His post–resurrectional Sunday appearances too.[48]

In connection with the concept of the eighth day, the early church emphasized the festive character of the Sabbath: a holy festival, celebrating the resurrection of the Lord Jesus Christ.[49]

Although the term *sabbath* would not be regularly used for the Lord's Day until after Constantine, references to the Lord's Day as Sabbath from the time of Constantine and even earlier are extant. Eusebius (ca. 260–339), a contemporary of Constantine, in a commentary on Psalm 92 showed the relation of the seventh-day Sabbath to the Lord's Day: "The Word, through the New Covenant, has changed and transferred the feast of the sabbath to the rising of the light and handed to us the image (*eikōn*) of a true rest, the Lord's Day."[50] Stott said:

45. *Didache* 14. For discussion of the textual variants see N. Lee, *The Covenantal Sabbath* (London: The Lord's Day Observance Society, 1966), 298–99.
46. Ignatius, *Magnesians* 9.1 (see n35 above).
47. Barnabas, *Epistle* 15:8–9.
48. Lee, *Covenantal Sabbath*, 241.
49. Beckwith and Stott, *Christian Sunday*, 64.
50. Eusebius, *Commentary on the Psalms* 91 (92), quoted in Beckwith and Stott, *Christian Sunday*, 76.

It is clear that there are mystical elements in it, but the references to "intervals of six days," "gatherings throughout the world," the allusions to the Eucharist, including the bread and "the blood of the Lamb which taketh away the sin of the world," the emphasis on "each Lord's day" several times, all suggest that it is a literal Sunday which Eusebius has in mind.[51]

Earlier, Origen (ca. 185–254) referred to the Lord's Day as the Sabbath. In the *Homilies on Numbers*, quoting Heb 4:9, he said, "Leaving the Jewish observance of the sabbath, let us see how the sabbath ought to be observed by a Christian."[52] Stott wrote, "While elsewhere Origen clearly saw the sabbath as a type of the rest from sin and evil works of all kinds, here he is dealing in a practical way with the observance of the Christian festal day."[53] Origen continued to discuss how the Sabbath should be spent, explaining that the Christian Sabbath was to be kept by abstaining from work and recreation:

On the sabbath day all worldly pleasures ought to be abstained from. If therefore you cease from all secular works (*saecularia*) and execute nothing worldly, but give yourself up to spiritual exercises, repairing to the church (*ad ecclesiam*), attending to sacred reading and instruction, thinking of celestial things, solicitous for the future, placing the judgment to come before your eyes, not looking to things present and visible, but to those which are future and invisible, this is the observance of the Christian sabbath.[54]

The highlight of the day was corporate worship, which Stott demonstrates would have required a number of hours. But, furthermore, there was an emphasis, as Origen indicated, on devoting the whole day to holy exercises. Origen's mentor, Clement of Alexandria (ca. 150–215), wrote:

---

51. Beckwith and Stott, *Christian Sunday*, 77.
52. Ibid., 70.
53. Ibid., 72. Earlier Stott deals with a difficult passage in Clement of Alexandria in which Stott believes Clement refers to the eighth day both as the Sabbath and the fulfillment of the Sabbath commandment: "And it (the eighth day) properly the sabbath, the rest, and the seventh (day of the week) a day of work" (68).
54. Ibid., 70.

Woman and man [probably "wife and husband"] are to go to church, decently attired, with natural step, embracing silence, possessing unfeigned love, pure in body, pure in heart, fit to pray to God. . . . But now I know not how people change their fashions and manners with the place. . . . So, laying aside the inspiration of the assembly, after their departure from it, they become like others with whom they associate . . . after having paid reverence to the discourse about God they leave within (the church) what they heard. And outside they foolishly amuse themselves with impious playing and amatory quavering, occupied with flute-playing and dancing and intoxication and all kinds of trash.[55]

Earlier the writer of 2 Clement (ca. 120–140) called his readers to a faithful observance of the day:

And let us not merely seem to believe and pay attention now, while we are being exhorted by the Elders, but also when we have gone home let us remember the commandments of the Lord, and let us not be dragged aside by worldly lusts, but let us try to come here more frequently, and to make progress in the commands of the Lord (17:3).

The importance of spending the whole day remained an emphasis throughout the remainder of this period. For example, Chrysostom, discussing the dangers of losing the spiritual benefits of the day, said in his commentary on Matthew:

For we ought not, as soon as we retire from the Communion, to plunge into affairs . . . unsuitable to the Communion, but as soon as ever we get home to take our Bible into our hands and call our wife and children to join us in putting together what we have heard and then, not before, engage in the business of life. . . . When you retire from the Communion, you must account nothing more necessary, than that you should put together the things that have been said to you. Yes, for it were the utmost folly, while we give up five or six days to the business of life, not to bestow on spiritual things so much as one day or rather not so much as a small part of one day. . . . Therefore let us write it down as an unalterable law for ourselves, for our wives and for our children, to give up this one day of the

---

55. Clement of Alexandria, *The Instructor* 3.11.

week entire to hearing and to the recollection of the things which we have heard.[56]

Commenting on 1 Cor 16:2 he called for the separation of the whole day:

[O]n the first day of the week . . . the separation from all work; the soul becomes more joyful from this laying of it aside. . . . Because of this (the blessings connected with the day of the Resurrection) it is fitting that we honor it with a spiritual honor . . . and every Lord's Day let the affairs connected with us as masters be laid aside at home.[57]

Stott pointed out that the early church also used Sunday for works of charity, baptisms, ordinations, and church discipline.[58] Hence, though most did not immediately relate the Lord's Day worship to the Sabbath commandment, the early church believed that the day of worship and rest had been changed to the first day and came to think of this day as the Sabbath. They taught that the whole day should be set aside for public and private worship and service.

By the fifth century the church was firmly committed to this high view of the Sabbath. At the fifth Council of Carthage (401), it was decreed that no plays might be performed on Sundays and it petitioned the emperor "that public shows might be transferred from the Christian Sunday . . . to some other days of the week."[59]

From the Seventh Day to the First Day

We have seen that during the days of the apostles, the church began to worship on the first day of the week and that this was the continued practice of the early church. What, then, was the basis of this change of day? We will attempt to answer this question by looking at Heb 4:9–10.[60] These verses begin the concluding argument of the exhortation that begins in 3:7 and concludes in 4:13.

56. Chrysostom, *Commentary on Matthew*, Homily 5:1. By "business of life" he is not referring to worldly occupations but the necessary work of the household.
57. Quoted in Beckwith and Stott, *Christian Sunday*, 135. For references to other fathers such as Augustine, see this same work and also Lee, *Covenantal Sabbath*.
58. Ibid., 99–102.
59. Lee, *Covenantal Sabbath*, 248.
60. Andrew T. Lincoln teaches that the rest described in Hebrews 4 is the accomplished work of Jesus Christ. Believers have already come to the heavenly Jerusalem and though the rest will not be finalized until the Second Coming, there is nothing left for the believer to

The book of Hebrews was written to encourage Jewish Christians who were tempted to return to Judaism. It demonstrates that in Jesus of Nazareth God had accomplished His covenantal purposes. To prove this the writer demonstrated the completion of all of God's saving work in Christ. Gaffin gave a helpful summary of this part of the message:

> The opening words of Hebrews give a pronounced eschatological, redemptive-historical orientation to the entire document: God's former speech through the prophets, "partial and piecemeal," not only contrasts with but culminates in his final speech in his Son "in these last days" (1:1–2). The present character of this "last days," eschatological revelation, embodied in the Son, is even more explicit in 9:26: In making sacrifice for sin, Christ has appeared once for all at the end of the ages; in terms of the fundamental historical-eschatological distinction between the two ages. Christ's death and exaltation inaugurate the coming eschatological age. Accordingly, through God's word and the Holy Spirit the church already experiences ("tastes") nothing less than "the powers of the age to come" (6:5). Similarly, "salvation" is a present reality resulting from God's eschatological speech "through the Lord" (2:3; cf. 1:1–2; 6:9). Again, believers have already come to the city of the living God, the heavenly Jerusalem (12:22) and are present in what is fairly described as the eschatological assembly gathered there (12:22–24).[61]

At the same time, however, the full reality is yet in the future when Christ shall appear to make all things perfect (Heb 9:26). According to Gaffin:

> For believers that future, second appearance will be for "salvation" (9:28, cf. 1:14; 6; 9). A "lasting city" is what they are still seeking; it is "the city to come" (13:14; cf. the "homeland" as well as the "city" in 11:10,13–16). The "appearance" of the Son, salvation, the heavenly city (homeland), then, all eschatologi-

---

enter into. Thus the Sabbath has been fulfilled and is abrogated. Lincoln, "Sabbath, Rest, and Eschatology in the New Testament," in *From Sabbath to Lord's Day*, ed. Carson, 197–220. We will answer this objection indirectly in our development of Heb 4:9–10. For a critical evaluation of Lincoln, see the chapter by R. Gaffin, "A Sabbath Rest Still Awaits the People of God," in *Pressing Toward the Mark*, ed. C. Dennison (Philadelphia: Committee for the Historian of the Orthodox Presbyterian Church, 1986), 33–51.

61. Gaffin, "A Sabbath Rest Still Awaits," 34.

cal in character, are both present and future in the view of the writer.[62]

This tension between the present and future nature of salvation gives rise to the theme of the book, an exhortation to the Jewish Christians to persevere. If they return to Judaism, they will be forsaking the full reality of the gospel for the shadows and types and will fail to enter into the rest of God. Of course, a true believer cannot permanently fall away, but the danger always remains that there are those within the church who, though professing faith, have not savingly experienced the powerful grace of God. A mere profession of faith does not save. True faith personally appropriates the promise of rest and manifests itself in perseverance.

The writer to the Hebrews pointed out the danger of failing to enter the rest by alluding to the apostasy of the children of Israel in the wilderness. Even though they had the promise pictured by the seventh-day Sabbath and the offer of rest in the land of Canaan, they failed to enter because of unbelief. Furthermore, he reminds the Hebrew Christians that the rest promised by God at creation in the establishment of the seventh-day rest was not fulfilled when Joshua brought them into the Promised Land. He bases these conclusions on the statement from Ps 95:7–11:

> Today, if you would hear His voice, do not harden your hearts, as at Meribah, as in the day of Massah in the wilderness, when your fathers tested Me, they tried Me, though they had seen My work. For forty years I loathed that generation, and said they are a people who err in their heart, and they do not know My ways. Therefore I swore in My anger, truly they shall not enter into My rest.

Since David wrote those words long after Joshua had led the children of Israel into the promised land, he was showing that the rest in the promised land did not fulfill the promise of rest given at creation. Therefore, as long as the promise remained, there was an urgent necessity for God's people to appropriate that rest (Heb 4:7–8). The fulfillment of God's promised rest had been provided by Jesus Christ, and those who believe in Him have begun to participate in its reality. But they will participate in His rest only if they

---

62. Ibid.

persevere (3:6). If they turned back, they would be like the children of Israel who did not enter the land because of unbelief (3:16–17; 4:1–2). Like Israel in the wilderness, they were pilgrims. They were to press on to the heavenly, eternal rest provided by the Lord Jesus Christ: "Therefore let us be diligent to enter that rest" (4:11).

The author concluded his exhortation with 4:9–13 and introduced it by saying, "So there remains a Sabbath rest for the people of God" (v. 9). The word *so* introduces a conclusion to the argument of 4:3–8. He exhorts the Hebrews not to look back but to look ahead since there remains a Sabbath rest for the people of God. By referring to the people of God, the writer draws a parallel between the covenant people of the New Testament church and God's people in the wilderness. He says the Sabbath rest with its promise of eternal life remains a reality for the new covenant people of God.

The word translated "Sabbath rest" (*sabbatismos*) is a rare word used only this one time in the Bible. The only other known use of the word not dependent on Heb 4:9 is in Plutarch's *Moralia* in which, according to some versions, he used *sabbatismos* to describe superstitious religious rest.[63] Hence, the word suggests religious observances.

Although the noun form of the word used in Heb 4:9 is found nowhere else in the Bible, the verbal form of the word (*sabbatizō*) occurs a number of times in the Septuagint (the Greek translation of the OT). The first use of the verbal form is in Exod 16:30, "So the people rested ["sabbatized," Gk. *esabbatisen*] on the seventh day"; that is, they observed a Sabbath rest. This verse concludes the section in which God tells them not to collect manna on the seventh day because it is the Sabbath (16:29). When they obeyed God and kept the Sabbath, they *sabbatized*.

This idea of Sabbath-keeping is involved every time this verb is used. For example, after a description of some feasts that were part of the worship of God's people, Lev 23:32 says, "It is to be a sabbath of complete rest to you, and you shall humble your souls; on the

---

63. BDAG, 909. Some critical editions of Plutarch suggest the reading *baptismos* in place of *sabbatismos*. In this section Plutarch is discussing barbarian superstitious practices, "because of superstition, such as smearing with mud, wallowing in filth, sabbath rests (*sabbatismos*) (or immersions, *baptismos*) casting oneself down with face to the ground, disgraceful besieging of the gods, and uncouth prostrations." Plutarch, *Moralia*, sec. 166. Some scholars agree with the emendation, since "resting" or even "superstitious ease" (in Plutarch's view) cannot fit the context here with the mud packs and hurling to the ground to overcome fears and sleeplessness. In the previous sentence, however, Plutarch says they "sit down on the ground and spend the whole day there." The context at least suggests the possibility of the use of *sabbatismos*, spending a day in religious rest.

ninth of the month at evening, from evening until evening you shall keep [Gk., *sabbatieite*] your sabbath." In Lev 26:34–35 the verb is used for the land keeping its Sabbath rest (cf. 2 Chron 36:21). In all of the above instances, the verbal form of *sabbatizō* is used to translate the Hebrew word meaning "to keep the Sabbath."

The early Christian writer Ignatius used this verb to describe OT Sabbath-keeping. In describing the change of day from the seventh to the first he says, "No longer living for the Sabbath [*sabbatizō*], but for the Lord's Day."[64]

Therefore, the verb suggests a specific rest of Sabbath-keeping. Whether the noun *sabbatismos* was in existence or the writer to the Hebrews coined it, he would have been familiar with the Septuagint's use of the verb *sabbatizō*. And in either case he chose this unique word with careful forethought for a particular purpose.

Throughout Hebrews 3 and 4, the writer used a more general word for "rest" (*katapausis*)[65] to depict God's rest, the eternal rest to be entered and the typical forms of that rest as they are expressed in the seventh-day rest and the rest of Canaan. Why, then, does the writer select the unique word *sabbatismos* in verse 9?

He used *sabbatismos* as a play on words. He emphasized that the spiritual, eternal rest promised by God has not been fulfilled; the promise of eternal rest remains, and they must enter it by persevering faith. That is, one enters this spiritual rest by faith in the Lord Jesus Christ, but it will be fully realized only when one enters the eternal rest of glory. Consequently, he emphasized the ongoing need to persevere.

But if this were all he wanted to say, he could have used the word *katapausis*. In fact, he used *katapausis* this way in verse 11: "Therefore let us be diligent to enter that rest [*katapausis*]." Neither does it make sense to say he chose *sabbatismos* for stylistic variety, as a synonym for *katapausis*. Such use does not make sense this late in the discourse. The uniqueness of the word suggests a deliberate, theological purpose. He selected or coined the term *sabbatismos* because, in addition to referring to spiritual rest, it suggested an observance of that rest by a "Sabbath-keeping." Because the promised rest lies ahead for the new covenant people, they are to strive to

---

64. Ignatius, *Magnesians* 9.1.
65. The noun *katapausis*, Heb 3:11,18; 4:1,3,5,11; the verb *katapauō*, Heb 4:8,10. The Septuagint uses this word in Gen 2:2 to describe God's rest.

enter the future rest. Yet as they do so, they anticipate it by continuing to keep the Sabbath.

Hence, the theology of redemption accomplished does not annul a continued Sabbath-keeping but requires it. And although we do not need a reinforcement or repetition of an OT moral command, yet since the Sabbath did have ceremonial and typical significance, God gives clear new covenant instruction. What better book to reiterate Sabbath observance than the book of Hebrews, which teaches most clearly how all old covenant ceremonial worship practices were fulfilled in Christ and therefore repealed? A. W. Pink concludes:

> Here then is a plain, positive, unequivocal declaration by the Spirit of God. "There remaineth therefore a Sabbath-keeping." Nothing could be simpler, nothing less ambiguous. The striking thing is that this statement occurs in the very epistle whose theme is the superiority of Christianity over Judaism; written to those addressed, as "holy brethren, partakers of the heavenly calling." Therefore, it cannot be gainsaid that Hebrews 4:9 refers directly to the Christian Sabbath. Hence we solemnly and emphatically declare that any man who says there is no Christian Sabbath takes direct issue with the New Testament Scriptures.[66]

So, as the old covenant people of God had the promise of future rest portrayed in its day of rest, the new covenant people of God, the church, also has the promise of future rest portrayed in its day of religious rest.

In addition to establishing the principle that there remains a present Sabbath-keeping, this passage also establishes the day of that Sabbath-observance. Verse 10 gives the grounds and explanation for verse 9. Notice that verse 10 begins with the word "For,"

---

66. A. W. Pink, *An Exposition of Hebrews* (Grand Rapids: Baker, 1967), 1:210. Gaffin reaches the same conclusion: "Certain effects, however, are unmistakable, or at least difficult to deny. [1] 'My rest' [in its local character, see above] is a place of Sabbath-rest. In explicit fashion, reinforced by the use of Gen 2:2 in v. 4, v. 9 ties God's rest, in its sweeping, eschatological scope, to the institution of the Sabbath and its observance. [2] There is an inner connection between ongoing Sabbath observance and eschatological [Sabbath-] rest; this ostensibly is the tie between anticipatory sign and reality. Although the writer does not say so explicitly, the clear implication is that recurring Sabbath observance has its significance as a sign or type of eschatological rest. [3] In view of the use of Gen 2:2 in v. 4, it would appear to be the seventh-day sign specifically, the typology of the weekly Sabbath, that the writer has in view, at least primarily" ("A Sabbath Rest Still Awaits," 41). See also R. L. Dabney, *Discussions: Evangelical and Theological*, 2 vols. (London: Banner of Truth Trust, 1967), 1:535.

which means "because." There remains a Sabbath-keeping *because* "the one who has entered His rest has himself also rested from his works, as God did from His."

In verse 10, the writer compared Christ's rest from His work of redemption with God's rest from the work of creation. Many commentators interpret verse 10 to refer to the believer's turning from sin to rest in Christ.[67] The NIV translates verse 10, "For anyone who enters God's rest also rests from their works, just as God did from his." The English Standard Version says, "For whoever has entered God's rest has also rested from his works as God did from his." The NASB is closer to the original when it says, "For the one who has entered His rest has himself also rested from his works, as God did from His." The American Standard Version (1901) and the KJV are closest to the Greek, "For he that is entered into his rest hath himself also rested from his works [he also hath ceased from his own works, KJV], as God did from his."

John Owen gave three reasons for applying verse 10 to Christ's rest and not the believer's.[68] First, the impropriety of comparing the believer's works and rest to God's work and rest; it is not proper to compare a sinner's works of sin and self-righteousness to the work of a holy God in creation. Gaffin pointed out that this interpretation

> does not seem to perceive the jarring incongruity of drawing a direct (and therefore positive) parallel between man's sinful works and God's works. Where else does the New Testament even remotely approach the notion that "repentance from dead works"{ is analogous to God's resting from his labors at creation? Does it really overstate to say that such a synthetic association is a glaring impossibility for any New Testament writer?[69]

---

67. For example, J. Calvin, *Epistle of Paul the Apostle to the Hebrews; and, the First and Second Epistles of St. Peter*, Calvin's New Testament Commentaries (Grand Rapids: Eerdmans, 1970), 48–49, and A. T. Lincoln, in *From Sabbath to Lord's Day*, 213–14, 365.

68. Owen, *Hebrews*, 2:331–36. Gaffin writes that "to refer 'the one who enters' to Christ [e.g., as Owen does], is not exegetically credible'" "A Sabbath Rest Still Awaits," 51, n. 31). Gaffin, though, gives no reasons for rejecting Owen's arguments. For further exegetical arguments enforcing Owen's position see H. Alford, *The Greek Testament*, 4 vols. (Boston: Lee and Shepard, 1877), 4:81–82.

69. Gaffin, "A Sabbath Rest Still Awaits," 45. Gaffin offered the interpretation that verse 10 refers to the positive works of a believer and that in heaven he shall rest from these (Rev 14:13): "In a word, the works of 4:10 are desert-works, the works of believers in the present wilderness, that is non-rest situation, looking toward the future, hoped-for, promised rest." To do this he must interpret the opening clause of verse 10 as presenting a future state to

As it is improper to compare the work of a sinner with that of God, it is also improper to compare the sinner resting from works of sin to God's rest. By referring to God's rest, the writer is building on Genesis 2:2–3 (cf. Heb 4:4). God's rest was not only a cessation of specific activity but also a joyful contemplation of His work. The believer's resting from his works is not a rest of contemplation and delight but rather a sharp breaking-off from sin. Therefore, the parallel is not between the believer's resting from his works and God's resting from His.

Owen's second argument involved the change of grammatical number. Throughout Heb 3:7–4:11, the writer referred to the rest of the believer in the plural: "Therefore, let us fear . . ." (4:1); "For we who have believed enter that rest" (v. 3); "Therefore let us be diligent." (v. 11). But in verse 10 he uses a singular participle ("the one who has entered"). The use of the singular suggests someone other than the people of God, that is, an individual who has entered his rest as God has entered His.

Some respond that the singular participle could refer to the antecedent "people" in verse 9, since the Greek word for "people" is collective (a singular noun referring to a group). Although "people" may take a singular verb and a singular relative pronoun, the writer to the Hebrews defined "people" by the plural word "brethren" (3:12). In Heb 7:5, the writer defined "people" by "brethren" and used the plural pronoun "their" and a plural participle "descended." Further-

---

the minds of the readers. Gaffin suggested that the aorist indicative verb *rested* has a "generalizing or gnomic force" (p. 45). The gnomic suggests a generally accepted truth. According to Burton the gnomic aorist "is used in proverbs and comparisons where the English commonly uses a General Present." E. de Witt Burton, *Syntax of the Moods and Tenses in New Testament Greek* (Edinburgh: T&T Clark, 1986), 21. New Testament examples that confirm this interpretation include 1 Pet 1:24; Luke 7:35; John 15:6; Jas 1:11,24. Hence, it is highly unlikely in this context that a gnomic use would apply to a future rest. Moreover, grammatically it is difficult to give any future force to the clause as a whole. The subject of the verb *rested* is the substantive participle, "he who has entered his rest." Dr. Baugh, in an unpublished class syllabus on Greek verbal aspect, writes of the substantive aorist participle "contrary to expectations . . . aorist substantive and attributive participles most often (but not always!) refer to an event that is past in respect to the main action, whether the main action is past, present, or future from the writer or speaker's perspective" (pp. 43–44). In this case the phrase "the one who has entered" precedes in time "rested from his works," which is a past main verb. More than likely the force in Heb 4:10 is, "By entering into his rest he rested." The action is still in the past. In a footnote Gaffin suggested also the possibility of a proleptical use, but as Burton pointed out, "This is rather a rhetorical figure than a grammatical idiom" (*Syntax*, 23). See for example 1 Cor 7:28: "If you should marry . . . " (NASB). Cf. John 15:8 and Jas 2:10. Furthermore, the development of the argument suggests a past tense for "rest," since verse 11 exhorts the believer to enter into that rest. The phrase "that rest" refers back to the rest established in verse 10.

more, he used plural pronouns with the singular noun "people" in 8:10 ("they," *autoi*) and 9:19–20 ("you" plural, *humas*). Thus, there seems to be no warrant for relating the singular participle "the one who has entered" in verse 10 to "people" in verse 9. Verse 10 refers to an individual, whereas throughout 3:7–4:11 the responsibility to enter into the rest is addressed to the people of God in the plural.

This leads to the third argument. In verse 10, the writer described a rest that is already completed, while in verse 11 he clearly stated that the responsibility to enter into the rest remains for the believer. Yes, we have begun to participate in God's rest, but we shall not fully enter into that rest until we are glorified with Christ in heaven. Gaffin recognized this problem and sought to interpret verse 10 as referring to a future rest. But this interpretation does not seem to be grammatically feasible (see note 69).

Some may object and ask, "Why an indefinite reference to Christ? Is it not awkward to introduce Christ in this fashion?" Actually, Christ and His rest are before us throughout this section. Remember the exhortation begins in 3:6, "But Christ was faithful as a Son over His house whose house we are, if we hold fast." Verse 11 refers to "that rest," namely, the rest provided by Christ. Furthermore, verse 14 reminds us that Christ has entered into His rest. Since grammatically one must take the entering as past and the impropriety of comparing the believer's resting from dead works with God's rest from creation, I see no other alternative than to interpret verse 10 in terms of Christ.

This understanding provides a parallel between the work of creation and the work of redemption. At the conclusion of creation, God rested on the seventh day to declare His work completed, to delight in that work, and to promise the eternal rest promised to Adam in the covenant of works. When Adam broke the covenant, God renewed the offer of eternal rest through a redeemer. The seventh-day Sabbath looked forward to that rest.

God the Son rested from His work of redemption on the first day of the week as a sign that His work had objectively been accomplished and nothing remained to be done. In the resurrection He entered into the joy of His work and confirmed that eternal life had been purchased (cf. Isa 53:10–11; Heb 12:2). By His example the day was changed. Vos wrote:

Inasmuch as the Old Covenant was still looking forward to the performance of the Messianic work, naturally the days of labor to it come first, the day of rest falls at the end of the week. We, under the New Covenant, look back upon the accomplished work of Christ. We, therefore, first celebrate the rest in principle procured by Christ, although the Sabbath also still remains a sign looking forward to the final eschatological rest. The Old Covenant people of God had to typify in their life the future developments of redemption. Consequently the precedence of labor and the consequence of rest had to find expression in their calendar. The N.T. Church has no typical function to perform, for the types have been fulfilled. But it has a great historic event to commemorate, the performance of the work by Christ and the entrance of Him and of His people through Him upon the state of never-ending rest. We do not sufficiently realize the profound sense the early Church had of the epoch-making significance of the appearance, and especially of the resurrection of the Messiah. The latter was to them nothing less than the bringing in of a new, the second, creation. And they felt that this ought to find expression in the placing of the Sabbath with reference to the other days of the week. Believers knew themselves in a measure partakers of the Sabbath-fulfillment. If the one creation required one sequence, then the other required another. It has been strikingly observed, that our Lord died on the eve of the Jewish Sabbath, at the end of one of these typical weeks of labor by which His work and its consummation were prefigured. And Christ entered upon His rest, so that the Jewish Sabbath comes to lie between, was as it were, disposed of, buried in His grave.[70]

The Old Testament alluded to the rest found in the resurrection on the eighth day that climaxed on the Feast of the Booths: "For seven days you shall present an offering by fire to the Lord. On the eighth day you shall have a holy convocation and present an offering by fire to the Lord; it is an assembly. You shall do no laborious work" (Lev 23:36). This high Sabbath at the end of the feast typified the rest promised to the pilgrim people and concluded the annual

---

70. G. Vos, *Biblical Theology: Old and New Testaments* (Grand Rapids: Eerdmans, 1968), 158.

cycle of feasts.[71] John apparently had this in mind in his Gospel when he referred to the first day of the week as the eighth day in John 20:26. The early church seized hold of the terminology of the eighth day to refer to the day of resurrection worship, the first day of the week. When the church celebrated the resurrection of the Lord Jesus Christ, they related the joy of the eighth day to the declaration of Ps 118:24: "This is the day which the Lord has made; let us rejoice and be glad in it." Wilfrid Stott gave the theological background:

> We must now, and in this connection, examine the origin of a very early name for Sunday, "the Eighth Day.". . . It seems more probable that we must look for the origin of the word in the Old Testament, inasmuch as the early church, having accepted the "first day" as the occasion of the resurrection and of Christian worship, saw the connection of passages in the Old Testament in which "first" and "eight" are linked together. The most likely passage is . . . Lev 23:36–39. It is the description of the feast of Tabernacles. The first day and the eighth day are special days. On the first and eighth days there are to be "holy convocations." There is to be no "laborious work." . . . The days are "feasts" (*heortai*) to the Lord, and there is to be "rest" (*anapausis*). The people are to "rejoice" . . . before the Lord. . . . There are other references to "the eighth day" in other connections. It is of course connected with circumcision and entry into the Covenant. . . .
>
> It seems likely, therefore, that it was the influence of the Old Testament references to the eighth day and its accompanying festal character of joy and rest that affected early Christian thinking. . . . Is it too much to see in the second appearance of Christ to the gathered disciples in the Upper Room a hint of what set their minds in this direction?[72]

As the apostles understood this theology by inspiration, they changed the day for celebrating the eternal rest from the seventh day to the first. The old covenant people looked forward to the accomplishment of redemption, so they kept the Sabbath at the end of the week. After the rest-giver had accomplished His work, the NT church kept its Sabbath on the day He entered into His rest,

---

71. G. Oehler, *Theology of the Old Testament* (Edinburgh: T & T Clark, 1883), 2:120. Cf. J. D. Davis, *Davis Dictionary of the Bible* (Grand Rapids: Baker, 1957), 756.

72. Beckwith and Stott, *Christian Sunday*, 64–65.

signifying that although we wait for the consummation, we already have begun to participate in this rest.

The church has always recognized that the change of day was first initiated by the resurrection appearances of Christ on the first day of the week when all of the New Testament's recorded appearances took place. Lange wrote with respect to John 20:26 that "the disciples already attribute a particular importance to Sunday, is evidenced by the numeric completeness of their assembly."[73] Philip Schaff, Lange's editor, added:

> This is the beginning of the history of the Lord's Day, which to this day has never suffered a single interruption in Christian lands, except for a brief period of madness in France during the reign of terror. Sunday is here pointed out by our Lord Himself and honored by His special presence as the day of religion, and public worship, and so it will remain to the end of time. God's word and God's Day are inseparable companions and the pillars of God's Church.[74]

This understanding was worked out in apostolic practice. In Acts 20:7 the church gathered for preaching and the Lord's Supper the first day of the week: "On the first day of the week, when we were gathered together." Apparently it was their custom. Luke does not say "on the first day of the week, when we gathered to say good-bye to Paul," but "on the first day of the week, when we were gathered together to break bread, Paul began talking to them." It was the custom of the early church to meet for worship on the first day of the week.

In 1 Cor 16:1–2, Paul assumed that the churches recognized the uniqueness of the day: "Now concerning the collection for the saints, as I directed the churches of Galatia, so do you also. On the first day of every week each one of you is to put aside and save, as he may prosper, so that no collections be made when I come." Just as it was the pattern in Galatian churches, so also in Corinth they gathered for worship on the first day of the week and took the collection for the poor. Paul was not instructing people to set aside money at home, since he wanted to avoid having to make a collection when

---

73. J. P. Lange, *Commentary on the Holy Scriptures*, 12 vols. (Grand Rapids: Zondervan, 1976), 9:621.
74. Ibid.

he arrived. He wanted the church to take a collection on the first day of each week, which is evidence that the apostolic church was committed to first-day worship.

Hence, the apostle John calls it the Lord's Day: "I was in the Spirit on the Lord's day" (Rev 1:10). The term John uses means a day that belongs peculiarly to the Lord Jesus Christ. It is not the often-used phrase "the day of the Lord" but a term that means a day "belonging to the Lord."[75] This term is used only one other time in the NT; Paul uses it in 1 Cor 11:20 to describe the Lord's Supper. The Lord's Supper is not an ordinary meal but a meal that belongs exclusively to the Lord and was appointed to celebrate His redeeming work and to communicate grace to His people. In like manner, the first day of the week is called the Lord's Day because it is a day that belongs peculiarly to the Lord and was appointed to commemorate His completed redemption and to communicate grace to His people.

We learn from Heb 4:9–10 that the practice of Sabbath-keeping remains for the people of God and that they are to keep the Sabbath on the first day of the week. Therefore, I conclude that by inspiration of the Holy Spirit, on the basis of Christ's resurrection, the apostles changed Sabbath-keeping to the first day of the week. Such Sabbath-keeping has been the practice and conviction of most Protestant Christians from the Reformation until 50 to 75 years ago. On the basis of this study, I assert that the position of the Westminster Standards is the position of Scripture.

The New Testament Practice

How then do we approach the day? God gives us a commentary on the application of the Sabbath commandment in Isa 58:13–14.

> If because of the sabbath, you turn your foot from doing your own pleasure on My holy day, and call the sabbath a delight, the holy day of the Lord honorable, and honor it, desisting from your own ways, from seeking your own pleasure and speaking your own word, then you will take delight in the Lord, and I will make you ride on the heights of the earth; and I will feed you with the heritage of Jacob your father, for the mouth of the Lord has spoken.

---

75. BDAG, 576.

In this passage the prophet was dealing with the lifeless formalism of the worship of God's people. He rebuked them for it: clinging to sin while going through the motions of worship; substituting external acts (fasting) for true obedience. In contrast to this formalism, he set before them the great principle of the Sabbath and the blessings that attend it. He said that the God of the covenant solemnly promises great spiritual blessings to those who keep the Sabbath day holy.

Some object, arguing that since God gave this commandment and promise to the OT people, it is not appropriate to apply this passage to the New Testament church. But we do not use this line of reasoning with the commandments and promises the OT gives concerning marriage or the place of our children in the covenant. Why use it here? The moral and spiritual commands as well as many of the OT promises apply to us, and we may not dismiss a threat or promise merely because it is found in the OT.

How, then, do we determine if this commandment and promise apply to the new covenant people? We begin to answer this question by considering the context of the promise. This entire section of Isaiah refers ultimately to Jesus Christ and the new covenant people. The section begins with the famous promise of the suffering Servant in chapter 53; then in chapter 54:1–3, the prophet assures the church of its worldwide outreach:

> "Shout for joy, O barren one, you who have borne no child; break forth into joyful shouting and cry aloud, you who have not travailed; for the sons of the desolate one will be more numerous than the sons of the married woman," says the Lord. "Enlarge the place of your tent; stretch out the curtains of your dwellings, spare not; lengthen your cords and strengthen your pegs. For you will spread abroad to the right and the left. And your descendants will possess nations and will resettle the desolate cities."

In Isa 55:1, he calls sinners to repentance: "Ho! Every one who thirsts, come to the waters; and you who have no money come, buy and eat. Come, buy wine and milk without money and without cost." All of these promises find fulfillment in the NT era.

In chapter 56, God relates the Sabbath to the New Testament people:

"How blessed is the man who does this, and the son of man who takes hold of it; who keeps from profaning the sabbath, and keeps his hand from doing any evil." Let not the foreigner who has joined himself to the Lord say, "The Lord will surely separate me from His people." Nor let the eunuch say, "Behold, I am a dry tree." For thus says the Lord, "To the eunuchs who keep My sabbaths, and choose what pleases Me, and hold fast My covenant, to them I will give in My house and within My walls a memorial. (Isa 56:2–5)

How do we know that this section applies to the New Testament era? Because only in the gospel era may a eunuch enjoy the privileges promised here. In Deut 23:1, God declares that a eunuch may not enter the house of the Lord. But in Isaiah 56, anticipating the reign of the Christ, God promises the eunuch that he shall receive a memorial name in the house of the Lord.[76] The prophet, therefore, relates Sabbath-keeping to the time of the new covenant.

We conclude that the commandment and promise of Isa 58:13–14 are for the New Testament church. How, then, does God apply the Sabbath commandment? God's people must honor and keep the Sabbath day holy. First, Isaiah states the condition negatively: "If because of the sabbath, you turn your foot from doing your own pleasure on My holy day." Anticipating the language of the NT—that Jesus is Lord of the Sabbath (Matt 12:8) and that the NT Sabbath is called the Lord's Day (Rev 1:10)—Isaiah refers to the Sabbath as God's "holy day" and "the holy day of the Lord." God calls the Sabbath a holy day because He sanctified it (Gen 2:2–3). Since it is the holy day of the Lord, we are to sanctify it as well, so if we pursue our own pleasures on the Sabbath, we are profaning God's holy day.

How, then, does one profane the day? By doing one's pleasure on it. This word *pleasure* is used throughout the OT to describe things in which people delight (Ps 1:2; Isa 44:28; 46:10; 58:3; Eccl 3:1,17; 8:6). "Doing your pleasure" describes those things you enjoy doing or have to do the other six days: business, work, play, and so on. By doing these things on God's holy day, you profane it. If you

---

76. E. J. Young, *The Book of Isaiah* (Grand Rapids: Eerdmans, 1974), 3:390–91. Delitzsch argues that this reference to eunuchs is to those who were forced into this condition by foreign service during the exile, C. F. Keil and F. Delitzsch, *Commentary on the Old Testament* (Grand Rapids: Eerdmans, 1969), 7:361–64. Nothing, however, in the context would favor this interpretation.

are to enjoy the promise of God, you must not desecrate the day by doing your own pleasure on it.

God, however, does not hinder our work or pleasure on the Sabbath to diminish our happiness. Rather, He calls us to turn aside from our pleasure in order to seek the pleasures He has in store for us on the day. Hence, He continues by teaching us to honor and revere the day, to "call the sabbath a delight, the holy day of the Lord honorable." We are to consider the Sabbath a delight. The word *delight* means to take exquisite pleasure. As we delight in those we love or beautiful things, so we are to delight in the spiritual exercises of the day. We are to take great pleasure in worship, fellowship, and Christian service.

We delight in the day as we honor it. Since God has sanctified it, we are to honor the day as "the holy day of the Lord." This is what the Sabbath commandment requires by the mandate, "Remember the sabbath day, to keep it holy." We remember the day by taking exquisite delight in it and honoring it.

"If this is the case," you ask, "how do I honor it?" You honor the day by doing three things: "Desisting from your own ways, from seeking your own pleasure and speaking your own word" (Isa 58:13). First, we "desist from our own ways" by not doing our regular work. With these words the prophet applies the prohibition of the Sabbath commandment, not to work and cause others to work. As we saw above, God has given us six days to do our business; the seventh belongs to Him. Thus, other than works of genuine necessity (Matt 12:1–8) or mercy (Matt 12:9–14), we ought not to pursue business. We ought not to be going into the office or working in the store; we ought not to be doing homework or unnecessary housework. Neither ought we to cause others to work unnecessarily, which means we should avoid eating out, going to the grocery store or mall, or traveling extensively.

Second, we are not to use Sunday as a day for recreational diversions, "seeking your own pleasure." The word *pleasure* is the same word He uses in the first clause of the verse when He says, "Turn your foot from doing your own pleasure on My holy day." Observe the relation between this stipulation and the promise: If we do not seek our own pleasure, we will find great pleasure in God. We ought not to pursue our own pleasure in playing or recreation. Rather, we are to seek the peculiar pleasures of the Sabbath, by finding exquisite delight in what it offers. Consequently, we ought not to be watching television, going to movies or ball games, or using the day for sports.

God is not opposed to our enjoyment; moderate recreation the other six days is His gift. We are to devote the Sabbath, however, to the peculiar spiritual pleasures of worship and service. We are to cease from our pleasures so that we might pursue greater and nobler things. We are to regard the Lord's Day as a spiritual vacation. God gives us a weekly vacation that we might have more time to enjoy Him.

Nevertheless, God does not prohibit all physical activity on the Lord's Day. Our children will need some physical activity. Some adults, as well, will need some physical activity in order to be alert for evening worship.

Third, we ought to avoid unnecessary conversation about work and recreation; we ought to "cease speaking [our] own word." The details of our work and recreation are not to be the focus of our attention; rather, we are to set our minds on the things of the Lord. This prohibition does not rule out conversation with Christian friends about work or family affairs; in order to have true fellowship, we will be concerned with what is going on in one another's lives.

The Shorter Catechism (Q. 61) gives an apt summary of what Isa 58:13 forbids:

> The Sabbath commandment forbiddeth the omission or careless performance of the duties required and the profaning the day by idleness or doing that, which is in itself sinful, or by unnecessary thoughts, words, or works about our worldly employments or recreations.

But mind you, it is not God's intention to leave us with merely negative notions with respect to this day. He wants us to define the day by what we *may* do. Why does God want us to cease from doing our own business? Why does God tell us to cease pursuing our own pleasure and speaking our own words? So that we may pursue His business, that we may seek the pleasures of His word and work, and that we may delight in His worship and Word.

How, then, should the day be kept? The principles by which the day is to be observed are also set forth in the Westminster Confession:

This Sabbath is then kept holy unto the Lord, when men, after a due preparing of their hearts, and ordering of their common affairs before-hand do not only observe an holy rest all the day from their own works, words, and thoughts about their worldly employments and recreations; but also are taken up the whole time in the public and private exercises of His worship, and in the duties of necessity and mercy.

True Sabbath-keeping begins by actively resting in God alone for our salvation. Without deliberately focusing on Christ and living in dependence on Him, there is no true Sabbath-keeping. When we turn aside from our work and pleasure, we are freed to worship Him. Corporate worship should be at the top of our list of pleasures. In addition, we should take advantage of the day to read and pray. Extended family worship and singing psalms and hymns is always a pleasure. We have the opportunity to serve Him by going to nursing homes, visiting the sick, going out to witness, teaching His Word, and fellowshipping with His people. God has given us this day as a great gift. He wants us to focus on the gift He has given us.

Those with young children will need to tailor the day's activities around their children: reading to them, working on Scripture and catechetical memorization, and playing games with them. This will instill in them a great delight for this day.

Though some declare that the Westminster approach to the Sabbath promotes legalism, the purpose of this careful observance of the Sabbath was not to create a legalistic entanglement that stifles people but to free the people of God for the wonderful privilege of worshipping and enjoying Him. In light of this purpose, God's Word offers great promises with regard to the Christian Sabbath in Isa 58:14: "Then you will take delight in the Lord, and I will make you ride on the heights of the earth; and I will feed you with the heritage of Jacob your father, for the mouth of the Lord has spoken." I do not know three greater things promised in the entire Bible than what God pledges here.

First, He promises exquisite, spiritual pleasure ("Then you will take delight in the Lord"). As noted above, the word *delight* means exquisite pleasure. To take exquisite pleasure in the Lord is to be overcome by His beauty, glory, attributes, and work (Job 22:26; Isa 61:10); to have our hearts ravished by the truths of the Word of God; and to have God manifest His love to us. God is promising you a communion and fellowship with Him that defies description. The Sabbath is like a wonderful garden adorned with beautiful flowers where God meets with us.

But He doesn't stop there. He adds, "And I will make you ride on the heights of the earth." This is language of victory, taken from Deut 32:12–13 and 33:29. In Deuteronomy, God promises Israel great victory over her enemies. As Isaiah speaks about returning to the land, He promises the people victory over their enemies (Isa 33:16). Their victorious return is a picture of the victory promised in the new covenant. We who are members of new Zion will also have victory. In Christ we are more than conquerors (Rom 8:37), and we shall have victory over Satan and sin. Sabbath-keeping is a means of grace that will help us die to sin and grow in holiness.

But there is still more. Not only will we find exquisite pleasure in the Lord and have victory over our enemies, but we will also enjoy the benefits of our salvation: "I will feed you with the heritage of Jacob your father." He is promising that God's people again will possess the land (Ps 105:10–11). We know that the possession of the land was symbolic of the inheritance of God's covenant people. Our inheritance includes the benefits of salvation—adoption, assurance of salvation, boldness in prayer, and our ultimate glorification. This promise means we will revel in our privileges as children of God (cf. WSC 36).

We have seen that the Sabbath is the "market day of the soul," appointed by God for special transactions with Him. In order to free us for the pleasures of the day, God allows us to lay aside our normal, daily affairs so that we may devote ourselves to the sanctification of His day. Again we are reminded that, like all of God's law, the Sabbath commandment is not a burden, but the way to true happiness. And as we structure the day according to God's revelation, we will enjoy the benefits promised in Isa 58:13–14.

CHAPTER 4

Responses to Joseph A. Pipa

Response by Skip MacCarty

Professor Pipa's Sabbath essay contains many contributions that resonate with sabbatarians. The Sabbath creation ordinance was established in Eden as a benefit for "all mankind" (p. 120). By declaring the Sabbath "holy," God set it apart for worship and service (p. 123). The Sabbath is "a perpetual moral law, rather than merely ceremonial" (pp. 123–28). Even in the OT era, "the Sabbath [applied] to Gentiles as well as Jews" (p. 127). Jesus observed the seventh-day Sabbath according to the OT divine guidelines, contrary to pharisaical accusations that He desecrated it: "He violated only Jewish traditions" (p. 135). Through His healing miracles, Jesus demonstrated that the Sabbath is "a day for the exercise of mercy" (p. 138). The theology of redemption articulated in Hebrews "requires" a continuation of Sabbath-keeping (*sabbatismos*) (p. 156). "All true Sabbath-keeping begins by actively resting in God alone for our salvation" (p. 170)—a spiritual truth, it should be pointed out, as applicable to OT believers as to NT believers. "Without deliberately focusing on Christ and living in dependence on Him, there is no true Sabbath-keeping" (p. 170). We agree that the day is all about Jesus—what He has done as our Creator (John 1:3; Col 1:16) and Redeemer (Eph 1:7); and again, it was as needful for OT believers to have focused and depended on Yahweh as for NT believers to focus and depend on Jesus.

I wish every modern sabbatarian could read Pipa's list of practical suggestions on how to keep the Sabbath holy. I say "suggestions" because the Bible is scant on Sabbath rules[1]—I counted 51 suggestions Pipa gave of what to do and not to do on the Sabbath (pp. 132–36, 141–44, 167–71). Against the charge that his list "promotes legalism," he explains its purpose: "To free the people of God for the wonderful privilege of worshipping and enjoying Him" (p. 170). Were the list generated by sabbatarians, who are considered legalists by many for merely worshipping on the seventh day specified in the Sabbath commandment, it would doubtless be considered further evidence of their legalism. For that reason, and because the Bible contains few rules, many Sabbatarian leaders shy away from providing such detailed guidelines for their members. Nevertheless, I find such thoughtful application of biblical principles to modern life refreshing to consider, though not on a level of biblical mandate.

Nevertheless, we find Pipa's premise that the "Christian Sabbath" is different from that found in the Decalogue seriously flawed. Challenging the commandment's divine specificity, Pipa writes, "I prefer the interpretation that refers to the seventh day as the seventh chronologically" (p. 145, n. 31). Where the Decalogue's Sabbath commandment reads, "the seventh day is a Sabbath to the Lord your God" (Exod 20:10 NIV), Pipa's would read, "One day in seven is a Sabbath to the Lord your God." We find Pipa's substitution of a "one-day-in-seven principle" (pp. 122, 123, 128, etc.) for the divinely ordained "seventh-day" Sabbath to be unwarranted, unscriptural, and misleading as a catechetical teaching.

We concur with A. T. Lincoln's statement:

> Many Sabbatarian arguments appeal to the fourth commandment and assert that the place of the Sabbath requirement in the Decalogue means that it is to be seen as binding moral law normative for all people in the same way as the rest of the Decalogue. Those who argue in this way, but apply the fourth commandment to Sunday, the first day of the week, are certainly not as consistent as those groups, such as the Seventh-day Adventists, who still observe the seventh day; they need to face

---

1. Biblical Sabbath prohibitions are few: Exod 20:8–11, working; Exod 35:3, lighting a fire (likely for cooking, a major and time-consuming task in those days); Neh 13:15–17, trading; Isa 58:13, "doing as you please" (likely secular activities that detract from the purpose of the day).

this inconsistency squarely. On their own presupposition, by what right do they tamper with an eternally valid moral law? What criterion allows them to isolate the seventh day aspect, which after all is at the heart of the commandment and its rationale (cf. Exod 20:11), as a temporary feature belonging only to the Mosaic period, while retaining the remainder of the Decalogue as normative for all ages?[2]

Pipa's essay replies that the Westminster Confession gives them that right, by declaring the "seventh-day" component of the Sabbath commandment a "positive" element of the Sabbath commandment that "can be changed without affecting the moral nature of the law" (p. 145). Declaring the "seventh-day" component of the Sabbath commandment "positive" makes it equivalent to "the ceremonial laws of the Mosaic covenant" (p. 145).

Pipa's second source of authority for this interpretation is "Ursinus (one of the framers of the Heidelberg Confession)" who wrote that "the [Sabbath] commandment has two parts: 'the one moral and perpetual, as that the Sabbath be kept holy; the other ceremonial and temporary, as that the seventh day be kept holy'" (p. 131).

These declarations were made in spite of the scriptural revelation that at creation "on the seventh day [God] rested," "God blessed *the seventh day* and made it holy," and of God's declaration in the Decalogue that "the *seventh day* is a Sabbath to the Lord your God"—sacred pronouncements never made anywhere else in Scripture regarding any other day of the week, and never revoked, but which are in fact reiterated in the NT (Gen 2:3; Exod 20:9, emphasis added; Heb 4:4).

Pipa cites Lev 23:1–25 as evidence that the seventh-day Sabbath was considered one of the "special holy days of Jewish worship" that Col 2:16–17 reveals were "fulfilled in [Christ]" and thus abrogated (p. 146). However, rather than *identifying* the seventh-day Sabbath with those feasts, Lev 23:1–38 *distinguishes* it from them. Keil and Delitzsch comment on Lev 23:3,38:

> As a weekly returning day of rest, the observance of which had its foundation in the creative work of God, the Sabbath was *distinguished* from the yearly feasts . . . which were generally called

2. A. T. Lincoln, "From Sabbath to Lord's Day: A Biblical and Theological Perspective," in *From Sabbath to Lord's Day: A Biblical, Historical, and Theological Investigation*, ed. D. A. Carson (Eugene, OR: Wipf and Stock, 1982), 355.

> "feasts of Jehovah" [23:4] in the stricter sense, and as such were
> *distinguished* from the Sabbath . . . (vers. 37, 38; Isa. i. 13,14;
> 1 Chron. xxiii. 31; 2 Chron. xxxi. 3; Neh. x. 34) (emphasis added).[3]

Even if Leviticus 23 had not clearly distinguished between the
seventh-day Sabbath and the ceremonial feasts and Sabbaths, that
would not provide license to tweeze the seventh day out of the Sabbath commandment and declare it "ceremonial and temporary."
God specifically blessed and sanctified the seventh day at creation
and enshrined it in the Sabbath commandment of the Decalogue to
set it apart and ensure its permanency.

The false assumption that the seventh-day component of the
Sabbath commandment is ceremonial and temporary permeates
Pipa's essay. Pipa's entire thesis for his essay in defense of Sunday
as the "Christian Sabbath" stands or falls on the premise that when
God said, "The seventh day is a Sabbath to the Lord your God," He
meant one day in seven is a Sabbath to the Lord your God and that,
for the time being during the OT period, that "one day" will be the
seventh day that is positive and changeable, ceremonial and temporary. His cited sources for this interpretation of the Sabbath commandment are Ursinus and the Westminster Confession. Ursinus
and the Westminster divines were undoubtedly godly men and their
confessions a blessing to the church, but they are not the Bible.

Pipa writes, "The Sabbath commandment, therefore, contained
ceremonial aspects—seventh-day worship, special Sabbaths (new
moon, seventh year, and jubilee), and religious feasts" (p. 128). But
the Sabbath commandment may be read a thousand times and still
be found to contain no hint of new moons, seventh years, jubilees,
or religious feasts (Exod 20:8–11). The complete lack of scriptural
support for this major and central pillar of Pipa's thesis—that the
seventh day is a ceremonial element of the Sabbath commandment—singlehandedly exposes the impotency of any attempt to
chisel "the seventh day" out of the Sabbath commandment and to
pencil in the "first day of the week" in its place.

In an attempt to mute the effect of singling out "seventh day"
as a ceremonial and temporary element of the Sabbath commandment, Pipa suggests that such a procedure is not unique since "all
of the Ten Commandments . . . have both civil and ceremonial

ramifications . . . [that] were types of Christ and His work and thus would pass away" (p. 127). While he makes attempts, failed in our view, to give examples from the commandments forbidding idolatry and commending the honoring of one's parents (p. 128), he steers clear of attempting to identify ceremonial and temporary elements embedded in the Decalogue's prohibitions against murder, adultery, stealing, coveting, and so forth.

Elsewhere Pipa ably and rightly defends the unity and permanence of the Ten Commandments as well as anyone I have read: The Ten Commandments "stand together as a unit. . . . They are the timeless expression of God's moral will. Therefore it is contrary to all sound reason to wrench out one commandment, claiming that it was ceremonial and consequently no longer binding" (p. 124). We consider Pipa a formidable ally in the struggle to defend the Decalogue against modern attacks made on it and agree wholeheartedly with his statement just quoted. However, it seems to us inconsistent and not only "contrary to all sound reason" but also contrary to Scripture for him to wrench "the seventh day" out of the Sabbath commandment and to declare it uniquely "positive" and "ceremonial," and therefore subject to abrogation in the NT era while the Sabbath commandment itself, with another day substituted in its place, remains permanent. Again, we concur with A. T. Lincoln on this issue, that it is inconsistent "to isolate the seventh day aspect, which after all is at the heart of the commandment and its rationale (cf. Exod 20:11), as a temporary feature belonging only to the Mosaic period, while retaining the remainder of the Decalogue as normative for all ages."[4]

Pipa's interpretation of the Sabbath commandment as a one-day-in-seven principle with a ceremonial and temporary seventh-day component becomes the lens through which he interprets other major debated passages such as Col 2:16–17 and Heb 4:9. When he states, "In Col 2:16–17 Paul abrogated the seventh-day Sabbath," he means that Paul abrogated the "ceremonial and temporary" sev-

---

4. Lincoln, "From Sabbath to Lord's Day," 355. Calvin, in typical Reformation diatribe toward those with whom they disagreed, branded "false prophets" those who "asserted that nothing but the ceremonial part of this [Sabbath] commandment has been abrogated (in their phraseology the 'appointing' of the seventh day), but the moral part remains—namely, the fixing of one day in seven." *Institutes of the Christian Religion*, ed. J. T. McNeill, trans. F. L. Battles, LCC 20–21 (Philadelphia: Westminster, 1950), 1:400 (2.8.34). He declared that those who establish Sunday as a replacement Sabbath in the Sabbath commandment "surpass the Jews three times over in crass and carnal Sabbatarian superstition" (ibid.).

enth-day component of the commandment, while still preserving the moral element of resting one day in seven (p. 146). Based on this interpretation, Pipa concludes that "the church was not free to continue the observance of the seventh day" (p. 146), meaning that those of us who continue to observe the seventh-day Sabbath enjoined at creation and enshrined in the Decalogue are breaking God's law!

However, Pipa says, the moral, one-day-in-seven Sabbath principle that remained in the NT era did not mean that the NT church was free "to set whatever day she preferred." The NT Sabbath established "by divine warrant" is the first day of the week (p. 146). What is the scriptural support for this? Pipa responds, "We learn from Heb 4:9–10 that the practice of Sabbath-keeping remains for the people of God and they are to keep the Sabbath on the first day of the week" (p. 165; cf. pp. 149, 153). But it is not at all clear how he can reach such a conclusion based on Heb 4:9–10, which reads: "There remains, then, a Sabbath-rest [Gk., *sabbatismos*] for the people of God; for anyone who enters God's rest also rests from their works, just as God did from his" (NIV).

I read Pipa's explanation (pp. 149–65) for his interpretation of this passage numerous times trying to follow his reasoning (which was not easy, but perhaps the fault was mine more than his). As best as I could follow it, the first step of his logical progression starts with this statement: "The Sabbath did have ceremonial and typical significance," and Hebrews "teaches most clearly how all OT ceremonial worship practices were fulfilled in Christ and therefore repealed" (p. 386). He therefore grounds his argument on the unscriptural premise that the "ceremonial" seventh-dayness of the Sabbath commandment has been "repealed."

Yet Pipa acknowledges that the *sabbatismos* that "remains . . . for the people of God" refers to keeping Sabbath: "Sabbath-keeping is involved every time this verb [*sabbatizō*, the cognate of *sabbatismos*] is used" (p. 156). And since, he says, the ceremonial seventh-day element of the Sabbath has been repealed, the NT Sabbath that remains for the people of God must be observed on another day. Pipa further argues that the key to establishing which day should be observed in the NT era is found in verse 10, which, he explains, refers to Jesus resting from His redemptive work on resurrection Sunday, thereby establishing Sunday as the

Christian Sabbath. In our view this argument from Heb 4:9–10 fails on multiple levels:

1. As noted above, there is no hint in Scripture that the seventh-day element of the Sabbath commandment is ceremonial and temporary. Indeed, God's specific creational blessing and sanctification of the *seventh day* of creation week forms the basis of the Sabbath commandment (Gen 2:3; Exod 20:11).

2. The seventh-day Sabbath was not a historical *type* like the sacrifices and OT feasts that foreshadowed Christ's future work. Rather, the Sabbath was God's chosen *sign* between Him and His people that He is their Creator and Redeemer who will make them holy (Exod 31:12,17). The NT reveals Jesus as our Creator (John 1:1–3) and Redeemer (Eph 1:7), thus investing the Sabbath with profound Christological significance. As Yahweh was Israel's true rest in the OT era, Jesus is new covenant Israel's rest in the NT era (Exod 33:14; Matt 11:28; Heb 8:8,10).[5]

3. Pipa implies that the Sabbath rest available to NT believers through faith in Jesus and the promise of future rest in the kingdom of God, represented by Sunday observance, was unavailable to OT believers who worshipped on the seventh day (pp. 158, 162). But the entire premise of Heb 3:7–4:13 belies that conclusion. The spiritual rest offered to the NT believer through faith in Christ was offered to the OT believer through faith in Yahweh, with the same heavenly hope available to both, as Hebrews attests (Heb 4:2,6,10–11; 11:8–16). Those who failed to enter that rest did so because of their unbelief and disobedience, not because it was not available (3:18–4:1).

4. Never in Scripture or early Christian extrabiblical literature does *sabbatismos*, or the cognate verb *sabbatizō*, ever refer to Sunday.[6]

---

5. See also, e.g., Heb 1:10–12, where God the Father attributes to Jesus what Ps 102:25–27 attributes to Yahweh.

6. The following list contains all biblical and extrabiblical references through the early church period. All biblical and apocryphal references containing the verb sabbatizō: Exod 16:30 (seventh-day Sabbath); Lev 23:32 (Day of Atonement Sabbath); 26:35 (the land will rest); 2 Chron 36:21 (the land rests); 2 Macc. 6:6 (seventh-day Sabbath). All early church extrabiblical references to *sabbatismos/sabbatismon* meaning observance of the seventh-

5. The interpretive key to the meaning of *sabbatismos* in Heb 4:9 is not verse 10, which makes no mention of a day, but verse 4, which does: "On the *seventh* day God rested from all his works" (NIV, emphasis added). Had there been a reference to Jesus' resurrection on the first day of the week here, it would have strengthened Pipa's argument that *sabbatismos* is being redefined in Hebrews 4, but it does not. Instead, it cites God's resting on the *seventh day* of creation as the point of reference for understanding the "Sabbath rest" (or, more literally, "Sabbath keeping," *sabbatismos*) that, according to Heb 4:9, *remains* for the people of God in the NT era. This reinforces the permanency and universality of the seventh-day Sabbath.[7]

6. If Heb 4:10 is a reference to Jesus' redemptive rest after His atoning death rather than to the sinner's rest in God, as Pipa attempts to prove (and quite persuasively if not yet conclusively for me, I might add), it enhances, rather than diminishes, the significance of seventh-day Sabbath observance. At the time of the evening sacrifice on Good Friday, Jesus cried out, "It is finished!" and then rested in the tomb on the seventh-day Sabbath from His redemptive work on earth (cf. Luke 23:50–24:1; John 19:30). As the original Sabbath celebrated God's finished work of creation, so in the NT era the seventh-day Sabbath celebrates Jesus' finished work of redemption on earth.

7. Ephesians 5:31–33 and Heb 4:4–9 provide parallel passages affirming in the NT era the creation ordinances of marriage and the seventh-day Sabbath, respectively:

---

day Sabbath as the Jews do: Plutarch, *De superstitione* 2 (166); Justin Martyr, *Dialogue with Trypho* 23.3; Epiphanius, *Refutation of All Heresies* 30:2.2; *Martyrdom of Peter and Paul* 1; *Apostolic Constitutions and Canons* 2.36.2,7. Origen, a Neoplatonist early Christian, used *sabbatismos/sabbatismon* five times allegorically, with figurative and often uncertain meaning: *Against Celsus* 5.59; *Commentarii in evangelium Joannis* 2.27; *First Principles* 27.16; *Selecta in Exodum* 12.289.7; and *Excerpta Psalmos* 17.144.31.

7. While Pipa makes no such claim, it should be pointed out that the "another day" God speaks of in Heb 4:8 is not a reference to another Sabbath but to the "today" of Ps 95:7, which the author of Hebrews just quoted in 4:7. In Ps 95:7–11 (quoted in full in Heb 3:7–11), David appealed for the people of God to enter the spiritual rest "today" (i.e., in David's day) that Israel of old had largely failed to experience under Joshua through unbelief. The author of Hebrews makes that same appeal for his own day (4:6–7).

(a) Ephesians 5:31 quotes Gen 2:24, the creation ordinance of marriage;

Heb 4:4 quotes Gen 2:2, the creation ordinance of seventh-day Sabbath.

(b) Ephesians 5:32 contains a spiritual analogy between marriage and the believer's spiritual union with Jesus;

Heb 4:6 speaks of the spiritual rest the Sabbath signifies—the rest in God and the gospel.

(c) Ephesians 5:33 affirms the literal application of the creation ordinance of marriage for NT people of God;

Heb 4:9 affirms the literal observance of the seventh-day Sabbath creation ordinance for NT people of God.[8]

Hebrews 4, rather than establishing Sunday as the Christian Sabbath, reaffirms that the seventh-day Sabbath of the creation ordinance and the Decalogue remains for the NT people of God as the authentic Christian Sabbath.

Pipa also includes some of the more traditional arguments for the establishment of Sunday worship. Following the purported repeal of the ceremonial and temporary seventh-day provision of the Sabbath commandment, Pipa claims that "the New Testament church immediately began to worship on the first day of the week (Acts 20:7; 1 Cor 16:1–2)" (p. 146). Pipa ignores that the breaking of bread, which Acts 20:7 reports occurred at a one-time meeting on the first day of the week, also occurred *daily* from house to house (Acts 2:46). And Paul's appeal in 1 Cor 16:1–2 for Corinthian believers to prepare a charitable gift for the poor in Jerusalem includes the Greek phrase *par' heautō*, which many if not most commentators agree with G. Lockwood "almost certainly means 'at home,'" not in a corporate worship service.[9] In addition, rather than use a

8. See this chart on p. 27 of my essay.

9. G. J. Lockwood, *1 Corinthians*, Concordia Commentary (St. Louis: Concordia, 2000), 609; cf. [note: no author] *The Analytical Greek Lexicon* (London: Samuel Bagster and Sons, n.d.), 110: *"with one's self, at home"*; G. Fee, *The First Epistle to the Corinthians*, NICNT (Grand Rapids: Eerdmans, 1987), 813; A. Thiselton, *The First Epistle to the Corinthians: A Commentary on the Greek Text*, NIGTC (Grand Rapids: Eerdmans, 2000), 1324; H. Conzelmann, *1 Corinthians: A Commentary on the First Epistle to the Corinthians*, Hermeneia (Philadelphia: Fortress Press, 1975), 296; W. F. Orr, *1 Corinthians: A New Translation*, AB 32 (Garden City, NY: Doubleday, 1976), 355,

Greek term for "giving an offering," Paul used *thēsaurizōn* ("storing up," NKJV; "saving it up," NIV; "save," NRSV). First Corinthians 16:2 refers to a private act of worship, not a corporate worship service. Paul invited "each one of you" (*hekastos humōn*) to plan ahead and have a contribution "saved up," accumulated for this special offering when he came so that the Corinthian believers would not have to collect it hurriedly from whatever money they might just happen to have available when he arrived.

Pipa states that "the change of the day was first initiated by the resurrection appearances of Christ on the first day of the week when all of the New Testament's recorded appearances took place" (p. 164). If Pipa means that after His resurrection Jesus never met with people except on the first day of the week, even if such were true, it would not provide evidence that God was establishing a new Sabbath day unless He announced such, which He did not. However, on unspecified days, with no mention of the first day of the week, "Jesus appeared to [the apostles] over a period of 40 days and spoke about the kingdom of God" (Acts 1:3), with several of those occasions specifically recorded (Matt 28:16–20; Mark 16:14–18; Luke 24:50–52; John 21; Acts 1:4–9); He also appeared to more than 500 believers on another unspecified day (1 Cor 15:6). The fact is, the Gospels record only two Sundays when Jesus appeared to people. The first was on the day Jesus rose from the dead, in apparently separate incidents, to the women who came to anoint His body (Matt 28:1–10), to Mary (John 20:10–18), to Cleopas and an unidentified companion (Luke 24:13–32), to Simon (Luke 24:34), and to the eleven (Luke 24:33–49; John 20:20–23), in each case to assure them that He had indeed risen and giving no hint that this was the beginning of a new Sabbath. The second Sunday was "a week later" (literally, "after eight days") when He again appeared to the disciples to convince doubting Thomas that He had risen (John 20:24–29), again giving no hint of any change in the Sabbath commandment.

Pipa suggests that John's mention of "after eight days" (John 20:26) refers to "the eighth day" of the OT Feast of Tabernacles or

---

et al. The objections of Llewelyn, "The Use of Sunday," 209, have been convincingly refuted by Young, "The Use of Sunday . . . A Response," 112–13, further noting that *para* followed by a dative pronoun can mean "at the house of" as in Acts 11:12 among other passages (citing A. T. Robertson, "Preface to the Fourth Edition," *A Grammar of the Greek New Testament in the Light of Historical Research* [Nashville: Broadman, 1934], xx).

Booths, which "concluded the annual cycle of feasts," corresponds to the first day of the week, and thus signifies a change of the Sabbath from Saturday to Sunday (pp. 162–64). This is problematic. First, John does not say "on the eighth day" (following tabernacles terminology in Lev 23:36,39), but "after eight days," a common Semitic expression signifying the period of a week (hence, NIV's translation, "a week later"). Secondly, the "first day" and "eighth day" "days of rest" (Lev 23:39–42) of the OT annual Feast of Tabernacle were not linked to the weekly cycle or to Sunday in particular. They occurred on the fifteenth and twenty-second days of the month of Tishri, and fell on different days of the week each year, as our Christmas on December 25 does. Third, John's reference to Jesus' appearance to the disciples on that day does not signify a worship service. They were meeting behind "locked" doors; compare when they met behind locked doors on resurrection day "for fear of the Jews," not for worship (John 20:19). "John seems to be at pains to make clear that all was just as it had been on the first occasion."[10] Fourth, the early church's reference to "the eighth day" to explain Sunday worship was not based on a connection to the Feast of Tabernacles but on each day of creation representing one thousand years, with Christ returning at the end of the seventh millennium and "the eighth day" symbolizing the eighth millennium when the new world supposedly would begin. Based on this fanciful typology, Sunday supposedly represented the church's advance celebration of new world time. R. Brown's assessment of such theological speculations is an understatement: "such imaginative interpretations are difficult to substantiate."[11]

The biblical basis for Pipa's guidelines on how to keep the Sunday Sabbath holy is Isaiah 58 (pp. 165–70). We concur that Isaiah's instruction on Sabbath-keeping is applicable for the NT era. However, we find quite amazing Pipa's suggestion that the whole of Isaiah 53–58 has a primarily NT, rather than an OT, application, thus suggesting that the Sabbath references in Isaiah 56 and 58 mean a Sunday Sabbath rather than the seventh-day Sabbath of the Decalogue. Following are his reasons and our responses:

---

10. L. Morris, *The Gospel According to John,* NICNT (Grand Rapids: Eerdmans, 1971), 852.

11. R. E. Brown, *The Gospel According to John XIII-XXI,* AB 29A (Garden City, NY: Doubleday, 1970), 1025.

1. *Isaiah 53 is a prophecy of Jesus and therefore meant for the NT believer* (p. 166). However, prophecies were also meant to benefit those to whom they were given, and that is especially true of any ethical instruction included in the prophecy (cf. ethical material in the descriptions of the new earth—Rev 21:2; 22:14,17).

2. *Isaiah's reference to a "worldwide outreach" (54:1–3) must refer to the NT era* (p. 166). However, God's mission for His covenant people in every historical era was to share the gospel with the entire world (e.g., Gen 28:14; Exod 19:5–6; Ps 67).[12]

3. *Isaiah's invitation to repentance and to seek God for spiritual nourishment (55:1) makes "promises [that] find fulfillment in the NT era"* (p. 166). However, in what possible way can this invitation to repentance be more applicable to a NT believer than to an OT believer, seeing as such appeals are replete throughout the OT era, and that without responding to them there is no salvation for anyone in any historical era?

4. *Isaiah's offer of a place in God's house for eunuchs who keep the Sabbath (56:2–5) was not applicable in the OT era according to Deut 23:1 (NIV): "No one who has been emasculated by crushing or cutting may enter the assembly of the Lord"* (p. 167). However, a number of major commentators argue that the prohibition in Deut 23:1 is "probably not intended to bar from the community those whose state of emasculation had been brought on by accident or illness,"[13] but rather "refers to people who have been ritually mutilated in the context of the worship of other gods."[14] Even if Deut 23:1 did refer to all OT eunuchs in general, Isaiah's prediction that such eunuchs will be allowed to enter temple worship in the eschatological age (56:3–5) does not imply that the Sabbath will be changed from the seventh-day Sabbath to the first day. In Isaiah 56 the same language describing worship on the Sabbath—"keeps from defiling the Sabbath"—is linked both to the present time of Isaiah's day (v. 2) and to the eschatological future (v. 6), clearly indicating that it is the same seventh-day Sabbath that is in view throughout this passage and applicable for both historical eras.

---

12. See W. Kaiser's insightful work, *Mission in the Old Testament: Israel as a Light to the Nations* (Grand Rapids: Baker, 2000).

13. P. Craigie, *The Book of Deuteronomy*, NICOT (Grand Rapids: Eerdmans, 1976), 296–97.

14. J. McConville, *Deuteronomy*, Apollos OT Commentary (Downers Grove, IL: InterVarsity, 2002), 348.

5. *God's reference in Isa 58:13–14 to the Sabbath as "my holy day" anticipates Jesus' statement seven hundred years later that He is Lord of the Sabbath (Mark 2:28) and therefore has in view a first-day "Christian Sabbath" rather than the seventh-day Sabbath of the creation ordinance and Decalogue* (p. 167). However, long before Isaiah's day, God referred to the seventh-day Sabbath as "a Sabbath to the Lord your God" (Exod 20:10 NIV) and "my Sabbaths" (Lev 19:3,30), synonymous to His reference to "my holy day" in Isaiah 58, which clearly have the seventh-day Sabbath of the Decalogue in view. Furthermore, Mark 2:28 says nothing about the change of the Sabbath but rather identifies Jesus as the Lord who instituted the seventh-day Sabbath at creation, enshrined it in the Decalogue, and is therefore the continuing authority on how it should be kept.

Therefore, there is no scriptural basis for applying the Sabbath references in Isaiah 56 and 58 to Sunday instead of the seventh-day Sabbath of the Decalogue. To do so usurps the original intention of these passages.

In his discussion of the record of early church history on the change of the Sabbath (pp. 146–53), Pipa is to be commended for his honest acknowledgment that "it is difficult to determine the attitude or practice of the early church on a number of issues because those who lived closest to the time of the apostles had the greatest difficulty in grasping the truth in a systematic fashion. . . . Clearly, such confusion was also the case with respect to the doctrine of the Sabbath" (p. 147). This should be a warning signal to those who try to read back into the NT later practices that developed in early church history, the precise history of which is largely disputed.

In three instances we take exception to Pipa's use and reading of early church historical sources. First, explaining the church's association of Sunday with the term, "Lord's Day," Pipa states (p. 149), "The church immediately adopted the phrase of the apostle John, 'Lord's day' (Rev 1:10)." He then refers to Ignatius and the *Didache* as early examples. However, the phrase "Lord's Day" does not occur in any of the earliest manuscripts of Ignatius or of the *Didache*. Translators have supplied the word *Day*. The first unambiguous connection between "Lord's Day" and Christian worship on Sunday does not show up in Christian literature until the second half of the second century.[15] Second, Pipa's use of the statement in

---

15. For further discussion see my essay, pp. 35–40 .

the Second Epistle of Clement (ca. 120–140) as an early example of instruction on how to keep Sunday in the Christian era is misleading as this document nowhere mentions the first day of the week or even implies worship on that day (p. 152). Finally, we find the influence of the Roman emperor Constantine on the establishment of Sunday worship in the church, as a replacement for the observance of the seventh-day Sabbath, to be considerably greater than the minimal role Pipa assigns to it (p. 150).[16]

Dr. Pipa's essay raises several additional questions for me:

- The Westminster Catechisms do not refer to Hebrews 4:9–10 to establish the first day of the week as a divinely ordained NT replacement day for the Sabbath commandment.[17] When did the Reformed tradition begin to so interpret this Scripture?

- Pipa writes in his essay: "The Sabbath commandment, therefore, contained ceremonial aspects—seventh-day worship, special Sabbaths (new moon, seventh year, and jubilee), and religious feasts" (p. 128). Where in the Sabbath commandment are references to "special Sabbaths (new moon, seventh year, and jubilee) and religious feasts" to be found?

- Pipa further claims: "All of the Ten Commandments, therefore, have both civil and ceremonial ramifications," and are thus "types of Christ and His work" that "thus would pass away" (p. 127). What specifically are the ceremonial elements of the Decalogue's commandments prohibiting murder, adultery, stealing, and coveting that were "types of Christ and His work" and "would pass away"? How would

---

16. J. Carroll's interpretation of the historical records is similar to our own. He regards Constantine's influence on Western civilization and the church as "the second greatest story ever told. . . . the most implication-laden event in Western history. If we rarely think so, that is because we take utterly for granted the structures of culture, mind, politics, spirituality, and even calendar (Sunday as holiday) to which it led. . . . when the power of the empire became joined to the Church, the empire was immediately recast and reenergized, and the Church became an entity so different from what had preceded it as to be almost unrecognizable." "For centuries, Christians' celebration of Easter coincided exactly with Passover, and their observance of the Sabbath continued to take place on Saturday. It took the order of Constantine, referred to earlier, and decrees of the fourth-century Church councils to draw fast distinctions between Jewish and Christian observances." *Constantine's Sword: The Church and the Jews, A History* (Boston: Houghton Mifflin, 2001), 171, 145.

17. Westminster Larger Catechism, Q. 116; Westminster Shorter Catechism Q. 69.

those commandments be restated with the ceremonial elements removed, as the essay has done with the Sabbath commandment?

- If the seventh-day Sabbath was exclusively for the Jews (p. 144), why would not the new covenant be exclusively for the Jews since God made it specifically with Israel (Heb 8:8,10)?

- In reference to John 20:26, Lange is quoted: "That the disciples already attribute a particular importance to Sunday, is evidenced by the numeric completeness of their assembly" (p. 164). What is meant by "numeric completeness of their assembly," and how does this "attribute a particular importance to Sunday"?

- The essay states: "So, as the old covenant people of God had the promise of future rest portrayed in its day of rest, the new covenant people of God, the church, also has the promise of future rest portrayed in its day of religious rest" (p. 158). How does the "future rest" available to the NT believer differ from the "future rest" that was available to the OT believer?

- We find alarming the suggestion that it would be spiritually healthy for our government to "legislate that businesses and shops be closed on the Lord's Day," and that the precedent for such Sunday closing laws might be the laws that prohibit "Muslims and certain Mormons" from practicing polygamy "if they want to live in this nation" (p. 134, n. 23). We wonder what might be considered appropriate penalties for those who would violate such Sunday closing laws. Our read on history is that whenever religion has mixed with political power the result has been explosive: conflict, witch hunts, war, atrocities, and now terrorism.

- Referring to Sunday as "the holy day of the Lord," the essay states, "God has sanctified it" (p. 168). Genesis 2:3 says, "God blessed the Seventh Day and made it holy" (NIV; "sanctified it," NASB; cf. Exod 20:11). What text says, "God sanctified the first day of the week?"

For the reasons stated in this critique, as well as in my original essay, we believe the seventh-day Sabbath of creation and the Decalogue to be the true Christian Sabbath and of continuing significance and blessing for the church today.

Response by Craig L. Blomberg

I am starting to type this reply on a Saturday afternoon and will finish it tomorrow on a Sunday afternoon. I suppose neither Skip MacCarty nor Joseph Pipa approves, though I don't know for sure. In fact, I wonder what each thinks of my entire weekend lineup of activity. Today involved sleeping late, a leisurely breakfast, and quiet time, answering e-mail and Facebook, playing a few Facebook games with friends (especially my wife), mowing my quarter-acre yard, lunch, reviewing for the sermons I'm preaching tomorrow morning and evening, reading Dr. Pipa's chapter, taking a brief nap, and now starting on this reply. Shortly we'll have dinner and then my wife and I are going to an outdoor concert this evening as an early wedding-anniversary gift to each other. Tomorrow, as best as I can anticipate it, will involve more serious time in prayer with my sermon notes, three hours for church (including drive time), lunch, finishing this response and other e-mail and Facebook odds and ends, probably another short nap, dinner, and another three hours for church.

Both MacCarty and Pipa agree that one day in seven must be set aside as special for worship and for rest (or the cessation of regular work). MacCarty believes it must be Saturday, while Pipa believes it must be Sunday. But each allows for exceptions, following his denomination's traditions, in the case of anything that is needed to help make worship happen for others and in the case of others' genuine needs. Presumably, writing this book will better help readers understand how and when to worship and/or rest, so it ought to be acceptable activity for me on either day. But wait! I teach, write, and minister as my professional occupation. So what I do on the weekends involving these activities is not taking a break from my regular work; so is it wrong? Mowing my lawn on the weekends is definitely unlike anything I do during the week, so maybe that is my most Sabbath-related activity. But of all the things I regularly do each weekend from April to October, it feels the most like work. Facebook is actually the most mindless and relaxing activity; does that then count as rest? My naps certainly should; I seldom get them during the workweek. But Pipa would limit even naps on Sundays to whether or not I need them in order to stay awake during the evening service. I can't honestly say I do; I just "take delight" in them. But that's not taking delight in something related to worship or to God's Word, so I guess my naps on Sunday are sinful?

Moreover, as every ministry professional knows, their day of worship (in my case Sunday) is often the least restful of the week. This fact has given rise to the notion of a different day of the week for the minister's Sabbath than for everyone else because we can't have one's ministers burning out all the time, working seven days a week even as everyone else works only five. (Maybe there's the rub; if we just had a six-day, 12-hour-a-day workweek like the ancients, we'd have no trouble worshipping and resting the entire seventh day. But how many employers are going to pay time-and-a-half or more for us to work overtime to recreate that workweek schedule so we can properly observe the Sabbath?)

So let's go back to the idea of one day in seven. Say the busy pastor takes it on Monday. It won't be a day of *corporate* worship for him or her, unless there is a church for him to attend somewhere nearby that worships on Monday. Even then, the pastor is not really following what both MacCarty and Pipa agree is the biblical mandate—one full 24-hour day different from all others with unique requirements of worship with one's own congregation and rest from one's regular work. Those activities actually get parceled out over different occasions on different days of the week. MacCarty and Pipa might agree this is acceptable for pastors but only as an exception to the general rule. But Jesus appealed to such exceptions in the Old Testament (Mark 2:23–28 par.) to justify more sweeping permissions for people who didn't qualify as Jewish "clergy." It is precisely the kind of casuistry that Pipa commends, especially from the days of the Puritans, that Jesus so regularly denounced when He found it among the Pharisees. Read the Scriptures and see how precious little is ever described in terms of just what constituted a Sabbath and then reread Pipa's chapter, especially with all of the quotations from the creeds and other Reformed theologians. My reaction, for whatever it's worth, was to sense that the Pharisees, with all the best intentions in the world, had returned with a vengeance 16 centuries later.

Pipa begins his chapter with an excellent overview of Sabbath-related theology in the beginning of Genesis. But one has to read carefully. Only two paragraphs after refuting the view "that God blesses [only] eternal rest, not [also] the seventh day," Pipa subtly shifts language (p. 122). Now it is God promising those who follow His example "of rest every seventh day" that He will bless them. The reader wonders if this means "not necessarily on Saturday, the seventh day" but one day in seven. Three paragraphs later Pipa confirms this is exactly what he means: "the observation of one day out of seven is a perpetually binding moral obligation because of this creation ordinance" (p. 123). I'm sure MacCarty would want to jump up and say, "Wait a minute! How did you shift from insisting the Sabbath had to be the seventh day of the week to saying it had only to be one day in seven?" I'd want to ask the same question.

A similar tension emerges after the proclamation that "the Ten Words, which were given in such an awesome manner at Mount Sinai and engraved by the finger of God in stone, stand together as a unit" (p. 124). But later we are told that there are both moral and ritual dimensions to the Sabbath command. The day of the week can be changed but not the fact of one full day each week. Two questions suggest themselves immediately. First, granting for the sake of argument that there are both moral and ritual dimensions to the Sabbath command, does not that observation in and of itself set this Commandment off as unique among the Ten? There aren't ritual dimensions to the commands against murder, adultery, or theft, are there? So, then, the Ten Words are not really quite the indissoluble unit of identically formed commands that we were first led to believe. Second, still granting Pipa's same premise, if the day on which we celebrate the Sabbath is part of the variable, ritual law, while the twin principles of worship and rest are the unvarying moral law, which is the principle of 24 full hours more like—the variability of the day of the week or the moral necessity of rest and worship? Surely to all but those immersed for a long time in the Puritan form of Sabbatarianism, the answer is obvious: it is far more like the ritual law since it too has to do with timing, than the moral law that involves humanity's central needs for rest and worship.

Not surprisingly, we soon read the first of several quotations from or references to the Westminster and Heidelberg Catechisms. For someone like me who has never been a Presbyterian or Reformed Christian, and despite my profound appreciation for the overall doctrinal syntheses that the sixteenth-century Reformers and their disciples produced, these bits about the Sabbath read very much like the product of so different a culture and mind-set, based on so little actual *exegesis* of Scripture, that I find it hard to see them very relevant to twenty-first century North America. As a Baptist, I appreciate why so many of my Baptist predecessors have looked with distrust at creedalism. However much any confession of faith attempts merely to summarize fundamental truths from Scripture, it is born out of key controversies of the time of its composition and has cultural blind spots that only those from quite different contexts will typically notice. More seriously, such confessions can easily and at times unnoticeably supersede Scripture in authority and interpretation by becoming the only acceptable way to understand the Bible. Reading Pipa's chapter as an outsider to his tradition certainly makes me feel like that is what has happened over and again in his work.

Pipa immediately attempts to bolster his quotation of the Westminster divines by references to the New Testament. But again we must read them carefully. "Jesus based His answer on two OT passages (Deut 6:5 and Lev 19:18) that summarize the Ten Commandments" (p. 125). Do they really? Or is it later Jewish and Christian theologians that have seen how aptly the first four commandments flesh out the command to love God and the last six to love one's neighbor? Nothing in either OT passage itself suggests a link with the Ten Words. Or consider Jesus' reply to the rich young ruler cited in Matt 19:18–19. Unambiguously, Christ refers to five of the Ten. That the first four are in the same sequence as in Exodus and Deuteronomy makes it highly likely he was thinking of them as they are recorded in Scripture. But honoring one's parents is put after the four commandments that it in fact precedes in its Old Testament contexts, and then Lev 19:18 is added as well. No reference to coveting appears and no reference to any of the first four commands, including the Sabbath. This is not quite the evidence that Pipa requires to refer to all Ten as a unique indissoluble unit.

Nor is it actually the case that we see here "that Jesus considered the second greatest commandment to be a summary of the last six commandments" (p. 125). What Jesus actually does is to include Lev 19:18 in his list of commandments as if it were a distinct command from the preceding five. *Maybe* He sees it functioning as a summary, but that's not what He actually says. *Maybe* He intends coveting to be included because, after giving five of the six last commands even if slightly out of sequence, we are meant to supply the last one on our own. But the case isn't really as clear as Pipa claims that it is. And even if it were, what would that prove about the Sabbath, which isn't even among these last six commands? It is not until later, chronologically, in His ministry, that Jesus will pair Deut 6:5 and Lev 19:18 as the *two* great commands (Matt 22:37–40). When He does, He labels them not a summary of the Ten Commandments but of the entire OT. There is the true, indissoluble unit. Pulling out the Ten Commandments and treating them differently from the rest of the Mosaic covenant or the OT is what is exegetically unsupported. And inferring anything at all about the first four of the Ten Words is utterly foreign to the contexts of Matthew 19 and 22.

When he turns to Col 2:16–17, Pipa employs the same exegetical sleight-of-hand as MacCarty to avoid the plain meaning of the text. Even though Paul speaks of "sabbaths," pure and simple, without any qualification, Sabbatarians, whether of the seventh- or first-day variety, cannot believe that the Sabbath commandment of the "Big Ten" could ever be assigned entirely to the ritual or ceremonial law. So they read in, with no actual warrant from the text, some limitation. For Pipa, it is only "the seventh-day Sabbath" that pointed to the Savior to come. But how could it have possibly done this? Remember, what Pipa means by "the seventh-day Sabbath" is the ritual aspect—the time of the celebration—of the command, not the moral aspects of rest and worship. Rest and worship could easily point forward to God's Messiah who would ultimately provide perfect rest and be worthy of our complete worship. But we are not talking about the moral dimensions of the Sabbath command, according to Pipa, in Col 2:16, merely the ritual dimension. In what way does ceasing from work on Saturday, apart from the practice of rest and worship, point forward to the Messiah? It points back to God's finished creative activity on the seventh day but not to anything the Messiah would ever do on a Saturday.

As in MacCarty's chapter, what is missing in Pipa's presentation is any exegetical grappling with Matt 5:17–20 and comparable passages in other New Testament writers. Pipa quotes all of Matt 5:17–19 and then proceeds to conclude, without any further discussion, that "Jesus asserted the perpetuity of God's moral law" (p. 136). No, not at all. To the extent that Jesus asserted the perpetuity of anything in these verses, it was of *the entire Old Testament* ("the Law and the Prophets"), which includes moral, civil, and ceremonial laws. There is no way from these verses to restrict his focus just to the moral law. But then we have to ask what "fulfill" means. It clearly does not mean "abolish," but as noted in my essay (pp. 323–25) neither does it mean "preserve unchanged." And the period of time during which not even the smallest part of the law will pass away lasts "until all is accomplished." Early Christians realized that everything pertaining to the sacrifices, to circumcision, to the dietary laws, to the civil government of Israel, and so on, *was* accomplished with Christ's death and resurrection. So the possibility that everything pertaining to the Sabbath was fulfilled—when Christ called all who were willing to come to Himself so that He might give them rest (Matt 11:28)—cannot be excluded *a priori* from an interpretation of His teaching in Matt 5:17–20.

There are a half-dozen recorded conflicts between Jesus and the Jewish leaders over the Sabbath. It is probably fair, with Pipa, to conclude that this means correct Sabbath observance is an important topic for Christ. It is not fair to assume this must mean one-day-in-seven observance, for that issue never remotely appears in any of the contexts in the Gospels dealing with Jesus and the Sabbath. It is just as possible that what Christ is working so hard to teach is that *no* one specific day in seven must be mandated for rest and worship so long as believers maintain a healthy dose of each. Pipa seems correct, in this context, to assert that "to fail to do good is to do harm, and the failure to save a life, when in one's power, is to destroy" (p. 140). But it does not appear that he recognizes the full significance of either half of this two-part principle. If I am employed in an occupation that I believe is consistent with my Christian allegiance because it provides some good service for humanity, then it remains just as good—no less and no more—no matter what day of the week I engage in it. Requiring me never to engage in that work on a particular day labeled the Sabbath might well prevent that good from happening, in which case it would follow that I was doing harm. But if the *only* good I am allowed to do is that which saves lives, then not one of Christ's conflicts with the Jewish leaders over the Sabbath was necessary because not one of

His controversial actions kept anyone from dying whose life was in demonstrable danger at the time.

To make the same point another way, Pipa captures the correct sense of Jesus' teaching when he concludes that "the Sabbath is a day for doing good to one's neighbor" (p. 138). But think of all the things that such good could involve: helping others with yard work, housework, babysitting, taking them out for a special meal, treating them by attending some other form of entertainment they might otherwise not be able to go to, playing games together with them for relaxation, repairing their technological gadgets, helping their kids with their homework, and on and on. Yet all of these activities, implicitly or explicitly, are precluded somewhere in either Pipa's or MacCarty's chapters. Apparently, it is only "religious good" that counts, even though nothing that Christ did on the Sabbath that drew the ire of the authorities was, directly, a religious good! Physical healings or providing food for the hungry could have religious side benefits for them, but so could any of my above-mentioned activities if neighbors became more open to the gospel because of our interest in them as complete persons.

In other words, after giving a correct and wide-ranging definition of Jesus' understanding of what is right on the Sabbath (doing good), Pipa then proceeds to backpedal from this definition in a variety of ways, some of them contradicting one another as well as Jesus' more sweeping principle. Later he refers even to saving a life only "if one has opportunity within one's calling and circumstance" (p. 140). Does this mean if my calling is not that of a medical doctor, I should not perform CPR on a person whose heart has stopped beating on the Sabbath? Later what is permitted is limited to "deeds of necessity and mercy" (p. 141). From this I deduce that CPR *is* OK for anyone to perform. But apparently none of the activities I envisioned above with my neighbors is in any way merciful. At least that's the way John Murray takes it when he allows only "deeds of piety, necessity, and mercy," with "mercy" defined as "works necessary for the preservation of life" (see p. 141 and n. 29). But Jesus' Sabbath healings and feeding fall under none of Murray's categories, so defined! Still later Pipa rephrases the principle of what is permitted on the Sabbath as "activity [that] promote[s] the purpose of the day" (p. 141). I could live with this criterion a lot better than with his previous three except that I suspect Pipa would disagree with me considerably over what actually does promote the purpose of the day. Almost everything I do outside of church on Sunday I find restful and/or God centered and at least most of what I do inside of church is at least God centered if not restful, but Pipa elsewhere in his chapter excludes much of what I would put into these categories.

Still one more criterion appears later in Pipa's chapter, which is not exactly coterminous with any of his previous ones: "work necessary for the good or well-being of our neighbor and the continuance of his or our lawful calling" (p. 144). With this wording I can justify working a 12-hour workday on the Sabbath if I am providing a good service for someone else's well-being (including retail sales, sporting events, education, and entertainment) and continuing my lawful calling that put me in that job in the first place! Nothing is said in this definition about the work being necessary or life saving, just good for someone else. So apparently the only thing I can't do on the Sabbath now is something that provides *me* with my much-needed rest but doesn't actually help anyone else! Isn't it time to end the bewildering string of casuistic and self-contradictory attempts to salvage a perspective (Sabbatarianism) that was never intended by God in the first place and let the NT speak with full force, however radical the results may be?

While I fully agree with Pipa, against MacCarty, that the New Testament *encourages* Sunday worship, I agree with MacCarty, against Pipa, that it nowhere *mandates* it. Notice again the self-contradictory entanglements Pipa lands in trying to defend his tradition's heritage. At first, "because the particular day is positive law, the day can be changed without affecting the moral nature of the law" (p. 145). Again, just for the sake of argument, let's grant this as a valid statement of NT teaching. It's all right for Christians to change the day of worship from Saturday to Sunday. But could a given church decide to worship exclusively on Tuesday nights? Apparently not. Despite the broader principle just cited, "The church was not free to continue the observance of the seventh day, nor was she permitted to set whatever day she preferred" (p. 146). But if this quotation is true, then the previous quotation is false. The day cannot be changed without affecting the moral nature of the law. Or, more precisely, the day could be changed once, in the first century, without affecting the moral nature of the law, but it had to be changed then (that sounds moral) and it could never be changed again (again moral). Excuse me if my reply is to question with bewilderment and say, "Excuse me?"

After extended and helpful discussions of early church practice, which of course cannot be normative for the evangelical but can at least give the lie to MacCarty's overly simplistic explanation of the shift from Saturday to Sunday Sabbath-keeping, we come to Pipa's treatment of Hebrews 4. Like Pipa, he manages to miss the inspired author's meaning altogether and to transform the text from a promise of rest in Christ throughout one's Christian life (partially) and throughout eternity (fully) into a sabbatarian command to practice Sabbath-keeping even in the new covenant age. Perhaps we need to reread the entire section to grasp the author's flow of thought rather than just citing isolated verses within it.

Beginning in 3:7, Hebrews warns its readers not to fail to enter God's rest as so many of the Israelites did in the wilderness. The author is not talking about Sabbath-keeping but about inheriting the promised land. A possible objection to his use of the Israelites as an analogy is that there no longer is such a thing as "God's rest" after they did occupy the land. Such an objection is unlikely even to have arisen were the first Christians Sabbatarians (on either Saturday *or* Sunday). As the entire book of Hebrews demonstrates, its author is worried about those who might commit apostasy (however that be explained theologically) and fail to be a part of God's people in the world to come. The reply to the potential objection is for our author to quote Ps 95:7–8 repeatedly. The psalmist could apply the concept of divine rest to God's people centuries after they inhabited the land because they were always subject to eviction by exile after too much disobedience. Again, what one does on one day of the week is nowhere an issue for discussion in this context. What the audience of Hebrews has to make sure it does properly is to share the faith of those who obeyed (4:2), that is, who believed God at His word that He would enable the Israelites to possess the land despite the odds, humanly speaking, being stacked against them.

Even the one time in the discussion when God's rest on the seventh day of the first week is mentioned, it is not for the sake of enjoining Sabbath-keeping but to contrast God's rest with the Israelites' failure to enter His rest, metaphorically speaking (4:4–5). The author of Hebrews then deduces that even in his day, after the coming of Christ, it is still a day when people can fail to enter God's rest, that is, to become true Christians and persevere so as to experience the full blessings of eternal life in the world to come (4:6–8,11). As a result, Heb 4:9 declares, "There remains, then, a Sabbath-rest for the people of God." Not only does becoming a Christian in this life and living with the triune God and all the company of the redeemed in the new heavens and new earth fulfill God's purposes for His people with respect to the theme of rest in general, it fulfills His purposes for them in the commands for *Sabbath-rest*. That is why Hebrews shifts from *katapausis* to *sabbatismos*. There is absolutely no way to make this verse mean anything about Christians having to worship and rest one day in seven without ripping the text away from everything else Heb 3:7–4:10 says. This remains the case irrespective of whether the person who enters God's rest in verse 10 is Jesus or the individual Christian.

I am grateful that Pipa's experience of a Sabbatarian approach to Sunday has been a positive one. As long as it remains so for him and his family and those in his orbit of influence, I would violate other biblical passages if I tried to discourage his practice. In my experience, however, most Sabbatarian Christians have not had nearly as positive an experience. If I were convinced that the Bible mandated sabbatarianism, then I would work at least as hard (!) as Pipa to make it a positive experience for myself, my family, and those I shepherd. Personally, I am glad I do not see the Scriptures as coming anywhere close to mandating it because it appears to me to have been one of those unnecessary obstacles that Paul wants to do away with in texts like 1 Cor 9:19–23, which over the centuries has kept too many Christians from really delighting in the Lord and too many unbelievers from ever coming to the Lord. For four years in the 1980s, I lived first in Scotland and then in England, where Sabbatarianism, at least among Christians and to a certain extent the general culture, was much more pronounced than it has been during any of the times and in any of the places I have lived in the U.S. It had its strengths to be sure, and, realizing that, as a guest to the British cultures, I would not overturn general Christian conviction singlehandedly, I applied Paul's "all things to all people" and tried to fit in. But I watched children consistently resist even the best, well-intentioned efforts of their parents to implement it, and many of those children are not following Jesus today. I am haunted by the question of whether things could have been different.

Response by Charles P. Arand

My first experience with "blue laws" occurred in the summer of 1980. I had spent most of my childhood growing up in southern Wisconsin around the Milwaukee area. It was strong Lutheran country with a larger German population. Then, in August 1980, my bride of two weeks and I moved down to St. Louis, Missouri, where I was to begin my program of theological education at Concordia Seminary. We moved into our apartment on a Saturday. After we came home from church the next morning, we changed our clothes and began to set up our apartment. But we needed to do a little cleaning first. So we went down to the local supermarket in order to purchase a broom, a dustpan, and some cleaning supplies. To our surprise, we were not allowed to do so. The checkout clerk informed us that it was contrary to Missouri law. Since then most of the blue laws in Missouri have been repealed. But that was my first experience.

And so it was with a great deal of interest that I read Dr. Pipa's paper in which he appeared not to be against those kinds of civil ordinances. In response, I'd like to make a number of observations, both positive and then critical.

The title of the paper immediately caught my attention: "The Christian Sabbath." As I read the paper, I realized that the title appears to have been taken from the Westminster Confession (21.7). At the same time, I thought, aren't all the views being presented here "Christian" views? What makes this *the* Christian view? To be sure, Pipa presents one Christian view, a view that insists on strict Sunday observance, based in part on biblical common sense, and based in part on cultural necessities arising out of specific English and Anglo-American concerns. It is a view that certainly had a significant impact upon the American Christian scene, particularly in the nineteenth century and the first half of the twentieth century.

As I read through the paper, I had much the same experience as I did when I read through MacCarty's paper regarding the Adventist view. I began reading it with a great deal of enjoyment, particularly as he explained the various features of God's rest on the seventh day. As one who believes that Christians have too often become exclusively second and third article (of the Apostles' Creed: redemption and sanctification) people, I appreciate a renewed emphasis on the first article (creation) as the context for the story of redemption and as providing the contours for God's story regarding the reclaiming and renewal of His creation. But what started out as an invitation to share in the restful delight of God soon turned into a sense of burden with regard to the requirements and obligations that subsequently emerged as Pipa expounded upon Sabbath obligations for Christians.

Pipa consistently uses language such as "correct observance" or "proper observance" of the Sabbath. Similarly, this involves observing "the entire day" or "the whole day." Why not simply say, "Observe the Sabbath. Rest! Listen to God's Word"? But his language makes it seem more that man was made for the Sabbath (that is, to observe it correctly, properly, and completely) than that the Sabbath was made for man (for rest and delight in the celebrating of God's works in creation and redemption through the hearing of the Word). In other words, at times it seemed as if the benefit of observing Sabbath-rest derived more from correct human observance and less from the Word of God as He speaks to us. But those are probably my Lutheran sensitivities manifesting themselves.

With regard to the section in which Pipa explained his understanding of Gen 2:2 (pp. 119–23), I have a few thoughts, most of which are in agreement. On page 120, Pipa makes the point that God established the "principle of Sabbath-keeping by resting." In his subsequent development, Pipa does a good job highlighting why God rested and what that might mean as pattern for our restful delight of the Sabbath. In spite of those parallels or similarities, it would have been good also to see what differences, if any, there might be. In other words, I would have also liked to see a little development of the contrast between God's resting and ours, and what each means for our understanding of God and of what it means to be human.

As he unfolded his explanation as to why God rested, I appreciated the emphasis that creation was exactly as God intended and that He "expressed delight in creation" and was "refreshed" (Exod 31:17). I couldn't agree more with the idea of God stepping back to contemplate with pleasure the beauty of His creation. Pipa's words reminded me how Protestants of all stripes need to work harder to develop a Christian aesthetic, not least in light of thinkers like A. Leopold, who has proposed an ecological aesthetic with regard to the creation.[18] "Beauty," and especially the creation of the beautiful as a Christian vocation, has received too little attention from the Puritan tradition but also from us Lutherans. We have done much better with music than with the graphic arts, in terms of actual creation or performance, as well as in terms of the theory or theology behind creation and performance of the beautiful.

The discussion on God's blessing the seventh day was intriguing, and there are points with which I concur. Certainly God blessed the day. I'm not quite sure how Pipa drew the conclusion from the blessing in Gen 2:2–3 that God thereby "consecrated the seventh day for man to keep the Sabbath" (p. 122). I do think he makes a good point two paragraphs later that when God blessed the day He "assigned it special purpose." Indeed, God's word of blessing is the power that results in fruitfulness and abundance. Pipa does a good job of showing this with regard to the procreation of the animals. But I would like to see a little more clarity on the "special purpose" for which God assigned the seventh day and how the blessing brings it about. Luther, for example, pointed to the importance of the proclamation of the Word in order to create and continue the conversation between God and His chosen people, which He initiates but in which they also participate, individually but also in community.

As we move on to the section in which Pipa speaks about the "moral ground for keeping the Sabbath," a number of questions arose in my mind. Pipa's argument is weakened a bit by his presumption (p. 124) that the nature and unity of the Decalogue is clear. The Sabbath commandment is an expression of God's universal moral will for all people, and all people have some sense of that in their own struggles to define proper worship, along with their frequent concentration on getting the sacred performance right, the proper rituals properly performed. But precisely how the Decalogue functions as moral law and how people recognize it as moral law, as something woven into the very fabric of creation or written on the heart, needs to be stated clearly for the sake of communicating this truth to the world, not least in the increasingly post-Christian West.

---

18. See A. Leopold, *A Sand County Almanac and Sketches Here and There* (London: Oxford University Press, 1968), 165–76. See also J. B. Callicott, "The Land Aesthetic," in *Companion to the Sand County Almanac: Interpretive and Critical Essays* (Madison: University of Wisconsin Press, 1987), 157–71.

In support of the Ten Commandments as moral law (and not ceremonial laws), Pipa cites Matt 22:37–40 where Christ speak about the two greatest commandments. Pipa sees this as a summary of the two tables of the Decalogue. I tend to agree. But Christ also concludes His statement with, "On these two commandments depend the whole Law and the Prophets" (NASB). It seems as if He uses the twofold command not only to summarize the Ten Commandments but to summarize the whole of covenant law ("law" here would refer to Torah in its entirety)—and for that matter, I would argue, of natural law. From a hermeneutical perspective, I'd have to ask, do only those things explicitly mentioned in the New Testament constitute moral law? To be sure, the New Testament brings into bold relief, at times, natural moral law. But as footnote 11 on page 125, indicates, moral law is "an unchangeable expression of God's moral will for mankind." That would include everyone, Christian and non-Christian.

Here it would be helpful to discuss clearly and thoroughly the relationship of natural law and biblical laws. Are moral laws accessible and knowable by all people, including non-Christians? This would seem to be a reasonable conclusion since they are woven into the fabric of creation and written on the hearts of all people. And certainly even non-Christian societies recognized the importance of honoring parents and not murdering or stealing. What might this mean for the Sabbath commandment? Or can moral law be recognized only on the basis of special revelation, namely, the Bible? Luther's position may have its problems in a post-Christian culture, but it at least suggests parameters and starting points for the discussion of how we communicate within a culture that does not accept biblical authority.

Pipa provides a helpful discussion on the relationship between moral laws, ceremonial laws, and civil laws. It would have been good, though, to provide stronger justification for the assertion that "all the ceremonial and judicial laws of Israel are based on the Ten Commandments" (p. 127). I agree that the Ten Commandments have ramifications in the realm of civil and ceremonial laws (p. 127). But one needs a well-developed hermeneutic in order to sort out which ones are prescriptive for all time and which ones are not (I think we'd agree that at least a few expectations and obligations were prescriptive for Israel but are not so for us).

In connection with this last point, Pipa also indicates the Sabbath commandment "teaches us how to structure the day *in or-*

der to derive the most benefit from it" (p. 132, emphasis added). I assume that "it" means to derive the most benefit from the day, as opposed to the rest potentially experienced on that day, for he goes on to write that this means we devote one "entire day" or "one whole day" to God. I couldn't help but wonder what additional benefit one receives from devoting an entire 24-hour day to the Sabbath versus, say, a 12-hour day? With regard to structuring our domestic life, he seems to suggest that "playing" should cease as well. With regard to social responsibility (p. 134), it would have been helpful for Pipa to have stated more precisely the logic that says one may not legislate going to church, but one may mandate the closing of businesses and shops. If one may legislate businesses and shops to be closed, why not legislate that people go to church? Or is it simply more of a pragmatic issue of enforcing such a law?

I am uneasy with the way Pipa moves easily from laws given to Israel in the OT to making them binding requirements upon Christians in the NT. What are the hermeneutics behind such moves? It seems as if Pipa does not see much of a difference between OT Israel and NT Israel. A discussion of the relationship between the old covenant and the new covenant would help to clarify that. Clearly, there are differences. One of those differences is promise and fulfillment. In Christ all the promises of the old covenant find their fulfillment. Christ is the new Israel. Among other things, the NT makes clear that Israel (the church) is no longer a theocracy. It is no longer a union of church and state. Those become two separate entities in the NT period as Christ declares that His kingdom is not of this world. Thus, the idea of laws made by the state (say, the United States or Great Britain) regarding matters pertaining to God (such as enforcing the Sabbath prohibition to cease from work) no longer makes sense.

While I do appreciate Pipa's drawing on confessional writings of his tradition, such as the Westminster Standards and the Heidelberg Catechism, I did not detect any sense that he was aware of the precise way in which the Standards or the Heidelberg Catechism are embedded in their own cultures. Within the Lutheran tradition, we have had to struggle with the changing cultural circumstances in which we find ourselves. In sixteenth-century Germany, our confessional writings carried with them a binding force that was enforced by the state. That is not the case in the United States. To recognize the historical contexts from which our confessions came and to which they were addressed need not diminish their abiding theological contributions. But it does need to be taken into account. And so, we recognize that even Luther's catechisms had in view the way in which the medieval church regarded holy things (relics versus the Word of God) and the legalistic demands connected with a medieval view of sin and penance.

With regard to Pipa's thoughts regarding Jesus and the Sabbath, several thoughts occurred to me. I agree with his emphasizing that we use the day of rest for the purpose of gathering for worship, edification, and fellowship (p. 142). Luther consistently did so as well. The woodcut that he used for his Small Catechism depicts a gathering of people within the church listening to the preacher. They are devoting themselves to the Word. Over their shoulders is a window through which we see outside to the hills and woods. On the hill is a man gathering wood rather than devoting himself to the Word. In one of the more important writings of his later years, "On the Councils and the Church," Luther defines the church in terms of the delivery of the Word in its oral, written, and sacramental forms. He then follows it up by describing the church's response (the response of faith) in terms of prayer, praise, and catechesis. This Word sanctifies the day for Luther, rather than any particular human action or observance.[19]

That brings us to the New Testament Sabbath day. I understand from Pipa's discussion that moral law is given to all people for all time. Positive law refers to commands given to certain people at certain times; thus, it refers to commands that are "not inherently right or wrong" (p. 145). Pipa appears to place the regulation of keeping the Sabbath correctly and entirely into the category of moral law, but he places the specific day (the seventh-day Sabbath) into the category of positive law (p. 145). In this reasoning, because the particular day observed belongs to positive law, that day may be changed. He then cites the Westminster Confession's assertion that "from the beginning of the world to the resurrection of Christ, [I presume the day for worship] was the last day of the week; and, from the resurrection of Christ [again, I presume the day for worship] was changed into the first day of the week, which in Scripture is

---

19. *Church and Ministry III*, Luther's Works 41, ed. J. Pelikan (Philadelphia: Fortress Press, 1966), 3–178.

called the Lord's Day, and is to be continued to the end of the world, as the Christian Sabbath."

Pipa's distinction between moral law and positive law helped me to understand his position, and yet it also created some confusion. The distinction allows me to see why he insists on a correct observance of the entire "Sabbath" day while not insisting that it be on the seventh day of the week. At the same time this point raised several questions.

First, how does one determine whether a particular command is moral law or positive law? I can see the distinction with regard to a command given to Moses to lead the people of Israel out of Egypt. That command was not given to everyone. But reference to the seventh day is located in Gen 2:3 as part of creation, which would seem to suggest that it provided a pattern for all people of all time. In addition, the Exodus 20 text grounds its command in Genesis 2. Now, if one were to say that the Decalogue in that particular form was given to one particular people (namely, the Israelites) and that God patterned their rest on His own rest on the seventh day, that would make sense.

Second, if the particular day is a matter of positive law rather than moral law, why insist on Sunday? I grant (and affirm) that there are good reasons for making Sunday the day of rest as well as the day we gather for worship. But the Westminster Confession seems to go beyond regarding this as a good idea and instead treats it as a command: "From the resurrection of Christ [the day for worship] was changed into the first day of the week . . . and *is to be continued to the end of the world*, as the Christian Sabbath." But if it belongs to positive law and is a command, where do we find the change commanded? And who commands the change? And when was the command given? I agree with the reasons cited by Pipa from the New Testament and the early church literature as to why the day was changed. But none of these involved a command. Thus, I hesitate to call it even positive law.

Interestingly, in footnote 31 Pipa acknowledges that some interpreters simply insist on one day out of seven (it doesn't matter which). But Pipa states, "Exegetically *I prefer* the interpretation that refers to the seventh day as the seventh chronologically" (emphasis added). This seems to suggest that the move of the day is less one that involves a command belonging to positive law than a matter of preference. Personally, I think that is the better route to go. But the Westminster

Confession seems to be saying much more than that with its declaration the shift in day "is to be continued to the end of the world."

Again I find helpful Luther's natural-law or law-of-creation criterion for determining what is binding universally for all time. To some extent everyone can recognize the need and value of a day of rest because it puts us in tune with God's design as it contributes to the flourishing of His creatures. Rather than speaking of moral law and positive law at this point, I suggest speaking of the distinction between God's moral/natural law and the way we appropriate that law into our lives through the use of our reason and imagination. Here I want to distinguish between *what* God mandated and *how* we carry it out. For example, God has commanded us to love our neighbor. We are to contribute to his or her well-being. But how we best can do that is given to us to use reason and figure out. That love must be tailored to the specific needs and personality of the person expressing the love and the person receiving it. The same applies with respect to the Sabbath question. *That* we rest and attend to the hearing of God's Word is a given. *How* and *when* we do so is left to the church to find the best ways.

Finally, at times I detected perhaps too sharp of a distinction between the secular and sacred in the sense that the secular is "bad" or at least inferior to the sacred. For example, in his discussion of how we profane the day, Pipa notes "by doing one's pleasure on it" (p. 167). I fail to see how taking pleasure in those things that one delights in on the other six days of the week (things that pertain to God's creaturely gifts) can profane the Lord's Day. Earlier in the essay, when Pipa spoke of the Sabbath as expressing delight, I took that to mean delight in *all* of God's handiwork in creation, as well as His work of redemption. I think it would also include delighting in the activities where we function as God's coworkers in creation. But I had the sense that Pipa has in view exclusively "spiritual pleasures of worship and service" or "greater and nobler things" (p. 169). Obviously, we are to seek the Lord's pleasures and not our own, but how to define them appropriately in each cultural setting and universally—both levels have to be taken seriously—is the question, which Pipa leaves unanswered.

Overall, I appreciated Pipa's argument as it forced me to grapple with a number of things about which I had not given much thought. It also compelled me to wrestle with and clarify my own thinking about how I make certain theological distinctions and hermeneutical moves, as well as the challenge of thinking through how each of us has been influenced in our readings by the specific cultural, historical, and traditional contexts from which we come.

Final Remarks
Joseph A. Pipa

My hearty thanks to Chris Donato for designing and managing an excellent project. I really appreciate the dialogical character of the book and the unique opportunity for each contributor to have a final clarifying word. I also want to thank my fellow contributors for their thoughtful and challenging articles and responses. My assignment here is to respond to the responders with a final word. I will divide my responses under the headings of clarifications, misunderstandings, and areas for further work.

First, though, a general remark about hermeneutics is in order. It is clear that the main issue behind my differences with Drs. Arand and Blomberg is hermeneutical, about which there are at least three areas of dispute. To begin with, how does one look at the unity of the Bible and the perpetual requirements of the Ten Commandments? I believe that whatever the New Testament does not abrogate remains binding; Arand and Blomberg are more subjective in determining what carries over from the old covenant to the new.

Second, how does one treat conclusions derived by good and necessary consequence (decidedly not proof-texting, but rather what does the Holy Spirit teach His church by inference)? "Good and necessary consequence" is the principle of deriving doctrines that are the natural deduction of things the Scripture states plainly. Christ responded to the Sadducees concerning the doctrine of the resurrection (Matt 22:31–32) by deriving the doctrine of the resurrection from how God speaks about Himself. This is the method the early church used to develop the doctrine of the Trinity, for example. In other words, there will not be a proof text for every point, but Arand and Blomberg seem, along with MacCarty, to limit all exegetical discussion to proof-texting. Third comes the principle that Scripture interprets Scripture. The interpreter does not need natural law or archeological findings to determine the meaning of Scripture or to figure out which of the Ten Commandments is binding and in what way. Their methods strike me as subjective and not grounded in the above principle. With these differences in view, obviously we will interpret the Bible differently.

Clarifications

I appreciate Dr. Arand's challenge to my title (the "Christian Sabbath") and see how it could appear arrogant. I chose the title not to say that mine is the only Christian approach, but because I maintain that the Sabbath commandment is binding on the New Testament church and that it is correct to refer to Sunday as the Christian Sabbath (indeed, just as the Westminster Confession 21.7 does).

Dr. Arand also objects to my use of the words "correct" or "proper observance" and concludes that my language makes it appear that man was made for the Sabbath and not the Sabbath for man. His mistake here is confusing careful obedience with a burden. I doubt that he would apply the same principle to precise prohibitions to murder or adultery. He further asks, "Are moral laws accessible and knowable by all people, including non-Christians?" And if so, "What might this mean for the Sabbath commandment?" (p. 200). I believe that human beings in their consciences have some grasp of all of the Ten Commandments (see Rom 2:14–16), and with respect to the Sabbath commandment, I would note that almost all—if not all—religions require special holy days. Hence, just as a person has some concept of the sanctity of life, he has a concept of the necessity of sacred time.

As to the question, How does one determine whether a particular commandment is moral or positive? I sought to answer that by the offering illustrations. When the Bible changes a law (laws of consanguinity or dietary laws, for example), that change is obviously positive. A moral law is as unchangeable as the God who gave it. Dr. Blomberg challenges me as to what other commandment had positive elements (p. 189). I direct his attention to the commandment to honor one's father and mother (cf. Deut 5:16 with Eph 6:3).

Dr. Arand wonders about the insistence on Sunday if the day is a positive law. I insist on Sunday as the new day because the Lord changed the day in the New Testament. The church is not free to set the day (Col 2:17). With respect to Dr. Arand's charge that I make a dichotomy between secular and sacred by emphasizing that one is not to do his own pleasure on the Sabbath (p. 204), I note that I am simply interpreting Isa 58:13; God is the one who makes the distinction with respect to the Sabbath.

I agree with Dr. MacCarty's assertion that the seventh-day Sabbath was different from the festival Sabbaths, but what I am seeking to demonstrate is that the phrase Paul uses, "festival, new moon, or a Sabbath day (days)" is a technical phrase that refers specifically to the seventh-day Sabbath as well as festival Sabbaths. He asks, "Where in the Sabbath commandment are references to 'special Sabbaths (new moon, seventh year, and jubilee) and religious feasts' to be found?" (p. 175). I point out in my chapter that these three terms are often used together to describe the special holy days of Jewish worship (2 Chron 8:13; 31:3; and Lev 23:1–25). I am operating on the principle that the Ten Commandments, called the Ten Words, are a summary of God's will for His people. All regulations may be traced back to them. The concept of holy convocation, which was first applied to the seventh-day Sabbath, was used of the festival days (Lev 23:2–4). The Day of Atonement is called "a Sabbath of complete rest" in Lev 23:32: "It is to be a Sabbath of complete rest to you, and you shall humble your souls; on the ninth of the month at evening, from evening until evening you shall keep your Sabbath." The festivals had special days of worship, and sometimes the Sabbath restriction of work was applied directly to them—"neither shall you do any work on that day" (v. 28). Furthermore, in my opinion, Dr. MacCarty has not interacted with my exegesis of Col 2:16–17 (on p. 146).

Dr. MacCarty asserts that Christ completed His work when He cried out, "It is finished!" and then rested on the seventh day (p. 179). I acknowledge that He had completed the active satisfaction of God's just wrath, but He still had to endure the punishment of death and burial. His work was completed on the first day when He rose from the dead, having paid the penalty of physical death. The prophecy in Ps 118:22–24 teaches this principle: "The stone which the builder rejected has become the chief corner stone. This is the Lord's doing; it is marvelous in our eyes. This is the day which the Lord has made; let us rejoice and be glad in it" (NASB). This psalm prophecies that Christ finished His work when He was vindicated by His resurrection. This vindication took place in the resurrection (see 1 Pet 2:7; also compare Ps 2:7 with Acts 13:33 and Heb 1:5; 5:5; see also 1 Cor 15:13–14).

With respect to the breaking of bread in Acts 20:7, I argue, in my response to Dr. MacCarty (p. 77), that the reference must be to the Lord's Supper since Paul delayed his trip until that Sunday. (In that same response, I deal with his interpretation of Acts 20:7; 1 Cor 16:1–2; and Rev 1:10.)

Dr. Blomberg takes exception (p. 190) to my development of the first great commandment referring to the First Table (Exod 20:1–12) of the Ten Commandments and the second great commandment to the Second Table (vv. 13–17). Regarding Matt 19:18, he asserts that the command to honor one's father and mother is mentioned out of order, and there is no reference to the coveting commandment in that summary (Exod 20:17). He concludes that the second great commandment—"You shall love your neighbor as yourself"—is not a summary of the Second Table of the Ten Commandments. Jesus changes the order for practical reasons, and his omission of the command not to covet in no way militates against the summary; He does not mention the command not to covet by direct quotation but rather by giving the rich young man a directive (Matt 19:21). By telling him to sell his possessions, Jesus exposes his heart. If He had said, "You shall not covet," the man's answer would have been the same ("I have kept all these," v. 20). But when Jesus commands him to sell everything and give the proceeds to the poor, He exposes his covetousness, which is seen in the result: "He went away grieving, because he had many possessions" (v. 22).

Neither is it of any significance that it was later in Jesus' ministry when He paired Deut 6:5 and Lev 19:8 as the two great commandments. He does so in Matt 22:37–40 in response to a question about the greatest commandment. The parallel, however, is clear: just like the First Table of the Ten Commandments has to do primarily with our relation to God and the Second Table our neighbor, so too do the two great commandments. Jesus goes on to say that these two fulfill the Law and the Prophets because the message of the prophets was the application of the law to the OT church. And as I have asserted, all of the laws of the Torah relate to the Ten Words. Moreover, Dr. Blomberg ignores my other arguments for the perpetual validity of the Ten Commandments (pp. 125, 136). To those arguments I would add that the new covenant promise of the law written on the hearts of the people (Jer 31:33) must be a reference to the Ten Commandments. Therefore, the Ten Commandments continue to be God's absolute moral standard in the new covenant.

Dr. Arand queries, "Do only those things explicitly mentioned in the New Testament constitute moral law?" (p. 200). I answer in the negative. The moral law is revealed in the Ten Commandments and worked out in both testaments. As I wrote above, what is not abrogated in the New Testament continues to be morally binding.

I would add to this that love divorced from law leads to a subjectivistic ethic. Dr. Arand writes, "But how we best can do that is given to us to use reason and figure out. That love must be tailored to the specific needs and personality of the person expressing the love and the person receiving it" (p. 204). The problem with this approach is that it implies we have no objective word from God. Both Drs. Arand and Blomberg leave us in an ethical wilderness with no objective compass.

I believe an unbiased reader will note that Dr. Blomberg does not deal fairly with my exposition of Christ's teaching on the Sabbath. With respect to Christ and the Sabbath, Dr. Blomberg concurs that the correct observance of the Sabbath was important to Jesus. But then he queries, How do we know that Jesus was committed to this as a one-day-in-seven observance (p. 192)? We know this because Jesus never did away with any of the requirements of God's moral law. While on the other hand, Scripture clearly delineates the laws Christ intended to abrogate.

Surely Blomberg knows the difference between lawful vocations and those things that are necessary exceptions to the requirement not to work on the Lord's Day. Just because something is lawful the other six days does not mean it is appropriate on the Lord's Day. He suggests that I say that the only good is that which saves lives (p. 192). But I never wrote that the only good is that which saves lives. The principle I sought to enunciate is that *every* activity is to be examined by answering three questions: (1) Does the work promote the purposes of the day? (2) Is it necessary for the preservation of life and property? and (3) Is it a necessary act of mercy? Nor did I suggest that one may only do "religious good." Furthermore, Blomberg twists my words ("saving a life only 'if one has opportunity within one's calling and circumstance'") when he asks the question should I not perform CPR if I am not a doctor (p. 193)? By the term *circumstance*, however, I am saying that if in God's providence one has opportunity to save a life, one should do so.

Dr. Blomberg's main problem in his response to this section is his failure to apply the principle that whatever promotes the purpose of the day is the standard for how one evaluates what is to be done. He does not accept that the primary purpose of the day is the worship and service of the Lord in a more narrow sense (while still recognizing that we do all things to God's glory). If one is committed to this purpose, one will make wise decisions about what one does or does not do on Sunday, the Christian Sabbath.

With respect to Col 2:16–17, Blomberg asks, "In what way does ceasing from work on Saturday, apart from the practice of rest and worship, point forward to the Messiah?" (p. 191). I answer, it is not that ceasing from work on Saturday pointed to Christ but that the observance of the day of rest at the end of the week pointed to the rest-giver who was yet to come. After all, Paul says the Sabbath (in the minds of his readers, the seventh-day Sabbath) was fulfilled in the work of Christ (Col 2:17).

Further, Blomberg accuses me of being inconsistent. He asserts that I say the church or a Christian may change the day (p. 194). However, with respect to the change of day, I clearly write that it is not the church's prerogative. A Christian is not free to decide; Christ, the Lord of the Sabbath changed the day. There is no contradiction in what I say. Moreover, there will be no change of the day in this age; only God can change a positive law; and as long as the law remains, there is a moral responsibility to keep it. For example, the church is not free to declare in the future that once again it is permissible for siblings to marry.

With respect to Heb 4:9, Blomberg asserts that the command for Sabbath rest has nothing to do with Sabbath-keeping, ignoring the import of *sabbatismos,* which means Sabbath-keeping. And I do not think my exegesis rips the verse out of the flow of the argument (p. 196). To the contrary, I invite the reader to evaluate my interpretation of Heb 4:9–10 in light of the inspired author's argument.

As to why I teach that the whole day is to be sanctified, that is the requirement of God's law. He is the one who distinguishes one day from the other six. He clearly does not say just have a time for sacred service; rather, He articulates that the seventh day is a day of complete rest (Lev 23:3; see also Chrysostom's comments on

p. 152). We observe the entire day so as not to lose the benefits of the day.

As to Dr. Blomberg's conclusion, that he submitted to a Sabbatarian church culture in order to be "all things to all people" (p. 196). Paul clearly distinguishes between those things that were cultural customs and those that were the law of God (see 1 Cor 9:21, where he equates the law of God and the law of Christ). The careful observance of the Lord's Day is not a cultural issue; it is a matter of God's law.

Misunderstandings

Dr. Arand misunderstands my application of the creation ordinance. He asks how I can draw the conclusion from blessing that the day is consecrated (p. 199). I remind him that God did two things to the day: He blessed it and He sanctified it. Its consecration grows out of both acts.

In response to Drs. Arand and Blomberg's calumny that I build my case on the Westminster Standards and not Scripture, I believe I anchored each part of my article on the biblical text and thus ask the reader to respond to the exegesis and not the straw man—that I built my case on confessional documents. Moreover, Blomberg's assertion is false that the Westminster Standards are based "on so little *exegesis* of Scripture" (p. 190). Apparently, he is unaware of the exegetical work that undergirded the Standards, not least as seen in his remark about the Baptist tradition (ibid.). The early Baptists of this country held to the Philadelphia Confession (1742), which took exactly the same position as the Standards on the Sabbath (22.7–8). I employ the Standards because I am convinced they are a good summary of what the Bible teaches. The same holds true with respect to the interpretation of the positive law application to the change of day from the seventh to the first. I seek to ground the concept in exegesis and quote from confessional sources to illustrate. I should, however, have recognized that these sources would not be as useful in certain contexts and thus used them more sparingly.

Dr. Blomberg asks with respect to the premise I build at the outset of my essay, "How did you shift from insisting the Sabbath had to be the seventh day of the week to saying it had only to be one day in seven?" (p. 189). But I am not shifting from the seventh day by this language, for I believe the commandment requires one day in seven. In the Old Testament the seventh day was the required day of worship, just like the first day is in the New Testament. Both Drs. Arand and MacCarty have misunderstood my comment in footnote 31: there I say that I prefer the *chronological* interpretation of one day in seven (as opposed to *any* day), namely, the day we call Saturday.

Dr. MacCarty misunderstands my remarks on page 127 : "All these things and practices were types of Christ and His work and thus would pass away." He asks, "What specifically are the ceremonial elements of the Decalogue's commandments prohibiting murder, adultery, stealing, and coveting that were 'types of Christ and His work' and 'would pass away'?" (pp. 185–86). My remarks here apply only to the commandment forbidding blasphemy, which is clear from the remainder of the line he quotes, "But the moral requirement of this specific commandment would remain." So, then, "all these things" are temple worship, sacrifices, and religious festivals.

As an aside, I do not think I leave unanswered the question, What are the appropriate pleasures of the Lord's Day? (See my essay on pp. 141–44). Also, I do not say that when Christ appeared after His resurrection that it was only on the first day of the week (p. 181). My claim with regard to the resurrection appearances is that where the Holy Spirit reveals the day in the Gospel accounts, it is always the first day of the week: "The church has always recognized that the change of day was first initiated by the resurrection appearances of Christ on the first day of the week when all of the New Testament's *recorded appearances* took place" (p. 164, emphasis added).

I do not ground my argument from Heb 4:9–10 on the ceremonial seventh-day aspect of the Sabbath commandment being repealed, but on the logic of the writer to the Hebrews: a Sabbath-keeping remains (v. 9); it was changed to the first day because Christ rested on the first day from His work that He had done. This is reinforced by clear New Testament and historical examples of the church worshipping on the first day of the week.

I do not say that the seventh-day Sabbath was a historical type like sacrifices but that it pointed to the completion of creation and the promise of redemption. While the first-day Sabbath points to the completion of redemption, we have already begun to participate in the rest that God has provided for us.

If I was unclear, I apologize. I did not intend to imply that the promised future rest was not available to Old Testament believers. Actually, what I wrote was, "The old covenant people looked forward to the accomplishment of redemption, so they kept the Sabbath at the end of the week. After the Rest Giver had accomplished His work, the NT church kept its Sabbath on the day He entered into His rest, signifying that although we wait for the consummation, we already have begun to participate in this rest" (pp. 163–64). They, like we, were saved by believing in God as Savior—for them the Savior to come; for us the Savior who has come.

Areas for Further Work and Unanswered Questions

I would agree that more should be done to show the relation of the ceremonial and judicial laws to the moral law. Basically, I assert the relationship on the basis of how the Old Testament works out these relationships. For example, the civil sanctions of the death penalty apply to the moral law, and all the worship laws spring out of the commandment forbidding idolatry (Exod 20:4–6). True, I did not do this for all the commandments, but since MacCarty mentions adultery, I will speak to that issue. Two ceremonial or judicial applications of the commandment against adultery (v. 14) would be the test of unfaithfulness in Numbers 5 or the degrees of consanguinity in marriage in Leviticus 18. In the same manner the various festival holy days, by the fact that they are called "days of rest," are related to the Sabbath commandment, which heads the discussion in Leviticus 23. Of course, in such limited space one cannot develop this hermeneutical principle more fully.

I do claim that ceremonial elements or positive-law elements are stated in the commandment to honor one's parents as well as in the Sabbath commandment. Notice in Eph 6:3 how the apostle Paul restates the ceremonial element of the commandment to honor one's parents, changing "living long in the land" (i.e., Israel) to "may live long on the earth."

Admittedly, I appear inconsistent in saying that the state should legislate the closing of shops and businesses but not compel one to attend church. I continue to wrestle with the application of the Ten Commandments to the contemporary civil code. I am opting for an application of the law of God that, on the one hand, does not demand faith in the true God while on the other does not publicly promote sin or idolatry. I think this is an area for further reflection. Since most everyone agrees that the Ten Commandments reflect natural law, then they should agree that they are not just for the church. In fact, the Sabbath commandment addresses the behavior of the sojourner (noncovenant inhabitant) in the land (Exod 20:10; see also Neh 13:15–22).

I think the so-called "blue laws" worked well in our country in the past. Dr. MacCarty accuses me of mixing religion with political power and writes, "Whenever religion has mixed with political power, the result has been explosive: conflict, witch hunts, war, atrocities, and now terrorism" (p. 186). I would ask in response, what is the difference in applying the creation ordinance of monogamous marriage to our criminal law and applying the creation ordinance of the Sabbath to our criminal law? What is the penalty for polygamy? Did public laws against blasphemy lead to radicalism or violence?

I would answer Arand's statement that "the idea of laws made by the state (either the United States or Great Britain) regarding matters pertaining to God (such as enforcing the Sabbath prohibition to cease from work) no longer makes sense" in a similar manner (p. 201). I do not think that one needs a theocracy to enforce these laws. Sunday laws, along with property and marriage laws, are creation ordinances and have been the basis of civil legislation in Western countries affected by the Reformation. One does not need a union between church and state to have such laws.

I would agree that there is a need to work more fully on the concept of the eighth day referring to the first day of the week. But note that the early church fathers who offered this interpretation also defended their worship on the first day of the week.

Dr. Blomberg is correct that I do not deal with Matt 5:17–20 and should do so (p. 191). Here I would simply point out that Christ Himself shows the continuing validity of the moral law, by freeing it from the erroneous interpretations of the Jews (Matt 5:21–48). Moreover, Christ's command to come to Him does not abdicate the clear requirements of the Sabbath commandment.

In concluding this section, I will seek to answer a number of Dr. MacCarty's concluding questions (pp. 185–86). In answer to his first question, When did the Reformed tradition first begin to apply Heb 4:10 to the change of day? John Owen, a contemporary of those who wrote the Westminster Standards, was the first I know of to offer this interpretation of that text; but there could have been others.

In the above section on "Misunderstandings," I address Mac-Carty's misreading of my claim that all the ceremonial law was fulfilled in Christ. I also addressed above MacCarty's third question, "How would those commandments be restated with the ceremonial elements removed?"

His fourth question was, "If the seventh-day Sabbath was exclusively for the Jews, why would not the new covenant be exclusively for the Jews since God made it specifically with Israel (Heb 8:8,10)?" I answer that the writer to the Hebrews applies this language about the new covenant to the church, which is God's Israel (Gal 6:16).

The fifth question revolves around the quotation from J. P. Lange: "That the disciples already attribute a particular importance to Sunday, is evidenced by the numeric completeness of their assembly."[20] MacCarty asks, "What is meant by 'numeric completeness of their assembly'?" I assume Lange was referring to the eighth day as the high day of the high Feast of Tabernacles, and the disciples applied that to the first day to show it fulfilled all that had been promised in the feast.

The sixth question, "How does the 'future rest' available to the NT believer differ from the 'future rest' that was available to the OT believer?" The rest is the same, but the writer to the Hebrews said they all died without receiving what was promised (11:39). They were saved, but they lived in the shadows of types and promises. We see the fulfillment of all in Christ; the Rest Giver has come.

I address above the seventh question on the legislation of Sunday laws. His eighth question, "What text says, 'God sanctified the first day of the week?'" can be answered by looking over the hermeneutical principles I laid out at the opening of this conclusion (i.e., it's deduced by good and necessary consequence from the text). Also, the section of my essay on the change of day seeks to answer this question. Add to this the fact that this interpretation of the change of day is confirmed by the near unanimous testimony of the church, and it would appear that it's not on the shaky ground MacCarty thinks.

Again, thank you to Mr. Donato and my fellow contributors. May the Spirit of Christ continue to lead us into all truth.

---

20. J. P. Lange, *Commentary on the Holy Scriptures* (Grand Rapids: Zondervan, 1976), 9:621.

CHAPTER 5

Luther's Radical Reading of the Sabbath Commandment

CHARLES P. ARAND

You are to hallow the day of rest.
What is this? Answer:
We are to fear and love God, so that we do not despise preaching or God's Word, but instead keep that Word holy and gladly hear and learn it.[1]

"You are to hallow the day of rest."[2] So reads the Sabbath commandment. Or does it? At least that is how it reads in the German

---

1. From Luther's Large Catechism (hereafter LC) in R. Kolb and T. Wengert, eds., *The Book of Concord: The Confessions of the Evangelical Lutheran Church*, trans. C. Arand (Minneapolis: Fortress, 2000), 352 para. 6.

2. The numbering of the Ten Commandments continues to be an issue for many. More specifically, which numbering is correct? The problem arises in the biblical text itself. It indicates ten commandments or "words" in Exod 34:28, Deut 4:13 and 10:4. But if you actually count them in either Exod 20:2–17 or in Deut 5:6–21, you will usually arrive at more than ten. There are basically three different ways in the history of the Christian church to categorize the commandments; see appendix C in C. Arand, *That I May Be His Own* (St. Louis: Concordia Publishing House, 2000), 195–97). Of the three traditions, Lutheranism follows the Western Catholic tradition. The question of numbering actually revolves around the prohibition of graven images. Once this is dealt with, everything else falls into place. It is worth noting, however, that the approaches to this commandment reveal not only how the graven images command was explicated but also reveals an underlying hermeneutical approach to the entire Bible.

text of the Ten Commandments in Martin Luther's catechisms. But that can't be right, can it? When it comes to the commandment regarding the Sabbath, Luther appears to exercise considerable freedom in how he renders it and how he interprets it. Three things in particular stand out: First, Luther renders the Sabbath as "a day of rest"[3] without identifying which day of the week this might be.[4] That might depend on when our bodies need rest. Second, Luther establishes a close connection between the First Commandment and the Sabbath commandment. Finally, one sanctifies the day not by obeying any particular regulations but by occupying oneself with the Word of God, which sanctifies all things.[5]

In fact, Luther's treatment of the Sabbath commandment provides an excellent point of entry to Luther's entire biblical hermeneutic that he develops in connection with his Reformation rediscovery of the gospel. Here, more clearly than anywhere else, a person can begin to see how the gospel of Christ gives him a radically Christocentric hermeneutic that many exegetes today might find to be more than a little uncomfortable by his rather free handling of the text. At the same time, in his rendering of the Sabbath commandment, one can also see how for Luther the gospel does not draw us out of this world as if it were some kind of an escape hatch. Instead, the gospel enables us to reembrace our identity as human creatures and with that to embrace our creaturely life as God had designed it.

Thus in order to deal with Luther's explanation of the Sabbath commandment, we need to broaden our investigation and study in order that we might see why he does what he does. To that end we will proceed in a series of concentric circles proceeding from the outer one and moving toward the inner one. We will first examine

---

3. In Luther's Large Catechism he explains that the words *holy day* (or *holiday*) is so called from the Hebrew word *shabbat*, which properly means to rest, that is to cease from work; hence our common expression for "stopping work" literally means "taking a holiday."

4. Luther wrote in "Against the Heavenly Prophets in the Matter of Images and Sacraments" (1525; see Luther's *Werke: Kritische Gesamtausgabe, Schriften* [Weimar: Böhlau, 1883–1993, hereafter *WA*], 8, 81, 26–82; and *Luther's Works*, ed. J. Pelikan [St. Louis: Concordia Publishing House, hereafter *LW*], 40:98): "It is not necessary to observe the Sabbath or Sunday because of Moses' commandment. Nature shows and teaches that one must now and then rest a day, so that man and beast may be refreshed. Moses also recognized in his Sabbath law, for he places the Sabbath under man, as also Christ does (Matt 12[:1ff.] and Mark 3[:2ff.]). For where it is kept for the sake of rest alone, it is clear that he who does not need rest may break the Sabbath and rest on some other day, as nature allows. The Sabbath is also to be kept for the purpose of preaching and hearing the Word of God."

5. Traditionally done by attending worship so that God's people may assemble to hear and discuss His Word and then to offer praise, song, and prayer to Him.

the creation and redemptive context in which Luther chooses to use the Ten Commandments and in light of which he then interprets them. Second, we will look at how he interprets the Ten Commandments as a unity by seeing the Second through the Tenth Commandments as daily expressions of the First Commandment. In other words, they are nine ways of living out the First Commandment. Finally, we will turn to Luther's explanation of the Sabbath commandment itself and show how it differs from the various medieval treatments that were commonplace in his day.

Luther's Interpretation in Light of Genesis and Natural Law

The most striking and perhaps surprising feature of Luther's treatment of the Ten Commandments lies in the larger context in which he interprets them. When most people think of the Ten Commandments, images come to mind of Mount Sinai and the handing of the tablets to Moses. This carries with it two possible implications.

First, we assume that the Ten Commandments were first given to the Israelites and thus to Christians. Are not Christians to obey them simply because they are given in the Bible? After all, we think, what was given to Israel was given to us. I suspect that many Christians today continue to think of the Ten Commandments as having a primarily "religious" character. In other words, they are exclusively a Judeo–Christian thing—although many might admit that they apply also to Muslims in that they acknowledge the Old Testament Scriptures in their Qur'an. The assumption that the Ten Commandments are primarily religious in character enters into our political debates too, like when we argue over whether the Ten Commandments should be posted in public places such as courthouses (and thus it's no surprise that these debates center on whether such a posting constitutes a violation of the separation of church and state).

Second, we then assume that the Ten Commandments should be interpreted within the context of the Israelites' exodus from Egypt, which means they should be interpreted within the context of Exodus 20 and Deuteronomy 5. Certainly that is a point that was brought to the forefront of biblical scholarship in the 1920s with the work of Gerhard von Rad.[6] It was also brought into the Lutheran

---

6. See G. von Rad, *From Genesis to Chronicles: Explorations in Old Testament Theology* (Minneapolis: Fortress, 2005), and *Deuteronomy*, OTL (Louisville: WJK, 1966).

catechetical tradition as expounded by Johann Michael Reu.[7] This means that the Ten Commandments should be interpreted in light of their prologue, which reads: "I am the Lord your God who led you out of Egypt." This verse highlights the gospel event of rescue from bondage, and when read in this manner the Ten Commandments appear to be given as a guide for how the rescued and covenant people should now conduct their lives. In other words, we're led to see them as Ten Words rather than Ten Commandments.

Neither of these assumptions (that the Ten Commandments are for Christians and that they should be interpreted in light of the prologue) should be taken for granted when reading Luther's interpretation on the topic. To be sure, Luther does hold that the Ten Commandments apply to the Christian. After all, he includes them in both of his catechisms! When Luther expounds upon the Ten Commandments in his lectures on Exodus (1525) and Deuteronomy (1525), he interprets them in light of the Exodus event, which he then interprets typologically for the Christian.[8] But when it comes to Luther's catechetical writings (as distinct from his exegetical writings), Luther interprets them within the wider context of Genesis rather than Exodus, which is to say that he interprets them in light of God's created order before interpreting them in light of redemption history.[9]

What does it matter? By doing it this way, Luther highlights the universal context of the Ten Commandments. In other words, they are not a distinctively Christian "thing" or ethic. They apply to everyone by virtue of the truth that everyone was created by God. Luther believed that the entire Ten Commandments applied to Christians not because they appear in Exodus or Deuteronomy but because they express the law of creation.[10] "The Ten Commandments . . . are written in the hearts of all people."[11] In terms of the form in which they come and the sequence in which they are numbered, those applied to the Israelites. Christians are free to use them

---

7. E.g., J. M. Reu, *Catechetics: Theory and Practice of Religious Instruction*, 3rd ed. (Chicago: Wartburg, 1931).

8. For example, baptism provides our counterpart to the exodus event in as much as it frees us from bondage under Satan's rule and dominion.

9. "Created order" simply means the way God intended things to be for all of creation before the fall of man.

10. C. Arand, "Luther on the God Behind the First Commandment," *LQ* 8 (1994): 397–423.

11. *Book of Concord*, LC, 440 para. 67.

of course, but they are not bound to do so simply by virtue of the fact that they appear in this form in Exodus 20 and Deuteronomy 5.

A Radical Christocentric Hermeneutic

Luther's approach to the Ten Commandments may strike some as alarming or perhaps even a bit antinomian. How can he seem to disregard the form and even the substance of the Ten Commandments? This becomes all the more evident by the somewhat radical way in which he both translates and interprets the commandment regarding the Sabbath. His approach can be deemed radically Christocentric. In other words, when the New Testament says that Christ is the end of the Mosaic law, Luther takes that to mean that Christ is the *end* of it—period. This applies to all of the Old Testament laws, whether they are civil or ceremonial. But it also applies to the Ten Commandments, which for Luther are a mixture of ceremonial (e.g., the Sabbath command in the form presented there), civil (e.g., adultery), and moral. In other words there is a sense for Christians that the Ten Commandments do not apply to them. They were literally given to the Israelites. They were not given to Christians. As Christians, we have been freed from all of the Old Testament laws and injunctions and now live in the freedom of the gospel.

This is not to say that Luther was an antinomian. He was not by any means, although this issue has been raised time and again. Already in 1528, there arose what has become known as the "first antinomian controversy" between Johannes Agricola and Philip Melanchthon.[12] In the wake of the first diet of Speyer, the Lutheran princes carried out visitations of the churches within their territories in order to assess their spiritual health and financial conditions. Melanchthon wrote "Instructions for the Visitors of Parish Pastors in Electoral Saxony"[13] in which he urged the visitors to make sure pastors proclaimed law and gospel from the pulpit.

Agricola (perhaps upset for not getting a position at the University of Wittenberg and now teaching at the girl's school in Eisleben) took issue with Melanchthon. Agricola contended that the law in general should be relegated to the courthouse. Pastors had no business

---

12. T. Wengert, *Law and Gospel: Philip Melanchthon's Debate with John Agricola of Eisleben over Poenitentia* (Grand Rapids: Baker, 1997).
13. "Instructions for the Visitors of Parish Pastors in Electoral Saxony," 1528 (*LW* 40, 263–320).

preaching law from the pulpit inasmuch as Christ had freed Christians from it. Christian repentance should be produced not from reflecting upon one's sins in light of the old law; rather, it flows from a reflection on the severe sufferings of Jesus on the cross. After the controversy erupted, Luther was hesitant to intervene right away. But eventually he had to weigh in on the issue. Timothy Wengert regards Luther's exposition of the Ten Commandments in the Large Catechism, published in 1529, as his answer to Agricola. It is worth noting that Luther's exposition of the Ten Commandments comprises the bulk of the Large Catechism, taking up nearly half of the entire book![14]

So no one can claim that Luther was an antinomian. At the same time, a cursory reading of the Ten Commandments in Luther's Large Catechism will yield few distinctively Christian references and allusions. Jesus is not mentioned at all (perhaps one place as judge). Few direct New Testament allusions can be found. Much of it (but not all) may strike the reader as surprisingly "secular" in nature although, to be sure, Luther consistently urges the reader to consider and take seriously the Word of God (i.e., the Commandments). So on what grounds does he do so?

This brings us back to Luther's Christocentric hermeneutic. To confess that Christ is the end of the old covenant law does not render Christians antinomians, much less anarchists. To the contrary, it gives Christians the freedom to go back into the Old Testament and see what is there that they can use for their daily lives. It is a little bit like what happens on Christmas morning with the unwrapping of all the gifts. After all the gifts are opened, mom and dad want to clean up. But before just grabbing boxes, paper, and ribbons to toss in the trash, they sift through all the paper on the floor to make sure they don't throw away something valuable that might be hiding underneath.

Luther is a bit like that when it comes to his approach to the laws in the Old Testament. Christians have been freed from those laws. Yet now they have the freedom to go back into the Old Testament to find that which continues to apply to them. What criterion should guide them—their own arbitrary preferences? No. For Luther, the criterion that guides Christians is natural law or the law of creation.[15]

---

14. For a more detailed analysis, see Arand, "Luther on the God behind the First Commandment."

15. To read more on the idea of natural law or the law of creation, refer to J. Budziszewski, *Written on the Heart: A Case for Natural Law* (Downers Grove, IL: IVP Academic, 1997).

Redemption does not overthrow creation, and so it does not overthrow the law of creation. Instead, redemption recovers and restores creation. For example, salvation in Christ does not do away with marriage (an "order of creation," established at the time of creation). Redemption enables Christians to recover creation and the orders of creation as the way in which God intended us to live out our lives. In a similar way Christians can reembrace God's created design for life as expressed in the Ten Commandments. It is not that the Ten Commandments provide only a distinctively Christian way of living.

The Way Is Opened Up to Embrace the Creaturely

One of the distinctive characteristics of the Reformation lies in the way it revalued the activities of daily life over and against the works of the monastic communities. In the late Middle Ages the Christian life was often bifurcated into two tiers so that there existed "average" Christians and "super" Christians. The former were called *carnali*, or carnal Christians. They could attempt to live according to the Ten Commandments like others, but this would only enable them to climb the ladder so far up to God. In order to climb all the way up, one had to move on to the so-called evangelical counsels—the vows of poverty, chastity, and obedience. In this way one could move toward the sanctified life. These were called the *perfecti*, or the sanctified ones. Luther's recovery of the gospel knocked the legs out of this way of thinking. It enabled one to come back to earth and embrace this earthly life as God's created form even for Christians. Rather than seeking to escape this world, one could embrace it in all of its fullness.

During the 1520s, one can see Luther moving away from a Neoplatonic view of life in which the spiritual was deemed to be of greater importance than the material. We can see this in a number of instances within his catechetical writings. For example, in the early 1520s, Luther tended to regard the threats and promises of the Old Testament as inferior to those of the New Testament. Why? Israel dealt with physical matters like floods, plagues, and droughts in a land flowing with milk and honey. By contrast, the threats and promises of the New Testament dealt with spiritual issues like heaven and hell. By 1529, he no longer thinks in this dualistic scheme. Similarly, in the early 1520s, Luther interpreted the fourth petition of the Lord's

Prayer ("give us this day our daily bread") as referring either to the Lord's Supper or the Word of God.[16] By 1529, he never does so again. Instead, he interprets "daily bread" with reference to the things that pertain to our physical life. "Everything included in the necessities and nourishment for our bodies, such as food, drink, clothing, shoes, house, farm, fields, livestock, money, property, an upright spouse, upright children, upright members of the household, upright and faithful rulers, good government, good weather, peace, health, decency, honor, good friends, faithful neighbors, and the like."[17]

Perhaps Luther is best known for his recovery of the idea of Christian vocation. In the late Middle Ages, vocation pertained primarily, if not exclusively, to those who served in the clerical office. Priests, monks, and nuns had callings from God. They lived and worked in "holy orders." The teaching that we are justified by faith alone and not by our works tore down those walls that separated "second-class" Christians from "first-class" Christians. Every Christian had a calling from God in whatever walk of life they found themselves. The needs of our neighbor within those various walks of life functioned as God's call to serve. Thus, the needs of a husband or wife functioned as God's call for the spouse to serve. The needs of a son or daughter functioned as God's call for parents to take care of their children.

The Ten Commandments functioned as the norm that God designed for how our various relationships (to God, to neighbor, and to creation) were to function. There was a sense in which these were woven into the very fabric of creation and written on the heart. They describe how life functions. In short, life works better when lived according to these norms. One did not even have to know the exact wording of the commandments as laid out in Exodus 20 or Deuteronomy 5. For example, life functions better when husbands and wives love and cherish each other. It is simply not possible for couples to rewrite the "rules" for marriage in such a way that if both agreed to abuse each other verbally, ignore each other, be unfaithful to each other, that they would have a long and happy marriage together. Similarly, a person cannot work 24–7–365 without rest. The body will break down. Blood pressure will climb. Heart attacks will occur.

16. P. Robison, "Luther's Explanation of Daily Bread in Light of Medieval Preaching," *LQ* 13 (1999): 435–47.
17. *Book of Concord*, Small Catechism (hereafter SC), 357 para. 14.

Here it is worth noting that for the most part, the Ten Commandments deal with what might best be called "creaturely matters." That is to say, there is nothing distinctively "spiritual" about the Ten Commandments, as far as Luther's explanations of them were concerned. The First Commandment deals with idolatry. But idolatry occurs only through the misuse of creaturely things where we confuse the Creator with the creature by "deifying" the latter. Second, as creatures of the Creator, we must call upon or name the one we trust. The Sabbath commandment deals with our bodily rest. The fourth deals with honoring our parents (hardly a distinctively Christian phenomenon). The fifth deals with the endangering or harming the lives of our neighbor. The sixth deals with our neighbor's spouse (in other words, adultery). The seventh deals with creaturely possessions. The eighth deals with our need for a good reputation in order to function properly in society. The Ninth and Tenth Commandments, then, deal with coveting the earthly possessions of one's neighbor.

If I were to rearrange Luther's Large Catechism, I would place the exposition of the Ten Commandments directly after the exposition of the first article and before the second article of the Apostles' Creed. In the first article Luther describes all the good things that God has given us. These are creaturely gifts necessary for our creaturely life. The Ten Commandments describe how to use these creaturely things in accord with the purposes for which God created them. It is not by accident that Luther concludes his explanation of the first article with the words, "For all of this I owe it to God to thank and praise, serve and obey him."[18] In the Large Catechism he adds the words, "according to the Ten Commandments." So, by placing them before the second article of the Creed, they would highlight our inability to keep them and hence our need for Christ.

There is a sense where one can find expressions of the Ten Commandments throughout Genesis, even though they are never formally given to human creatures as they were given to Moses on Mount Sinai.[19] Cain knew that it was wrong to kill Abel. Joseph fled Potiphar's wife, for he knew that it was wrong to commit adultery.

---

18. Ibid., 355 para. 2.

19. See J. Barr, "Biblical Law and the Question of Natural Theology," in *The Law in the Bible and in Its Environment,* ed. T. Veijola, Publications of the Finnish Exegetical Society 51 (Helsinki: The Finnish Exegetical Society; Göttingen: Vandenhoeck & Ruprecht, 1990), 1–22.

But nowhere does Genesis describe a direct command to that effect. This is what Luther would call natural law.

And so Luther uses natural law as a criterion for identifying those things in the OT that still apply to Christians. So why does he settle on the Ten Commandments? There are a couple of reasons. First, in large measure, Luther finds them to be the best summary of natural law within the Bible. Theoretically, he could have used Jesus' twofold command: "You shall love the Lord your God with all your heart and with all your soul and with all your mind. This is the great and first commandment. And a second is like it: You shall love your neighbor as yourself."[20] Or he could have selected any one of the series of exhortations with which the apostle Paul concludes many of his letters. But the Ten Commandments provides as handy of a summary as can be found within the Bible.

Second, Luther inherited the Ten Commandments from the tradition. While he was a reformer, he didn't seek to throw out the baby with the bathwater in many instances. Augustine may have been the first to promote the Decalogue's use as such as standard, perhaps as a result of his conflict with the Manicheans. He focused on the twofold command of love for God and love for neighbor as a summary of the Decalogue, which he pointed out is the foundation of Christian morality.[21] Although the Ten Commandments had not been used consistently for the first thousand years after Christ for the most part, the church in the early Middle Ages adopted an ambivalent attitude toward the Decalogue. The reason for this ambivalence may have been the hostility between the synagogue and the church at that time, namely, the tension between the church's roots and its future. On the one hand, Christians saw themselves as recipients of a new covenant that had been sealed with the ultimate sacrifice of Jesus' death, and now a new and better law (encapsulated in the Sermon on the Mount) guided them. In other words, Christianity had superseded Judaism, and thus the NT had superseded the OT.[22] The Ten Commandments became an important catechetical component fairly late in the church's tradition. In the early church the doctrine of the two ways (the way of life and the way of death), as laid out in the Didache and Apostolic Constitutions of the second

---

20. Matthew 22:37–39. All Scripture references are taken from the ESV unless otherwise noted.

21. Arand, *That I May Be His Own*, 35.

22. Ibid.

and third centuries, provided the basis of most moral teaching.[23] Luther was somewhat conservative in these matters. He sought to use what he had inherited but to purge them of any sense of works-righteousness, which undermined the gospel. And so he used the Ten Commandments as they were fairly well established within the catechetical and confessional tradition in his day. In this regard, he even tended to use the version handed down that was memorized among the laity for the sake of not confusing people by changing the words.

Ultimately, Luther's approach to the Ten Commandments gave him a certain freedom when dealing with them. For example, in his catechisms he "rearranged" the Ten Commandments by placing the "appendix" of the First Commandment after the Tenth Commandment (see next section below). Similarly, he chose not to include the specific prohibition regarding graven images (seeing it as a further exposition of the First Commandment). He also did not include the blessing that was attached to the Fourth Commandment in Exodus 20.[24]

Prologue and Epilogue

A good example of Luther's unique approach to the Ten Commandments can be seen in the ways he deals with its "prologue." In Exodus 20, the Decalogue is introduced with the words, "I am the Lord your God who led you out of Egypt." Most commentators today will see this as an indispensable hermeneutical key for interpreting the Commandments. With these words God declares what He has done for His people. Now that He has rescued them from Egypt, God describes how His redeemed people will live. This prologue sets forth the gospel, as it were. What follows sets forth the way in which a redeemed people now live. And so, in light of the prologue (the "gospel"), one must give the Commandments a positive interpretation.

Luther chooses not to include the prologue of the Commandments in either one of his catechisms. For that matter, he does not refer to it in any of his catechetical sermons either. Its exclusion seems odd to us who live in the twenty-first century since we know how foundational the exodus event was to the entire OT. It shaped

---

23. Ibid. Much more information in understanding the origin of the Decalogue can be found in chap. 1 of *That I May Be His Own*.

24. Ibid., 195–97.

and formed the core identity of the Israelites. They recalled the story when observing the Sabbath. The prophets reminded God's people of the story time and time again. Luther does not ignore that observation—much less deny it. He knew the importance of the exodus for the Old Testament. He was, after all, primarily an Old Testament scholar. So what does he do with the prologue? Here it may be helpful to qualify the earlier assertion that Luther does not include the prologue in any of his catechetical writings: occasionally he does cite a portion of the prologue. For example, he will quote the words, "I am the Lord your God," but he generally does not follow it up with the clause, "who led you out of Egypt." Whether or not one agrees with Luther's approach in this matter, it is fascinating to see how he deals with the two clauses in light of creation and redemption.

Luther includes the first clause "I am the Lord your God" because this clause applies to all people—Christian and non-Christian alike. How? Because as maker of heaven and earth, God is the Creator of all people. This is what makes God "God." For Luther, what defines God above anything else is His creative activity. In this he simply follows the pattern of the Old Testament prophets, especially Isaiah. Neither he nor the prophets define God by the *via negativa*. They do not describe God by what He is not (e.g., we are finite, so He is infinite; we are corporeal, so He is spirit; we are limited in power, so He is omnipotent). Instead, God's creative activity defines Him as God. God created everything that exists; ergo, He is God! And so Luther occasionally includes this clause in his discussion of the Ten Commandments: "I am your Creator." This has two advantages.

First, it makes clear that God has a claim on every person on earth whether or not they are Israelites, whether or not they are Christians. He has a claim on every person by virtue of being their Creator. Second, the creation context enables Luther to stress that the Ten Commandments are not capricious commands issued by a capricious God. Instead, the commandments describe the grain of the universe. It is as if the Creator said: "Here is how I designed the world to work, and these commands are the instruction guides for using all the creaturely gifts that I gave you. Life works better when they are used in accord with their purpose!"

If the clause "I am the Lord your God" identified God as the Creator of every person who ever lived, the clause "who led you out of Egypt" revealed the identity of that Creator. The qualifying phrase "who led you out of Egypt" thus applies directly and immediately only to the people of Israel. This again makes clear that the literal Ten Commandments do not pertain to Christians, for God never led us out of Egypt.[25] That is to say, if one were to ask an old covenant Israelite the question, "What is the Creator's name?" they would answer, "I am the Lord your God." For Luther the act whereby God rescued the Israelites from Egypt became the defining event that shaped their identity and the single act that identified for them who the Creator was. It was the redemptive act by which the Creator revealed Himself. It became part of the name of God, so to speak. We might say that this phrase came to function much like the second article of the Apostles' or Nicene Creed functions for many Christians. So what does that mean?

Luther gives an example of how it should have functioned for the Israelites particularly toward the end of their 40 years of wilderness wandering. He suggests that as the Israelites were about to enter the promised land, Moses gathered them together and spoke to them about what they would encounter and how they should conduct themselves in Canaan. In brief, it might have gone something like this:

> Now when you enter the land of Canaan, you are going to find people who worship many other gods (idols). In fact, your eyes will be dazzled by the glitz and glitter of the Canaanite gods. But whenever you are tempted to follow one of those gods, you should ask yourselves this question: "Did this god lead you out of Egypt?" If the answer is no, then avoid that god. That is not your God!

In brief, the clause "who led you out of Egypt" served to distinguish for the Israelites the true identity of their Creator from all other competitors and false gods.

And so the people of Israel recited this historical deed on a regular basis throughout their history. It often went like this:

> And you shall make response before the Lord your God, "A wandering Aramean was my father. And he went down into Egypt and sojourned there, few in number, and there he became a nation, great, mighty, and populous. And the Egyptians treated

---

25. Arand, "Luther on the God Behind the First Commandment," 401.

us harshly and humiliated us and laid on us hard labor. Then we cried to the Lord, the God of our fathers, and the Lord heard our voice and saw our affliction, our toil, and our oppression. And the Lord brought us out of Egypt with a mighty hand and an outstretched arm, with great deeds of terror, with signs and wonders. And he brought us into this place and gave us this land, a land flowing with milk and honey." (Deut 26:5–9)

In other words, this clause functioned as something of a creedal statement for the Israelites. It does not apply to Christians today. We do not rehearse this event on a weekly basis as a way of identifying God within the Christian story. Why not?

Hermeneutically, Luther sees in the Old Testament a day when that historical recital would cease to function as a creed for the Israelites. For this he turns to Jeremiah 31. There it states:

Behold, the days are coming, declares the Lord, when I will make a new covenant with the house of Israel and the house of Judah, not like the covenant that I made with their fathers on the day when I took them by the hand to bring them out of the land of Egypt, my covenant that they broke, though I was their husband, declares the Lord. But this is the covenant that I will make with the house of Israel after those days, declares the Lord: I will put my law within them, and I will write it on their hearts. And I will be their God, and they shall be my people. And no longer shall each one teach his neighbor and each his brother, saying, 'Know the Lord,' for they shall all know me, from the least of them to the greatest, declares the Lord. For I will forgive their iniquity, and I will remember their sin no more. (Jer 31:31–34)

Luther sees this passage as a prophecy pointing to the coming of Christ. And so today when Christians gather in worship, they do not cite the story of the miraculous deeds of their God by saying, "He led us out of Egypt." Instead, Christians pray, "Lord, you have redeemed us through the blood of your Son."[26] Where it was once important to stress "out of Egypt," it is now necessary to speak of the God who "suffered under Pontius Pilate, crucified, dead, and was buried." In other words, this redemptive act replaces the redemptive act of the

---

26. See Arand, *That I May Be His Own*, 6.

exodus as the defining event in history that now shapes Christians as a people in terms of identity, values, and ethics.

Thus Luther suggests that Moses' speech (or for that matter, any pastor speaking to his people) to Christians today might go as follows: "Whenever you are tempted to follow another god and find your security and meaning in success, money, clothes, or power, you should ask yourselves this question: 'Did this god (money, success, fame, power) suffer and die for you on the cross?' If the answer is no, then avoid it! That is not your god." So the death and resurrection of Christ come to identify for Christians the Creator who is bringing about His new creation. By reciting that story Sunday after Sunday, we Christians not only identify who our God is but identify ourselves as part of that story. Christ's story is our story as we were incorporated into it through baptism. It is the story that shapes who we are and how we live.

In both cases, however, the exodus account for the Israelites and the crucifixion-resurrection account for Christians, people are restored to be the people that God had originally envisioned for them in creation. In other words, the Ten Commandments are *not* new instructions given to a redeemed people. Instead, they are in a sense "regiven" to God's people. We can now live as God first created us to live. We can reclaim our created identity as creatures and rejoice in that creatureliness. There is no need for us to become little gods ourselves or seek to become in some way divine, as that would reject our creatureliness. Luther provides one of his longest rejoicings in creatureliness in his sermon of 1537:

> I am called and am a creature and work of the one and highest God. The world seeks great honor with money, power, and all other such things, godliness it is not, that it rightly looks for this, that we here in faith through the young child's mouth pray, that God is our master, who has given us body and soul and daily preserves them.[27]

The First Commandment as the Organizing Center

For Luther, the Sabbath Commandment also cannot be interpreted apart from the First Commandment ("first" according to Lutheran enumeration; Exod 20:3–6). In this regard one can hardly

27. *WA* 45, 14, 1–5.

overstate the importance of the First Commandment in Luther's theology, and with him all of Lutheran theology. How the human creature stands in the presence of the judging eye of the Creator is basic to the entire body of Lutheran teaching. And so the Lutheran Formula of Concord[28] (1577) discusses original righteousness not in terms of the original capacities and abilities of the human being apart from God, that is, in terms of how the various parts of the human being (reason, will, passions, body) function together; instead, it interprets original righteousness personally and relationally, in terms of how the individual stands with God. Similarly, the Augsburg Confession[29] (1530) describes original sin in the personal language of the First Commandment. Original sin is in large part the inability to fear, love, and trust in God above all things. With regards to justification, the Lutherans charged that Rome focused on the Second Table of the Law (which focuses on caring for our neighbor) to the exclusion of the First Table (which focuses on God), most notably, the First Commandment.

For Luther, the First Commandment stood out as the summary of all summaries (*summa summarum*) of biblical teaching. The whole Psalter was nothing other than a collection of meditations and exercises based on the First Commandment.[30] It also was "the ocean out of which the prophets have drawn both their message of consolation and their message of condemnation."[31] Beyond that, Luther contended that "the first commandment is the chief part of our entire Christianity; it is the fountain of our faith, of all understanding, wisdom, knowledge, and law and all that is good."[32] For this reason we must ever remain pupils of the First Commandment.

> Therefore, however long we live, we shall always have our hands full if we remain pupils of the first commandment and of faith throughout all work and sufferings, and never cease to learn. Nobody knows what a great thing it is to trust God alone except him who begins to trust and tries to do faith's works.[33]

---

28. The Formula of Concord can be found in the *Book of Concord*, 481–660.
29. The Augsburg Confession can be found in the *Book of Concord*, 27–105.
30. *Book of Concord*, LC, 382 para. 18.
31. Source? [NOTE: No idea.—Rob Bowman]
32. *WA* 28, 10–12, 601.
33. *A Treatise on Good Works* (1520), *LW* 44:61.

The First Commandment provides an important vantage point from which Christians can interpret all of life theologically. In other words, it provides the critical part of the framework for their view of the world, in which our relationship to God is defined by our dependence on God. He gives; we receive (over and against our relationships with our neighbors where we give and they receive). The nature of these relationships give the lives of God's human creatures their direction and purpose. To that end Luther not only explains the First Commandment as an epitome of the Decalogue but also sets it as the cornerstone that determines the lines and direction of the entire catechism! The Ten Commandments highlight and show us our need for faith and God. The Apostles' Creed provides us with the gifts of God whereby our faith is aroused and strengthened. The Lord's Prayer then becomes the expression of the Christian's struggle to believe over against the challenges to faith; it serves as the battle cry of faith.

The primacy of the First Commandment in the Small and Large Catechisms appears in two ways and may be illustrated by Luther's use of two metaphors: the hoop of a wreath and the heart of a body. In the first metaphor, the First Commandment serves as the unifying thread of the Decalogue. In the second metaphor the first Commandment functions as the source or the fountainhead of the entire Decalogue. As Luther put it, the First Commandment is the "very first, highest, and best from which all others must proceed, in which they must exist and abide, and by which they must be judged and assessed." [34]

The First Commandment as the Commandment

Not only did Luther have a high appreciation for the First Commandment, but he plumbed the depths of it as perhaps no other expositor before him. Johannes Meyer observed that in the Middle Ages only a few commentators ranked the First Commandment above all the others, but in these isolated cases the First Commandment was simply laid alongside the remaining nine commandments as though it were simply the most prominent pearl in a strand of pearls. The individual commandments remained disconnected from one another and were expounded as isolated actions of the mouth and hand. In many ways this approach fit in nicely with the need for

---

34. *LW* 44:30.

a confessional mirror wherein one could reflect on the actual sins rather than on the inclinations of the heart.[35] Since the time of the First Lateran Council (AD 1215) every Christian was required to attend confession at least once a year in preparation for receiving the body and blood of Christ on Easter. This provided a priest with the opportunity for one-on-one pastoral care in which he could catechize as well as hear confession.

Luther went beyond making the First Commandment the most important of the Ten Commandments; it became for Luther the first among equals, so to speak. In his catechisms he demonstrated how the First Commandment lies at the heart of the remaining nine. In the process he wove the Ten Commandments into a single, seamless tapestry, a unity that Johann Michael Reu described as "an achievement of truly reformatory significance, an absolutely unique accomplishment."[36] In doing so, he made clear that our life with God is defined not by the individual actions we choose to carry out; rather, it is defined by a relationship in which we live solely from the gifts of God, and we are to live by faith alone.

In order to highlight the unity of the Decalogue in the First Commandment (as noted above), Luther drew upon the metaphor of a wreath. A wreath is bound by an inner hoop or frame made of board or wire that is bent into a circle in which the ends are bound to one another. Luther describes the First Commandment as a "clasp or the hoop of a wreath that binds the end to the beginning and holds everything together."[37] The "clasp"(*schele*) probably refers to the fastener with which both ends are bound together. The "hoop" (*bögel*), again, refers to the circular frame around which branches are wound together.[38] In other words, Luther contends that the First Commandment is the beginning, middle, and end of all the other commandments. Luther unfolds this unity of the Ten Commandments in both the structure and logic of his explanations.

35. J. Meyer, *Historischer Kommentar zu Luthers Kleinem Katechismus* (Gütersloh: C. Bertelsmann, 1929), 170ff. Luther's earlier writings served the purpose of confession as well. He provided lists of how the commandments were kept and how they were broken.

36. Reu, *Catechetics: Theory and Practice of Religious Instruction*, 103.

37. *Book of Concord*, LC, 430 para. 326.

38. Reu, "Hints for an Understanding of the First [and Second] Chief Part," quoted in P. I. Johnston, *An Assessment of the Educational Philosophy of Johann Michael Reu Using the Hermeneutic Paradigms of J.F. Herbart and of J.C. K. Von Hofmann and the Erlangen School,* Volume 4, April 1989 (Dissertation at University of Illinois at Urbana-Champion), 812.

Luther held that everything in the biblical texts of the Decalogue—from the prologue, "I am the Lord your God, who brought you out of the land of Egypt," through the prohibitions, "You shall have no other gods before me," and, "You shall not make for yourself a carved image," to the epilogue, "I the Lord your God am a jealous God"—fell under the rubric of the First Commandment.[39] These verses all together form a single, undivided unity. Throughout his catechetical writings, Luther consistently interpreted these statements as parts of a whole that comprised the entire first commandment.

The Clasp of the Wreath

Just how the First Commandment serves to unify the whole appears in Luther's exposition of the opening and concluding words of the Decalogue in the Small Catechism. He begins by explaining that the First Commandment requires that "we should fear, love, and trust God above all things."[40] He then brings the commandments to a close with the threats and the promises of the epilogue—all in the context of the first commandment:

> What is this? Answer: God threatens to punish all who break these commandments. Therefore we are to *fear* His wrath and not disobey these commandments. *However*, God promises grace and every good thing to all those who keep these commandments. Therefore we also are to love and trust him and gladly act according to his commands.[41] Here the triad "fear, love, and trust" appears in both the first Commandment and in the epilogue. That is to say, they appear in the first Commandment and then again after the tenth Commandment. For Luther, they are of one piece. One assists in explanation of the other. The epilogue (or what Luther calls the "appendix to the first Commandment") provides the interpretive backdrop for drawing out the meaning of the first Commandment as op-

---

39. See Exod 20:2–5a; Deut 5:6–7. With this enumeration Luther stood in the stream of the Western church since Augustine. B. Reicke, *Die Zehn Worte in Geschichte und Gegenwart: Zählung und Bedeutung der Gebote in den verschiedenen Konfession* (Tübingen: Mohr, 1973), 9; Cf. Arand, *That I May Be His Own*, Appendix B, 193–94.

40. *Book of Concord*, SC, 351 para. 2.

41. Ibid., 354 para. 22, emphasis added.

posed to the prologue ("I am the Lord your God, who brought you out of the land of Egypt").[42]

While Luther interprets the First Commandment together with its threats and promises as a single unit, he does not locate them alongside one another in the Small Catechism. Instead, he takes the threats and promises of the First Commandment (which follow the prohibition against images in the biblical text) and relocates them at the end of the Tenth Commandment as an epilogue of the entire Decalogue. This move was unique in the history of catechetical expositions of the Decalogue.[43]

Fear		Fear
Love	2nd–10th Commandment	Love
Trust		Trust

Luther thereby made the First Commandment the Alpha and Omega, the beginning and the end of the Decalogue. You could say that the First Commandment functions as bookends for the other nine commandments. The Large Catechism brings out this *inclusio* even more clearly. "Thus the first commandment is to illuminate and impart its splendor to all the others."[44] Here Luther expounds the close of the Commandments twice: immediately after the First Commandment and following the Tenth Commandment. The First Commandment thereby functions like the clasp of a wreath that binds the beginning to the end.

The "Hoop" of the Wreath

With the First Commandment standing at the beginning and the end of the Decalogue as a clasp, Luther then threads the First Commandment through the other nine by opening each commandment with the words "we should fear and love God." In his 1528 sermon series, Luther declares that the First Commandment "must

---

42. "This [fear and trust] is exactly the meaning and right interpretation of the first and chief commandment, from which all the others proceed" (*Book of Concord*, LC, 429 para. 324). "Let this [conclusion] be enough for the First Commandment" (ibid., 392 para. 48). Finally, Luther's third series of sermons in 1528 reiterate the same thought: "To the conclusion of the commandments add the threat and promise of the first commandment" (*LW* 51:161).

43. Although the enumeration of the Commandments differed between Jewish, Roman Catholic, and Reformed commentators, as a rule they all kept the epilogue in its biblical sequence. Arand, *That I May Be His Own*, Appendix B, 193–94.

44. *Book of Concord*, LC, 430 para. 326.

run through all commandments because it is the sum and the light of all the others."[45] For example, his explanation to the Second Commandment reads: "We are to fear and love God, so that we do not curse, swear, practice magic, lie, or deceive using God's name, but instead use that very name in every time of need to call on, pray to, praise, and give thanks to God."[46]

After weaving the First Commandment forward to connect the second through the tenth as the hoop of the wreath, Luther applies the threats and promises of the epilogue retroactively to the previous nine commandments. In the Small Catechism he introduces his conclusion to this section with the question: "What then does God say about *all these* commandments?" (emphasis added). Luther explains the epilogue in such a way that it embraces all of the preceding commandments. Exodus 20:5–6 states, "I the Lord your God am a jealous God, visiting the iniquity of the fathers on the children to the third and the fourth generation of those who hate me, but showing steadfast love to thousands of those who love me and keep my commandments." Luther understands this statement to mean that those who hate God break the Commandments while those who love God keep the Commandments.[47]

Luther makes numerous statements in the Large Catechism that confirm these structural observations. He repeatedly refers to the importance of the epilogue for all of the Commandments in the same language with which he speaks of the First Commandment itself:

> Although primarily attached to the First Commandment, as we heard above, this appendix was intended to apply to all the commandments, and all of them as a whole ought to be referred and directed to it. . . . This appendix ought to be regarded as attached to each individual commandment, penetrating and pervading them all."[48]

A few paragraphs later, Luther explains that by attaching the epilogue to all of the Commandments, he applies the First Commandment to each of them:

---

45. *LW* 51:144.
46. *Book of Concord*, SC, 352 para. 4.
47. Ibid., 354 para. 21–22.
48. *Book of Concord*, LC 429 para. 321.

Thus the First Commandment is to illuminate and impart its splendor to all the others. In order that this may be constantly repeated and never forgotten, therefore, you must let these concluding words run through all the commandments, like the clasp or the hoop of a wreath that binds the end to the beginning and holds everything together.[49]

In his Third Series of Sermons of 1528,[50] Luther speaks of the threat and promise, death and life, wrath and grace, curse and blessing, evil and benefit, as "the cord with which one binds the garland together."[51] Again, "to the conclusion of the commandments add the threat and promise of the first commandment."[52] Luther carries this out in the Large Catechism by integrating the threats and promises of the epilogue into the explanations of each commandment. At times he expresses them in a general way, namely that God threatens those who break the Commandments and promises those who keep them.[53] At other times the specifics of the threats/promises correspond directly to the particulars of the commandment under consideration.[54] In this manner, the First Commandment serves as the hoop of a wreath that holds everything together.

The First Commandment as Fountain of all the Others[55]

In addition to viewing the First Commandment as the unifying thread that weaves the individual commandments into a single wreath, Luther identifies the First Commandment as the source

49. Ibid., 430.

50. Luther preached his catechisms four times a year over a two-year week period. For 1528 we have those series. First series: May–June. Second series: September. Third series: December.

51. *LW* 51:161. Cf. *WA* 30, 180–81, 1.

52. *LW* 51:161.

53. *Book of Concord*, LC, 429 para. 322; 430–31 para. 330; 431 para. 333.

54. For example, the First Commandment threats: "How angry God is with those who rely on anything but himself" (*Book of Concord*, 390 para. 32); "takes vengeance upon men who turn away from him" (ibid., para. 34); "strike and punish them so severely . . . those who persist in their stubbornness and pride" (ibid., 391 para. 38); "God will tolerate no presumption or trust in anything else" (392 para. 47). The promises: "how kind and gracious he is to those who trust and believe him alone" (para. 32). Note also the Second Commandment (p. 393, para. 57); Third Commandment (again, the Sabbath commandment in Lutheran circles; 399 para. 95), "the Word . . . never departs without fruit. It always awakens new understanding" (p. 400, para.101); and Fourth Commandment (404 para. 134; 405 para.139; 406 para. 146; and 408 para. 161.

55. See A. Peters, *Kommentar Zu Luthers Katechismen, Band 1: Die Zehn Gebote* (Göttingen: Vandenhoeck & Ruprecht, 1990), 127–29.

and fountain for the fulfillment and keeping of the remaining nine commandments. It is the chief commandment "from which all others proceed."[56] To bring out its importance, Luther commonly uses the metaphor of the relation of the head or heart to the entire body. "If the heart is right with God and we keep this [first] commandment, all the rest will follow on their own."[57] Or, "Where the head is right, the whole life must be right, and vice versa."[58]

With this single insight, Luther reverses the manner in which the fulfillment of the Commandments had traditionally been defined.[59] In the catechetical tradition of the Middle Ages, the First Commandment was generally regarded as being fulfilled by adhering to the remaining nine. But for Luther, all the Commandments are fulfilled by keeping the first! The breaking or keeping of each commandment depends upon the attitude of one's heart toward God. This conviction is conveyed consistently throughout Luther's writings.[60] All actions flow from the believer's heart, which is defined by fear and faith. This conviction shapes Luther's catechism in a number of ways.

By focusing on the First Commandment, Luther does not look to the isolated actions of the individual; rather, he takes into account the entire person of the believer.[61]

> The Christian life is no more regarded as a series of separate works, but as the organic development of fear and love which God himself kindled in the heart. Instead of bewildering the child, or common man, or mature Christian with an almost countless number of virtues, Luther shows him the one and indispensable requirement; fear and love embraces, and produces everything else. And by representing as perfectly worthless all

---

56. *Book of Concord*, LC, 429–30 para. 324.
57. Ibid., 392 para. 48; 429–30 para. 323–24, 326.
58. Ibid, 390, para. 31–32.
59. Arand, "Luther on the God behind the First Commandment," 397.
60. Already in his *Decem praecepta* (1518), Luther stated that the First Commandment contains all the others within itself. In 1520, the first Commandment "is the very first of all commandments and the highest and the best, [the one] from which all other proceed, in which they exist and by which they are judged and assessed" (*LW* 44:30; *WA* 6, 202–76). In his "Treatise on Good Works," Luther says, "First, there must be health (*gesundheit*), then the functions of all members will work" (*WA* 6, 213). Elsewhere, he speaks of the First Commandment as "the measure and yardstick of all the others, to which they are to yield and give obedience" (*LW* 9:70; *WA* 14, 611–12). The first Commandment is *the* Commandment out of which all others flow (*WA* 16, 463, 3–5).
61. Cf. Meyer, *Historischer Kommentar zu Luthers Kleinem Katechismus*, 171.

other works if detached from this source, he emphasizes most effectively the important evangelical principle that works are not acceptable to God unless the person has first become acceptable. Thereby an end is made of the "bargain features" of Romanism; no longer is work added to work in the hope that the sum of them all will suffice to earn God's favor.[62]

We have seen that, structurally, Luther places the First Commandment at the head of each commandment by using the first as an introduction to each of the others. Syntactically, Luther's exposition of each commandment breaks down into two parts consisting of a main clause and a subordinate clause. Into the main clause, Luther places the words of the First Commandment, "We should fear and love God." Into the subordinate clause he places the distinctive contents of the particular commandment under discussion. As an example: In the text of the Second Commandment Luther writes, "Just as the First Commandment instructs the heart and teaches faith, so this commandment leads us outward and directs the lips and tongue into a right relationship with God."[63]

Luther demonstrates the headship of the First Commandment by means of the subordinating conjunction *das*. Over the years there has been some debate over the best way to translate the word *das* and express the syntactical relationship of the two clauses in a manner that is faithful to Luther's theology.[64] Two options have prevailed: either regarding it as introducing a purpose clause or introducing a result clause.

If one understands the *das* as introducing a purpose clause, it then answers the question, "For what purpose do we fear and love God?" Its translation might be rendered: "We should fear and love God *in order* that we do not" (or "may not") despise the preaching of His word. In the latter case, the subjunctive *may* is used in the subordinate clause. Several factors weigh in favor of the purpose clause. Meyer finds evidence in the use of the subjunctive *seien* in the Eighth Commandment: "*might* be of help and service to him."[65]

---

62. Reu, *Catechetics*, 103.

63. *Book of Concord*, LC, 392 para. 50.

64. Reu contends that the translation must express this thought in the exact words in such a manner that everyone can grasp it, *Luther's Small Catechism: A New English Translation* (Minneapolis; Augsburg, 1929), 645.

65. J. Meyer, *Historischer Kommentar zu Luthers Kleinem Katechismus* (Gutersloh: Druck and Verlag, 1929), 172–73.

Also, two Latin translations of the Catechism seem to support this sense of purpose by using *ut* and *ne* in all the Commandments. Thus, the exposition of the Sabbath commandment reads: "We ought to fear and love God lest we despise the divine saying of his Word, and conversely that we may hold it sacred."[66] From a negative standpoint the First Commandment might be viewed more as a means to an end, namely, that it leads to obedience, than as the beginning, middle, and end of all the Commandments. From a positive standpoint, this approach would highlight the proper motivation for keeping the Commandments.

As an alternative, Reu argues that Luther looked upon the conjunction *das* as introducing "the contemplated result."[67] The subordinate clause would then answer the question: "What is the result of fearing and loving God?" Reu thus proposed translating *das* as: "We should fear and love God *and. . .*" (emphasis added).[68] Luther's conclusion in the Large Catechism of the Commandments would then lend support as he replaces the subordinating conjunction *das*, seen in his exposition of Commandments 2–10, with the coordinating conjunction *und* in order to connect our fearing and loving God with our actions and living.[69] In translating Luther's exposition of the Commandments according to this view, the subordinate clause is put into the indicative. The advantage of viewing the subordinate clause as a result clause is that it highlights the latter as the fruit of the former. It keeps the emphasis on the main clause, that is, on the fearing and loving.

Interestingly, in addition to using *das*, Luther occasionally uses *auf das* in his Small Catechism. When he does, he always uses it exclusively to introduce a purpose clause.[70] This would suggest that *das* cannot by itself be taken exclusively in the sense of purpose. It

---

66. Reu, "Hints for an Understanding," 814. See Reu, *Catechetics*, 330–31; Reu, "Hints for an Understanding," 813–14; and Reu, *Luther's Small Catechism*, 644–45. Historically, it would appear that the catechisms of the Missouri Synod adopted this approach as evidenced in the Dietrich Catechism, the 1943 Synodical Catechism, and the Triglot. However, the subjunctive verb *may* was placed only into the negative clause.

67. Reu, *Catechetics*, 330.

68. Ibid. Cranmer's translation went with "and, for his sake, not . . ."

69. Following Reu's lead, the Tappert edition of the *Book of Concord* (Minneapolis: Augsburg Fortress, 16th ed., 1989) translates the *das* to read: "We should fear and love God *and* so . . . " (emphasis added). Most recently, the 1986 translation of the Missouri Synod's new catechism seems to follow suit as it expresses the coordinating conjunction thus: "We should fear and love God so that we do not . . . "

70. *Book of Concord*, Second Article of Creed; Second Petition of Lord's Prayer; Sixth Petition of Lord's Prayer.

would either introduce a result clause or introduce a combination of both purpose and result but not a purpose clause alone. Hence, both sides could be captured by rendering *das* as "so as to." In this way a certain amount of ambiguity is allowed to stand.

This ambiguity may be deliberate on Luther's part. At times, when he expounds the Second through the Tenth Commandments, he stresses that the motivation for keeping them must arise from the First Commandment. Thus he says that our actions are to "proceed from a heart that fears God alone and from such fear . . ."[71] In these cases, he notes why we should observe the Commandments.

At other times, when he addresses the fulfillment of the First Commandment itself, he points to the results. For example, when people consider the threats and promises, "there will arise a spontaneous impulse and desire gladly to do God's will."[72] Or, as seen earlier, "where the head is right, the whole life must be right, and vice versa."[73] Or, in the case of the heart, where it is "right with God and we keep this commandment, all the rest will follow on their own."[74] In his third sermon series of 1528, Luther also points in the direction of result, this time expressed as a descriptive after the fact. If you fear God, "you will not mistrust him, you will not blaspheme, you will not be disobedient to your parents, you will not kill. . . ."[75]

The First Commandment as Prohibition and Precept

As Luther links the First Commandment to all the others, he generally distinguishes between fear on one side and love and trust on the other side. This comes to the forefront in the epilogue of the Ten Commandments in the Small Catechism, the entire exposition in the Large Catechism, and all three sermons series on the catechism in 1528. Against the backdrop of the epilogue, Luther warns, "God threatens to punish all who break these commandments. Therefore we are to fear his wrath and not disobey these commandments." Conversely, Luther encourages, "God promises grace and every good thing. . . . Therefore we also are to love and trust him and gladly act according to his commands."[76] Even Reu concedes the

---

71. *Book of Concord*, LC 429–30 para. 323, 326–27.
72. Ibid., 430–31 para. 330.
73. Ibid., 390 para. 31.
74. Ibid., 392 para. 48, 429–30 para. 324, 326.
75. *LW* 51:161.
76. *Book of Concord*, SC, 354 para. 22.

242 — PERSPECTIVES ON THE SABBATH

point, albeit reluctantly, that "Luther meant to correlate the fear of
God rather with the negative features of the commandments, and
the love of God with the positive ones, is a view doubtless warranted
by the facts."[77]

Fear and Prohibition

As noted, fear and the prohibition belong together. This is, for
Luther, the clear scope of all biblical prohibitions.[78] In particular,
fear leads to the avoidance of evil. Already in 1515, Luther states
that fear serves as a *schutz* (protection) against the transgression.[79]
It functions as a dam against the onrush and rising tide of all disobedience.[80] A decade later it remained the same. As he expressed it in
1528, we "must fear God if we are to cease to do evil."[81] The fear of
God leads one to avoid all that is contrary to His will lest we provoke
God to wrath.[82] "Because of this fear, avoid all that is contrary to his
will."[83] Fear avoids sin.[84] As Kolb has noted, "Dread determines daily
decision-making, whether consciously or unconsciously."[85]

The kind of "fear" Luther constantly speaks of is filial fear. There
are, of course, so many interpretations for fear. But Luther is speaking of a healthy respect for God. What God says, He means. One is
to take proper precautions when dealing with Him; one is to have a
proper respect, a proper "yes, sir" kind of fear.

---

77. Reu, *Catechetics*, 330. He hastens to add, however, that not much weight ought
to be attached to this distinction for this does not hold true in the Commandment prohibiting adultery. This one example, however, is clearly the exception that need not dis-
prove the rule. Cf. G. Hoffmann, "Der kleine Katechismus als Abriß der Theologie Martin
Luthers," *Luther* 30 (1959): 49–63.
78. Peters, *Kommentar Zu Luthers Katechismen*, 132.
79. Meyer, *Historischer Kommentar zu Luthers Kleinem Katechismus*, 182.
80. Ibid., 187.
81. "For they [the young] must fear God if they are to cease from doing evil for his
sake and [they must trust God if they are to do good for his sake]" (*LW* 51:140).
82. "By means of warning and threat, restraint and punishment, children [shall] be
trained in due time to beware of lying and especially to avoid calling upon God's name in
support of it" (*Book of Concord*, LC, 395 para. 69). The fear of God prevents the outbreak
of evil, subdues our desire for revenge (411 para. 187, 413 para. 195), and restrains wan-
tonness (417 para. 232).
83. *Book of Concord*, LC, 406 para. 145, and 417 para. 232.
84. Cf. Meyer, *Historischer Kommentar zu Luthers Kleinem Katechismus*, 172. Meyer cites several Luther passages which treat this theme: WA 30 I 62 (12, 14); 63 (1); 64
(20); 65 (2); 66 (8, 17, 21); 68 (5); 75 (7); 79 (15); 85 (9).
85. R. Kolb, *Teaching God's Children His Teaching* (Hutchinson, MN: Crown, 1992),
2–11.

For Luther, the prohibitions we face reflect our true situation over against God and His creation. On the one hand, they presuppose the *dona creata* (God's good gifts, mercy, grace, blessings all that is unmerited) and the created orders of God. On the other hand, "the prohibitions remind us that all created orders of God are subject to human interference and destruction."[86] While we do not create God's good gifts of this life, we can lose them, destroy them, or forfeit them through abuse and misuse. So we are "enjoined to refrain from the crimes that destroy community."[87] The prohibitions thus function as protective fences around God's creation, around this present life, as a boundary between good and evil,[88] and as a "wall, fortress, refuge."[89] They show that God wants every husband and wife guarded and protected[90] as well as their property.[91] They serve as God's instruments to preserve creation. Luther can even compare God's activity here with that of a kind father who intervenes to stop bloodshed.[92] This would correspond to the statement in his exposition of the first of the Apostles' Creed where Luther confesses that God protects, guards, and defends us from all evil.[93]

Love and the Precept

Interestingly, Luther places love and trust alongside fear. Whereas fear held in view the punishment and the wrath of God, love and trust look to the gracious father.[94] And so Luther moves beyond the negatively framed statements ("you shall not") of the biblical text to set forth the positive actions that spring from faith. Threats are reactive, promises are proactive, and punishment is merited—you get what you deserve; thus, God's grace and blessings are all unmerited—you get what you don't deserve.

---

86. W. Elert, *The Christian Ethos*, trans. C. J. Schindler (Eugene, OR: Wipf & Stock, 2004), 74.

87. R. W. Jensen, "A Large Catechism: The Decalogue," *Lutheran Forum* 23:4 (Advent 1989): 12–14.

88. Cf. *Book of Concord*, LC, 411 para. 183.

89. Ibid., para. 185.

90. Ibid., 414 para. 205–6.

91. Ibid., 413 para. 195.

92. In the end, fear and the prohibition seem to suggest that Luther has in view here a first use of the Law. See Peters, *Kommentar Zu Luthers Katechismen*, 132–33, 136.

93. *Book of Concord*, SC, 354 para. 2.

94. Peters, *Kommentar Zu Luthers Katechismen*, 137.

244 — PERSPECTIVES ON THE SABBATH

Unlike the actions that result from the fear of God's threatened wrath, Luther notes that the actions that result from love and trust are carried out not grudgingly but "willingly and gladly."[95] When one views married life as a good gift of God, "chastity always follows spontaneously without any command." [96] Luther reiterates this in the explanation to the first article of the Apostles' Creed in the Large Catechism. There he suggests that when we take note of God's manifold blessings, His *dona creata*, "our hearts will be warmed and kindled with gratitude to God and a desire to use all these blessings to his glory and praise."[97] Luther acknowledges that Christians in particular "have this advantage, that they acknowledge that they owe it to God to serve and obey him for all these things."[98] Through knowledge of the promise we come to "love and delight" in all the commandments of God because we see that God gives his gifts completely.[99]

One who loves and trusts God is not content with doing the bare minimum needed to get by and avoid punishments. Instead, the person who delights in God's law goes "above and beyond the call of duty." Love and trust, for Luther, lead to the positive ordering of one's own life and the proper use of God's gifts according to His Commandments.[100] Luther concludes his analysis of the First Commandment in the Large Catechism with these words:

> God will tolerate no presumption or trust in anything else; he makes no greater demand on us than a heartfelt trust in him for every good thing, so that we walk straight ahead on the right path, using all of God's gifts exactly as a shoemaker uses a needle, awl, and thread for his work and afterward puts them aside, or as a traveler makes use of an inn, food, and lodging, but only for his physical needs. Let each person do the same in his or her walk of life according to God's order, allowing none of these things to be a lord or an idol.[101]

---

95. In fact, "where men consider this [God's promises] and take it to heart, there will arise a spontaneous impulse and desire gladly to do God's will" (*Book of Concord*, LC, 431 para. 330).

96. *Book of Concord*, LC, 415 para. 219.

97. Ibid., 433, para. 23.

98. Ibid., para. 22.

99. Ibid., 440 para. 69.

100. Ibid., 414, 417, 419 para. 207, 233, 251.

101. Ibid., 392 para. 47.

Looking to God for all we need restores creatures and creaturely gifts to their rightful place. Thus, those gifts are not turned into idols but are used according to the purpose for which they were given. As Peters puts it, "God does not simply want us to live alongside our fellow human being in Stoic composure; he also looks for our imaginative and active neighborly love."[102]

A First-Commandment Orientation to the Decalogue

A number of implications may be drawn from the structure of Luther's explanations together with the content of those explanations. This provides for a theological understanding of his treatment of the Decalogue in his Small Catechism.

The prominence of the First Commandment brings out the intensely personal character of all the commandments and indicates that they all must be understood in interpersonal terms.[103] The Law is a personal address that will not replace the Lawgiver but will bind a person directly to his or her God.[104] Each commandment drives the hearer back to the person of God. Luther brings out this intensely personal character of the Commandments by fastening our attention more on our relation to their Giver than on our obedience to the particularities of the Commandments themselves. This is the main key, for it is not about what we creatures do; instead, the focus is all about what our gracious God has done for us. The Commandments thus may not be regarded as impersonal principles, words of wisdom, abstract regulations, or codes of ethics. They are the personal will of the Creator for His human creatures.[105] The catechisms' concentration on the First Commandment guards against all attempts to loosen the individual commandments from the person and will of God.[106]

By preventing any separation of the Commandments from their author, Luther's explanations discourage a keeping score of sins so

---

102. A. Peters, "Die Bedeutug der Katechismen Luthers innerhalb der Bekenntnisshriften," *Luther und die Bekenntnisschriften, Veroffentlichungen der Luther-Akademie Ratzburg, Band 2* (Erlangen: Martin Luther-Verlag, 1981), 68; quoted in J.F. Hebart, "Luther's Large Catechism: the Path of Faith" in *Luther's Large Catechism,* Anniversary Translation (Adeline, South Australia: Lutheran Publishing House, 1983), xxix.

103. For more on this, see T. E. Fretheim, "The Reclamation of Creation: Redemption and Law in Exodus," *Interpretation* 45.4 (Oct. 1991): 354–65.

104. Cf. A. Siirala, *Gottes Gebot bei Martin Luther: eine Untersuchung der Theologie Luthers unterbesonderer Berücksichtigung des ersten Hauptstücke im Grossen Katechismus* (Helsinki, 1956), 47.

105. Ibid., 24–25.

106. Ibid., 44.

as to develop a list of dos and don'ts, of vices and virtues. Such lists were used for confessing sins before the priest when sin was viewed primarily in terms of voluntary actions by the individual.[107] Luther himself, however, ceased using catalogues of sins after 1522 (up until that time he continued to provide a list of the ways he kept or broke each commandment). As a corollary, Luther's explanation of the Decalogue also discourages the partitioning of one's life into distinct and unrelated categories (such as one's religious life, business life, family life, etc.). Everything is pulled to God and places us under the eyes of God (*coram Deo*). The First Commandment provides the key for understanding the human predicament of sin by diagnosing every sin as an attack on God as God.[108] Every sin is in its own way an attempt to dislodge God from our lives. In this regard, the First Commandment diagnoses the heart of the problem while the remaining commandments identify only the symptoms. As Luther states at the close of his exposition on the First Commandment, "If the heart is right with God and we keep this commandment, all the rest will follow on their own."[109]

The First Commandment also imparts a value to all of the Commandments as the most important things that can be done in life, not to mention the most difficult. One of the remarkable things about the Small Catechism is the essentially nonreligious nature of Luther's explanations to the Commandments. But consider exhortations of the Ten Commandments: Obey parents, help those in danger, cherish your spouse, support and protect the possessions of others and their sources of income, speak well of your neighbor, and so on. As G. Wingren expressed it, "This is a shockingly trivial list of works!"[110] These are not the types of things that get people excited about when it comes to serving God. Indeed, Luther himself laments that because the Commandments deal with ordinary, everyday matters, people treat them as if they came "from some loudmouthed street vendor"[111] and thus seek more exciting and attractive things to do. Yet no matter how trivial, ordinary, or mun-

---

107. For a historical discussion on the topic of confession see T. Tentler, *Sin and Confession on the Eve of the Reformation* (Princeton: Princeton University Press, 1977).

108. Cf. P. Althaus, *The Theology of Martin Luther*, trans. R. C. Schultz (Philadelphia: Fortress, 1966), 169.

109. *Book of Concord*, LC, 392 para. 48.

110. G. Wingren, *Credo: The Christian View of Faith and Life*, trans. E. M. Carlson (Minneapolis: Augsburg, 1981), 76.

111. *Book of Concord*, 407 para. 152.

dane they may be, the First Commandment reminds us that they remain the very commands of God![112] For that reason they set forth the greatest and most precious things we can do.

The New Content Imparted by the First Commandment

All this suggests that when one is teaching the Commandments within a limited time frame, a much larger portion of time should be devoted to the First Commandment than to the remaining nine. As the First Commandment sums up within itself all the others, the Second through the Tenth Commandments have become nine different ways of teaching the First Commandment, that is, nine commentaries on the First Commandment. We are to use the other nine to illustrate how the First Commandment is to be lived out. It's personal, and it all goes back to God. God confronts us face-to-face.

The First Commandment imparts a new content to all the others. It reveals that in every commandment the central issue or content is God's lordship over our lives. We are related to God in such a way that in every circumstance, in every situation of life, we need to hang on to someone or something. The First Commandment warns against the ever-present danger of turning to the creaturely things of life and of ourselves and elevating them to the status of the Creator. Thus it stands as a wall of protection around the gifts in the other commandments so that we do not seek from them (and thereby misuse) what we should expect from God alone. Thus the breaking of the Commandments involves not only sin against God because He so commanded them but also involves a particular type of sin, namely, a refusal of God's gifts, a rejection of His lordship, and a desire to reorder creation according to our own ideas and wishes.

God's standing in our lives as God is revealed from two sides and in two seasons of life: fear and love, tragedy and prosperity. For Luther, whatever we regard as being able to do us the greatest harm is as much a god as that which we believe can do us the greatest good. Indeed, one is the flip side of the other. That which I most want is also what I most fear losing or not getting. Therefore, that which we most fear losing reveals our god. "The test of such idolatry is seen when such things are taken away, and [despair and]

---

112. Wingren, *Credo*, 76. He also suggests that "the trivial nature of the deeds to be done is the best protection against the danger that attends all legal righteousness—the notion that the works of the law are evidences of the doer's goodness."

depression overwhelm the idolater."[113] Despising or defiance of His wrath and doubt of His goodness both involve the rejection of God's claim upon us.

In some ways Luther's explanation of the First Commandment as "fear and love" (the latter often a synonym for faith) serves as the source of all the Commandments. It suggests a law–gospel dialectic in understanding the Ten Commandments. To fulfill the Commandments out of fear is a reflection of the first use of the law, namely, coercion. To be clear, Lutherans teach three uses of the law. This first serves as coercion to external discipline, the second as a curb to sin, and the third as a mirror or reflection of how to live and walk in the law, by God's Spirit.[114] Consequently, when fear is the primary motivator, one does only the bare minimum and not an iota more than necessary. At this point the law is prescriptive. Love and trust, on the other hand, lead one to live gladly according to the Commandments. This points us in the direction of a joyful, spontaneous obedience. At this point the law is more descriptive of the life that is lived in such a way. Accordingly, the positive dimensions of the Second through the Tenth Commandments reveal that one should want to go beyond the bare minimum to embrace those things that are above and beyond the call of duty.

Summary

Thinking through the structure and logic of Luther's explanations to the Decalogue provides crucial insights into its central themes. These themes in turn carry important implications for teaching the catechisms. At the very least it suggests a two-step sequence in the reflective process. The greatest emphasis should be placed on the First Commandment within the context of the epilogue. The second step would involve reflection upon the way in which the First Commandment informs all of the subsequent Commandments. With this understanding in place, the student of the catechisms will be prepared to perceive rightly the nature of created reality and our responsibility as creatures to the Creator. Having learned *that* they are to expect and receive all that is good from God alone through the analysis of the Ten Commandments in the catechisms, catechists are then ready to hear and ponder the depth

---

113. Kolb, *Teaching God's Children*, 2–4.
114. *Book of Concord*, Article 6, Formula of Concord, 587.

and riches of God bestowed in the Apostles' Creed (which exposition comes immediately after in both catechisms).

The Sabbath Commandment

Having considered the context of creation for the Ten Commandments, and the Ten Commandments as the context for the Sabbath Commandment, we are now ready to look at the Sabbath Commandment itself.

In the Large Catechism, Luther develops the flow of the first three commandments as moving from faith to name to word. The heart that seeks God calls upon His name. To use God's name properly, we need to be trained in the use of God's Word, for God's name is made known to us in the Word. This becomes the theme of Luther's explanation for the Sabbath Commandment. If we are only able to believe through the hearing of the Word, then may we never finish learning, neither the catechism nor the Scriptures. "We can never conclude that we have had too much of the Word of God (*acedia*)."[115] In order to see how Luther comes to make the Word the centerpiece of the Sabbath Commandment, it is necessary to take a look at the medieval church's understanding of the biblical text on the eve of the Reformation.

As in the case of other commandments, and with the tradition preceding him, Luther used an abbreviated text for the purpose of making it easier for children to learn the command by heart. The full text of the Sabbath Commandment in Exodus 20:8–11 reads:

> Remember the Sabbath day, to keep it holy. Six days you shall labor, and do all your work, but the seventh day is a Sabbath to the Lord your God. On it you shall not do any work, you, or your son, or you daughter, your male servant, or your female servant, or your livestock, or the sojourner who is within your gates. For in six days the Lord made heaven and earth, the sea, and all that is in them, and rested on the seventh day. Therefore the Lord blessed the Sabbath day and made it holy.

Luther rendered the biblical text, "Remember the Sabbath day, to keep it holy," as, "You are to hallow the day of rest" (*"Du sollst den*

---

115. F. Mildenberger, *Theology of the Lutheran Confessions*, ed. R. C. Schultz (Philadelphia: Fortress, 1986), 145.

feiertag [*ruhetag*] *heiligen.*"). The medieval memory text typically rendered it, "You shall cease to work on the holy day" ("*Du sollst die heiligen Tage feiern*" [*ruhen*]).[116] In doing so, Luther focused on more the first part of the text (Exod 20:8) than on the second part (vv. 9–10), which speaks of the cessation of work. We will make two observations based on Luther's rendering: first, with regard to the word *Sabbath*; and, second, with regard to his focus on *resting* and *hallowing* or *sanctifying*.

The Sabbath

In the late Middle Ages the Hebrew word for *Sabbath* was either transliterated as *sabbat* or was translated into the German as *feiertag* ("feast day" or "festival"). In either case the Sabbath referred to a liturgical designation of religious days known as feasts or festivals (*kulttagen* or *feriae*).[117] Each day of the week when used for religious purposes could be considered as a feast day or festival.

This broader understanding of the Sabbath found expression in the actual way the Sabbath commandment was translated or presented. In fifteenth-century France, for example, Jean Gerson explained the Sabbath Commandment in his popular *L'ABC des simples gens* as follows: "You shall keep the Sundays and the commanded feast days."[118] Dietrich Kolde, in his well-known "Mirror for Christians," explains the Sabbath Commandment this way: "To all the holy days be true."[119] What are the holy days to which they refer? To find this, we must first look at the medieval church's liturgical calendar, which took three main forms.

First was the divine office or series of daily prayers. Monastic institutions wanted to provide the world a role model for living the Christian life. This was done by the ringing of the town bells. The monastic *horarium* split the day into a series of seven celebrations hours: *matins/lauds* (sixth and fourteenth hours), *terce* (seventh hour), *sext* (the ninth hour), *none* (tenth hour), *vespers* (eleventh hour), *compline* (twelfth hour), and the midnight vigil at the thirteenth hour (the cycle then begins again as it returns to *matins/*

116. Meyer, *Historischer Kommentar zu Luthers Kleinem Katechismus*, 207.
117. Ibid., 206.
118. J. Gerson, *An Hebt Sich Das ABC Der Götlichen Leibi* (Memmingen: Albrecht Kunne, 1493). 155.
119. D. Kolde, "Mirror for Christians" in *The Reformation Catechisms: Catholic, Anabaptist, Lutheran* (New York: Edwin Mellen, 1982), 47.

lauds on the fourteenth hour).[120] This ordering of the day according to these hours provided people (particularly monks and nuns)
the opportunity to praise God and meditate on His word. Laypeople
could also participate in their own limited ways. The impact upon
their lives more often took place through the ringing of bells to
announce the hours. This made people aware of the monastic devotional life and gave them the opportunity to engage in some form of
commemoration such as a saying of the Lord's Prayer.[121]

The second form of the liturgical calendar consisted of weekly rounds. Although the weekly rounds centered on Sunday, they
included a full range of services in the congregation on other days
as well. In other words, the devotional life of the people was not
confined to Sunday. Fridays served as a recollection of Good Friday;
Saturdays came to be dedicated to the Virgin. And so services could
be held throughout the week.[122]

The third form of the liturgical calendar consisted of the annual
cycle. The church year was divided into a festival half and a non-
festival half. The former centered on the life of Christ and moved
from Advent through Christmas, Lent, Good Friday, Easter, and
culminated with the feast of the Ascension of Christ into heaven.
The latter half of the church year began with Pentecost followed by
Trinity Sunday. The weeks that followed were often simply designated as Sundays after Trinity. These Sundays and feasts reflected the
narrative of God's activity in history and provided opportunity for
reflecting on the ways in which God related to His human creatures.

Over the course of time, many other feasts or days of commemoration were inserted into the yearly round so that the yearly calendar
became increasingly crowded. New spiritual concerns gave rise to
new "holy days" that were officially sanctioned by the church. Often

---

120. R. Taft, *The Liturgy of Hours in East and West* (Collegeville: Order of St. Bene-
dict, 1986), 85.

121. R. N. Swanson, *Religion and Devotion in Europe, c. 1215–1515* (Cambridge:
Cambridge University Press, 1995), 93.

122. J. Geffken, *Der Beldercatechismus des funfzehnten Jahrhunderts und die cateche-
tischen Hauptstucke in dieser Zeit bis auf Luther* (Leipzig, 1855). See also T. N. Tentler,
Sin and Confession on the Eve of the Reformation (Princeton: Princeton University Press,
1977), 63, in which he notes that in addition to Sunday, the Sabbath included other feast
days, according to Guido de Monte Rocherii: the Nativity of Christ, feast of St. Stephan,
John the Evangelist, *sanctorum Innocentum, Silestri, Circumcistio*, Epiphany, Purification
of Mary, *Sanctum pasca cum tota ebdomada*, three days of Rogantide, the Ascension of
Christ, Pentecost, John the Baptist, Sts. Peter and Paul, Laurentii, Assumption of the Virgin
Mary, St. Michael, All Saints, and St. Martin and its attendant festivals.

these additional festivals were included in a piecemeal manner. Many of these commemorations were observed by the entire church while others were more localized to a particular territory or city.[123] Many of these "holy days" were extra-liturgical or para-liturgical in nature and focused more on social relationships within the community.

The additional feast days inserted into the yearly round included, for example, those that marked the turning point from winter to spring and that were celebrated within the first couple months of the church year. Thus the feast of Fabian and Sebastian (Jan. 20) was tied to new sap rising in the trees. On St. Agnes's (Jan. 21) a lamb would be blessed with holy water. There followed in short order, St. Vincent's day (Jan. 22) and St. Paul's day (Jan. 25). On the Purification of the Virgin (Feb. 2), candles were blessed to symbolize purity and light of the world. On St. Blasius's day (Feb. 3) horses and cattle were given blessed water. On the feast of St. Dorothea (Feb. 6), people were promised protection against frost on tender plants. On St. Gallus's day (Oct. 16) in Augsburg each year, they observed a ritual expulsion of prostitutes.[124]

Given the number of liturgical days and the importance accorded them, the focus of various interpretations of the Sabbath commandment centered on how one should observe those days, particularly through the cessation of work. In this regard, catechists tended to focus on Exod 20:9–10, which spoke about rest on the Sabbath, but now they applied it to all holy days of the church year. In the process an extensive catalog of requirements arose about the kind of "rest" that was required of the people in connection with the various holy days.

As a general rule one could say that "except in cases of dire need all work and trading had to cease; entertainment opportunities were limited."[125] For example, Kolde explains that violators of the Sabbath include:

> those who gamble or play out of avarice, passing their time with ball games, block throwing, nine pins, doubling, dice games and the like, or those who fail to attend services because of such games. . . . Those careless ones who live immodestly and impurely in the taverns and unnecessary meals with dis-

---

123. Swanson, *Religion and Devotion*, 93–96.
124. R. W. Scribner, *Popular Culture and Popular Movement in Reformation Germany* (London: Hambledon Press, 1987), 3–5.
125. Swanson, *Religion and Devotion*, 93.

honorable women. Those who buy or sell on the holy day, when it is not necessary. . . . Those who do tailoring, or sew, or shoe horses, or do washing or the like. . . . Those who spend practically the whole morning of a holy day putting on new shoes or clothes. . . . Those who go to church and disturb the service with chatting, laughing and other mischief.[126]

On the annual calendar, a large number of "minor" or quasi-liturgical feasts interrupted the year and thus "increased the demands of devotion, and had their own impact on daily life, often in a ban on trade and labour."[127] "The feasts and seasons of the Christian calendar were not just dates: they impacted daily life in dietary and other restrictions—the abstinence from meat on Friday and Lent; a ban on sexual activity at certain seasons (notably during Advent and Lent) or on particular days, prohibitions on trade and labour, the halting of judicial processes."[128] Other days had their special restrictions: Saturdays dedicated to the Virgin with special Masses; Fridays, in recollection of Good Friday, with meat-eating banned except for fish. Local festivals and commemorations added their own customs and requirements.

A Day of Rest

When Luther undertook the task of translating and explaining the Sabbath commandment, he chose not to interpret *sabbat* or *feiertag* with reference to the church's designated liturgical days (*kulttagen* or *feriae*). Instead, he chose to interpret it in connection with a general day of rest (*ruhetag*).[129] In other words, for Luther *sabbat* and *feiertag* should be ways of designating any "day of rest" (*ruhetag*).[130] In his "September Sermons" (1528) Luther put it succinctly: "The Sabbath means that one rests."[131] He thus shifts the focus of the commandment away from the religious days (together with their required observances) that had been specifically designated or established by the church, and instead he concentrates on

---

126. Kolde, "Mirror for Christians," 54–55.
127. Swanson, *Religion and Devotion*, 94.
128. Ibid., 96.
129. Just as one would call the time of rest in the evening an "evening rest" (*feierabend*) so the day of rest (*feiertag*) is in a similar sense a rendering/reproduction of the Sabbath. Cf. Meyer, *Historischer Kommentar zu Luthers Kleinem Katechismus*, 206.
130. Ibid., 207. Luther simply defined rest (*feiert*) as a cessation of work ("September Sermon Series," *WA* 30, I, 32).
131. *WA* 30, I, 31, 37.

the day of rest as established by God in creation. Again, he simply states, "God has appointed a day of rest."[132] Moreover, hearkening back to our earlier discussion of creation as the context for the commandments, Luther continues that "nature has taught it ever since" (i.e., that we need bodily rest). Our Creator did not design us to be on the go 24–7, 365 days a year.

The shift to creation as the context allowed Luther to make the point that the Sabbath was made for man and not man for the Sabbath (Mark 2:27). In other words, the Sabbath commandment was not given in order to require our obedience to humanly devised devotional acts. Instead, the observance of the Sabbath was intended to serve the needs of God's human creatures for rest and refreshment. On this basis Luther would criticize the multiplication of festival days since they go beyond natural law.[133]

The appeal to natural law would become a particularly strong argument against those who insisted upon the observance of the literal Sabbath. In light of his radical Christocentric hermeneutic for reading the Old Testament, Luther simply noted that Christian freedom did not require Christians to observe the literal seventh day, namely, Saturday.[134] Instead, in light of his Christocentric hermeneutic and his revaluation of creation, Luther could dare to call the literal Sabbath an "external" matter. He placed the literal Sabbath into the same category as the ordinances and regulations of the Old Testament: "It is an entirely external matter, like the other regulations of the Old Testament associated with particular customs, persons, times, and places, from all of which we are now set free through Christ."[135] They "have no validity for Christianity."[136] In "Against the Sabbatarians," he writes, "In the New Testament the Sabbath is annihilated as it regards the crude external observance, for every day is a holy day."[137] Again, Luther roots it all in natural law.[138]

---

132. "Ten Sermons on the Catechism, November 30–December 18, 1528," *LW* 51:143.

133. Meyer also appropriately points out that one should not misunderstand Luther's criticism to mean that he pleaded for the elimination of all religious days (*Historischer Kommentar zu Luthers Kleinem Katechismus*, 207–8).

134. See "Against the Sabbatarians," *LW* 47:91–93. Luther further argues, "Where then the Mosaic law and the natural law are one, there the law remains" ("Against the Heavenly Prophets," *LW* 40:97).

135. *Book of Concord*, LC, 397 para. 82.

136. H. Girgensohn, *Teaching Luther's Catechism* (Philadelphia: Muhlenberg, 1959–1960), 57–58.

137. *LW* 35:166.

138. Natural law was deeply rooted in Luther's thinking. See "How Christians Should Regard Moses" (*LW* 35:155–74); J. T. McNeill, "Natural Law in the Thought of Luther,"

Luther also argues that since this day had been established for bodily rest, God does not fix "the time when the day of rest shall occur."[139] In "Against the Heavenly Prophets," he states, "Nature also shows and teaches that one must now and then rest a day, so that man and beast may be refreshed. . . . It is clear that he who does not need rest may break the Sabbath and rest on some other day, as nature allows."[140] Again, Luther observes, "Nature teaches and demands that the common people . . . should also retire for a day to rest and be refreshed."[141]

So even though Luther did not include in his rendering of the Decalogue those verses that require abstention from work (Exod 20:9–11), he retained the sum and substance with his word "day of rest." But he did not turn that day of rest into a catalog of do's and don'ts at which point it would no longer be restful! Instead, he notes that "we observe [holy days], first, because our bodies need them."[142] As H. Girgensohn notes, even in this more secularized form, "the Sunday rest has significance for the whole structure of life" that is not to be underestimated.[143] The well-known Lutheran historian, M. Marty, observes in a little commentary on Luther's Large Catechism, "If God owns man's rest time, and man really believes in God, then man is asked to rest in God, as part of God's plan."[144]

This "creational" approach to the Sabbath marks a bit of a departure from the way in which Luther interpreted the Sabbath in his earlier writings. In those writings Luther stressed that the bodily rest was a symbol of an inner spiritual rest, a Sabbath of the soul.[145] This was more in line with Augustine's spiritualized understanding. "Within, in the Heart, is our Sabbath!"[146] Luther received this meaning handed down through the Middle Ages. It was interpreted as the unreserved abandonment of one's will to the divine will. In his *Decem Praecepta* (1518),[147] Luther included the

---

in *Church History* 10 (1941): 211–27; and H. Bornkamm, *Luther's Doctrine of the Two Kingdoms in the Context of His Theology*, trans. K. H. Hertz (Philadelphia: Fortress, 1966).

139. Girgensohn, *Teaching Luther's Catechism*, 57.
140. "Against the Heavenly Prophets," *LW* 40:98.
141. *Book of Concord*, LC, 397 para. 83.
142. Ibid.
143. Girgensohn, *Teaching Luther's Catechism*, 62.
144. M. Marty, *The Hidden Discipline* (St. Louis: Concordia, 1974) 10.
145. Peters, *Kommentar Zu Luthers Katechismen*, 17.
146. Ibid., 169.
147. M. Basse, "Luthers frühe Dekalogpredigten in ihrer historischen und theologischen Bedeutung," *Luther: Zeitschrift der Luther-Gesellschaft* 78 (2007): 6–17.

spiritual meaning alongside the five works of sanctification.[148] In his "Sermon on Good Works" (1520), spiritual rest meant not only that we rest from the work of our hands, but much more—we must allow God to work in us. "'You shall sanctify the Sabbath-day' that I may work in you."[149] In brief, this "commandment requires a person to be poor in spirit, to sacrifice his nothingness to God so that He may be that soul's only God and that in that soul God's deeds may be glorified."[150]

To Sanctify the Day of Rest

It is worth noting that neither the bodily rest (Large Catechism) nor the Sabbath rest for the soul (which he leaves behind completely) is picked up by the Small Catechism. Little by little, Luther pushes the hearing of God's Word into the center of the Commandment itself and finally displaces all other topics in the Small Catechism.[151]

While Luther understands the Sabbath or *feiertag* as a period of rest—especially in the Large Catechism—he focuses his attention on what we are to do with that day, namely, we are to sanctify it (to put it aside). And so he renders the biblical text as "hallow [sanctify] the day of rest." Put another way, Luther concentrates on the purpose of bodily rest. In his Ten Sermons, he stresses, "God has appointed a day of rest and on that day our bodies are to rest from physical labor. . . . It is not enough, however, that you only rest; you are also *to keep this rest holy*. The commandment does not say: You shall be idle or get into mischief on the day of rest; but rather, you shall keep it holy (emphasis added).[152] "A person refrains from work

---

148. This is different from the works of sanctification Luther had listed in *Decem Praecepta* according to the medieval list that enumerated five works of sanctification: namely, hear the Mass, hear the word, pray, make offerings, and be reconciled, but with clearer critique of the evangelical elements. See Meyer, *Historischer Kommentar zu Luthers Kleinem Katechismus*, 212; WA 1, 398–521.

149. Peters, *Kommentar Zu Luthers Katechismen*, 170; WA 11, 39, 14–19.

150. *LW* 43:22. The entire section reads as follows: "Yield to God so that all we do is done by him alone through us. This commandment requires a person to be poor in spirit [Matt 5;3], to sacrifice his nothingness to God so that He may be that soul's only God and that in that soul God's deeds may be glorified [2 Cor 9:13] as the first two commandments require. Here belongs everything required of us: serving God, listening to what is preached about God, doing good deeds, subjecting the body to the spirit [1 Cor 9:27]. And so that all we accomplish is God's and nothing our own."

151. Cf. Peters, *Kommentar Zu Luthers Katechismen*, 162.

152. *LW* 51:143.

for the sake of hallowing the day."[153] And so Luther will not place the emphasis of the commandment upon enumerating various forms of resting or different restrictions on human activity as a way of keeping the commandment. Instead, he will focus on what we are to do with our times of rest. The accent in Luther's catechisms will fall not on the "rest" but on "sanctifying" the day of rest.[154]

What does it mean to sanctify the day of rest? It does not mean that we can somehow make the day or time holy as if it were not holy prior to our sanctifying it. God himself had made the day of rest holy. Here Luther picks up the thought of Exod 20:11b, which gives reference to the seventh day of creation and states, "Therefore the Lord blessed the Sabbath day and made it holy." The day has already been sanctified or set apart by God's Word. God had given the day of rest the highest worth when he bound the Word of blessing to it. Luther referenced the biblical sentence "God sanctified the Sabbath (Exod 20:11)" to mean that the day of rest had the Word as its "holy thing" (*heiligtum*): "The Word of God is the thing (*heiligtum*) that makes the holy day holy."[155] So people and their actions are holy through the Word. "For the Word of God is the true holy object above all holy objects. . . . But God's Word is the treasure that makes everything holy. By it all the saints themselves have been made holy."[156] This places emphasis upon the Word as the holy thing. By 1528 this replaces earlier thoughts that the devotional exercises are the key to sanctifying the holy day.[157]

In the establishment of the Sabbath day at the beginning of the world, the way had been prepared for worship days. They provide time and opportunity for the preaching and hearing of the Word and in turn are made holy through that Word (even as the original Sabbath). These worship days are holy not inasmuch as they contain a series of churchly ordained ceremonies but inasmuch as they provide times and places for the proclamation of the Word of God that incites faith; and, therefore, the Word for Luther pushes into the center of all worship practices. "Places, times, persons, and the entire outward order of worship have therefore been instituted and

---

153. Girgensohn, *Teaching Luther's Catechism*, 57.

154. Peters, *Kommentar Zu Luthers Katechismen*, 162.

155. Meyer notes that he takes the expression *heiligtum* from the language of the cult, which was the name for the relics of the saints of the church buried in the altar, by which the church received its holiness. *WA* 30, 32.

156. *Book of Concord*, LC, 399 para. 91.

157. Meyer, *Historischer Kommentar zu Luthers Kleinem Katechismus*, 211.

appointed in order that God's Word may exert its power publicly."[158] The Word is the heart of worship.

From this it becomes clear why Luther explains the sentence "to hallow the day of rest" is to "hold the day sacred. . . . For this day is given to us in order that we may use it for the exercise of holiness."[159] But this is nothing else than to hold sacred that which makes the day holy, namely, the Word of God and using it for the purpose that God gave it. Above all else it takes place through the preaching and hearing of the Word. Therefore, it presupposes that the Word of God stands at the center of the worship day, and establishes/determines above all else, that the sanctifying of the day of rest is expounded as a "holding the Word sacred."[160]

Do Not Despise . . .

Luther interprets the "despising" of the Word as refusing to "hear and learn it." This also includes those who only from habit go to the service of the Word without seriousness and care to hear it and learn nothing, alongside those who from *geiz order leichtfertigket* (avarice and gross negligence) generally do not come to the divine service.[161]

God "wills that we should keep the holy day by receiving the gifts he offers. The full seriousness and severity of the commandment lies in our not spurning his outstretched hand, lest we lose God himself." In other words, "this commandment is aimed at all our human laziness and slackness, our tendency to do what we feel like doing, our disinterest and unconcern."[162]

> Therefore this commandment is violated not only by those who grossly misuse and desecrate the holy day, like those who in their greed or frivolity neglect to hear God's Word or lie around in taverns dead drunk like swine. It is also violated by that other crowd who listen to God's Word as they would to any other entertainment, who only from force of habit go to hear the sermon and leave again with as little knowledge at the end of the year as at the beginning.[163]

---

158. *Book of Concord*, LC, 399 para. 94.
159. *LW* 51:143–4.
160. Meyer, *Historischer Kommentar zu Luthers Kleinem Katechismus*, 211.
161. Peters, *Kommentar Zu Luthers Katechismen*, 163.
162. Girgensohn, *Teaching Luther's Catechism*, 64.
163. *Book of Concord*, LC, 399 para. 96.

So much depends on God's Word that "we must realize that God wants this commandment to be kept strictly and will punish all who despise his Word and refuse to hear and learn it, especially at the times appointed."[164] Hold it sacred, and willingly hear it and learn it!

"The day itself does not need to be made holy, for it was created holy. But God wants it to be holy for you."[165] How does this take place? "When we make use of God's Word and exercise ourselves in it."[166] In the second chief section of the LC, "*heilig Halten*," Luther pushes the Word into the center of the commandment as its focus "as the divinely instituted means for sanctification into the center and binds in it the [Sabbath] commandment with the first."[167] "Accordingly, I constantly repeat that all our life and work must be guided by God's Word if they are to be God-pleasing or holy."[168] Only in this way does "rest become that real rest which lifts one out of toil and trouble, out of futility and care, out of sin and shame, in short, out of the whole sphere of earthly life."[169]

Did you notice the turnaround of events that takes place? We sanctify the day by devoting ourselves to God's Word, but the Word ends up sanctifying us and thus the day.

> Note, then, that the power and force of this commandment consists not in the resting but in the hallowing, so that this day may have its special holy function. Other work and business are really not designated holy activities unless the person doing them is first holy. In this case, however, a work must take place through which a person becomes holy. This work, as we have heard, takes place through God's Word.[170]

But here a work must be performed by which the doer himself is made holy; this, as we have heard, takes place only through God's Word. Luther continues: "Remember, then, that you must be concerned not only about hearing the Word, but also about learning it and retaining it."[171] Luther then speaks about what that word produces within our lives.

---

164. Ibid., para. 95.
165. Ibid., 398 para. 87.
166. Ibid., para. 88.
167. Peters, *Kommentar Zu Luthers Katechismen*, 173.
168. *Book of Concord*, LC, 399 para. 92.
169. Girgensohn, *Teaching Luther's Catechism*, 63.
170. *Book of Concord*, 399 para. 94.
171. Ibid., 400 para. 98.

When we seriously ponder the Word, hear it, and put it to use, such is its power that it never departs without fruit. It always awakens new understanding, pleasure, and devotion, and it constantly creates clean hearts and minds. For this Word is not idle or dead, but effective and living.[172]

So the Lucas Cranach woodcut that Luther included with the Sabbath Commandment in his translation of the Bible depicted a congregation listening attentively to the Word as it is being proclaimed by the pastor. Meantime, through the window the reader can see a man gathering firewood on the hillside. He is not devoting himself to the Word of God. And so Luther declares, "It is commanded that you should not remain idle at home and thus despise the Word, but go to church and hear it."[173]

Conclusion

Luther's approach to the Sabbath Commandment set the direction for most subsequent Lutheran treatments of the topic. The one notable exception in American Lutheran history is that of Samuel Simon Schmucker. In the nineteenth century, Schmucker sought to "Americanize" Lutheranism and thus promoted a general Protestantism that had a decidedly German Reformed character. To that end he even proposed that Lutherans revise the Augsburg Confession (known as the "American Recension of the Augsburg Confession") to eliminate teachings regarding baptismal regeneration, private confession, the real presence of the Lord's Supper, amillennialism, and a nonliteral Sabbath. But Schmucker was decidedly rejected by a growing tide of confessional Lutheranism in the second half of the twentieth century. Since that time there has really not been any significant debate regarding the Sabbath or the interpretation of the Sabbath Commandment.

So Luther's explanations in both the Small and Large Catechisms continue to shape the way in which the Sabbath Commandment is taught to both children and adults. Part of the reason is that these two catechisms remain integral documents within Lutheran confessional writings. In other words, they are official confessional statements of the Lutheran church throughout the world. Hav-

---

172. Ibid., para.101.
173. *LW* 51:146.

ing said that, it must be admitted that many Lutherans today are unaware of Luther's hermeneutical approach to dealing with the Sabbath in particular and the Ten Commandments in general. That is to say, many today are unaware of both Luther's Christocentric hermeneutic to the Old Testament and his understanding of the Commandments in connection with creation. In this regard, many Lutherans have been shaped in their reading of the Ten Commandments by contemporary exegetes who have highlighted the importance of the biblical prologue for reading the Ten Commandments. This in itself, however, has not necessarily led to a reinterpretation of the Sabbath and its applicability to the Christian life today.

CHAPTER 6

Responses to
Charles P. Arand

Response by Skip MacCarty

Dr. Arand is to be commended for his scholarly and informative essay on Luther's, and Lutheranism's, position on the Sabbath commandment. Luther's contribution to the Reformation and the development of evangelical theology is seminal: His commitment under great adversity to the primacy of Scripture, grace, and faith stoked the fires of the Reformation. His Large Catechism stands among the classics of Christian literature and has blessed me personally. The evangelical church, including the Sabbatarian movement, owes much to Luther.

Rich homiletical material punctuated this essay, such as: "Our inability to keep [the Commandments] and hence our need of Christ" (p. 224); "the first Commandment instructs the heart and teaches faith . . . highlight[ing] the proper motivation for keeping the Commandments" (pp. 239–40); though the Ten Commandments may seem trivial to some, "they remain the very commands of God," and "for that reason, they set forth the greatest and most precious things that we can do" (pp. 246–47). I could cite many other examples.

Remarkable for its absence, however, is any discussion of the biblical material related to the Sabbath. The essay discusses Luther rather than Scripture, focusing primarily on Luther's interpretation of his own rendering of the Sabbath commandment in the Large Catechism:

"You shall sanctify God's holiday,"[1] a rendering Luther believed expresses the "natural law" behind the commandment in the Decalogue.[2]

As Arand acknowledges, Luther devotes 50 percent of his Large Catechism to explaining the Ten Commandments. The other four sections are devoted to The Faith (Apostles' Creed), the Our Father (Lord's Prayer), Baptism, and the Sacrament (Lord's Supper), with priority given to the first three sections. All Christians, Luther said, should "be obligated to learn and know the Ten Commandments, the Creed, and the Lord's Prayer. Indeed, the total content of Scripture and preaching and everything a Christian needs to know is quite fully and adequately comprehended in these three items. . . ."[3] In his treatise, "Against the Antinomians," he wrote:

> It is most surprising to me that anyone can claim that I reject the law or the Ten Commandments, since there is available, in more than one edition, my exposition of the Ten Commandments, which furthermore are daily preached and practiced in our churches. . . . I myself, as old and as learned as I am, recite the commandments daily word for word like a child.[4]

Thus Luther leaves no doubt as to the importance he attributes to the Ten Commandments, as the following statements from his Large Catechism further attest:

- "These commandments are not trivialities put together by human beings. They are the commandments of God's great majesty. He keeps a watchful eye on them, and angrily punishes those who look down on them, just as he is quite extravagant in rewarding those who keep them."[5]
- "We should prize and value the commandments more highly than any other teachings. They are the greatest possible treasure—and it has been given to us by God."[6]
- In his section on The Faith/Apostles' Creed:

---

1. *Luther's Large Catechism: Anniversary Translation and Introductory Essay by Friedmann Hebart* (hereafter *LC*; Adelaide, Australia: Lutheran Publishing House, 1983), 1:78.
2. Since Arand relies so heavily on Luther in his essay, I will do the same in this critique.
3. *Luther's Works* (hereafter *LW*), J. Pelikan and H. Lehmann, gen. eds. (St. Louis: Concordia; Philadelphia: Fortress; Philadelphia: Muhlenberg Press, 1955–86).
4. *LW* 47:109.
5. *LC* 1:330.
6. *LC* 1:333.

[The Faith] tells us everything we are to expect and receive from God. In short, it teaches us to know him completely. This is meant to help us do what we are supposed to do according to the Ten Commandments. . . . It's just as necessary to learn this section as it is to learn the other [the Ten Commandments], so that we can know how to go about keeping the commandments, and where and how to get the strength we need.[7]

- In his section on the Our Father:

What we need most of all is to keep on pestering God with our prayers, and to ask him to give, keep on providing, and develop in us faith and power to do what the Ten Commandments expect. We need to be at him to clear away whatever lies in our path and prevents us from believing and keeping them.[8]

- In his section on the Sacrament: "The Sacrament is like the Ten Commandments, the Our Father, and the Faith: they remain what they are and always apply, even if you never keep them, pray them, or believe them."[9]

A Sabbatarian reading these statements would think that Luther was surely one of us. Luther would reply, "No, for you sabbatarians have bound yourselves to the Ten Commandments written by Moses, but I speak of the Ten Commandments written by nature." Throughout his essay Arand adeptly points out the difference.

Luther's concept of "natural law" did not originate with him. He acknowledges his own indebtedness in part to Plato for this concept:

The heathen Plato writes that there are two kinds of justice—that which is by nature and that which is just by law. I am going to call them the healthy law and the sick law. Whatever is done with nature's power succeeds very smoothly without any law; in fact, it overrides all the laws.[10]

---

7. *LC* 2:1–2.
8. *LC* 3:2.
9. *LC* 5:5.
10. *LW* 13:163–64.

Greek philosophers, whom Luther described as "the wisest people on earth,"[11] distinguished "natural law," an eternal moral order, from "positive law," civic legislation imposed by governments on their citizens. They considered the ideal to be a perfect congruence between the two.[12]

In 1521, Melanchthon, ahead of Luther, adapted this philosophical "natural law" concept into a theological one. He defined "natural law" as "a common judgment to which all men alike assent, and therefore one which God has inscribed upon the soul of each man."[13] Luther expresses his own understanding of "natural law" in his commentary on Ecclesiastes, in which he also equated "natural law" with "human reason":

> This Book of Ecclesiastes . . . does not, indeed, legislate or prescribe laws for the governance of the state or the family. This is taken care of in great detail by the natural law or human reason, to which, according to Gen 1:28, earthly things have been subjected; this has been, is, and must remain the source, the criterion, and the end of all laws, whether political or domestic.[14]

Luther sees "natural law" behind many of the biblical laws, especially love as expressed in the Golden Rule (Matt 7:12 and Luke 6:31)[15] and the Ten Commandments, but also including prohibitions against avenging wrongs against us (Deut 32:35),[16] against a couple eloping without parental consent (which he saw reflected in Exod 21:9),[17] against "forced engagements" (which he saw reflected in Gen 24:58),[18] and so forth.

Luther believed that such "natural laws" are written on the hearts of all humanity and that everyone will be held accountable for obedience to them. He writes in his commentary on Romans 2:12: The Gentiles "have received a spiritual law . . . . This law is impressed upon all people, Jews and Gentiles, and to this law all people are bound . . . the natural law, which cannot be unknown to anyone

---

11. *LW* 46:269.
12. *LW* 13:163–64 n. 31.
13. Ibid.
14. *LW* 15:4.
15. *LW* 45:127 n. 117, cf. 25:180; 46:114.
16. *LW* 46:25.
17. *LW* 46:269.
18. *LW* 46:304–305.

and on account of which no one can be excused."[19] He speaks of "the divine and natural law, which all the heathen keep."[20] And yet elsewhere he laments that "the noble gem called natural law and reason is a rare thing among the children of men."[21]

Further on in his commentary on Rom 2:12, Luther writes: "'They will perish without the Law' just as they are saved without the Law if they have kept their law, the law that is inborn and present in creation, not given; found at hand, not handed down to them; alive, not contained in letters."[22]

We see numerous problems with Luther's "natural law" schema. On the one hand we do not deny that to the heathen who have not had access to His written revelation in Scripture, God has provided a sufficient knowledge of truth to which they can respond and be either saved or lost (Rom 1:18–21; 2:14–16; cf. Eccl 3:11). On the other hand, such divine revelations of truth sufficient to save were nonetheless considered times of spiritual "ignorance" that God mercifully "overlooked" (Acts 17:30) when compared to His manifold written revelation in Scripture. Furthermore, Rom 3:10–18 describes natural man after the fall not as having the law of God inborn and written on the heart but rather in a condition where "no one understands, no one seeks God. All have turned away, they have together become worthless; there is no one who does good, not even one." Whatever spiritual light sufficient for salvation that those who were without the Scriptures have received from God over the centuries has been a revealed light, not one "inborn." John describes Jesus as "the true light that gives light to every man" (John 1:9; biblical quotations from the NIV). The NT is clear that fallen and unconverted humanity, unaided by the Spirit, can neither perceive nor obey spiritual truth. Jesus' declaration that "no one can see the kingdom of God unless they are born again. . . . You must be born again" applies equally to all fallen humanity in all historical ages (John 3:3–5). It is only after conversion and the new birth experience (i.e., "whenever one turns to the Lord," 2 Cor 3:16) that God fulfills His new covenant promise: "I will put my laws in their minds and write them on their hearts" (Heb 8:10 NIV).

---

19. *LW* 25:180.
20. *LW* 46:27.
21. *LW* 13:161.
22. *LW* 25:180–81.

Second, Luther makes "natural law" the source of written revelation. He writes: "At present people are beginning to praise natural law and natural reason as the source from which all written law has come and issued. This is true, of course, and the praise is well placed."[23] Luther repeatedly refers to the Ten Commandments recorded in Exodus 20 and Deuteronomy 5 as Jewish adaptations of the more ancient and universal natural laws that were "implanted at creation in the hearts of all men" and which Moses simply discerned and "fitted . . . nicely into his laws in a more orderly and excellent manner than could have been done by anyone else."[24] Luther refers to the seventh-day Sabbath commandment in Exod 20:8–11 as "Moses' commandment . . . [and] his Sabbath law,"[25] which Moses "imposed"[26] on Israel:

> The Sabbath, of which the Jews make so much, is per se a commandment that applies to the whole world; but the form in which Moses frames it and adapts it to his people was imposed only on the Jews . . . a temporary addendum and adaptation intended solely for this people which was brought out of Egypt.[27]

On this basis Luther declares the seventh-day Sabbath of Exod 20:8–11 to be "an entirely external matter,"[28] "only ceremonial,"[29] and "annihilated as it regards the crude external observance,"[30] "entirely abrogated through the Messiah,"[31] "finished . . . forever abandoned."[32] For Luther, the universal "natural law Sabbath (from which the Exod 20:8–11 Sabbath commandment was only a "crude" and "temporary" adaptation for the Jews) pertains to "the teaching and preaching of God's word, which is the true, genuine, and sole meaning of this commandment—has been from the beginning and pertains to all the world forever."[33]

---

23. *LW* 13:160.
24. *LW* 47:90; cf. 54:52, "What Moses teaches [in the Ten Commandments] is also taught by nature. To be sure, he expressed it better than the Gentiles, but they nevertheless taught the same thing."
25. *LW* 40:98.
26. Ibid.
27. *LW* 47:92.
28. *LC* 1:82.
29. *LW* 54:52.
30. *LW* 35:166.
31. *LW* 47:80.
32. *LW* 47:81.
33. *LW* 47:92.

Third, for Luther the "natural law" supersedes the written revelation of Scripture, and thus his natural law Sabbath replaces the Sabbath commandment of Exod 20:8–11. So Luther can write: "Where Moses gives commandment, we are not to follow him except so far as he agrees with the natural law,"[34] and "where then the Mosaic law and the natural law are one, there the law remains."[35] It is on this basis that Arand can suggest that Christians do not have "to obey [the Ten Commandments] simply because they are given in the Bible" (pp. 218, 220). This leaves to anyone's own personal judgment what laws of Scripture may have a corresponding, valid, and enduring natural law behind them, and what that more enduring natural law actually is, compared to what is written. Luther's statements that "nature also shows . . . nature allows . . . nature teaches" (p. 255) supposedly justify his bold statement that when it comes to "rest" one "may break the Sabbath [commandment of the Decalogue] and rest on some other day."[36] What would result if that same reasoning were to be logically extended to the other Commandments?

Suppose two teenagers met, fell passionately in love in a couple of days, and within weeks faced a decision regarding a resultant pregnancy. If they defended their actions based on what "nature taught" them and what "nature allowed" in the heat of the moment, what credence would that have with their concerned parents, or what justification before God? I have counseled couples in the midst of an adulterous affair who defended their actions with the claim that they were both having the most wonderful spiritual experience of their lives—"we have never felt so close to God as when we pray together and experience shared intimacy," they say. It sounds sophisticated to trump a scriptural command of God by appealing to a higher "natural law" that supersedes it, something "taught by nature" and that "nature allows," one that promotes one's own spiritual experience beyond what they suppose the literal written commandment provides. But such theological reasoning is perniciously dangerous and can easily become a runaway train of rationalization leaving no command of God in the OT or the NT safe from subjective manipulation.

To this Luther responds: "The commandment concerning the Sabbath is different from the other commandments of the Decalogue. . . . The others are general and are all taught by nature. . . .

---

34. *LW* 35:173.
35. *LW* 40:97.
36. *LW* 40:98.

The Sabbath is special and applies only to the Jews."[37] But this is an entirely arbitrary distinction based on Luther's highly subjective and speculative natural law theology.

It is our conviction that the only safe guide for the Christian is, "What does the Bible say?" Orthodox Christian doctrine is not based on natural law but on Scripture alone (2 Tim 3:16). When tempted by Satan in the desert, Jesus did not respond, with "Nature teaches . . . nature allows," but with, "It is written" (Matt 4:4,7, 10).[38] For believers in any historical era, the "It is written" Word of God supersedes any speculation regarding "natural law." The "It is written" Sabbath commandment of the Decalogue reads:

> Remember the Sabbath day by keeping it holy. Six days you shall labor and do all your work, but the seventh day is a Sabbath to the Lord your God. On it you shall not do any work, neither you, nor your son or daughter, nor your male or female servant, nor your animals, nor the foreigner residing in your towns. For in six days the Lord made the heavens and the earth, the sea, and all that is in them, but he rested on the seventh day. Therefore the Lord blessed the Sabbath day and made it holy (Exod 20:8–11 NIV).

In our view Luther's replacement of the "It is written" Sabbath with his "natural law" sabbath was not the product of a "radically Christocentric" hermeneutic as Arand suggests, but of a Lutherocentric one philosophically and speculatively based on his "natural law" theology. Luther chided the papal clergy of his day for preaching "faith" on the one hand, but neutering it on the other by

> divid[ing] faith into many parts . . . natural faith and spiritual faith . . . general and particular faith . . . explicit and implicit

---

37. *LW* 54:52.

38. The only place in Scripture that the term "nature teaches" appears is 1 Cor 11:14–15: "Does not the very nature of things teach [*phusis autē didaskei*, 'nature herself teaches'] you that if a man has long hair, it is a disgrace to him, but that if a woman has long hair, it is her glory?" This has been generally understood by scholars to be an appeal for Christians not to live so out of harmony with their cultural customs on nonmoral issues that they become an offense to the gospel. It has not been taken to mean that there is a law of hair length inborn in every human and taught by nature, the violation of which would be a sin against God. Nor has anyone suggested that short hair for men and long for women are among the "requirements of the law . . . written on the hearts . . . [and] consciences" of Gentiles, by which they will be accused or excused in the final judgment (Rom 2:15).

faith. The gospel knows nothing of these manifold distinctions; it proclaims the faith which puts its trust in nothing but God's grace, without any merit of works.[39]

Well said, Luther. Similarly, the Bible knows nothing of a Sabbath commandment divided into a "natural law" Sabbath that applies to all humanity and an "It is Written" Sabbath that applies only to the Jews. It proclaims only the Sabbath commandment that God wrote with His own finger and enshrined in the Decalogue—the seventh-day Sabbath on which God rested at creation and upon which He blessed and sanctified for holy purposes, with permanent and universal application.

Against the Sabbatarian teaching of Andrew Karlstadt, a Wittenberg colleague, Luther raised four objections.[40] First, "How do they propose to prove that Saturday is the seventh day? . . . It has not yet been established whether Christ died on a Saturday or a Friday." This objection is answered by Luke 23:50–24:3, which clearly identifies the biblical Sabbath as the day between Good Friday and Easter Sunday. Furthermore, the Jewish nation which has observed the seventh-day Sabbath throughout its history still does so today, on Saturday.

Second, Luther claims "the Sabbath is only ceremonial." This was answered millennia earlier when God enshrined the Sabbath commandment in His moral law of Ten Commandments, rather than including it among the many ceremonial rituals that were shadows of Jesus' atoning earthly ministry and thus abrogated when He died and rose for our justification.

Third, Luther says the Ten Commandments are not "to be applied to and imposed on us Christians" except at those points where they are also "taught by nature." I have answered this objection above in my discussion of Luther's speculative "natural law" theology.

And finally, Luther declares that "those who insist on the Sabbath ought to be circumcised as well." But Luther's association of circumcision with the Sabbath is completely arbitrary, not scriptural. Circumcision was neither a creation ordinance nor enshrined in God's moral law of Ten Commandments; the seventh-day Sabbath was both. My own Sabbatarian faith community has never advocated circumcision as a religious rite. The Holy Spirit rescinded circumcision at the Jerusalem Council. Hebrews 4:4,9 affirms

39. *LW* 52:241.
40. *LW* 54:51–52.

that seventh-day Sabbath observance "remains . . . for the people of God." "Circumcision is nothing and uncircumcision is nothing. Keeping God's commands [*entolōn,* 'commandments'] is what counts" (1 Cor 7:19).

Concerning his "natural law" Sabbath, Luther taught in his catechism that

> nature teaches and demands that ordinary people . . . should pause for a day of rest and recreation. Secondly, above all, there is a rest day, so that people will take the time and opportunity to go to divine service—because they wouldn't get there otherwise—that is, to come together to hear and busy themselves with God's word, and then praise God, sing, and pray.[41]

Luther chose Sunday for the NT day of worship, not because the Bible mandates it, as Arand takes care to point out, but because Sunday had become a traditional day of worship long before Luther's time. Then, once Luther gave his interpretation of how he believed the Sabbath that nature teaches should apply particularly to Christians, he added, as Arand notes, that "we must realize that God wants this commandment to be kept strictly and will punish all who despise his Word and refuse to hear and learn it, especially at the times appointed."[42] Luther not only dispenses with the "It is written" seventh-day Sabbath of the Decalogue, he also creates another Sabbath experience and corporate rest day in its place and threatens divine punishment on all who do not abide by it strictly, while at the same time touting this as Christian freedom (pp. 220–22). In other words, Luther commands a commandment the Bible does not command, and then he commands that his commandment be strictly obeyed on pain of divine punishment—all in the name of Christian freedom. This seems to us a curious irony.

Our view on the role of the Ten Commandments corresponds with the Protestant position on the three uses of the law, which Arand (p. 249) and the Formula of Concord[43] testify is also a Lutheran teaching. The three uses are summarized well in the Solid Declaration of the Formula of Concord:

---

41. *LC* I:83–84.
42. Cf. Arand's essay, p. 50 ; *LC* 1:95.
43. *The Book of Concord: The Confessions of the Evangelical Lutheran Church* (hereafter *BC*), ed. R. Kolb and T. Wengert, trans. C. Arand, et. al. (Minneapolis: Fortress, 2000), 502–3, 587–91.

> The law of God is used (1) to maintain external discipline and respectability against dissolute, disobedient people and (2) to bring such people to a recognition of their sins. (3) It is also used when those who have been born anew through God's Spirit, converted to the Lord, and had the veil of Moses removed for them live and walk in the law.[44]

The Holy Spirit is at work in all three uses. But it is particularly during the second use that the Holy Spirit works through the law to expose sin and bring conviction and a sense of the need of Christ, leading to conversion (Rom 3:20; Gal 3:24). At conversion under the Holy Spirit's supervision "the law of sin and death" (second use) becomes "the law of the Spirit of life" (third use) (Rom 8:2). Using Arand's terminology, the first use of the law is "prescriptive" (p. 248), wherein the law is viewed strictly in terms of commands and demands, and obedience is motivated by fear or a sheer sense of duty, even legalism. By contrast, in the third use the law may be described as Arand's "descriptive" phase (p. 248), wherein God's commandments are viewed as new covenant promises describing the kind of people He is making of us, restoring us to our original creation design: "I will put my laws in their minds and write them on their hearts" (Heb 8:10). Under the third use, the literal observance of the seventh-day Sabbath reminds God's people that they belong to Him by creation and redemption (Exod 20:11; Deut 5:15) and that He is the one who makes them holy by His Spirit who works within them (Exod 31:12). It also represents His invitation to find rest in Him from their temporal and spiritual labors, worries, anxieties (Matt 11:28; Heb 4:9–10).

Several other items in Arand's essay deserve comment. I found enlightening Arand's explanation of the medieval church's association of "Sabbath" with all of the holy days on the church's liturgical calendar and the regulations required for each. Luther initially and rightly shifted the Sabbath focus away from the myriad liturgical holy days to the day of rest appointed by God at creation (p. 253).[45] In light of our present Sabbath discussion, perhaps the real significance of the medieval church lies in how it solidified the early

---

44. *BC* 587.
45. Though as Arand insightfully points out, Luther eventually moved away from the "rest" concept of the Sabbath in favor of its provision for "the hearing of God's word" (p. 47).

church's gradual departure from the biblical Sabbath in its development of a liturgical tradition.

Arand suggests that Luther's treatment of the Ten Commandments is "surprisingly 'secular' in nature" (p. 221) and "nothing distinctively 'spiritual'" (p. 224). I found His treatment of the commandments, especially in his Large Catechism, to be profoundly spiritual, examining with spiritual discernment and depth the practical life of a believer in relation to God and others. Had he not considered them deeply spiritual, it seems unlikely that he would have described them as "the greatest possible treasure" from God which ought to be valued "more highly than any other teachings."[46] Of course he did not value them more highly than he valued Jesus or faith, but neither did he consider them "secular" or as "nothing distinctively spiritual."

Arand describes the priority Luther gave to the First Commandment over the others, for love and trust lead to a willing and delightful obedience to all of the other commandments (pp. 230–32). He said that Luther's focus on the First Commandment was meant to direct our attention more on "their Giver than on our obedience to the particularities of the Commandments themselves" (p. 245). This is a beautiful truth. But Arand then makes the curious statement that the Ten Commandments are "not about what we creatures do," nor "codes of ethics" (p. 245). And yet that is exactly what they are— a code of ethics about what we creatures are to do in our relationship to God and others. One does not have to choose between the commandments as pointing our attention to God or comprising a divine code of ethics for humanity. They serve both functions. What if the human race had never considered the prohibitions against murder, adultery, stealing, bearing false witness, and so forth, as a code of ethics, but only spiritual concepts to focus our attention on God? The only reason we can see for not considering the Ten Commandments a divinely provided code of ethics for humanity would be to divert attention away from the divine specificity of the blessed and sanctified *seventh day* embedded in the Sabbath commandment.

In our view, any discussion of God's law for the NT era must pass through Jesus' statement in Matt 5:17–18:

> Do not think that I have come to abolish the Law or the Prophets: I have not come to abolish them but to fulfill them. I tell

46. *LC* 1:333.

you the truth, until heaven and earth disappear, not the smallest letter, not the least stroke of a pen, will by any means disappear from the Law until everything is accomplished.

Referring to this statement, Luther writes: "When he said that the
law will not pass away . . . our Lord Christ is here not at all speaking of circumcision or of the law of ordinance of Moses, but rather
is speaking of the Ten Commandments."[47] We agree. But we believe
that the Ten Commandments that Jesus affirmed would not pass
away were not speculative ones based on natural law but were the
"It is written" law inscribed with Christ's own finger and contained
in Scripture.

In the Large Catechism, in defending baptism, the Lord's Supper, and the commandment to honor one's parents against those
who questioned the necessity of these practices for Christians,
Luther emphatically answered that they are commands of God and
need no further defense![48] Because the Lord's Supper is God's commandment, Luther went so far as to say that those who regularly
absented themselves from participating in it "can't be regarded as
Christians."[49] While Sabbatarians do not go so far as to judge who
are Christians based on their observance or nonobservance of the
Sabbath commandment, the only basis we have for the stance we
take regarding the divinely specified seventh-day element of the
Sabbath commandment is simply that it is the command of God. It
should need no other defense.

In addition to the issues discussed above, Dr. Arand's Sabbath
essay and further reading of Luther have raised several questions
for me.

- As the essay acknowledges, Luther claims that the prologue
  to the Ten Commandments, namely, "I am the Lord your
  God, who brought you up out of Egypt, out of the house of
  bondage," demonstrates that the Sabbath commandment
  of the Decalogue applies only to the Jews and not to Christians. And yet, if on this basis the Sabbath were only for the
  Jews and not Christians, then why is not the new covenant
  only for the Jews and not Christians, for the new covenant

---

47. *LW* 47:88.
48. *LC* 4:38 (baptism); 5:4–5 (Lord's Supper); 1:112–13 (honor one's parents).
49. *LC* 5:42.

was explicitly addressed to Israel? "I will make a new covenant with the house of Israel . . . . This is the covenant I will make with the house of Israel." (Heb 8:8,10).

- In defense of natural law as a basis for nine of the Commandments as they occur in the Decalogue, Luther wrote:

> For all creatures rightly regard God as God and honor his name, as do also the angels in heaven. Thus we and all human beings are obligated to hear his word, to honor father and mother, to refrain from killing, from adultery, from stealing, from bearing false witness, from coveting one's neighbor's house or anything else that is his. All the heathen bear witness to this in their writings, laws, and governments, as can be clearly seen; but nothing is said therein of circumcision or of the laws Moses gave to the Jews for the land of Canaan.[50]

This is a primary reason Luther rejects the specifics of the Sabbath commandment of the Decalogue because a seventh-day sabbath does not occur in the laws of heathen writings and governments, and is not something "which all the heathen keep,"[51] and therefore it must not be natural law and applicable for all humanity. But we ask, Where does the law prohibiting coveting show up in heathen legislation or writings? And where may the "natural law" Sabbath (in contrast to the seventh-day Sabbath of the Decalogue) that Luther defends be found in these sources? What did this natural law Sabbath look like as it was observed among the heathen—did they meet one day of the week for worship, consider every day a holy day, or just take care to get enough rest as they needed it and as "nature allowed"? Furthermore, on what scriptural basis do heathen writings and laws become the criterion on which the permanency of the Word of God in Scripture is to be assessed, especially in light of such revelations as Isa 40:6–8: "All men are like grass, and all their glory is like

---

50. *LW* 47:89–90. Cf. 46:27, 269, where Luther seems to assess "natural law" by observing "the natural law among the heathen, and also with the Greeks who were the wisest people on earth," laws "which all the heathen keep."

51. *LW* 46:27.

the flowers of the field. . . . The grass withers and the flowers fall, but the word of our God stands forever"?

- The essay states that "in light of his radical Christocentric hermeneutic for reading the Old Testament, Luther simply noted that Christian freedom did not require Christians to observe the literal seventh day, namely, Saturday" (p. 254). The Augsburg Confession, giving "an example of Christian freedom" says, "It was not necessary to keep the sabbath (Sunday) or any other day."[52] And yet Luther's own Sabbath commandment involves Christians setting Sunday aside to "assemble to hear and discuss God's word and then to offer praise, song, and prayer to God," and that "God wants this commandment to be kept strictly and will punish all who despise his Word and refuse to hear and learn it, especially at the times appointed."[53] On the one hand, Lutherans speak of Christian freedom in terms of not having to observe any particular day as a holy day. On the other hand, Luther claims that God will punish you if you do not strictly keep Luther's own sabbath command which includes attending divine service on Sunday.[54] This seems self-contradictory to me.
- Luther considers Exod 20:8–11 to be Moses' modification, exclusively for the Jews, of the natural law Sabbath that is universally written on the hearts of all humanity.[55] Did Luther, do modern Lutherans, believe that God wrote the Ten Commandments as recorded in Exodus 20 with His own finger (Exod 31:18)?

At his defense before papal interrogators at the Diet of Worms in 1521, at which he faced excommunication and possible death, Luther declared with consummate courage: "My conscience is captive to the Word of God. . . . Here I stand. I cannot do otherwise." Several months later Luther wrote the following taken from one of his sermons, which was also undoubtedly preached by pastors in hundreds of Lutheran pulpits across Germany:

---

52. *BC* 101, Augsburg Confession 28:60.
53. *LC* 1:82–98.
54. *LC* 1:83–85.
55. *LW* 47:90–92.

We should not look to the works and teachings, the glosses and lives of men, but rather fix our eyes on the pure Scriptures and retain what is best from the lives and teachings of all the saints, so that we may not undertake to snatch up everything they do and say, but judge all things carefully and choose with discrimination what is born of the Scriptures. Whatever the saints have devised themselves, without the Scriptures, that we should consider human and abstain from, as St. Paul teaches us in II Thessalonians 3 [1 Thess 5:21]: "Test everything; hold fast what is good."[56]

This is the Martin Luther we remember, the one who valued fidelity to Scripture more highly than preserving his own life. He acknowledged that great saints of the past made invaluable contributions to our understanding of Scripture. We should learn from them. But where they depart from Scripture, we need to part company with them. We revere Martin Luther as a great man of God and have learned much from him. But it is our understanding that due to his "natural law" hermeneutic based on philosophy rather than Scripture, Luther had a blind spot relative to the integrity of the seventh-day Sabbath of the Decalogue. And in this regard we should follow his own counsel that "whatever the saints have devised themselves, without the Scriptures, that we should consider human and abstain from, as St. Paul teaches us [in 1 Thess 5:21]: 'Test everything; hold fast what is good.'"

Response by Joseph A. Pipa

I thank Dr. Arand for his chapter, from which I learned a great deal. As I understand it, Dr. Arand's purpose is to state the Lutheran confessional position on the Sabbath commandment. He lays the foundation for this position by leading us through the exegetical process Luther used in arriving at this position.

Luther's approach to the Mosaic law, particularly the Sabbath commandment, may be termed minimalist. According to Arand, Luther taught that the Commandment teaches the need of a day of rest, without specifying which day in the week; the day is to be sanctified by the careful use of the Word of God.

---

56. *LW* 52:177.

According to Luther, the primary requirement of the Sabbath commandment is the careful use of God's Word. In his summary of it he wrote: "You are to hallow the day of rest. What is this? Answer: We are to fear and love God, so that we do not despise preaching or God's Word, but instead keep that Word holy and gladly hear and learn it." He rightly demonstrated that the Christian is not bound to keep the seventh-day Sabbath or any other holy days of the old covenant. He taught that God does not require any specific day to be observed, but that the church settled on Sunday "so that people will have time and opportunity . . . to attend worship services."[57] Furthermore, as already noted, we must not despise preaching and the Word by neglecting public worship.

How did Luther reach this interpretation? Arand says that Luther's approach to the Ten Commandments may best be understood through his radical "Christocentric hermeneutic" (p. 217). In order to understand how Luther applies this hermeneutic to the Sabbath, Arand develops three concentric circles: the creation and redemptive context by which Luther interprets the Commandments; the primacy of the First Commandment in interpreting two through ten; and Luther's interpretation of the Sabbath commandment.

The First Circle: Creation and Redemption Context of Interpretation

Under the creation and redemption context of Luther's hermeneutic, Arand asserts two things: first, that Luther viewed the Ten Commandments as given for all people and not primarily for the church; and second, that the Ten Commandments should not be interpreted within the context of the exodus. He concludes: "Neither of these assumptions (that the Ten Commandments are for Christians and that they should be interpreted in light of the prologue) should be taken for granted when reading Luther's interpretation on the topic." He continues: "By doing it this way Luther highlights the universal context of the Ten Commandments. In other words, they are not a distinctively Christian 'thing' or ethic. They apply to everyone by virtue of the truth that everyone was created by God. Luther believed that the Ten Commandments applied to Christians not because they appear in Exodus or Deuteronomy but because they express the law of creation" (p. 219).

---

57. Large Catechism, in *Book of Concord*, 397 para. 84.

In setting forth his first assertion, Arand commits the fallacy of a false alternative. He seems to assert that if one believes that God gave the Ten Commandments to govern the church, one cannot believe they also are for all mankind. He fails to understand that the Ten Commandments are a summary of God's moral law for all people, which God gave to the church as her standard of obedience. I would agree with Luther's statement that God's law "is written in the hearts of all people." If this fact is true (and it is), then His law would apply to the believer primarily since God redeemed His people to serve Him according to it.

Arand, however, goes on to admit the Ten Commandments had a particular application to Israel: "In terms of the form in which they come and the sequence in which they are numbered, those applied to the Israelites" (p. 119). But then he concludes: "Christians are free to use them of course, but they are not bound to do so simply by virtue of the fact that they appear in this form in Exodus 20 and Deuteronomy 5" (pp. 119–20). The first statement seems to concede that the Ten Commandments had a unique role for Israel, which Arand seems earlier to deny. The conclusion is a non sequitur. How does it follow from the fact that they receive their form and order for Israel that the Commandments are not binding on the Christian? More importantly if they are written on the hearts of all people, why ought not Christians to be governed by them?

As Reformed Christians, we concur that God's law binds all people. The Reformed approach to the Ten Commandments is summarized in the Westminster Larger Catechism:

> *What is the moral law?* The moral law is the declaration of the will of God to mankind, directing and binding everyone to personal, perfect, and perpetual conformity and obedience thereunto, in the frame and disposition of the whole man, soul and body, and in performance of all those duties of holiness and righteousness which he oweth to God and man: promising life upon the fulfilling, and threatening death upon the breach of it.[58]

Moreover, Dr. Arand does not appear to prove his statement: "Luther believed that the entire Ten Commandments applied to Christians not because they appear in Exodus or Deuteronomy but because they express the law of creation" (p. 119).

---

58. Westminster Larger Catechism 93.

I agree that the law of God was on Adam's heart at creation and that the remnant of that law (what Arand would call natural law) remains and functions through conscience. Although the Ten Commandments are binding on all, they were written on tablets of stone in particular to govern the church and are by nature religious, for they are God's direction to human beings as to how they should live.

This leads to his second assertion that the Ten Commandments should not be interpreted within the context of the deliverance from Egypt—that is, interpreted in light of the prologue: "I am the Lord your God, who brought you out of the land of Egypt, out of the house of slavery" (Exod 20:2 NASB). Is it valid to say that since Luther does not treat the prologue in the catechisms, he does not see the Commandments as having a covenantal setting? Arand points out that in Luther's lectures on the Ten Commandments "he interprets them in light of the Exodus event, which he then interprets typologically for the Christian" (p. 219).

Arand's conclusion based on his two assertions is that Luther did not find the Ten Commandments necessarily binding since Christ is the end of the Mosaic law. He concludes: "Christians have been freed from those laws. Yet now they have the freedom to go back into the Old Testament to find that which continues to apply to them. What criterion should guide them—their own arbitrary preferences? No. For Luther, the criterion that guides Christians is natural law or the law of creation . . . redemption recovers and restores creation. . . . Redemption enables Christians to recover creation and the orders of creation as the way in which God intended us to live out our lives. In a similar way, Christians can reembrace God's created design for life as expressed in the Ten Commandments. It is not that the Ten Commandments provide only a distinctively Christian way of living" (pp. 221–22).

First, I would ask, "Where is the exegetical basis for saying that since Christ has fulfilled the Law, the Christian is not to order his life by it?" In fact, the Ten Commandments, on the basis of Arand's principle, do provide a distinctive Christian way of living because only the Christian, by redemption and regeneration, can begin by God's grace to live this way. If the Ten Commandments are the objective record of God's law on man's heart, since that law does not change, they remain an objective standard. Luther wrote in the Small Catechism 87: "God wants us to keep His Commandments *perfectly in thoughts, desires, words,* and *deeds.*" And in discussing the three uses of the law (90): *"Thirdly,* the Law teaches us Christians which works we must do to *lead a God-pleasing life"* (emphasis original).[59]

Surprisingly, Arand asserts that "at the same time, a cursory reading of the Ten Commandments in Luther's Large Catechism will yield few distinctively Christian references and allusions" (p. 221). In the "Conclusion to the Ten Commandments," Luther wrote:

> For it will be a long time before they will produce a doctrine or estates equal to the Ten Commandments, because they are so high that no one can attain to them by human power; and whoever does attain to them is a heavenly, angelic man far above all holiness of the world. Only occupy yourself with them, and try your best, apply all power and ability and you will find so much to do that you will neither seek nor esteem any other work or holiness.[60]

And in the very next line, he wrote that they are "the first part of the common Christian doctrine, both for teaching and urging what is necessary." Luther, in fact, emphasizes their use by the Christian. Commenting on the First Commandment in the Large Catechism, he wrote: "Therefore it is the intent of this commandment to require true faith and trust of the heart which settles upon the only true God and clings to Him alone. That is as much as to say: 'See to it that you let Me alone be your God, and never seek another.'" Later in that section,

> Let every one, then, see to it that he esteem this commandment great and high above all things, and do not regard it as a joke. Ask and examine your heart diligently, and you will find whether it cleaves to God alone or not. If you have a heart that can expect of Him nothing but what is good, especially in want and distress, and that, moreover renounces and forsakes everything that is not God, then you have the only true God. If on the contrary, it cleaves to anything else, of which it expects more good and help than of God, and does not take refuge in Him, but in adversity flees from Him, then you have an idol, another god.[61]

In examining the Small Catechism, we find the same emphasis.

---

59. *Luther's Small Catechism* (St. Louis: Concordia, 1943), 86.

60. F. Bente and W. Dau, *Concordia, or Book of Concord: The Symbols of the Evangelical Lutheran Church* (St. Louis: Concordia, 1922), 12.

61. Ibid, 16.

There is also a problem with the assertion "that for the most part, the Ten Commandments deal with what might best be called 'creaturely matters'" (p. 224). This comment may apply to the second table (Exod 20:12–17) but surely not to Luther's exposition of the first table (vv. 3–8).

One other problem with this section is Arand's remark that "Luther includes the first clause 'I am the Lord your God" because this clause applies to all people—Christian and non-Christian alike. How? Because as maker of heaven and earth, God is the Creator of all people" (p. 227). Of course God is the creator of all, but the name Lord (Yahweh) is His covenantal name and expresses His peculiar relationship to His church.

I would conclude that Luther's approach in the two catechisms is to distil what he considers the essence of each Commandment. His catechetical approach is not intended to give a comprehensive exposition of the Ten Commandments. In my opinion Arand's first circle does not explain Luther's approach to the Sabbath commandment. The question remains, Does Luther's interpretation of the Commandment correctly distil its essence?

The Second Circle: The First Commandment as the Organizing Center

I found this section illuminating. Arand points out that Luther's entire exposition of the Mosaic law focuses on God because the First Commandment defines all the others. His emphasis on the personal nature of the Commandments is refreshing. But I think he goes too far and creates another false alternative when he says, "Luther brings out this intensely personal character of the Commandments by fastening our attention more on our relation to the Giver of the Commandments than on our obedience to the particularities of the commandments themselves" (p. 245). There really is no conflict between the personal nature and the fact that God requires our obedience to particularities of the Commandments.

Arand continues, "By preventing any separation of the Commandments from their author, Luther's explanations discourage a keeping score of sins so as to develop a list of do's and don'ts, of vices and virtues" (p. 245). The NT, however, makes many specific applications of the Ten Commandments in applying the law of Moses (Matt 5:21ff; Gal 5:13–24; Jas 2:1–13 for example).

One other problem with this section is Arand's assertion that the last nine Commandments are but ways of teaching the First

Commandment. On the contrary, I maintain that the NT writers apply the second table as distinct moral obligations (Rom 13:8–10 and Jas 2:1–13).

Third Circle: The Sabbath

In this section Dr. Arand develops Luther's exposition of the Sabbath commandment. In his early writings Luther taught that the bodily rest of the Sabbath was a symbol for spiritual rest—"a Sabbath of the soul" (p. 255). In the Large Catechism, in reaction to the medieval multiplication of holy days, Luther emphasized that the Commandment provides for physical rest. He based this requirement on natural law and rejected the observance of the literal Sabbath, which he believed to refer to the seventh-day Sabbath. He argued that God does not appoint any particular day of the week. He also wrote: "Second and most important, we observe them so that people will have time and opportunity on such days of rest, which otherwise would not be available, to attend worship services, that is, so that they may assemble to hear and discuss God's Word and then to offer praise, song, and prayer to God" (Large Catechism, "Third Commandment").

By the time he wrote the Small Catechism, he dropped the emphasis on physical rest and focused on how one uses the day. Rest is so one may pursue the spiritual purposes of the day. In his "Ten Sermons on the Catechism" he said that "God has appointed a day of rest and on that day our bodies are to rest from physical labor. . . . It is not enough, however, that you only rest; you are also *to keep this rest holy.* The commandment does not say: You shall be idle or get into mischief on the day of rest; but rather, you shall keep it holy" (p. 256).

Arand quotes Luther as emphasizing that we sanctify the day by focusing on the Word of God: "The Word of God is the thing . . . that makes the holy day holy." Through the word used on the sanctified day, God sanctifies His people holy. Arand concludes, "We sanctify the day by devoting ourselves to God's Word, but the Word ends up sanctifying us and thus the day" (p. 259). Luther made the Word of God the centerpiece of the Sabbath commandment. He arrived at this interpretation by teaching that the first Commandment deals with faith, the second the name, and the third the Word. "In like manner such fear, love, and trust is to urge and force us not to despise

His Word, but gladly to learn, hear, and esteem it holy, and honor it" (Large Catechism, "Conclusion to the Ten Commandments").

Luther said that the "gross sense" of the Commandment does not concern Christians: "It is an entirely external matter, like the other regulations of the Old Testament associated with particular customs, persons, times, and places, from all of which we are now set free through Christ" (Large Catechism, "Third Commandment").

Moreover, he emphasized that the rest was to be used in the pursuit of holiness: "Accordingly, when you are asked what 'You are to hallow the day of rest' means, answer: 'Hallowing the day of rest means to keep it holy. What is meant by 'keeping it holy'? Nothing else than devoting it to holy words, holy works, and holy living" (Large Catechism, "Third Commandment').

As to the day, Luther taught that the Commandment does not set aside a particular day; the church may select the day and since Sunday has been the day traditionally, we should use it in the same way for order.

In conclusion I have three problems. First, Luther misunderstood the purpose of the Sabbath commandment when he wrote:

> In the Old Testament, God set apart the seventh day, appointed it for rest, and commanded it to be kept holy above all other days. As far as outward observance is concerned, the commandment was given to the Jews alone. They were to refrain from hard work and to rest, so that both human beings and animals might be refreshed and not be exhausted by constant labor. In time, however, the Jews interpreted this commandment too narrowly and grossly misused it. They slandered Christ and would not permit him to do the very same things they themselves did on that day, as we read in the gospel—as if the commandment could be fulfilled by refraining from work of any kind. This was not its intention, but rather, as we shall hear, it meant that we should sanctify the holy day or day of rest (Large Catechism, "Third Commandment"). Bente and Dau translation, p. 64.

He fails to note that the creation ordinance, which is the basis of the Sabbath commandment, emphasizes sanctifying the day, and not simply physical rest. Moreover, Lev 23:3 teaches that the purpose of the old covenant Sabbath is worship: "For six days work may be done; but on the seventh day there is a sabbath of complete rest, a holy convocation. You shall not do any work; it is a sabbath to the Lord in all your dwellings" (NASB). The day of complete rest was for corporate worship. Therefore, Luther failed to note that the commandment was never simply concerned with external matters.

Second, although I would agree that public worship is the chief purpose of the day, this approach is too minimalistic. He seems to neglect the private acts of devotion and worship that also contribute to our sanctification.

Third, I have a problem with Luther's assertion that the Bible does not teach which day the commandment is to be observed. He admits that God sanctified and blessed the seventh day. Arand summarizes Luther's position: "The day has already been sanctified or set apart by God's Word. God had given the day of rest the highest worth when he bound the word of blessing to it" (p. 257). Since the Sabbath has been set aside from creation and this sanctification is the basis of the Sabbath commandment, it is surprising that Luther consigned the Sabbath to the dustbin of ceremonies. Luther said, "It is an entirely external matter, like the other regulations of the Old Testament associated with particular customs, persons, times, and places, from all of which we are now set free through Christ" (Large Catechism, "Third Commandment"). As I seek to show in my chapter, the apostles changed the day to the first day of the week, and because of their appointment, the church since then observed the first day.

At the end of the day, however, there is a good deal of conformity between Luther's approach and the practices of those who see Sunday as the Christian Sabbath. He advocated keeping a whole day for rest, meditation, and worship: "Although the Sabbath is now abolished, and the conscience is free from it, it is still good, and even necessary, that men should keep a particular day in the week for the sake of the word of God, in which they are to meditate, hear, and learn, for all cannot command every day; and nature also requires that one day in the week should be kept quiet, without labour either for man or beast."[62]

---

62. Quoted in P. Fairbairn, *Typology of Scripture* (Grand Rapids: Kregel, 1989), 2:452.

Response by Craig L. Blomberg

I was raised in one of the more liberal parishes within the old Lutheran Church of America, the most liberal of the three branches of American Lutheranism that later merged to create the Evangelical Lutheran Church in America (in which "evangelical," like the German *evangelische,* basically means Protestant as opposed to Catholic, not theologically conservative as opposed to liberal). Nevertheless, these were the transitional years of the 1960s (I was confirmed in 1968, the year of the assassinations of Martin Luther King Jr. and Robert Kennedy, and of the riots in Chicago during the Democratic National Convention there). So while our clergy, including professors representing the even more radical developments at the nearby Lutheran college, were young and liberal, many of our older members, including my parents, still adhered to the gospel in a form that Luther would probably have recognized.

It was only, of course, as my theological training progressed through three academic degrees that I was able to sort out the kinds of views to which I had been exposed and plot them on the larger landscape of Christian options. The supernatural elements in the Bible had not always been well served; often they were, to use Bultmann's famous term, demythologized. The historicity of Scripture was likewise frequently called into question; the Gospel parallels, for example, we were "shown" were full of contradictions. But somehow, between my grandparents, parents, certain Sunday school teachers and occasional sermons, I still managed to learn well the classic Lutheran emphases on justification by faith, the preeminence of grace, and the strong contrast between law and gospel, closely analogous (though scarcely identical) to the contrast between Old and New Testaments.

It was not until I began to participate in a Campus Life / Youth for Christ club during my sophomore year in high school, however, that I remember learning about the possibility of a personal relationship with Jesus *and* saw peers my own age who spoke of having such a relationship and lived in ways that demonstrated its reality and difference it made in their lives. For all too many young people in the church I grew up in, confirmation had devolved into a rite of passage that was one's ticket to leave church, not the beginning of participation in it as an adult with mature understanding, as it had been designed to foster. It was in high school also, in my senior year, that an independent Baptist friend of mine insisted that I had to be immersed as a believer in *his* kind of church in order to be saved. By that time I had already read enough of the Bible and met enough genuine believers to know he could not possibly be right. So I did not seriously investigate the prospect that believers' baptism by immersion might be the *right* thing to do, even if not salvific, until eight years later. Meanwhile, I migrated through the Evangelical Free Church, which allowed both Baptists and Paedobaptists into membership. It was a good place for me during those transitional years, allowing me to be an active evangelical in a formal ecclesiastical context without having to come to grips with the possibility of rejecting my upbringing more directly and the likelihood of hurting my family in the process.

All this is to say that before I ever read any of the other three essays in this volume, I was confident that I would gravitate much more enthusiastically to the Lutheran one than to either the Calvinist or the Seventh-day Adventist one. Although I became a Baptist during doctoral study in Scotland and have discovered plenty of Sabbatarianism in my adopted legacy on both sides of the Atlantic, it is not part of *my* theological psyche. Indeed, when he was first projecting this volume, Chris Donato, the editor, asked me if my view was sufficiently different from Luther's even to merit separate treatment. I told him I thought that it was, but that ours would certainly be the two closest ones in perspective in this volume.

As I have now actually read Charles Arand's essay, my reaction, while still highly appreciative, is not quite as enthusiastic as I first thought it might be. I think the main reason for that has to do with its format. While MacCarty, Pipa, and I all, without coaching, spent the majority of our chapters in exegetical study—explaining in fair detail what we believed about specific texts of Scripture from both Testaments—Arand has chosen primarily to quote Luther himself, along with those he most immediately influenced. Because Luther, unlike Calvin and numerous more recent theologians, did not primarily write *commentaries* on individual books of the Bible, Arand has followed the structure of those portions of Luther's *Works* that impinge on the Ten Commandments more generally, especially his Large and Short Catechisms. As a result there is little actual exegesis in Arand's chapter.

What did Luther think about Matt 11:28–30 and Christ's call to come to Him for rest? What about Col 2:16 and the Sabbath as

a shadow, the substance of which is Christ? Or Heb 4:1–10 and the
Sabbath rest that yet remains for the people of God? I've never taken
the time to do the research to see if Luther made substantive comments about texts like these and many others with which we could
compare the other exegetical approaches represented in this anthol-
ogy of perspectives. Perhaps he did not. That would make the structure and contents of Arand's chapter all the more understandable.
But Lutherans in more recent years have written commentaries on
all of the books in which these passages appear; one could at least
consult them and see what they say. For whatever reason, Arand
has chosen not to do this. As an exegete, then, rather than either a
systematic theologian or a church historian, much less a historical
theologian, I find it much harder to know how to respond to Arand's
chapter than to MacCarty's and Pipa's.

What is more, Arand spends a lot of his chapter not even talking
about the Sabbath at all. Instead he develops the concept at length,
and with considerable repetition of concepts and even individual
sentences and phrases, that the First Commandment is the key for
Luther to all the other Commandments, so that any exposition of
the Ten Commandments should give disproportionate attention to
the first one. That's not the same as saying any exposition of any
individual Commandment other than the first, like Arand's, should
give over a majority of its study to the First Commandment, but it
appears that is how Arand interpreted things. More puzzling is that
when he finally does turn to the specifics of the Sabbath commandment, we are told almost nothing of how the First Commandment
helps us interpret it. It is as if all the prolegomena that dominated
most of the essay was one section, largely unrelated to the final section and major area of interest for this book!

Still, there are a few comments I may make related to points
more or less in the order that they arise in Arand's chapter. I gravitate to the notion that fundamental biblical, ethical norms can often
(perhaps always) be defended on the basis of natural law as well as
divine revelation. Romans 1:32 seems to me legitimately to form
a key scriptural basis for the moral argument for God's existence
(which all people should acknowledge), while both Gen 1:26–28
and Eph 4:24 interpreted in light of Col 3:10 suggest that a central
dimension of the *imago Dei* in which all humans are created is the
capacity for a relationship with God characterized by righteousness

and holiness. Principles as foundational as the Ten Commandments, then, it makes sense to me, should "ring true" to many unregenerate humans, at least when they are being honest, insofar as the divine image in their lives is not entirely obliterated, only marred. Indeed, rest and worship appear in virtually every culture, though the rhythm for these varies widely, suggesting that these two components reflect the timeless portion of the Sabbath command, not a particular day, length of time, liturgy, or prescribed set of activities one cannot or must perform on a given day.

I likewise gravitate to Luther's Christocentric hermeneutic, even if, as an exegete, I find it at times a little overdone and, among his orthodox followers, sometimes slightly more exaggerated. With this hermeneutic, worshipping and resting on Sunday rather than Saturday makes perfect sense. Yet the Lutheran approach does not try to justify this switch in days, as Pipa did in his chapter, by arguing from specific NT texts and early church practice. Nor does one come away from Arand's chapter with the sense that Luther saw worship and rest on Sunday (or on any set day) as something *mandatory*, at least not in the same way Sabbatarians do. This appears to be the more responsible exegetical and historical way to defend "keeping Sunday special" (instead of some other day of the week), rather than trying to prove more from specific Old or New Testament texts than their authorial intents can bear.

There is also something very biblical, very true to the gospel, to Jesus and the apostles and to their teachings and writings about the notion, first attributed, I believe, to Augustine, of "love God and do as you please." Or perhaps it is better to rephrase it as, "Love God and you will, as a result, do what pleases Him." Although my German isn't up to the finer points of *das*, Arand's conclusions here make sense (pp. 239–41). If you love God, moreover, and let your life flow from that commitment, you may well wind up worshipping Him more often than once on a weekend, perhaps much more often, perhaps even corporately much more often. If you love Him as He has disclosed Himself in Christ, you will likewise adopt a Christological approach to the Scriptures and see that in Him is our perfect rest 24–7. What you will not do is heap a guilt trip on yourself, or allow anyone else to, if you miss a week, or choose a day other than Saturday or Sunday, or choose no one day consistently but many days often, or choose parts of several days frequently but without any mandatory itinerary. At the same time, as a product of the 1960s, I also watched what happened with Joseph Fletcher and his "situation ethics" movement and realize that we still need moral absolutes or we may have no morals at all. As fallen creatures, we need incentives to worship Christ and rest in Him, even after we are believers. But our absolutes must be moral ones, not ritual or ceremonial ones like fixed days of the week. And our incentives must be out of gratitude to God for all He has done for us that we could never have done for ourselves, a point Luther stressed better than any other reformer. This, rather than sheer obedience or hope for further reward, must be the key to the Christian life.

Although Arand touches on the relationship between the First and Fourth (Third for him) Commandments only briefly and obliquely, I take it that at least part of the connection is that we do not celebrate the Sabbath in any idolatrous fashion. Prescribing what does or does not constitute work or rest, whether as the ancient Pharisees did or as more recent Reformed and SDA sabbatarians have done, may start us down a path that could end in our worshipping (and therefore idolizing) the Sabbath rather than worshipping God. I like Arand's concept that taking away what we most fear losing may disclose our true gods. Almost all Sabbatarians I have ever met or read, sooner or later speak somewhat wistfully of a bygone era of Sabbath observance they wish would return and lament how contemporary society is simply deteriorating in this regard. Reading some of the Puritan discussions discloses the identical wistfulness and lament, making one wonder if there *ever* really were any "good old days" worth recreating! Might such attitudes represent the first steps toward worshipping the Sabbath rather than the Christ who gives us permanent Sabbath rest in Him?

One can scarcely study Luther's theology for very long, of course, without learning about the centrality of the proclaimed Word of God. Here non-Lutheran evangelical churches often far outstrip nonevangelical Lutheran ones in remaining true to the great reformer's emphasis. The shallowness, brevity, and lack of true biblical rootedness of much of what passes for sermons in many ELCA churches make many merely mediocre evangelical pulpit ministries seem stellar in comparison. Arand, of course, speaks for the more faithful, conservative Missouri Synod Lutheran tradition, of which I have much less firsthand in-church experience, because I am not welcome as a full communicant in the Missouri Synod since I am now a Baptist. Ironically, I remain welcome in the ELCA, even though I have far more in common theologically with the Missouri Synod than with the ELCA!

What is missing in most Lutheran treatments of the relationship between the testaments, or between law and gospel, and thus of the Sabbath commandment, is an adequate exegesis of 2 Tim 3:16–17 and related Scriptures. If "*all* Scripture is God-breathed and profitable for reproof, rebuke, correction and training in righteousness so that the person of God might be equipped for every good work," and if for Paul all Scripture meant what we call the Old Testament in its entirety, then we cannot merely jettison the civil or ceremonial law. We must learn to understand how every pericope in the entire Christian Bible remains relevant in some way for us, and not just to show us how sinful and in need of a Savior we are. Here is where Paul's *tertius usus legis* (third use of the law), the guide for believers, comes into play. If the Sabbatarians of both first- and seventh-day varieties do not adequately distinguish Christ's fulfillment of the Law (Matt 5:17) from the concept of simply preserving it unchanged, it appears that Lutherans do not adequately distinguish Christ's fulfillment of the Law from the concept of His abolishing it. Christ is the end of the Law (Rom 10:4), but as its goal not just its termination. Fulfillment is a true *via media* between preservation and abolition, as I have argued in my chapter.

The end results for Christian practice, when one compares the Lutheran view and the fulfillment view, may look extremely similar, just as the two sabbatarian perspectives look extremely similar, apart from the day chosen for worship. But the routes taken to arrive at the destination vary considerably (just as they do for the sabbatarian views). The fulfillment view argues that the commands in Exodus and Deuteronomy, in the passages that present the Decalogue and as part of inspired Scripture, have an application of some kind that is binding on believers today. But it is not one to be found through either natural law (via Luther) or all the painstaking exegesis of the Old Testament imaginable (via Sabbatarianism), *apart from understanding how any given command is fulfilled in Christ.* That is to say, every commandment of the Decalogue, or of any other portion of the Old Testament, or the application of any other Old Testament genre besides Law, must be filtered through the grid of New

Testament teaching on the same topic (or, lacking anything directly on the topic, whatever comes closest to it). Then and only then can we begin to envision how Christians should implement that part of inspired Scripture today. This is the methodology for which I look in vain in Arand's chapter, even if he and I come up with approximately the same conclusions about rest and worship for Christian believers.

Final Remarks
Charles P. Arand

In some ways I suspect that my essay was the most difficult essay about which to write a critique. I did not lay out the biblical material in the same way as the other authors. Instead, I adopted to go with more of a historical-theological and hermeneutical approach. I approached the topic of the Sabbath in this way in large part because I was asked to take a confessional approach to the topic. Much of my academic career has been devoted to researching, writing, and teaching on the Lutheran confessional writings as they were set forth and collected in *The Book of Concord* at the end of the sixteenth century. This collection includes among others, the three ecumenical creeds and the well-known Augsburg Confession—a statement that influenced many other confessional statements coming out of the Reformation.

Martin Luther's Small and Large Catechisms occupy a prominent place within *The Book of Concord*. These texts have been perennially popular as Luther's down-to-earth language has spoken to the hearts of average people in the pew over the course of the past five centuries. These texts have shaped the hearts and minds of those who have learned them by heart. More specifically, they have shaped the way people think and live. To that end they provide Christians with a worldview, an orientation to our life within the church, and guidance for our life out in the world. One could say that they teach both children and adults the art of living by faith. So it seemed only natural in many ways to turn to them in order to understand how Lutherans have understood the Sabbath, shaped as they are by Luther's treatment of the Third Commandment.

Like many others, Lutherans today recognize that no one approaches the Bible without some prior assumptions, presuppositions, and past experiences. These shape the way we read the Bible. Our daily experience, including the exchange we have enjoyed in this book, has taught us that no one reads the Bible in a purely objective way. The only issue is whether we let people know upfront what our assumptions are when reading the Bible. By approaching the topic of the Sabbath from the standpoint of Luther's catechisms, I was trying to "lay my cards on the table," as it were. Lutherans certainly do not place their catechisms above the Scriptures, but we do see them as guides to the Scriptures, guides bequeathed to us by generations of Christians who have gone before us. One might think of them as something akin to a road map. The map does not replace the trip, but it does provide guidance along the way. Thus, the catechisms guide us in our travels through Scripture and orient us to Christ. Or we can think of them as something like the cover of a jigsaw box (an updating of Irenaeus's mosaic analogy). The cover does not replace the pieces of the puzzle, but it does help us put the pieces of the puzzle together so as to see the big picture of Scripture centered on Christ.

Having said that, the historical context and theological arguments made in creeds, catechisms, and confessions are not always evident to the contemporary reader. In some ways that is the case with Luther's explanation in the Small Catechism. It is hard to miss the distinctive way in which he retranslates and then explains the Third Commandment, particularly when set against the backdrop of many medieval catechisms. One of my goals, therefore, was to explicate the rationale and retrace the steps by which Luther arrived at that particular understanding. I quickly realized that this approach to the Third Commandment could not be isolated from a much larger hermeneutical understanding regarding the purpose of the Scriptures being centered in Jesus Christ and how to read them in light of His work.

While the Lutheran confessional writings define Lutheran teaching, not all who claimed to be Lutheran have agreed with them. One notable person, Samuel Simon Schmucker, published a revision of the Augsburg Confession in America during the nineteenth century in which he "corrected" what he deemed to be five errors. One of those involved the Sabbath. At that time there were few Lutherans in America and even fewer Lutheran writings available in English. Schmucker's dream was to develop a distinctively American Lutheranism, but it turned out to be one strongly influenced by the Moravian and German Reformed traditions. Also during that time, the move toward legislating Sunday as a day set aside from work and for worship had picked up steam among many American Christians. In the end, however, Schmucker's revisions were rejected by a growing number of Lutherans who were part of the confessional revival in the second half of the nineteenth century because they found this position out of accord with Scripture.

Response to MacCarty

I must commend Dr. MacCarty. His response showed that he had not only a great deal of familiarity with Luther's teaching but with the Lutheran Confessions as well (he even cited the Formula of Concord!). Regrettably, I must admit that he has a more thorough knowledge and understanding of the Lutheran tradition than I have of the Adventist tradition. As it turns out, he shared with me that over the years he had frequently consulted a little document jointly produced by Lutherans and Adventists in Cartigny, Switzerland, on May 15, 1998, entitled "Adventists and Lutherans in Conversation." That is a most helpful text and well worth consulting. [63] I also appreciate MacCarty's acknowledgement of the insights that he has found in Luther's Large Catechism.

MacCarty opens his response by noting the importance of the Ten Commandments in the Large Catechism. It is clear that he has a working familiarity with it, even as he quips that a Sabbatarian reading of Luther's statements "would think that Luther was surely one of us." But that concurrence is short-lived as he turns to a discussion of natural law. On this point MacCarty does a good job at summarizing in an evenhanded manner Luther's (and Melanchthon's) understanding of how the Ten Commandments are related to natural law. This is not to say that MacCarty doesn't see any problems with Luther's "natural law schema." He acknowledges that non-Christians have been provided sufficient knowledge of the truth from God's revelation in creation and so are without excuse for not turning to the true God. Still, he points out that such knowl-

---

63. Interested readers can find this document at: http://www.adventtikirkko.fi/opetus/advluth.html.

edge was considered to be spiritual "ignorance" by the Scriptures. He notes further that the NT consistently declares that the human person apart from the Spirit can "neither perceive nor obey spiritual truth" (p. 266). I agree.

But I would like to make an important distinction: I agree that non-Christians are without excuse; God has left sufficient knowledge of Himself available in His creation. However, I would like to distinguish between the knowledge that creation provides about God as Creator of all that exists and the knowledge that only the gospel of Jesus reveals regarding God's redemption of the human race. It is with regard to the former that non-Christians are left without excuse. One can discern the goodness of God in creation (though even here, sin, more often than not, obscures and diverts our vision). But with regard to God's redemptive grace, it can be said truly that human creatures are blind and ignorant in spiritual matters. In other words, there is no way that any person could know about the redemption accomplished by Christ unless it were revealed by the Spirit through the Word. It is to this that humans are blind. So, with regard to items involving creation and our creatureliness, we still retain a modicum of knowledge (however little) regarding God's law. But when it comes to spiritual matters involving the gospel, we are blind until the Spirit enlightens us (1 Cor 2:13–16; 12:3). This becomes the subject for the Lutheran understanding of the bound will that the Formula of Concord lays out in exhaustive biblical detail. This requires nothing less than that we are born anew, as MacCarty rightly points out (ibid.).

MacCarty also takes issue with Luther's comment that the natural law is the source of written revelation. Perhaps "source" is not the best choice of words since it is meant to be taken more in terms of "foundation." Natural law precedes written revelation, and it is hardwired into creation by God. Thus, for example, it precedes the need for the written law given by Moses on Sinai. The written or revealed law is congruent with the law that God has written into our hearts. It says the same thing, for it is the same God who ordered the world in this way.

MacCarty also takes issue with Luther that natural law supersedes the written revelation of Scripture with the result that the natural-law Sabbath replaces the Sabbath commandment. He then quotes my question as to whether Christians must "obey [the Ten

Commandments] simply because they are given in the Bible" (p. 218). That's perhaps a bit overstated. The point is that the commandments have a universal import for all people, whether one has ever read the Bible or come into contact with divine revelation. If we obey them only because they are in the Bible, that would deny their relevance for all people until they came to accept the Scriptures as the written Word of God. Had the Ten Commandments not been given by Moses, we would still have to obey them. We follow them because that is how God designed and ordered His world to function.

MacCarty's concern is that such an approach to natural law could leave it merely to personal judgment as to what laws have a naturally enduring law behind them. I certainly understand the concern. I didn't mean to imply that we didn't need the written law today. We need it precisely to clarify natural law in a world where we do everything we can to evade it. When we hear the law proclaimed in the Scriptures, it, in a sense, resonates with people for the very reason that it was first written on their hearts but now needs to be brought into bold relief on account of sin.

To use an analogy, think of an Etch A Sketch with a picture drawn upon it by rotating those two little white knobs on the bottom corners. After we're done drawing, we shake it to erase the picture. In some ways that is the case with us and natural law. God wrote it on our hearts, and at one time it was crystal clear. But through sin we have attempted to erase it, just like that Etch A Sketch. But when you look closely at the screen, you can still see the faint lines of the original drawing. It is still there, however obscured it might have become. In any case, MacCarty does have a legitimate concern about rationalizing away the commands of God in Scripture by subjective manipulation, especially with so clear a guide as the revealed Word.

Now we come to the heart of the issue, specifically, Luther's setting aside the Sabbath as a different commandment from the others. MacCarty regards it as an "entirely arbitrary distinction based on Luther's highly subjective and speculative natural law theology" (p. 269). He believes that Luther's approach is due less to a radical Christocentric hermeneutic than to a Lutherocentric one that is "philosophically and speculatively based on his 'natural law' theology" (p. 269). He then discusses Luther's response to Andrew Karlstadt, in which Luther compares the seventh-day Sabbath to circumcision, with both belonging to old covenant ceremonial traditions (p. 270).

As I would expect, MacCarty stumbles over and rejects the designation of the seventh-day Sabbath of Exodus 20 as only "an external matter" or only "ceremonial." In particular, he cannot see how one can regard the seventh-day Sabbath of the Decalogue as a ceremonial law and then "create another Sabbath experience and corporate rest day in its place" (p. 271). In other words, he believes that Luther "commands a commandment the Bible does not command" (p. 271). And to make matters worse, Luther contends that we risk incurring God's disfavor should we not attend services on Sunday. This seems self-contradictory to MacCarty.

Here I think the key is not to focus on the fact that Luther insists on another day, such as Sunday, to be the day upon which the people of God *must* gather. Luther's concern is not about attending *Sunday* services per se but about attending to the Word. Attending services on the first day of the week is simply a means to an end, in that those services provide the opportunity to hear the Word. Without that Word one does not hear the gospel of forgiveness and thus remains in sin. To ignore the Word of God is to despise the Word of God. I don't believe Luther is simply commanding another day—replacing the old Sabbath for a new one. When he talks that way, it is always with reference to the opportunity to hear the Word. Of course, in Luther's day that ordinarily occurred on Sunday, but it would not have to. In Christian freedom, which day offers the best opportunity for hearing the Word? The point for Lutherans is that all Christians should occupy themselves with the Word of God continually.

With regard to the point that the Ten Commandments are surprisingly "secular" in nature (p. 273), this was set forth specifically in contrast to all churchly ordinances, traditions, and commands that have no basis in Scripture. In other words, going to shrines and carrying out certain devotional activities do not necessarily sanctify a person. Nor, for that matter, do they provide helpful devotional practices. So my use of the term *secular* should not be construed as something bad or inferior. To the contrary, the point is that the Ten Commandments are rooted in and tied to our daily lives; they're profoundly practical. They pertain to how we handle the gifts of creation within our daily activities. I agree with MacCarty that they are "deeply spiritual" in the sense that they align us with God's will for how he had created us to be and to live within His magnificent creation. The same applies with regard to my suggestion that the commandments are more than merely a "code of ethics" (p. 245). The point there is that the Ten Commandments are much more than a checklist of actions to keep or to break. Instead, they pertain to a fundamental orientation that shapes the way we act throughout our lives.

Response to Pipa

I thank Dr. Pipa for giving my essay a close reading. I thought that his summary of the essential thrust of the argument was cogent and accurate, and he captured well the development of my article as it worked outward through a series of three concentric circles. I realize that the task of evaluating the historical material is not an easy task, and I appreciate the way Pipa brought Luther's texts into conversation with other Reformation texts of the Christian Reformed tradition—such as the Westminster Confession—in order to explore the ongoing applicability of the moral law in the life of the Christian. Dr. Pipa also raises a number of good questions that seek further clarification in order to see the consistency of the arguments that I put forward.

With regard to the first circle of the article, the creation and redemption context for interpretation, Dr. Pipa argues that I committed a fallacy of false alternatives. It appears that I gave the impression that God gave the Commandments either for all humankind or only for the church. I'm sorry if I gave that impression, as that was not my intention. I agree that the Ten Commandments are a summary of God's moral law for all people. The key word here is *summary*. That is not to say that there are no other summaries to be found. Nor is it to say that there aren't ceremonial elements in the specific form of the Ten Commandments as given to Israel and thus applicable only to Israel. Having said that, it's fair to say I argued that because the Ten Commandments are God's design for all creation, they also continue to be God's design also for the church. The reason is that in Christ, God has restored His people to His creation.

I also would maintain that the Ten Commandments given on Sinai did play a unique role for Israel. What I meant when I stated that Christians are free to use them (or not) had to do with the specific form and sequence of them—not their moral force or content. The twofold commandment to love God and neighbor is a terrific summary, and the church could just as well use that in its catechesis to teach the moral life. Or for that matter, we could use Jesus' Sermon on the Mount. Each of these in a different way summarizes God's created intention for us. When I speak about form, I have in view also, for example, the commandment for a child to honor his father and mother (Exod 20:12), the promise of which seems to apply specifically to the promised land that God would give to Israel. I'm not sure how the promise would apply to us. So, while the command to honor father and mother applies, the specific promise ("that your days may be long in the [promised land]") does not. To be sure, in a more general way, the promise does apply, just as Luther notes in the Large Catechism when he asks, "Why is it that some families turn out so badly, generation after generation?"

Dr. Pipa also looks at the way that I handled the "prologue" to the Ten Commandments, namely, the opening clause, "I am the Lord your God, who led you out of Egypt" (Exod 20:2). He asks, "Is it valid to say that since Luther does not treat the prologue in the catechisms that he does not see the commandments as having a covenantal setting?" (p. 280). That is an interesting question, but my point is that Luther's treatment of the Ten Commandments in his catechisms is tailored to fit into a diagnosis/cure/life-after-cure plan for the hearer and so is different from the approach that he takes to Exodus 20 and Deuteronomy 5 in his exegetical commentaries. If Pipa means, however, a "covenant" in the broadest sense—that God designed life to work in a particular way, and that when we in a sense "go with the grain" life works better, then yes, I would see the Ten Commandments couched in a covenantal setting. But this would reach back toward creation as the context for such a covenant or agreement. So, for example, cherishing one's spouse would lead to a happier marriage (were it not for the wild card of sin).

Pipa also asks about the exegetical basis for saying that since "Christ has fulfilled the Law, the Christian is not to order his life by it" (p. 280). Again, I meant the specific form and sequence of the Ten Commandments, as well as the other ceremonial laws, not the universal moral law to which the previous two specific sets of laws give expression. To be sure, they are in our catechisms; we teach them as God's will for our lives. I would concede that to an extent they do provide a "distinctive Christian way of living" within the world in the sense that the Christian who is redeemed can begin to live according to God's will. But that distinctive form has to do with a life of faith that only God can see. Outwardly, in terms of what human eyes can see, I cannot always distinguish the good things that a Christian does from the good things that a non-Christian does (such as taking care of creation). I see other people worshipping God and living moral lives. If one says it is distinctive to worship the triune God, then fair enough. But because the law is written on the heart, we can expect that there will be some external conformity to the law in society and in its expectations. Pipa does have a point, however, that as we move into a post-Christian age, living according to the Ten Commandments will become more distinctively identified with Christians. In an age when Christianity held much more influence, it often shaped the way even non-Christians were expected to live. That is no longer the case. With regard to the three uses of the Law, I'm afraid that Pipa (due to no fault of his own) is quoting from subsequent Lutheran interpretations of Luther's texts. Having said that, I of course agree with his quotation from Luther's Small Catechism regarding the third use of the Law (p. 281).

Pipa also sees a problem with my assertion "that for the most part, the Ten Commandments deal with what might best be called 'creaturely matters'" (p. 281). He suggests that this does not apply to the first table. Well, yes and no. To be sure, the first table involves our relationship with God. But we only deal with God through creation and through the means provided therein. Idolatry can only occur when we confuse the Creator with the creature or with creaturely things. For example, Exod 20:7 has to do with our naming and identifying God. Do we call our God "money" or Yahweh? Also, the Sabbath commandment involves bodily rest. In an important sense, then, the first table does deal with creaturely things, but in relation to God. The second table also deals with creaturely things but in relation to neighbor.

I'm glad Dr. Pipa found the second circle of my article illuminating and helpful. Personally, I think the centrality and prominence of the First Commandment within the Decalogue and its connection to all the other Commandments brings out one of the great insights of Luther. But Pipa fears that I have set up another false alternative by distinguishing too sharply between the personal character (that they all deal ultimately with God) of the Commandments and the particularities of the individual Commandments (p. 282). My only intention was to emphasize that Luther sees an organic connection between them all. The First Commandment (Exod 20:3–6) is certainly lived out in the particularities of the other nine Commandments (vv. 7–17).

Now we come to the specifics of the Sabbath commandment itself in the third circle of my essay. Pipa again does a good job summarizing it, but here he sees three problems. First, Luther appeared to misunderstand the purpose of the Sabbath commandment. Pipa does not see Luther grounding it in the specific seventh day of creation as recorded in Gen 2:4. More specifically, "He [Luther] fails to note that the creation ordinance, which is the basis of the Sabbath commandment, emphasizes sanctifying the day, and not simply physical rest" (p. 284). Here Pipa quotes Lev 23:3, which speaks of the purpose of the seventh day as worship in a holy convocation. This again goes to the issue of what sanctifies the day. For Luther it is the Word of God, not the performance, or lack thereof, of certain activities. Second, Pipa argues that restricting the Sabbath to public worship is too minimalistic. I agree. For Luther it really involves spending time with and in the Word. To that end, Luther's recommendations for daily prayers in the catechism provide opportunity to meditate on the Word throughout each and every day, in what Walter Brueggemann refers to as "brief sabbaths."[64] Third, Pipa takes issue with my point that the Bible does not teach how the Sabbath commandment is to be observed. He does not like how Luther supposedly "consigned [it] to the dustbin of ceremonies as an external matter" (p. 285). My only response is to point out that this problem cuts more deeply in the "Christian Sabbath" direction—although many in the early church worshipped on Sunday, the first day of the week, it is nowhere handed down as a divine mandate in Scripture.

Response to Blomberg

I suspect that Dr. Blomberg knows the Lutheran tradition fairly well given his theological journey and migration from Lutheranism to the free church tradition. I realize that my paper provided greater frustration given the historical-systematic approach that I took. Nonetheless, I do thank him for his patient reading of it and his subsequent response. Blomberg is right about the critical importance

---

64. W. Brueggemann, *Genesis*, Interpretation: A Bible Commentary for Teaching and Preaching (Atlanta: John Knox, 1982), 39.

of texts such as Matthew 11, Colossians 2, and Hebrews 4 when dealing with the subject of the Sabbath. Indeed, Colossians 2 proves to be crucial for how the sixteenth-century Reformers developed their evaluations of the medieval church's practices (see pp. 392–93).

Blomberg indicates that he finds himself drawn to several of Luther's ideas, and he indicates that he finds himself gravitating to the belief that the basic biblical norms can "be defended on the basis of natural law as well as divine revelation" (p. 288). In other words, he suggests that it is right to say that they should "ring true" when people hear them, whether or not they are Christian. He also gravitates toward Luther's Christocentric hermeneutic but cautions that it may be overdone among some of Luther's subsequent followers. I agree. At times it has probably been used in order to run roughshod over (or at the very least ignore) the historical context and theological argument of the individual books. This has probably been done more with regard to the books of the Old Testament than the New Testament. The danger then exists that certain parts of the Bible are deemed not important if one cannot read Christ into them. Admittedly, a Christocentric hermeneutic does make the point that even though everything in the Bible is inspired, not everything in the Bible is equally central to the Christian faith.

Blomberg is right that Luther does not see worship and rest on Sunday or another specified day as mandatory. I appreciated his quote from Augustine, "Love God and do as you please," or, as Blomberg rephrases it, "Love God and you will, as a result, do what pleases Him" (p. 289). Here he expresses appreciation for Luther's understanding of the First Commandment as the basis of the others. I do like how Blomberg developed the dangers of making mandatory certain Sabbath observances as a form of idolatry. That was well done and in the spirit of Luther's thought too.

Blomberg cautions, however, about the danger of situation ethics and with it the loss of moral absolutes, such as happened, for example, in the wake of the 1960s. He rightly notes that as fallen creatures "we need incentives to worship Christ and rest in Him" (p. 290). I agree with that assessment, and those incentives come in the form of a written norm of commandments. Luther simply argues for an organic relationship between the commandments as that which brings us face-to-face with the Creator.

Blomberg did find lacking a treatment of the relationships between the Old Testament and the New Testament in Luther, particularly with reference to the ongoing value of the civil and ceremonial laws of the OT. He suggests that here is where the third use of the Law comes into play (which Lutherans affirm). Blomberg suggests that Lutherans "do not adequately distinguish Christ's fulfillment of the Law from the concept of His abolishing it" (p. 291). He contends that Christ's being the end of the Law means that Christ is its goal, not just its termination. Well said! Here, again, I would want to distinguish between the "what" of the law and the "how" of the law. The former is divinely mandated. The latter is left for us to figure out how best to live it out. For example, that I love my neighbor is a given, but how I love my neighbor will vary from person to person and in each passing age and place. How I love my neighbor will depend on my means, personality, skills, as well as the particular needs and personality of my neighbor. And so how we love our neighbors will differ (though in each case it should be recognizably an act of love). In this regard, the ceremonial and civil laws of the Old Testament (not to mention the wisdom literature) provide helpful suggestions and guidelines.

Quo Vademus?

Reading and responding to the three authors in this volume was a treat. I acquired a greater appreciation for their respective traditions and found that they had given me much to think about. In the end, each of our traditions and their positions are shaped by those circumstances and eras out of which they arose. And thus they represent specific responses to specific historical questions and issues revolving around the subject of this volume. To some extent, that makes it difficult to bring the different positions into conversation. Aside from the debate regarding whether we are obligated to observe or set aside for worship one particular day of the week (over against others), there are a number of issues on which I suspect we could find significant agreement. In particular, I would find it helpful to explore the entire issue of rest. Why do we rest? Why did God cease His creative work and begin to rest on the seventh day? What does it mean to pattern our rest after God's rest on the seventh day? What do we do with that day of rest? Nothing? Worship? To enjoy and find pleasure in the works of God's hands? What is the relation of that Sabbath rest to the rest about which the author of the book of Hebrews speaks? What might it say about the nature of God's human creatures? These are all questions that touch on some great theological issues.

In this regard, I found the other essays to be helpful for my own thinking. What I liked about the articles by MacCarty and Pipa was the emphasis on the Sabbath in terms of a delightful rest. It would well be worth exploring the scriptural basis for the concept of delight and rest such as we have in Exod 31:17 and Prov 8:31. I'd like to think that it has to do with God's regarding what He had made as good. In that case, delight gives us an avenue to the proper use and enjoyment of all created things—and thus we come into accord with God's view of His creation. In this regard, it seems to me that the goal of God's work, our coworking with Him and the goal of evangelizing, is to lead people into the delightful rest of all God's work. This includes God's work of creation and the work of restoring and renewing His creation.

I liked Blomberg's emphasis on Christian freedom not to avoid rest or worship but in order to find time for it throughout the week. With regard to some of the specifics of the debate over the Sabbath, I'm not sure how helpful it is to focus so much on which day one rests and worships or whether that day is a full 24 hours. In a certain sense it appears to miss the whole point of the Sabbath. For example, if "apostasy focused, among other things, on desecration of the Sabbath and drew a strong response from the prophets" (p. 18), should not the "other things" become just as necessary for Christian observance? Many of them, of course, are, but all of them are symptoms of the failure to fear, love, and trust God above all things.

Finally, I can't say that I had ever given this topic much thought prior to working on this project. I discovered fortuitously that it fit well with work that I've been doing regarding the Christian obligation to care for God's creation. In that regard, I've been developing the thesis that God has called us to care for His earth as creatures among fellow creatures. This thesis has led me to explore not only God's creative work but His valuing of His creation. More specifically to our discussion about the Sabbath, it has prompted me to wrestle with the theological significance of the days of creation, particularly as they reach their culmination on the seventh day, the day on which God rested, and how that relates to the call of creation care.

CHAPTER 7

The Sabbath as Fulfilled in Christ

CRAIG L. BLOMBERG

> Remember the Sabbath day by keeping it holy. Six days you shall labor and do all your work, but the seventh day is a Sabbath to the Lord your God. On it you shall not do any work, neither you, nor your son or daughter, nor your male or female servant, nor your animals, nor any foreigner residing in your towns. For in six days the Lord made the heavens and the earth, the sea, and all that is in them, but he rested on the seventh day. Therefore the Lord blessed the Sabbath day and made it holy. (Exod 20:8–11)[1]

The longest of all of the Ten Commandments is also the most controversial. Was it intended uniquely for Israel? If it carries over to Christians, can seventh-day rest be transferred to Sunday (first-day) observance? If not, how do we justify *worshipping* on the Sabbath when the original commandment said nothing about worship, and worship is hardly rest? These and related questions are what the various essays in this volume seek to address.

---

1. All Scripture references are taken from the TNIV unless otherwise noted.

Historical Perspectives

Old Testament Times

The first reference to a Sabbath in the Scriptures actually appears four chapters before the giving of the law on Mount Sinai in Exodus 20, quoted above. In Exod 16:23–29, in the context of God's provision of manna in the wilderness, instructions were given so that the Israelites would collect a double portion on the sixth day of the week in order for them not to have to collect on the Sabbath. Some use this observation to argue that, because the principle of Sabbath rest predated the giving of the Law, it survives beyond the Old Testament as well. On the other hand, circumcision began considerably earlier (Gen 17) and yet does not carry over into the NT age (Acts 15).[2] In the second recounting of the Decalogue, a new motive is given for Sabbath observance—that the Israelites might remember that God brought them out of Egypt (Deut 5:12–15). This rationale has been used by some others to argue that the Law is a provision uniquely for Jews, yet the NT regularly refers to believers as the spiritual descendants of Israel. Complicating matters, the OT contains just over 100 references to the Sabbath, many of them in contexts that makes clear just how central the practice was supposed to be for God's people in that era (see esp. Exodus 31; Leviticus 23; 2 Kings 11; Nehemiah 13; Isaiah 56; Jeremiah 17; Ezekiel 20, 46).[3] The Law as a whole was, of course, viewed as eternal and immutable, perfect and delightful (see esp. Psalm 119).

Only a tiny minority of Christians, however, have believed that it was their responsibility to practice the Jewish Sabbath unchanged.[4]

---

2. Some have even argued that the Sabbath was part of an original general revelation to all humankind, still preserved in corrupted form in the various ancient cultures' practices of holy days of all different kinds. Still useful for a survey of both close and distant parallels is H. Webster, *Rest Days: The Christian Sunday, the Jewish Sabbath, and Their Historical and Anthropological Prototypes* (New York: Macmillan, 1916).

3. See further H. H. P. Dressler, "The Sabbath in the Old Testament," in *From Sabbath to Lord's Day: A Biblical, Historical, and Theological Investigation*, ed. D. A. Carson (Grand Rapids: Zondervan, 1982), 21–41.

4. For an excellent historical overview, see the three chapters by R. J. Bauckham entitled "Sabbath and Sunday in the Post-Apostolic Church," "Sabbath and Sunday in the Medieval Church in the West," and "Sabbath and Sunday in the Protestant Tradition," in ibid., 251–341. For an even broader survey that includes Jewish and Muslim practice as well, see C. D. Ringwald, *A Day Apart: How Jews, Christians, and Muslims Find Faith, Freedom, and Joy on the Sabbath* (Oxford: Oxford University Press, 2007). For a Seventh-day Adventist understanding of each phase of biblical and church history,

Even then, only Jewish Christians or Messianic congregations have ever attempted to reconstruct the full spectrum of ancient Jewish worship practices, applying them to the Sabbath, even though the OT is itself silent on whether any of these ever began in pre-Christian times. Indeed, if all we had were the Hebrew Scriptures we might never guess that a day of rest eventually also became a day for worship.[5] Even in the intertestamental period, the most extensively documented development involves the enunciation of specific prohibitions of Sabbath activity, unpacking just what constituted forbidden work (see esp. Jub 2:25–33; 50:6–13; cf. CD 10:14–11:18). But weekly synagogue worship began at *some* point during this period, the forms of which provided the foundation for early Christian worship.[6] The majority viewpoints in Christian history on the application of the Sabbath laws subsequently unfolded and may be identified by surveying several broad periods of time in which one particular approach dominated.

The Earliest Centuries

During the first three centuries, believers rarely had the freedom to rest from work on the Sabbath, the last day of the week (or what we call Saturday), or any other day of the week with any consistency. Jewish Christians, of course, often preserved the practice of their non-Christian Jewish ancestors, whom Rome had allowed the privilege of ceasing from labor on their Sabbaths. But by the middle of the second century, Jews comprised only a tiny minority of the Christians scattered throughout the empire.[7] Greeks and Romans took off work several days every month according to an

---

see *The Sabbath in Scripture and History*, ed. K. A. Strand (Washington, DC: Review and Herald, 1992). For the papers from a conference of Jews and Christians that deals with biblical, rabbinic, historical theological, liturgical, legal, and ecumenical perspectives, see *The Sabbath in Jewish and Christian Traditions*, ed. T. C. Eskenazi, D. J. Harrington, and W. H. Shea (New York: Crossroad, 1991).

5. For "A Summary of Sabbath Observance in Judaism at the Beginning of the Christian Era," see the article so entitled by C. Rowland in *From Sabbath to Lord's Day*, ed. Carson, 43–55.

6. The origins of the synagogue are hotly debated, with dates ranging from the fifth century B.C. during the exile in Persia to barely before the time of Christ. The former are probably closer to the truth. See esp. A. Runesson, *The Origins of the Synagogue: A Socio-Historical Study* (Stockholm: Almqvist & Wiksell, 2001).

7. The important, recent volume *Jewish Believers in Jesus: The Early Centuries*, ed. O. Skarsaune and R. Hvalvik (Peabody: Hendrickson, 2007) demonstrates, however, that this group remained by no means negligible or uninfluential even through the fifth century.

annual calendar of festivals, but these could fall on any day of the week and afforded no one particular day as a regular holiday.

The New Testament contains three texts that demonstrate that, already in the first century, some Christians transferred their day of worship from Saturday to Sunday, the day of Jesus' resurrection. Acts 20:7a describes how "on the first day" of a certain week, most likely in AD 59, Paul, Luke, and their companions "came together to break bread" in Troas. Like other churches in the area, this one would have almost certainly contained numerous Gentiles, so the service no doubt started after dark either on Sunday or, because Jews considered evening to be the beginning of the new day, perhaps on Saturday. Breaking bread would thus have involved the evening meal, shared communally by the believers.[8] This timing appears to be confirmed when Luke adds that Paul addressed the people and "kept on talking until midnight" (v. 7b) and eventually even "until daylight" (v. 11). Gentile or mixed congregations elsewhere in the empire would likewise have had to meet either Saturday nights, Sunday mornings before dawn, or Sunday evenings.[9]

The second probable reference to early Christians' Sunday worship appears in 1 Cor 16:1–4. In this passage Paul prepares the Corinthians in or around AD 55 for his more detailed instruction in 2 Corinthians 8–9 on the collection for Judean believers impoverished after the famine in the late 40s that hit that part of the empire particularly hard. He writes, "On the first day of every week, each one of you should set aside a sum of money in keeping with your income, saving it up, so that when I come no collections will have to be made" (1 Cor 16:2). While it is theoretically possible that Paul is referring simply to weekly individual savings,[10] in a community-oriented context like the ancient Mediterranean world, this is much less likely. Far more probable is that this is the oldest existing reference to a regular offering as part of the weekly Christian worship service, especially because Paul explains that he does not want any collections to have to be made when he arrives. If each individual or family were just saving

---

8. See further D. L. Bock, *Acts* (Grand Rapids: Baker, 2007), 619–20; and C. K. Barrett, *A Critical and Exegetical Commentary on the Acts of the Apostles*, vol. 2 (Edinburgh: T & T Clark, 1998), 950–52.

9. See S. R. Llewelyn, "The Use of Sunday for Meetings of Believers in the New Testament," *NovT* 43 (2001): esp. 210–19.

10. N. H. Young, "'The Use of Sunday for Meetings of Believers in the New Testament': A Response," *NovT* 45 (2003): esp. 112–16.

up their own money week by week, one or more collections would indeed have needed to be made when Paul came to Corinth.[11]

The final NT reference to Sunday worship does not depict a worshipping community but a worshipping individual—the apostle John in exile for his faith on the Greek island of Patmos in the Aegean Sea, probably in the mid-90s (Rev 1:9). In Rev 1:10, John recalls that "on the Lord's Day I was in the Spirit, and I heard behind me a loud voice like a trumpet." Here begins the series of divine visions that will form the backbone of this magnificent Apocalypse. What is important to observe is that a given day of the week has already come to be known in Gentile contexts as "the Lord's day," a term that early church fathers would pick up and clearly identify as Sunday, the Christian day of worship.[12]

Worshipping and resting, however, are two quite different activities. It was natural for the Jewish Sabbath to come to be the day of worship because God's commandments from Mount Sinai had already designated it as the day on which the Israelites should rest from their work and as a day to keep holy.[13] But when Christians, many of them Gentiles, began to worship consistently on what they called the first day of the week, without any regular opportunity to refrain from their occupations on that day, the concepts of rest and worship obviously became separated. A variety of quotations from patristic writers from the first four centuries shows that attempts to enforce Sabbath rest one day a week were frequently labeled as Judaizing and viewed as a danger to the gospel of salvation and spiritual living by grace through faith alone.

To this end, Ignatius, early in the 110s, wrote, "For if we still live according to the Jewish law, we acknowledge that we have not

---

11. See further A. C. Thiselton, *The First Epistle to the Corinthians*, NIGTC (Carlisle: Paternoster; Grand Rapids: Eerdmans, 2000), 1321–23; and D. E. Garland, *1 Corinthians*, BECNT (Grand Rapids: Baker, 2003), 753.

12. See further G. R. Osborne, *Revelation*, BECNT (Grand Rapids: Baker, 2002), 83–84; G. K. Beale, *The Book of Revelation*, NIGTC (Carlisle: Paternoster; Grand Rapids: Eerdmans, 1999), 203. We need not enter here into the dispute of how immediately in the second century this occurs; the point is merely that it did.

13. But pre-Christian Jewish sources tell us almost nothing about when and how this practice developed. Even the Jewish literature contemporaneous with and immediately after the NT discloses only a little more. See H. A. McKay, *Sabbath and Synagogue: The Question of Sabbath Worship in Ancient Judaism* (Leiden and Boston: Brill, 2001). Perhaps the best guess is that Sabbath worship sprang up at the same time as the earliest hints of synagogue worship (as a gathering of Jews, not necessarily in a distinctive building, during the exile under Persia). See G. Robinson, *The Origin and Development of the Old Testament Sabbath: A Comprehensive Exegetical Approach* (Frankfurt am Main and New York: Peter Lang, 1988).

received grace." This perspective becomes a little anachronistic as Ignatius continues, "For the divinest prophets lived according to Jesus Christ" (*To the Magnesians* 8). Nevertheless, in his next section, Ignatius enjoins his readers not to live as if Christ had not come, and he uses those Israelites who had become believers in the gospel of Jesus Christ as good examples of living rightly in light of the Messiah's advent. He deduces in passing that "those who were brought up in the ancient order of things have come to the possession of a new hope" no longer "[observed] the Sabbath, but [lived] in the observance of the Lord's day" (*Magn.* 9). In so doing, presumably, they would be laying aside "the evil, the old, the sour leaven," for "it is absurd to profess Christ Jesus, and to Judaize" (*Magn.* 10).[14]

In about AD 170 Justin Martyr proclaimed:

> The new law requires you to keep perpetual sabbath, and you, because you are idle for one day, suppose you are pious, not discerning why this has been commanded you. . . . The Lord our God does not take pleasure in such observances: if there is any perjured person or a thief among you, let him cease to be so; if any adulterer, let him repent; then he has kept the sweet and true Sabbaths of God. (*Dialogue with Trypho* 12)

The concept of Sabbath-keeping is thus entirely spiritualized to refer to repentance and moral living in general. Indeed, Justin viewed the Sabbath as akin to circumcision (*Dial.* 11). Despite being a fundamental ritual in the Mosaic law, it was not a practice for Christians to observe literally.

Approximately 70 years later, Origen apologized for the special observance of any day at all, explaining to Celsus that it was a concession to those fellow Christians who were unable or unwilling to keep every day as holy (*Against Celsus* 8.22–23). Origen explicitly cites part of Paul's discussion of the topic in Col 2:16 (on which, see below, pp. 341–48). Nor did these opinions disappear as soon as Constantine, the first Christian emperor of Rome, legalized Sunday worship in the early fourth century. Athanasius in around 345 still declared, "The Sabbath was the end of the first creation, the Lord's day was the beginning of the second, in which he renewed and

---

14. Unless otherwise indicated, all translations of patristic writers or documents are taken from the *ANF* or *NPNF* series. For more on these statements of Ignatius, see H. B. Porter, *The Day of Light: The Biblical and Liturgical Meaning of Sunday* (Greenwich, CT: Seabury, 1960), 19.

restored the old in the same way as he prescribed that they should formerly observe the Sabbath as a memorial of the end of the first things, so we honor the Lord's Day as being the memorial of the new creation" (*On the Sabbath and Circumcision* 3).[15] The very title of Athanasius' work discloses the same linkage and logic as Justin's. And the excerpt cited shows that Athanasius did not understand Sunday as the Christian Sabbath but as a different kind of day for a very different purpose—to remember Jesus' resurrection rather than to cease from one's weekly labor.

Strongest of all was Canon 29 of the Council of Laodicea in 363, all the more significant for being a conciliar declaration rather than just the pontification of an individual church leader, however influential he might have been: "Christians must not judaize by resting on the Sabbath, but must work on that day, rather honouring the Lord's Day; and, if they can, resting then as Christians." This mandate appears to violate both Col 2:16 and Romans 14–15 (on which, see below, pp. 341–48), in which believers are not to judge one another on their diverse practices in this arena. But it shows how far from actual Sabbath-keeping the early church had come. Even as rest is suggested for Sunday, it is only for those who are able to do so. Jerome, also writing in the late fourth century, describes how even after Sunday mornings were freed up for Christian worship, even in as historic a center of Judaism as Bethlehem, even in monasteries, believers resumed their normal work for the rest of the day after their church services (*Letters* 108.20).[16]

The "Holy Roman Empire" and Its Aftermath

With the legalization of Christianity in Europe, however, gradual changes would set in. Sunday became a weekly holiday so that some Christians began to recombine cessation from labor and religious worship on the first day of each week. Some Christian theologizing had already begun to pave the way for this transfer;[17] now it could actually be implemented in practice. Throughout the millennium-plus of Roman Catholic dominance in the West and the proliferation of

---

15. http://www.catholic.com/library/Sabbath_or_Sunday.asp, accessed on October 14, 2008.

16. For a thorough survey of this topic in the first three Christian centuries, see W. Rordorf, *Sunday: The History of the Day of Rest and Worship in the Earliest Centuries of the Christian Church* (Philadelphia: Westminster, 1968). See also R. L. Odom, *Sabbath and Sunday in Early Christianity* (Washington, DC: Review and Herald, 1977).

17. E.g., *Didache* 14; *Epistle of Barnabas* 15:6–8; Tertullian, *Answer to the Jews* 2.

312 — PERSPECTIVES ON THE SABBATH

ethnically related Orthodox churches in the East, this pattern of apply-ing the Sabbath commandment prevailed. As early as 386, Theodosius forbade all litigation on Sunday, along with theatrical and circus per-formances. In 585, all businesses were closed by the Council of Macon, and Sunday was declared a day of perpetual rest. At the same time, older views continued to linger during this transitional period. Augus-tine, who sends mixed signals in his writings in various places on the topic, in one sermon applied the Sabbath commandment as follows:

> [This] commandment imposes a regular periodical holiday—quietness of heart, tranquility of mind, the product of a good conscience. Here is sanctification, because here is the Spirit of God. Well, here is what a true holiday, that is to say, quietness and rest, means. "Upon whom," he says, "shall my spirit rest? Upon one who is humble and quiet and trembles at my words." So unquiet people are those who recoil from the Holy Spirit, lov-ing quarrels, spreading slanders, keener on argument than on truth, and so in their restlessness they do not allow the quietness of the spiritual Sabbath to enter into themselves. (*Sermon* 8.6)

Clearly Augustine is taking the Sabbath commandment here to enjoin a spiritual demeanor that applies throughout one's Christian life, not an injunction to rest one day in seven.

While Eusebius already in the fourth century applied the pagan term "Sunday" to the first day of the week and to the wor-ship Christians were practicing thereon, it was not until the eighth century that Alcuin became the first explicitly to identify Sunday as the Christian Sabbath.[18] At this point, the Seventh-day Adventists and Seventh Day Baptists best the Roman Catholics in their histori-cal argumentation. Neither in the Bible nor in the first 600 years of church tradition is rest as a divine mandate for Christian behavior on Sunday ever unambiguously promoted. In the Scriptures and first three centuries of the church, an even clearer distinction is maintained. Sabbath, for whoever practices it, means cessation from labor; the first day of the week is for worship. The one is not interchangeable with the other. With the enormously influential work of Thomas Aquinas and his endorsement of the transfer of

---

18. For an excellent collection of excerpts from primary sources on the Sabbath throughout the first centuries of Christianity, see T. K. Carroll and T. Halton, *Liturgical Practice in the Fathers* (Wilmington, DE: Michael Glazier, 1988), 17–76.

Sabbath rest to Sunday practice, however, the biblical and early church approach all but disappeared from view in Catholic thought. Indeed, Aquinas's support virtually guaranteed that the newer approach would prevail for centuries as a major Christian approach to the issue, even within various strands of Protestantism, who otherwise broke from Catholic dogma.[19] Still, even during the Middle Ages, only work and a few forms of entertainment were prohibited on Sunday, while many other forms of recreation and amusement continued to be encouraged for centuries.

The Protestant Reformation broke from Catholicism in numerous ways and to varying extents, depending on the reformer. With respect to our topic, Luther in his larger catechism agreed that Christians should rest and worship one day in seven, but he recognized that some people needed to work on Sundays and that it didn't matter which day of the week formed a person's Sabbath (*Luther's Works* 40.93). Calvin in his *Institutes* declared, "It being expedient to overthrow superstition, the Jewish holy day was abolished, and as a thing necessary to retain decency, order and peace in the Church, another day was appointed for that purpose." And, lest one think he was merely endorsing Sunday as the Christian Sabbath, he continues, "The observance of days among us is a free service and void of all superstition" (2.8.32, 34).[20] The Second Helvetic Confession 24 explicitly enunciates the voluntary nature of this practice: "The Lord's Day itself, ever since the apostles' time, was set aside for them and for a holy rest, a practice now rightly preserved by our Churches for the sake of worship and love." Thus, "in this connection we do not yield to the Jewish observance and to superstitions. For we do not believe that one day is any holier than another, or think that rest in itself is acceptable to God. Moreover, we celebrate the Lord's Day and not the Sabbath as a free observance."[21] The mingling of a day of

---

19. For a brief introduction, see M. Dauphinais and M. Levering, "Law in the Theology of St. Thomas Aquinas," in *The Ten Commandments: The Reciprocity of Faithfulness*, ed. W. P. Brown (Louisville: WJK, 2004), 45–50.

20. In a fuller treatment of the topic, however, Calvin vacillates. See his sermon on Deut 5:12–14, from 1555, in *John Calvin's Sermons on the Ten Commandments*, ed. B. W. Farley (Grand Rapids: Baker, 1980), 97–113. Here he clearly states that the ceremonial aspects of the law have been abolished but that the civil practice of a day on which stores are closed, transferred to Sunday, should be required. Later Calvinists would typically reject or play down the civil law in favor of arguing that a moral dimension of the Sabbath command remained in force.

21. http://www.christianobserver.org/Helvetic-chapters/helvetic24.htm, accessed on October 14, 2008.

worship and a day of rest continues for this period of the Reformation so that we have not gone back to the pre-Constantinian era of thinking, but neither may we speak of this as Sabbatarianism—the mandated cessation of certain activities and practice of others on one specific day each week based on the Ten Commandments.[22]

That development (Sabbatarianism) would be due largely to the rise of Puritan theology a century later in the mid-1600s. This breakaway movement from the Church of England spawned sufficient official legislation and unofficial tradition surrounding what could or could not be done on Sundays that it came to resemble the legalism on this matter entrenched in first-century Judaism against which Jesus so strenuously contended.[23] The Westminster Confession, birthed at just this time (1648), repealed the freedom articulated by both Calvin and the Second Helvetic Confession. Its pronouncements on the Sabbath (21.7–8) read as follows:

> As it is the law of nature, that, in general, a due proportion of time be set apart for the worship of God; so, in His Word, by a positive, moral, and perpetual commandment binding all men in all ages, He has particularly appointed one day in seven, for a Sabbath, to be kept holy unto Him: which, from the beginning of the world to the resurrection of Christ, was the last day of the week; and, from the resurrection of Christ, was changed into the first day of the week, which, in Scripture, is called the Lord's Day, and is to be continued to the end of the world, as the Christian Sabbath.
>
> This Sabbath is to be kept holy unto the Lord, when men, after a due preparing of their hearts, and ordering of their common affairs beforehand, do not only observe an holy rest all the day from their own works, words, and thoughts about their worldly employments and recreations, but also are taken up

---

22. J. H. Primus, *Holy Time: Moderate Puritanism and the Sabbath* (Macon: Mercer, 1989), 11. For an excellent nuanced understanding of Calvin, which still stresses the discontinuities between his theology of the Sabbath and puritan practice, see idem., "Calvin and the Puritan Sabbath: A Comparative Study," in *Exploring the Heritage of John Calvin*, ed. D. E. Holwerda (Grand Rapids: Baker, 1976), 40–75.

23. See, e.g., D. S. Katz, "Jewish Sabbath and Christian Sunday in Early Modern England," in *Jewish Christians and Christian Jews: From the Renaissance to the Enlightenment*, ed., R. H. Popkin and G. M. Weiner (Dordrecht and Boston: Kluwer, 1994), 119–30.

the whole time in the public and private exercises of His worship, and in the duties of necessity and mercy.[24]

Now sports on Sunday would be banned, along with most other forms of recreation and "worldly amusement." Schoolmasters could not teach and students could not study nonreligious subjects. Judges could no longer examine evidence or try cases, nor magistrates undertake their civil obligations. Masters could not command their servants to work. All fairs, nonessential travel, marriage feasts, and loitering in the taverns were outlawed, and farmers were strongly discouraged from harvesting their fields on this Christian Sabbath.[25] Particularly in parts of Great Britain, many of these practices would continue well into the late twentieth century. Little wonder that William Barclay, eminent mid-twentieth-century Scottish pastor and scholar, bound by this doctrine and many of these traditions as a Church of Scotland minister, assessed the two paragraphs of the Westminster Confession cited above with clear frustration: "Almost from beginning to end it is a departure from Reformed doctrine, particularly in its identification of the Sabbath and the Lord's Day, an identification which can be supported neither from the Scriptures nor from the doctrines of the Reformation."[26]

American Church History

Christianity in the colonies and the early days of the republic imposed Puritan Sabbatarianism almost universally and crushed most all dissent.[27] Of course, many of its devout practitioners recognized the benefits of so sustained a focus on worship and rest. seventh-day denominations grew out of this Puritan environment; they merely returned to Saturday, thus clashing with the dominant culture, to implement their Sabbatarianism.[28] Only in the nineteenth and early twentieth centuries do we begin to see a loosening

---

24. *The Westminster Confession of Faith*, 3rd ed. (Atlanta, GA: Comm. for Christian Ed. and Pub., PCA, 1990), 72–73.

25. For all these developments, see R. L. Greaves, "The Origins of English Sabbatarian Thought," *Sixteenth Century Journal* 3 (1981): 19–34.

26. W. Barclay, *The Plain Man's Guide to Ethics: Thoughts on the Ten Commandments* (Glasgow: Collins, 1973), 37.

27. For a thorough history of Sabbath practices during this period, see W. U. Solberg, *Redeem the Time: The Puritan Sabbath in Early America* (Cambridge, MA: Harvard University Press, 1977).

28. See B. W. Ball, *The English Connection: The Puritan Roots of Seventh-day Adventist Belief* (London: James Clarke, 1981), 138–58.

of the many Puritan restrictions, but to quite different degrees and by very different means in the various epochs and subcultures of the U.S. From the second half of the twentieth century to the present, the rate of change increased dramatically as did the abolition of old proscriptions.

Today Christian practice, like the theological justification for that practice, spans a broad spectrum of options.[29] Seventh-day Adventists and Seventh Day Baptists still insist on Saturday rest and worship. Evangelical and fundamentalist churches in the heart of the Bible Belt sometimes observe Sundays with staunch traditions about what can and cannot be done on those days. Blue laws, mandating that business (or certain kinds of businesses—often liquor stores) close for part or all of Sundays, remain on the books in many parts of the country, though many are also being repealed at an ever more rapid pace. Presbyterian and Reformed theologians typically defend Sunday as "the Christian Sabbath."[30] Many others recognize that an exact equation between the two is not possible, while still holding Sunday to be the right or best day of the week on which to gather in "God's house." These believers often lament those businesses and sports that interfere with participants attending church on Sunday mornings should they desire to do so. Still others are content to support regular, weekly Christian worship and fellowship no matter the day of the week or speak of the need for believers to rest one day in seven. Many of these individuals are in professional Christian ministry and recognize that their responsibilities each Sunday thoroughly prevent *that* day from being a day of rest for them!

By their actual practices, including sporadic attendance at worship and little sense that anything is "off limits" during the portion of Sundays they are not in church, possibly the majority of American Christians today behave as if the Old Testament Sabbath legislation did not apply to Christians at all. Due to the workaholism endemic in our high-tech society, periodically certain believers discover the marvelous, refreshing, and renewing value in regular retreat from work, enhanced all the more when it is combined with exercises

---

29. As demonstrated by the diverse contributions to this volume! For a succinct overview of the main positions and an analysis of the hermeneutical issues involved, see W. M. Swartley, *Slavery, Sabbath, War and Women: Case Issues in Biblical Interpretation* (Scottdale, PA: Herald, 1983), 67–95.

30. See, e.g., J. Douma, *The Ten Commandments: Manual for the Christian Life* (Phillipsburg: P & R, 1996).

in spiritual formation, discipline, and fasting from a whole array of activities that otherwise dominate their lives. Some of these individuals will then vociferously champion the restoration of the Sabbath in Christian living, whether via resting and worshipping every Saturday, every Sunday, or at least one day a week.[31] What they rarely discuss (and have never demonstrated) is if all human beings are wired so similarly that one 24-hour period every seven days is the optimal way for every person to achieve these otherwise healthy goals. It is one thing to maintain that all people need regular rest from work and times of corporate as well as private worship, undoubtedly a true claim; it is quite another to insist that such physical and spiritual health cannot be maintained even if one rests, say, for a half day every Monday, every second Saturday, and every third Friday (or by an even less predictable itinerary) and worships in church twice weekly every other week (or however else one cares to set up one's routine).

Evangelical Christians, who by definition are supposed to take their "marching orders" primarily if not exclusively from Scripture,[32] must therefore return to the Bible and ask what *it* teaches, how those teachings are best interpreted in their original contexts, and how they are most probably to be applied in today's world. Because the relevant texts span both testaments, such Christians must also make explicit their hermeneutic (or methodology of interpretation) of the role of the Old Testament law in the New Testament age. In fact, it is this that largely accounts for the different approaches represented by the contributors to this volume. Before we can analyze specific passages, therefore, we must consider which of the competing Christian approaches to the Hebrew Scriptures more generally should guide us in our thinking and acting.[33]

Applying the Old Testament Law in the New Testament Age

Four well known approaches merit consideration here. Two of these form a pair of natural opposites. Indeed, they may be thought of as the opposing ends of a spectrum of options. We will consider

---

31. See, e.g., M. J. Dawn, *Keeping the Sabbath Wholly: Ceasing, Resting, Embracing, Feasting* (Grand Rapids: Eerdmans, 1989).

32. See esp. D. W. Bebbington, *Evangelicalism in Modern Britain: A History from the 1730s to the 1980s* (London: Unwin Hyman, 1989), 2–3.

33. See Rordorf, *Sunday*, 296.

these two first and then move on to the two others that prove most common.

Dispensationalism

One option is to hold that nothing in the OT law applies to Christian living unless the NT repeats and endorses it. This approach has often characterized dispensational thought, though it is not limited to it.[34] Consider, for example, the miscellany of laws that comprises Leviticus 19, the first chapter in the so-called Holiness Code. We don't leave the edges of our fields to be gleaned by the poor and the foreigner (vv. 9–10), we don't worry about not mating two different kinds of animals, not planting our fields with two kinds of seed, or not wearing clothes woven of two kinds of material (v. 19), and we aren't concerned about eating the fruit of a newly planted tree during the first three years it bears fruit or about offering the fourth year's fruit to the Lord as a sacrifice of praise (vv. 23–24). The NT takes up none of these specific laws, so, the argument goes, we understand them as unique to ancient Israel.[35]

On the other hand, neither does the NT say a thing about not cursing the deaf or putting a stumbling block in front of the blind (v. 14), yet most of us would intuitively sense that such things are still bad and wrong. The NT does not discuss divination or omens even once (v. 26b), yet most Christians would find such practices abhorrent. And the distinctively Christian Scriptures make no mention of mediums or spiritists (v. 31), yet surely they remain forbidden. So perhaps we should move on to another option for a more consistently applicable model.

Covenant Theology

The opposite approach therefore argues that everything in the OT carries over to the NT age unless the NT explicitly rescinds it. This option has typically characterized the legacy of Calvin in Presbyterian and Reformed thought and what is traditionally called

---

34. See, e.g., W. G. Strickland, "The Inauguration of the Law of Christ with the Gospel of Christ," in *The Law, the Gospel, and the Modern Christian: Five Views*, ed. W. G. Strickland (Grand Rapids: Zondervan, 1993), 229–79. See also C. C. Ryrie, *Basic Theology* (Wheaton: Victor, 1986), 302–6.

35. Or, in Strickland's words, "When Israel failed in its stewardship responsibilities under the Mosaic dispensation, the law in its regulatory function ceased in its validity" ("Law of Christ," 278). In essence, then, only NT ethics are binding on the believer.

covenant theology.[36] Now we can rule out the use of mediums or spiritists, the use of divination or omens and anything that would intentionally make life more difficult for the disabled than it already is. But is it really incumbent on believers not to wear clothes woven from two different kinds of fabric? If so, most of us are in constant violation of this law! Must farmers raise only one crop in any given field and leave portions around its edge unharvested? If they did, would today's poor and foreigners even be able to come and glean if they wanted to, since they reside mostly in urban centers and the most destitute have no access to transportation to even the nearest farms? It appears we need to move on to still further options.

Moral, Civil, and Ceremonial Laws

A third common approach in the history of Christian interpretation, going back at least to Thomas Aquinas, has been to argue that the *moral* parts of the OT laws remain in force for believers, but the *civil* and *ceremonial* (or ritual) portion of the laws do not (see throughout *Summa Theologica* 100.3–11). The ceremonial laws are those that have to do with the animal sacrifices, the dietary laws, the annual festivals held in Jerusalem, and the like. They are those laws the violation of which rendered an Israelite ritually defiled or unclean until a period of time had elapsed and/or a sacrifice had been offered. The civil laws are those that were given to Israel for the establishment of its government, the ordering of its communities and its land, along with the people's civic responsibilities, many of them unique even among the cultures in the ancient Near East. The moral laws, then, are the remaining commandments that deal with fundamental issues of right and wrong, often found in many of the world's cultures and religions, which humans, perhaps by general revelation or the image of God that remains in them (though marred) even as unbelievers, almost universally acknowledge as dictating how people should or should not behave. These include commands against murder, adultery, theft, and greed, as well as

---

36. In its purest form, this leads to what today is called theonomy. See G. L. Bahnsen, "The Theonomic Reformed Approach to Law and Gospel," in *The Law, the Gospel, and the Modern Christian*, ed. Strickland, 93–143. As one of his 12 concluding affirmations, Bahnsen summarizes, "We should presume that Old Testament standing laws continue to be morally binding in the New Testament, unless they are rescinded or modified by further revelation" (142). And by "standing laws," Bahnsen explains that he means policy directives "applicable over time to classes of individuals" in contrast to particular directives to single individuals (n. 36).

stipulations in favor of loving God and others, honoring one's parents, giving generously to the needy and dispossessed, and so on.[37]

This threefold division of the laws of ancient Israel proves more helpful than the first two options presented. Many laws fairly clearly fall into one of the three categories. Leviticus 19:1–4 commands holiness and honor of parents, while proscribing idolatry. Surely these are all moral laws. Verses 5–8 deal with ritual laws that accompanied ancient animal sacrifices, while gleaning reflects the civil law for everyday life in ancient Israel (vv. 9–10). Similarly, the laws that span verses 11–18 can all be viewed as moral: prohibitions of swearing falsely, defrauding, endangering, slandering, hating, retaliating, and denying justice. Verse 19 with its triad of "match, don't mix" laws would appear to fall into the category of ritual injunctions, much like the dietary laws included specifications for not mixing different kinds of food in the same meal.[38] Other portions of legal material in Exodus through Deuteronomy likewise group together multiple examples of one of these three discrete categories of legislation.

But Leviticus 19, like numerous other portions of Torah, scarcely creates such groupings with any consistency. Moreover, plenty of laws defy simple categorization according to the taxonomy of moral, civil, and ceremonial. What, for example, are we to make of verse 27: "Do not cut the hair at the sides of your head or clip off the edges of your beard"? First of all, it is not even clear what this means at the level of original interpretation—that all men are to have forelocks that are never trimmed? that they must let their beards grow without ever shaving? or that it somehow offends God if, when they do shave, their beards become jagged-edged rather than neatly trimmed? Even if we could answer all these questions,

37. See, e.g., W. A. VanGemeren, "The Law Is the Perfection of Righteousness in Christ," in *The Law, the Gospel, and the Modern Christian*, ed. Strickland, 13–58; and W. C. Kaiser Jr., "The Law as God's Gracious Guidance for the Promotion of Holiness," in ibid., 177–99. Kaiser views his position as more of a conscious mediation between dispensationalism and covenant theology, but there is little difference in substance between VanGemeren's views and his.

38. "Lev. 11 pronounces unclean those animals that do not fit the normal categories. The division within the animal kingdom mirrored those within the human world, between clean and unclean men, between Israel and the nations. . . . This ban on all mixtures, especially mixed breeding, shows man following in God's steps. He must keep separate what God created separate. As God separated Israel from among the nations to be his own possession, so they must maintain their holy identity." G. J. Wenham, *The Book of Leviticus* (Grand Rapids: Eerdmans, 1979), 269. The decrees "against the mixing of things also contribute to the social consciousness that the holy is pure and unadulterated." J. E. Hartley, *Leviticus*, WBC 4 (Dallas: Word, 1992), 318.

would this be a ceremonial or a civil law?[39] It certainly doesn't seem to be a moral law, but then a nagging thought comes to mind. Can anything that the God of the universe commands any people to do or not do be treated as *a*moral?

Indeed, doesn't the source of all 613 commands of Torah somehow make it inherently a moral issue whether we obey them or not? Notice how often the commands of Leviticus 19—moral, civil, and ceremonial alike—end with a declaration such as, "I am the Lord (your God)" (vv. 3,4,10,12,14,16,18,25,28,30–32,34,36–37). Going back to the issue of gleaning, shouldn't this law be treated as a moral law even in the narrower sense of the expression since it has to do with care for the poor and outsider? And what on earth are we supposed to make of the command against tattoos in verse 28? About the only category this falls into that makes sense in a modern, scientific age is that it probably is a physically unhealthy practice. But this is never given as a rationale for the prohibition, and it is doubtful if the ancient Israelites even thought much in terms of its impact, good or bad, on one's physical health.[40]

Possibly even more puzzling is the lack of any logical sequence of the laws in Leviticus 19 and in numerous other portions of the Torah. If the inspired writer had *any* fixed categories in mind, he has certainly not disclosed them through his outline or structure. Verses 20–22 deal with sacrifices (a ceremonial issue), but they also deal with fornication (a moral one). The laws of harvesting and eating fruit could readily be viewed as either ceremonial or civil. After that the progression seems virtually random—from not eating meat with blood still in it, to divination, to beards and tattoos, to prostitution, to mediums, to standing in the presence of the aged, to not mistreating foreigners, to using honest standards in the marketplace, and closing with a call to keep *all* of these laws. Equally "randomly," tucked into this chapter are two references to keeping the Sabbath (vv. 4b and 30)! And we haven't even asked yet into which of our three categories the Sabbath law would fall. The little NT letter of James, nevertheless, alludes to or quotes Leviticus 19

---

39. As a result, C. J. H. Wright, *God's People in God's Land: Family, Land, and Property in the Old Testament* (Exeter: Paternoster, 1990), helpfully suggests that we need to create thematic categories of the Mosaic laws that go well beyond the simple moral, civil, and ceremonial divisions.

40. See esp. M. Douglas, *Purity and Danger: An Analysis of the Concepts of Pollution and Taboo* (London and New York: Routledge, rev. 2001).

in at least seven places, recognizing the abiding validity of at least the verses it cites. And these range from the foundational calls to holiness and neighbor love (vv. 2, 18) to specific injunctions like not holding back a hired worker's wages overnight and not showing partiality to the poor or favoritism to the rich (vv. 13, 15).[41] The Sabbath commands, however, like many other parts of the chapter, are not mentioned.

Privileging the "Big Ten"

A fourth main approach, finally, elevates the Ten Commandments above all the others.[42] At first glance this seems attractive. They alone were given to Moses written by the finger of God on stone tablets. Nine of the ten seem clearly "moral" and fairly fundamental moral obligations as well. The first five focus on obligations to God; the second five on interpersonal responsibilities. Many of the remaining 603 laws of the Torah can be viewed as an unpacking of one or more of the "big ten"; occasionally scholars have argued that, with a little creativity, they all can be so assigned.[43] The OT itself three times refers back to these tablets given on Mount Sinai, recognizing their unique role as transcribed by the finger of God, preserved in the ark of the covenant and forming the heart of God's covenantal stipulations for Israel (Exod 24:8; Deut 4:13; and 10:4). At the same time, all three of those are narrative passages recounting the foundational events of Israel's time at Sinai, but nowhere else in either testament are the Ten referred to again as a group, much less in any didactic passage that would set them apart as uniquely timeless or cross-cultural in application. All but the Sabbath law *are* taken up and endorsed in the NT, so on *any* of the approaches to the OT law in the NT age believers can recognize their abiding validity. But, as we shall see, the only references to the Sabbath commands in the NT are ones that relativize their application in various ways.

---

41. See esp. L. T. Johnson, "The Use of Leviticus 19 in the Letter of James," *JBL* 101 (1982): 391–401.

42. See, e.g., throughout P. G. Ryken, *Written in Stone: The Ten Commandments and Today's Moral Crisis* (Wheaton: Crossway, 2003); and F. Catherwood, *First Things First: The Ten Commandments in the 20th Century* (Downers Grove, IL: InterVarsity, 1979).

43. With respect just to Leviticus 19, M. F. Rooker, *Leviticus*, NAC 3A (Nashville: Broadman & Holman, 2000), 252, presents a chart in which he believes he has established how each command of this chapter unpacks one or more of the Ten Commandments.

Perhaps, therefore, the solution to our question of how to deal with Torah in the Christian era is best handled in an altogether different way than assessing the strengths and weaknesses of the major approaches adopted throughout church history. Perhaps the solution is to turn to the NT itself and see what guidance Jesus and the apostles provide.

New Testament Witness to the Abiding Role of Torah

The Synoptic Gospels and Acts[44]

One scarcely has to read beyond the opening chapters of Matthew to encounter texts that bear on our topic. Beginning the thesis paragraph of the Sermon on the Mount, Jesus declares, "Do not think that I have come to abolish the Law or the Prophets; I have not come to abolish but to fulfill them" (Matt 5:17). The concept of fulfillment is the key to understanding the role of the OT in the NT age. Jesus is not abolishing the Law; every last verse remains an inspired authority for believers (cf. 2 Tim 3:16–17). But Jesus does not contrast "abolish" with its natural opposite, such as "preserve unchanged." Instead he uses a verb (Gk., *plēroō*; Heb. *mālē'*) that implies here "to give the true or complete meaning to something," or "to provide the real significance of" that item.[45] Not the tiniest part of the Law will be superseded "until everything is accomplished" (v. 18). But in the case of the sacrificial laws, everything was accomplished on the cross of Christ, so believers no longer offer animal sacrifices. We do not set aside various laws as irrelevant (v. 19), but we do recognize that the way they are obeyed in the age of the new covenant may be quite different. Kosher laws that created ritual purity need not be literally followed (Acts 10:1–11:18; Mark 7:19b), but they do remind us about the need for moral purity (cf., e.g., the transfer of language of ritual purity to the moral arena in Jas 1:27).[46] The rest of Matthew 5 quotes or alludes to the Old

44. See further P. G. Nelson, "Christian Morality: Jesus' Teaching on the Law," *Themelios* 32 (2006): 4–17; J. P. Meier, "The Historical Jesus and the Historical Law: Some Problems within the Problem," *CBQ* 65 (2003): 52–79; and D. J. Moo, "Jesus and the Authority of the Mosaic Law," *JSNT* 20 (1984): 3–49.

45. J. P. Louw and E. A. Nida, eds., *Greek-English Lexicon of the New Testament Based on Semantic Domains*, vol. 1 (New York: United Bible Societies, rev. 1989), 405.

46. "Purity, to be sure, carries no palpable 'ritual' function for Gentiles, and yet the inherited Jewish view of immorality as pollution ensures that New Testament

Testament six times, in each case to *contrast* Jesus' interpretation of its application to His followers from conventional Jewish understanding in His day. At the end of the body of His Great Sermon, Jesus summarizes all the Law and the Prophets with what has come to be called the Golden Rule—that believers treat others as they would want to be treated themselves (Matt 7:12).[47]

Not surprisingly, then, when near the end of His ministry a scribe asks Him to identify the greatest or most important commandment (Mark 12:28 pars.), Jesus replies by citing the Shema and its sequel: "'Hear, O Israel: The Lord our God, the Lord is one. Love the Lord your God with all your heart and with all your soul and with all your mind and with all your strength'" (vv. 29b–30; cf. Deut 6:4–5). Then He ties a second one to the first: "'Love your neighbor as yourself.' There is no commandment greater than these" (v. 31; cf. Lev 19:18). Matthew's account of this same conversation adds that Jesus concluded, "All the Law and the Prophets hang on these two commandments" (Matt 22:40). Scot McKnight's wonderful primer, *The Jesus Creed: Loving God, Loving Others*, shows how all the major themes of Jesus' own ministry and teaching can similarly be summed up in the double love command.[48]

Luke recognizes the identical relationship between Jesus and the Law as do Matthew and Mark. In Luke 24:44, the risen Lord declares to Cleopas and his unnamed companion on the Emmaus Road that "this is what I told you while I was still with you. Everything must be fulfilled that is written about me in the Law of Moses, the Prophets and the Psalms." The patristic commentators rightly recognized that a Christian appropriation of the OT understood every major segment of the text to point forward to Jesus in some way, even if some of their applications wound up overly allegorizing the text. In the Acts of the Apostles, Luke portrays the disciples

---

Christianity retains a vital concern for the *moral* purity of believers—i.e., above all in the cardinal areas of idolatry, sex, and bloodshed." M. Bockmuehl, "Keeping It Holy: Old Testament Commandment and New Testament Faith," in *I Am the Lord Your God: Christian Reflections on the Ten Commandments*, ed. C. E. Braaten and C. R. Seitz (Grand Rapids: Eerdmans, 2005), 118.

47. For this approach to the Sermon on the Mount and its understanding of the Law, see R. Banks, "Matthew's Understanding of the Law," *JBL* 93 (1974): 226–42; and R. Deines, "Not the Law but the Messiah: Law and Righteousness in the Gospel of Matthew—An Ongoing Debate," in *Built upon the Rock: Studies in the Gospel of Matthew*, ed. D. M. Gurtner and J. Nolland (Grand Rapids and Cambridge: Eerdmans, 2008), 53–84.

48. Brewster, MA: Paraclete, 2004.

applying this model to scriptural interpretation immediately after the ascension. Judas is replaced "because the Scripture had to be fulfilled" (1:16); Peter's sermon on the day of Pentecost is strewn with Scripture that he believed prophesied the Christ event and explained the supernatural phenomena of that specific day (2:1–36). In Acts 3:18, Peter refers explicitly to the fulfillment of messianic prophecy. One is not surprised to hear a speaker refer to the fulfillment of writings of the prophets, but Jesus' own words apply the concept of fulfillment to the Law as well.[49]

The Letters of Paul

The apostle Paul demonstrates agreement with this hermeneutic. When one looks at the OT laws that he cites to support his exhortational material, which are not all that frequent in the first place, one discovers that Paul spans the gamut of what we have labeled moral, civil, and ceremonial law. In 1 Tim 5:18, he appeals to the commandment not to "muzzle an ox while it is treading out the grain" (Deut 25:4), part of the civil law of Israel, to support his call for "elders who direct the affairs of the church well" to receive "double honor" (1 Tim 5:17; cf. a related use of the same text in 1 Cor 9:9). In similar fashion he applies the civil principle that "every matter must be established by the testimony of two or three witnesses" (Deut 19:15) to his third visit to Corinth (2 Cor 13:1). In 2 Cor 6:17, he appeals to the laws of ritual separation from unclean objects (Lev 26:12) to justify his proscription of idolatry. And, of course, he most commonly quotes fundamental moral principles, including most of the Decalogue (e.g., Rom 7:7, 13:9; Eph 6:2–3).[50]

What, then, is Paul's overarching understanding of the role of Torah for believers? Gal 3:19–4:7 suggests two key answers: as a temporary deterrent for humanity so that it does not become as bad as it otherwise might and to point out our fundamental need for a

49. On which see esp. D. L. Bock, *Proclamation from Prophecy and Pattern: Lucan Old Testament Christology*, JSNTSup 12 (London: Sheffield, 1987). Bock summarizes this concept as a prophetic and Christological understanding of the law.

50. For a concise catalogue of references to NT endorsements of nine of the Ten commandments, save the Sabbath-law see C. L. Feinberg, *Sabbath and the Lord's Day* (Whittier, CA: Emeth Publications, 1957), 22. On Paul's use of the OT Law more generally, see esp. E. E. Ellis, *Paul's Use of the Old Testament* (Grand Rapids: Eerdmans, rev. 1960); R. B. Hays, *Echoes of Scripture in the Letters of Paul* (New Haven: Yale University Press, 1989); C. D. Stanley, *Paul and the Language of Scripture* (Cambridge: Cambridge University Press, 1992); and B. S. Rosner, *Paul, Scripture, and Ethics: A Study of 1 Corinthians 5–7* (Grand Rapids: Baker, 1994).

Savior. Romans 6:20–8:10 unpacks these concepts in considerably greater detail. But for our study the most directly relevant purpose of the Law for Paul is the third—as a moral guide for believers.[51] Even more specifically, "the entire Law is fulfilled in keeping this one command: 'Love your neighbor as yourself'" (Gal 5:14). Assuming that God can be thought of as one's most important neighbor, there is no tension here with Jesus or the Gospel writers. Paul certainly knows and insists that God in Christ is to be the primary object of our worship and devotion (Rom 1:19–32; Phil 3:7–14).

Two opposite errors must be avoided in order to understand correctly Paul's teaching on the law as fulfilled in the love command(s). On the one hand, Paul is no situation ethicist—"love God and do as you please"—in the sense of rejecting all moral absolutes save love.[52] As already noted, he believes that murdering, committing adultery, stealing, lying, coveting, dishonoring parents, and many other offenses remain sinful (see also esp. the vice lists of Rom 1:29–31; 1 Cor 6:9–10; Gal 5:19–21; Eph 5:3–5; and 1 Tim 1:9–10). On the other hand, there is no commandment of Torah, even from the Ten Commandments, that Paul promotes *simply* because it appears in the Hebrew Scriptures. He filters each piece of legislation through its fulfillment in the law of love—the teaching and ministry of Jesus—to see how it applies in the Christian era.[53]

For this reason, Paul twice speaks about "the law of Christ" as that to which he is most directly subject. In Gal 6:2, after enunciating the freedom of the believer from the yoke of the Torah in chapter 5, he declares, "Carry each other's burdens, and in this way you will fulfill the law of Christ." After thoroughly rebuking the Judaizers who insisted on keeping the Torah as a requirement for salvation in chapters 1–4, Paul enunciates the true Christian way—freedom from Torah. But he immediately guards against the opposite and perhaps equally dangerous alternative—antinomianism or lawlessness. So he proclaims, "You, my brothers and sisters, were called to be free. But do not use your freedom to indulge the sinful nature; rather, serve one another humbly in love" (Gal 5:13).

---

51. Dubbed by many Reformers as the *tertius usus legis* (the "third use of the law") and vigorously debated ever since!

52. As in the famous work of J. Fletcher, *Situation Ethics: The New Morality* (Philadelphia: Westminster, 1966).

53. See D. R. de Lacey, "The Sabbath/Sunday Question and the Law in the Pauline Corpus," in *From Sabbath to Lord's Day*, ed. Carson, 159–95.

This leads immediately into his enunciation of the fulfillment of the entire Law in the love command (vv. 14–15), his warning to walk by the Spirit and not pursue the works of the flesh (vv. 16–26), and his directive to restore sinning believers gently (6:1). Carrying one another's burdens is thus not likely to be the sum total of the "law of Christ" but the last in this series of teachings on ethical behavior for followers of Jesus in the NT age.[54] Being a disciple does not mean being amoral, much less supporting immorality. But neither does it mean that we adhere to *any* OT law simply because it is in the Hebrew Scriptures. Rather, we run it through the grid of fulfillment in Christ to see how, if at all, its application in the era of the new covenant has changed.[55]

The context of Paul's other reference to "the law of Christ" proves equally revealing. In 1 Cor 9:19–23, Paul describes how he bends over backwards not to put unnecessary obstacles in the way of people coming to Jesus. He has already made clear how the scandal of the cross—the account of Christ's substitutionary atonement and the concomitant "foolishness of the gospel" that our message and cruciform lifestyle seems to be in the eyes of the world—is unavoidable (1:18–2:5). But here he is thinking of doctrines and practices that do not form part of that small core of fundamentals of the faith apart from which salvation cannot be experienced. On morally neutral issues, Paul's lifestyle can be remarkably flexible: "Though I am free and belong to no one, I have made myself a slave to everyone, to win as many as possible" (v. 19). For Jews this means that he is willing to follow elements of the Mosaic law in the company of Jews, so long as they understand that these are not prerequisites for salvation, in the hopes of winning as many Jews as possible to Christ. Verse 20 repeats this principle first with explicit reference to "Jews" and then by means of the descriptor, "to those under the law." But

---

54. At the same time, B. Witherington III, *Grace in Galatia: A Commentary on St. Paul's Letter to the Galatians* (Grand Rapids: Eerdmans, 1998), 423–24, observes that "this pattern of burden bearing and self-giving is seen as the essence of what Christ was about and so rightly at the heart of what Paul means when he speaks of the Law (or main principle) of Christ."

55. J. M. G. Barclay, *Obeying the Truth: Paul's Ethics in Galatians* (Edinburgh: T&T Clark, 1988), 134 (after an excellent, thorough survey of the exegetical options on pp. 126–33). Witherington arrives at basically the same results by more sharply distinguishing the law of Christ from the law of Moses but then observing that Christ himself "endorsed a certain amount of the principles within the Mosaic law as part of his own teaching, in particular the love commandment, but he also declared void other parts, and intensified yet other parts of the Mosaic law"; *Grace in Galatia*, 424, n. 23.

he stresses that he himself, Jewish Christian though he is, is "not under the law"; this is entirely a voluntary and tactical action.[56]

On the other hand, with Gentiles ("those not having the law") he does not worry about following distinctively Jewish practices, while recognizing his continuing subservience to what he calls both "God's law" and "Christ's law" (v. 21). In the larger context of chapters 8–10, the "weak" in verse 22 probably refer back to the Jews who still think themselves to be under God's law. This creates a perfect chiasm, with verses 19 and 23 articulating the basic principles of all things to all people for evangelistic reasons, with verses 20 and 22 reiterating the theme of acting like a Jew to win Jews, and with the climactic center focusing on Paul's freedom (within God's larger trans-covenantal framework of how He wants His people to live) to act like a Gentile to win Gentiles.[57]

Second Corinthians 3:1–4:6 forms the most detailed, sustained treatment in Paul of the role of the Law in the age of the gospel and of the need to recognize a clean break between the two even as numerous principles carry over from the old age to the new age. One ministry (the Mosaic covenant) brought death for those who do not see its fulfillment in Christ; the other (the age of the Spirit) brings life precisely through that same fulfillment (vv. 6–7a, 14–16). The former was glorious even though transitory and provisional; the latter is far more glorious because of its permanence and completion (vv. 7b–11).[58] Rom 7:7–13 clarifies that it was not the Law that was evil or deficient in any way. It was God's perfect covenant for its era. But to try to continue to follow the Law after its fulfillment has

---

56. "To put it in more contemporary terms, when he was among Jews he was kosher; when he was among Gentiles he was non-kosher—precisely because, as with circumcision, neither mattered to God (cf. 7:19; 8:8). But such conduct tends to matter a great deal to the religious—on either side!—so that inconsistency in such matters ranks among the greatest of evils." G. D. Fee, *The First Epistle to the Corinthians*, NICNT (Grand Rapids: Eerdmans, 1987), 427.

57. "The greater difficulty for all who would so preach Christ is our inherent resistance, due to the Fall, to the imitation of Christ expressed in v. 19, that freedom leads to making oneself the servant of all in order to win them" (ibid., 433). "Paul *is* boldly liberal here. Even as he tries to limit the freedom of those who use it in a destructive way, his affirmation of the radical freedom of the Christian life is unmistakable." L. D. Vander Broek, *Breaking Barriers: The Possibilities of Christian Community in a Lonely World* (Grand Rapids: Brazos, 2002), 101.

58. See further L. L. Belleville, *Reflections of Glory: Paul's Polemical Use of the Moses-Doxa Tradition in 2 Corinthians 3.1–18*, JSNTSup 42 (London: Sheffield, 1991); and S. J. Hafemann, *Paul, Moses, and the History of Israel: The Letter/Spirit Contrast and the Argument from Scripture in 2 Corinthians 3* (Tübingen: Mohr, 1995).

come is like a woman who tries to remain married to her deceased husband after she is widowed. Christians are freed from the law as the covenant to which they are obligated (7:1–6).[59] Thus, when Paul declares in Rom 10:4 that Christ is the *telos* (end) of the law "so that there may be righteousness for everyone who believes," he means that Christ is both its goal and termination, as nicely captured in the TNIV's translation "culmination."[60]

The Rest of the New Testament

The remaining NT witnesses do not deal as frequently with the continuities and discontinuities of the old and new covenants as do the Synoptics, Acts, and Paul. But what they do contain reinforces what we have already observed. John 1:17 contrasts the "law . . . given through Moses" with "grace and truth [that] came through Jesus Christ." That this is not an absolute contrast is made clear by verse 16, again more accurately translated in the TNIV than in other English versions: "Out of his fullness we have all received grace in place of grace already given."[61] But just as the glory of the new covenant makes the glory of the old pale in comparison, so likewise the grace of the new far outstrips the grace of the old. The most pervasive way the Gospel of John shows the law as fulfilled in Christ is by highlighting Jesus' claims during His several trips to Jerusalem (or elsewhere during festival times) in which His person and ministry bring to fruition the full meaning of the various Jewish feasts (John 5–10). He heals a lame man at a festival that is either the Tabernacles or Passover but definitely on the Sabbath (chap. 5), shows Himself to be the Bread of Life at Passover time (the Feast of the Unleavened Bread, chap. 6), and presents Himself as the light of the world and living water at Tabernacles, when the two major rituals were the daily water drawings with their priestly processions from the pool of Siloam to the temple and the daily temple services with brightly lit, giant candelabra (chaps. 7–9). Finally, He is the Good Shepherd at the Feast of the Dedication (Hanukkah), which celebrated the

---

59. D. J. Moo, *The Epistle to the Romans*, NICNT (Grand Rapids: Eerdmans, 1996), 421–22.

60. Ibid., 641–42. See also G. R. Osborne, *Romans*, IVP New Testament Commentary (Downers Grove, IL: InterVarsity, 2004), 264–66.

61. See esp. R. B. Edwards, "χάριν ἀντὶ χάριτος (John 1.16): Grace and the Law in the Johannine Prologue," *JSNT* 32 (1988): 3–15.

liberation of Israel under the Maccabees and the installation of righteous leader-shepherds (cf. Ezek 34) over the nation.[62]

Hebrews is steeped in the OT to buttress its claims at almost every turn. But the dominant pattern of this epistle's use of the Hebrew Scriptures is to show how typologically they pointed to Christ. In terms of the Mosaic covenant, per se, Hebrews 8 provides the most directly relevant sustained instruction. This chapter also contains the longest uninterrupted quotation of the OT anywhere in the New (Heb 8:8–12), as it cites the longest and clearest OT prediction of the coming of a new covenant (Jer 31:31–34). In this passage we learn of both continuity and discontinuity with the first covenant. On the one hand, it is still promised to involve the houses of Israel and Judah (v. 8), and it will bring about obedience to God's laws (v. 10). But the enumeration of differences noticeably exceeds the listing of similarities. "It will not be like the covenant" God made with the Israelites on Mount Sinai (v. 9). It will be a covenant to which God's people will remain faithful (v. 10a). God's legislation will be internalized (v. 10b). People will not need to keep on instructing their fellow covenant community members to know the Lord because all will truly know Him (v. 11). Permanent forgiveness of all their sins will be accomplished (v. 12). Thus, the author of Hebrews summarizes the import of this extended quotation with the strongest statement in all of Scripture of the contrast between old and new covenants: "By calling this covenant 'new,' [God] has made the first one obsolete, and what is obsolete and outdated will soon disappear."[63]

The epistle of James is often alleged to be the clearest NT example of an early Jewish-Christian community that still remained Torah observant. James cites various portions of the Mosaic law, especially Leviticus 19, positively. But he also sounds Pauline when he declares that

> whoever keeps the whole law and yet stumbles at just one point is guilty of breaking all of it. For he who said, "You shall not

---

62. See F. J. Moloney, *The Gospel of John* (Collegeville, MN: Liturgical Press, 1998), 164; B. D. Johnson, "'Salvation Is from the Jews': Salvation in the Gospel of John," in *New Currents Through John: A Global Perspective*, ed. F. Lozada Jr. and T. Thatcher (Atlanta: Society for Biblical Literature, 2006), 98.

63. See, most recently, P. Gräbe, "The New Covenant and Christian Identity in Hebrews," in *A Cloud of Witnesses: The Theology of Hebrews in Its Ancient Contexts*, ed. R. Bauckham, D. Driver, T. Hart, and N. Macdonald (London: T & T Clark, 2008), 118–27.

commit adultery," also said, "You shall not commit murder." If you do not commit adultery but do commit murder you have become a lawbreaker (Jas 2:10–11).

James sandwiches these undeniable references to the Mosaic law inside two references to a "law" distinct from the Mosaic one. The first is a reference to the "royal law" of loving one's neighbor as oneself (vv. 8–9), using an adjective (*basilikos*) to modify law that comes from the same root as the noun for "kingdom." This expression is probably a reference to Jesus' central emphasis on the kingdom of God. The second is a reference to "the law that gives freedom" (v. 12), as opposed to the Mosaic law that condemns as soon as one breaks even one of its laws. By contrast, this liberating law focuses on mercy rather than judgment; indeed, that mercy triumphs over judgment (v. 13). Just as for both Jesus and Paul, for James the royal or kingdom (or supreme) law of neighbor love sums up the Mosaic law, which is then implemented in a radically new way for Christian believers as it is understood in light of Jesus' and the apostles' teaching and supplemented by that same teaching.[64]

The writings of Peter and Jude do not directly address the role of the law in the NT age, but 1 Pet 1:10–12 clearly recognizes that a new stage in salvation history has arrived. Prophets, and even angels, knew only partially about the salvation the Messiah would bring, but now Jesus' followers know and experience these blessings much more fully. First and 2 Peter, along with Jude, understand that with the death and resurrection of Jesus, the last days or end times have begun, and judgment day will soon arrive, soon at least by the arithmetic of eternity (1 Pet 4:17, 2 Pet 3:3–10, Jude 14–19). The Johannine epistles echo these themes and add that in this last hour "antichrists" portending a final "antichrist" have even begun to appear on the scene (1 John 2:18, 2 John 7). The book of Revelation closes the biblical canon by then depicting the visions God gave the apostle John about some of the details of what we might call "the end of the end times" or "the last of the last days."[65]

---

64. See esp. M. J. Evans, "The Law in James," *VE* 13 (1983): 29–40. See C. L. Blomberg and M. J. Kamell, *James*, Zondervan Exegetical Commentary on the NT (Grand Rapids: Zondervan, 2008), 258–59 *et passim*.

65. For the new era of fulfillment of the Hebrew Scriptures and, hence, eschatology more generally as the unifying theme or center of NT thought more generally, including the theology of these final books of the canon, see esp. G. E. Ladd, *A Theology of the New Testament*, rev. and ed. D. A. Hagner (Grand Rapids: Eerdmans, 1993).

Preliminary Conclusions

Pervasive throughout the NT is the concept that Christians live in the era of the fulfillment of everything to which every part of the Hebrew Scriptures pointed. Every portion of the law remains an inspired, relevant authority for believers; but none of it may be applied properly until one understands how the new covenant has fulfilled that particular law or part of the law. A new age has been inaugurated that potentially changes everything. In some cases the application of a segment of Hebrew Scripture involves appreciating how it is fulfilled in the life, death, and resurrection of Jesus so that we obey certain OT laws simply by trusting in Christ for our salvation. In other cases, especially with broad moral principles, applications may remain virtually unchanged. In many instances there will be both continuity and discontinuity of application.[66] We dare not assume in advance where on this spectrum Sabbath observance in the NT era will fall by some methodological presupposition that would *a priori* push obedience to this command to a particular place on our spectrum of possible applications. We must rather turn to the specific NT texts that impinge on the issue of Sabbath-keeping and see what pattern, if any, emerges from their teaching.

New Testament Teaching on the Sabbath

The Synoptic Gospels

On numerous occasions in the Synoptic Gospels, Jesus healed an individual or engaged in some other activity that at the very least violated Pharisaic *halakah* or oral law ("the traditions of the elders," Matt 15:2; Mark 7:3,5) about working on the Sabbath. In Mark 2:23–28 and parallels, His disciples picked grain from some fields on the Sabbath and were accused by the Pharisees of doing what was "unlawful" (v. 24). In Mark 3:1–6 and parallels, Jesus healed a man with a shriveled hand on the Sabbath. Nothing suggests that anyone was in danger of dying of starvation in the first

---

66. Closest to my perspective in *The Law, the Gospel, and the Modern Christian* (ed. Carson), though stressing discontinuity just a little more than I would, is D. J. Moo, "The Law of Christ as the Fulfillment of the Law of Moses: A Modified Lutheran View," 319–76. Almost exactly identical to my views is the detailed survey of "The Law and Salvation History," in T. R. Schreiner, *New Testament Theology: Magnifying God in Christ* (Grand Rapids: Baker, 2008), 617–72.

episode, while the malady afflicting the man who was healed was the kind he would have lived with for a long time. From the perspective of this group of Jewish leaders, both activities could easily have been postponed by a day.[67] Luke 13 and 14 add accounts of two additional Sabbath healings not included in Matthew or Mark. Luke 13:10–17 presents the account of the healing of a crippled woman who had suffered from her deformity for 18 years (v. 11). If ever there were a "patient" who, by Pharisaic logic, could wait one more day, she would be it. But Jesus intentionally heals her on a Sabbath, in a synagogue no less, provoking the immediate ire of the synagogue leader (v. 14). In 14:1–6, Jesus heals a man of dropsy in a prominent Pharisee's home as a Sabbath banquet was being prepared. This man had actually contracted what eventually would have become a life-threatening ailment, but again nothing suggests he was anywhere close to being in danger of dying had Jesus waited 24 hours to cure this individual (or less—perhaps as few as six hours from a midday banquet until sundown and the start of a new day).[68]

Nothing suggests Jesus actually broke the written law of Moses in any of these incidents. Indeed, nowhere in the Gospels do we see Jesus unambiguously breaking one of the Pentateuchal commandments. He was a Jew, "born under the law" (Gal 4:4), so that it was appropriate for Him to obey God's inspired commands. To be a spotless, sinless sacrifice for our sins, He actually *had* to obey the law perfectly. But the emphasis in these Sabbath episodes is hardly on Jesus following convention or expectation.[69] And when we analyze the statements He actually makes to justify His behavior, it is hard not to see the foundations being laid for a more sweeping challenge to and change in the law that would begin after His death and resurrection among His followers, even if it would only gradually dawn on them just how sweeping those ramifications were.

Thus, in Mark 2:27–28, Jesus insists, "The Sabbath was made for people, not people for the Sabbath. So the Son of Man is Lord even of the Sabbath." Two points jump out immediately. First, a wholesale application of the first declaration fits poorly with any list, however

67. *Yoma* 8:6 forbade healing of non-life-threatening illnesses or injuries on the Sabbath.
68. W. Braun, *Feasting and Social Rhetoric in Luke 14* (Cambridge: Cambridge University Press, 1995), 41.
69. The classic Mishnaic passage with the 39 forms of work ultimately prohibited on the Sabbath appears in *Shabbat* 7:2 and includes reaping and threshing.

short, of proscribed activities on whatever day is deemed to be today's equivalent of the Jewish Sabbath. If the principle of Sabbath rest was designed to benefit humanity, then there will always be circumstances in which what actually benefits a given person more than cessation of work is some important activity that someone else will consider to be work.[70] Second, and even more radically, if Jesus as the Son of Man is sovereign over the Sabbath law, because of His divine origin, then we should not be surprised if He were setting the stage here for some more systemic change to the implementation of the Sabbath command than merely recognizing a broader range of exceptions to it than many of His contemporaries did.[71] After all, the specific OT practice to which Jesus appealed as precedent for breaking the Sabbath was one in which the written law itself was broken (Mark 2:26: David "entered the house of God and ate the consecrated bread, *which is lawful only for priests to eat*. And he also gave some to his companions" [italics mine]).[72]

Mark 3:4 (and Luke 6:9) pushes things still further. Here Jesus asks His critics, "Which is lawful on the Sabbath: to do good or to do evil, to save life or to kill?" Taken seriously, this rhetorical question suggests that there will always be meaningful and appropriate work for believers on every day of the week since there is always much good, including the saving of lives both physically and spiritually, that needs doing 24–7 (to use the current vernacular).[73] Luke 13:15

---

70. Thus R. T. France, *The Gospel of Mark: A Commentary on the Greek Text*, NIGTC (Carlisle: Paternoster, 2002), 144: "While few could object in theory to the notion that the Sabbath exists to benefit people (after all, it is repeatedly declared to be a day of joy) and is a time for 'doing good,' to make such broad principles the basis for the decision on what is and is not permissible is to threaten to overturn the whole halakhic process."

71. J. M. Lochman, *Signposts to Freedom: The Ten Commandments and Christian Ethics* (Minneapolis: Augsburg, 1982), 64, observes, "People are free to order their Sunday as a free day. When our contemporaries actually choose to use this day in the way that suits them, to sleep in (and so skip church attendance), to go off on an outing, to potter around, to play or watch games, to laze around or even to kill time, the reaction of the Church should not be simply one of grim displeasure. There is one radical saying of Jesus in the gospels which should by rights have deprived church people of their fondness for complaints on this score: 'The sabbath was made for human beings, not human beings for the sabbath!' (Mk 2:27)."

72. Exodus 25:30 and Lev 24:5–9 provide the Mosaic legislation being referenced here. On the legal importance of the words I have italicized, see W. L. Lane, *The Gospel According to Mark*, NICNT (Grand Rapids: Eerdmans, 1974), 117.

73. J. Marcus, *Mark 1–8: A New Translation with Introduction and Commentary*, Yale AB (New York: Doubleday, 2000), 252, observes that "the Markan Jesus makes withholding the cure of the man's paralyzed hand, even for a few hours, tantamount to killing him, and performing the cure immediately tantamount to saving his life. . . .

and 14:5 highlight the inconsistency of the Pharisees' behavior—
they are willing to work to provide normal sustenance for their animals on the Sabbath, and they will rescue an animal or a child who
has fallen into a well, but they object to Jesus' miraculous cures of
other maladies on this special day. Judging from the history of Sabbatarianism in both Judaism and Christianity, it is impossible ever
to devise a system of specifications as to what counts as work and
what does not that is free from such inconsistencies. It would seem,
therefore, that Jesus is implying that a new approach to Sabbath-
keeping is needed altogether, free from any such casuistry.[74] It is
difficult otherwise to account for the depth of hostility indicated in
Mark 3:6—that the Jewish leaders already began to plot Jesus' death
this early in His ministry.

The other references to the Sabbath in the Synoptics merely
denote the day on which certain events happened: teaching in the
Capernaum synagogue and exorcising on the Sabbath (without criticism; Mark 1:21 par.), teaching in the Nazareth synagogue (Mark
6:2 pars.), and the day of the week before the resurrection (Mark
15:42 pars., 16:1 pars.). Matthew includes a short addition to Mark's
version of the Olivet Discourse so that we learn Jesus taught His disciples to pray not merely that their having to flee Jerusalem might
not occur in winter but also not on a Sabbath (Matt 24:20; cf. Mark
13:18). Commentators have often argued that this addition demonstrates Matthew to be more focused on law-keeping than Mark since
having to travel more than approximately a kilometer on the Sabbath was forbidden. But there is nothing unlawful about traveling
in the winter! In the larger context, both Matthew and Mark have
just warned how hard such flight would be on pregnant women and
nursing mothers. Winter travel in Israel was often made more difficult by the colder, rainier weather. Likewise even if Jesus' followers
were not practicing Sabbath-keeping, non-Christian Jews would be,
and it would be difficult to buy provisions, get emergency help, or
escape the rebukes (or worse) of onlookers if Christ's followers did

For Mark's Jesus, the eschatological war is already raging, and on that battlefield every
human action either strikes a blow for life or wields one for death; the cautious middle
ground, upon which one might wait a few minutes before doing good, has disappeared."

74. J. R. Edwards, *The Gospel According to Mark*, Pillar NT Commentary (Grand
Rapids: Eerdmans, 2002), 99. Edwards adds, "It is thus not simply permissible to heal
on the Sabbath but *right* to heal on the Sabbath, whether or not it is 'lawful.' A litmus
test of true versus false religion is its response to injustice."

travel farther on a given Saturday.[75] In any event, there is nothing prescriptive in this passage about ceasing from work on Sabbaths.[76]

The Gospel of John

Two additional examples of Jesus' provoking controversy by healing on a Sabbath occur in the fourth Gospel. In John 5, Jesus heals yet another invalid, this time a man whose condition had remained unchanged for 38 years (v. 5). Talk about a non-life-threatening situation! Still, Jesus actually takes the initiative to ask this man if he wants to be healed (v. 6) and then performs the miracle on the spot. Unlike the Synoptic Sabbath controversies, the Sabbath healings in John provoke extended discourse and debate. In this context, to justify His behavior, Jesus replies, "My Father is always at his work to this very day, and I too am working" (v. 17). God does not stop creating new life, providentially upholding the universe, fixing the times for the end of life, and so on, once a week for 24 hours. No Jew would have disputed that. But Jesus' logic makes sense only if He is in some sense also God, an implication the authorities immediately recognize (v. 18).[77]

Now, to support this seemingly blasphemous claim, Jesus launches into a lengthy discourse that makes the main point that He is doing nothing but what the Father does and has commis-

75. See esp. G. N. Stanton, "'Pray That Your Flight May Not Be in Winter or on a Sabbath' (Matthew 24.20)," *JSNT* 37 (1989): 17–30. W. H. Shea, "The Sabbath in Matthew 24:20," *AUSS* 40 (2002): 23–35, disputes this line of interpretation by pointing out ways in which such flight just prior to the destruction of the temple in AD 70 need not have been so onerous. But his various scenarios all depend on careful thought and advance planning, not always in abundant supply in the times of panic precipitated by war. Plus, his scenarios prove entirely irrelevant if Jesus is looking to a conflagration later in history than (or in addition to) the destruction of Jerusalem by Rome.

76. Particularly thorough and exegetically convincing on Matthew's presentation of the Sabbath in general is Y.-E. Yang, *Jesus and the Sabbath in Matthew's Gospel* (Sheffield: Sheffield Academic Press, 1997). Yang concludes, "For Matthew, the Sabbath is perpetual only until its fulfillment, like the temple (chap. 24; cf. 12.6) and accordingly the priesthood and sacrifices. After Jesus' fulfillment of the Sabbath, the function of the Sabbath as the sign/type is replaced by Jesus' redemption, the antitype of the Sabbath, and thus is no longer required. Matthew may then have had enough reason even to encourage his community to give up Sabbath observance and instead to focus on Jesus, the Lord of the Sabbath, and on his redemption, the ultimate goal of the Sabbath. Such advice may even have been necessary especially if the community had to face the danger of legalism within it and also the threat of casuistic Pharisaism outside it, both of which endangered the true meaning and significance of Jesus' fulfillment of the Sabbath" (307–8).

77. J. W. Pryor, *John, Evangelist of the Covenant People* (Downers Grove, IL: InterVarsity, 1992), 26–27. See A. Köstenberger, *John* (Grand Rapids: Baker, 2004), 185.

sioned Him to do (vv. 16–47). On the one hand, this preserves His subordination to the Father, while at the same time demonstrating His equality with God.[78] He does not return to the specific issue of Sabbath activity in this context, but the implications seem clear. Just as Jesus claimed transcendent authority over the law when He was challenged for "harvesting" grain on the Sabbath, here He claims even more explicit divine authority to reinterpret the Sabbath command, not arbitrarily but precisely as God the Father has called Him to do. The Son can give life to whomever He wishes exactly as the Father does (vv. 20–21). If Jesus' disciples are likewise called to imitate Jesus, then we too can be engaged, and perhaps should be engaged in active and productive activity, consistent with God's kingdom principles, every day of the week.[79]

John 7:21–24 returns to this topic. Back in Jerusalem, this time for Tabernacles, Jesus alludes back to His earlier miracle, explaining to the crowds:

> 'I did one miracle, and you are all amazed. Yet, because Moses gave you circumcision . . . you circumcise a boy on the Sabbath. Now if a boy can be circumcised on the Sabbath so that the law of Moses may not be broken, why are you angry with me for healing a man's whole body on the Sabbath? Stop judging by mere appearances, but instead judge correctly.

Apart from the last sentence, a fair Pharisaic reply would have been, "Ah, but that is in a case where a law of Moses will be broken no matter what one does. If we leave the boy uncircumcised we break the commandment to circumcise him on his eighth day of life outside the womb. If we circumcise him, yes, we do a kind of work. But God would not command something that would regularly involve breaking another Law, so circumcision must not be work. As for you, nothing in the Law required you to heal the man by the pool on the Sabbath, so you have broken the Sabbath commandment."[80]

---

78. See U. C. von Wahlde, "He Has Given to the Son to Have Life in Himself (John 5.26)," *Biblica* 85 (2004): 409–12; D. A. Carson, *The Gospel According to John*, Pillar NT Commentary (Grand Rapids: Eerdmans, 1991), 251.

79. See also S. M. Bryan, "Power in the Pool: The Healing of the Man of Bethesda and Jesus' Violation of the Sabbath (Jn 5:1–18)," *TynB* 54 (2003): 7–22.

80. In the Mishnah, circumcision on the eighth day of a baby's life *had* to be performed, even if that day fell on the Sabbath. See *Shabbat* 18.3; 19:1–2; *Nedarim* 3.11. Elsewhere, even the "how much more" (*a fortiori* or *qal-wa-homer*—"from the lesser to

With verse 24, however, it becomes plain that Jesus is making a much bigger point. The fact that the Jewish leaders condemn Him for what externally looks like a violation of the Sabbath *halakah*, without understanding His motives or His reasons or, for that matter, God's real heart and concern for the crippled man in this situation, shows that they are judging incorrectly. Ironically, most forms of Sabbatarianism throughout history have themselves actually fostered the kind of externalism Jesus eschews. Observant participants tend to focus on what they have successfully refrained from doing and at times obsess over determining precisely what those things should be, and miss the real purpose behind rest—physical and spiritual refreshment and renewal. Conversely, it is possible to become physically and spiritually rested via many activities and breaks from activity in the course of life without ever identifying a particular 24-hour period every week in which certain kinds of behaviors, otherwise commendable, are taboo.[81]

In John 9 Jesus heals the blind man by telling him to wash in the pool called Siloam. This time we learn that the man was born with this disability (v. 1), and the fact that he is "of age" means that he is at least 12 years old, so again the deficiency is a long-standing one. Jesus' unprecedented miracle (v. 32) leads to a sharp debate between the authorities and the man and his parents. Not only did Jesus choose the Sabbath day on which to work this healing, but He deliberately applied a small mud pack, as it were, to the man's eyes (v. 6), again violating the traditions of the elders. Whatever else this behavior accomplished, it made crystal clear that Christ was flaunting the oral law. Not surprisingly, some who learned of the event were convinced that Jesus had sinned and could not possibly be the divine Messiah. Others recognized the undeniable miracle worked

---

the greater") form used here was employed on this issue. See *Mekilta Exodus* 31.13b; *b. Yoma* 85b.

81. C. K. Barrett, *The Gospel According to St. John* (London: SPCK, rev. 1978), 320–21, elaborates: "John carries the whole argument a stage further [than the rabbinic discussion] with the assertion that Jesus' action was not a transgression of the word of God in the Old Testament but a fulfillment of it; his action was not permitted, but demanded by the Law for its own fulfillment. This gives a striking and important turn to the Sabbath controversy which plays so large a part in the Synoptic Gospels but is never really explained in them. Jesus' attitude is not a sentimental liberalizing of a harsh and unpractical law . . . nor the masterful dealing of an opponent of the Law as such; it is rather the accomplishment of the redemptive purpose of God towards which the Law had pointed. There is a similar, but by no means identical, controversial treatment of the practice of circumcision on the Sabbath in Justin, *Trypho* 27."

for good and not for evil purposes and could not imagine Jesus as anything else (v. 16 and throughout). Clearly the latter perspective is the one the fourth Gospel endorses, which means that divine judgment will come upon those who do not correctly identify Jesus' nature and origin (vv. 38–41). Not only does Jesus fulfill the Passover by becoming the Bread of Life, and Tabernacles by becoming living water and the light of the world,[82] he also fulfills the Sabbath law by becoming our rest. Just as believers are no longer required to practice the other Jewish holidays that occurred annually, there is no reason for them literally to observe the weekly holiday known as the Sabbath. Jesus has fulfilled that as well.[83]

The Book of Acts

Many Christians quickly recognize that just because Jesus appears to have observed the basic Mosaic law of Sabbath rest and clearly worshipped in the synagogue on that day doesn't mean that believers necessarily have to do the same. After all, the vast majority of Christians who have practiced Sabbath observance have not done so on the day commanded by the law of Moses or followed by Jesus, namely, Saturday. But what about after Jesus' death, resurrection, ascension, and sending of the Spirit on Pentecost? Now the new covenant was fully in place. As late in the unfolding of these events as Luke 23:56, we read of the women who prepared spices and perfumes for Jesus' corpse resting "on the Sabbath in obedience to the commandment." Even after Pentecost, we are not to imagine a Christian town herald arriving at the temple precincts of Jerusalem announcing, "New covenant arrived. Law fulfilled in Jesus. Followers of Yeshua, stop all animal sacrifices. Circumcision and Sabbath-keeping now optional!" The implications would dawn on Jesus' followers only gradually, at different speeds with different people and in different places, and not without controversy (hence Acts 15).[84] Nevertheless, it is interesting that there is not a single

---

82. For details see G. R. Beasley-Murray, *John* (Nashville: Nelson, rev. 1999), 113–14; and H. M. Knapp, "The Messianic Water Which Gives Life to the World," *HBT* 19 (1997): 109–21. See also 2 Baruch 77:11–16.

83. See esp. D. A. Carson, "Jesus and the Sabbath in the Four Gospels," in *From Sabbath to Lord's Day*, ed. Carson, 57–97.

84. See H. Weiss, "The Sabbath in the Synoptic Gospels," *JSNT* 38 (1990): 24–25: "Sabbath observance among early Christians was, like circumcision and Temple worship, part and parcel of their religious heritage and they did not reject it radically and abruptly under the leadership of Jesus himself." But, "in time, Christians elaborated

reference to the Sabbath in the first 12 chapters of Acts, which form the "half" of Luke's narrative that focuses more on the Jews, under Peter's leadership, before he turns to the segment (chaps. 13–28) that focuses more on the Gentiles, under Paul's leadership.

The first reference to the Sabbath in Acts, then, comes in chapter 13, where we see Christian Jews in Acts worshipping in the synagogue with other Jews on the Sabbath. In Acts 13, Paul and his companions go to the synagogue in Pisidian Antioch one Sabbath soon after they arrive in town (v. 14) and wind up being invited to deliver the morning's sermon (v. 15), which Paul does (vv. 16–41). They subsequently bring the message the next two Sabbaths as well (vv. 42–44). Attending a worship service on Saturday, however, does not demonstrate Torah observance. The original commandment in the Decalogue in fact said nothing about worshipping on the Sabbath. This practice began centuries later, understandably so, because it was the one day each week Jews were consistently available during daylight hours to gather for something other than work. But even in the rest of the OT, Sabbath worship never appears as a command. In the immediate context of Acts 13, moreover, Paul and company do not continue to attend the synagogue because enough Jewish leaders there rejected the gospel that Paul declares he is turning with his message from them to the Gentiles in the community (vv. 45–48).

This is a recurring pattern that Paul experiences throughout his missionary journeys, illustrated in several subsequent passages in Acts (14:4–7; 17:5–10a, 13–15; 18:6–8; 18:23–28), and explained by Paul himself in Rom 1:16: "I am not ashamed of the gospel, because it is the power of God that brings salvation to everyone who believes: first to the Jew, then to the Gentile." As the people chosen by God to be those through whom all the nations of the earth would be blessed (Gen 12:1–3), it was necessary to begin by offering the gospel to Jews in every newly evangelized city.[85] In light of 1 Cor 9:19–23, already discussed, Paul may well have observed quite a number of the distinctively Jewish laws as he began ministry in cities with significant Jewish populations. But he would not have

---

more concrete positions toward these three institutions in Judaism . . . independently of each other . . . conditioned as much by sociological as by theological considerations."

85. So, too, W. J. Larkin Jr., *Acts* (Downers Grove, IL: InterVarsity, 1995), 206.

thought of this as anything binding on him as a Christian.[86] One can see the identical pattern of behavior already during Jesus' ministry as He first sends out his 12 apostles only to the Jews in cities in Israel (Matt 10:5–6,23); but after His death and resurrection, He commissions them to go and make disciples of all peoples on the planet (28:18–20).

The remaining references in Acts to Christians attending Jewish places of worship on the Sabbath all match this same model. In Philippi there are too few Jews for even the quorum of ten male heads of household to establish a synagogue. But Paul presumably knows the Jewish tradition that the next best alternative is to meet by a place of flowing water, no doubt used for various purification rites.[87] That is how he finds a small group of Jewish women in town and preaches the gospel to them (Acts 16:13–15). Acts 17:2 finds Paul and his traveling companions in Thessalonica, again preaching in the synagogue (for three Sabbaths) to try to convince them from the Hebrew Scriptures that Jesus was their Messiah (17:1–4). In Corinth, it appears he was able to speak for a considerably longer period of time in this format and venue because Luke writes that "every Sabbath he reasoned in the synagogue, trying to persuade Jews and Greeks" (18:4). Of course, verses 6–7 clarify that Luke means "every Sabbath" until the hostility forced Paul to leave and turn to ministry in the nearby house of a key Gentile believer.[88]

Paul's Letters

The only appearance of the word *Sabbath* in the rest of the NT occurs in Col 2:16. But this passage may also be the most important one in all of the NT for confirming the preliminary conclusions that have been pressing themselves upon us. Although gallons of ink have been spilled debating the precise nature of the false teaching afflicting the Colossian church, it is obvious from 2:8 on that Paul is exercised that these young believers not fall prey to "hollow and

86. See further M. B. Turner, "The Sabbath, Sunday and the Law in Luke/Acts," in *From Sabbath to Lord's Day*, ed. Carson, 99–157; C. L. Blomberg, "The Christian and the Law of Moses," in *Witness to the Gospel: The Theology of Acts*, ed. I. H. Marshall and D. Peterson (Grand Rapids and Cambridge: Eerdmans, 1998), 397–416.

87. For details, see Barrett, *Acts*, 2:781.

88. For more on the ways in which literal Sabbath observance was a nonissue for Luke in his two-volume work, see J. B. Tyson, "Scripture, Torah, and Sabbath in Luke-Acts," in *Jesus, the Gospels, and the Church: Essays in Honor of William R. Farmer*, ed. E. P. Sanders (Macon: Mercer, 1987), 89–104.

342 — PERSPECTIVES ON THE SABBATH

deceptive philosophy, which depends on human tradition."[89] From 2:16–23, then, we learn that a key component of what Paul wants to combat is an approach to the Christian life in which believers judge one another based on their observance or nonobservance of practices that are not core to the gospel. He commands the Colossians to "not let anyone judge you by what you eat or drink, or with regard to a religious festival, a New Moon celebration or a Sabbath day. These are a shadow of the things that were to come; the reality, however, is found in Christ" (vv. 16–17). There could scarcely be a clearer pair of verses proving that Sabbath observance is optional for believers.[90]

To be sure, a tiny handful of scholars have proposed all kinds of alternatives to avoid the plain meaning of the text: these are special ceremonial Jewish Sabbaths separate from the weekly day of rest, only the nonbiblical Jewish traditions about Sabbath-keeping are in view, some Greco-Roman practice is in view and not the Jewish one at all, or only the Sabbath sacrifices are revoked.[91] But in the broader context of chapter 2, it is difficult to imagine that Paul had *only* one or more of these narrower ranges of practices in mind. In the immediately preceding paragraphs, he explains how the Gentiles now experience salvation on equal terms with Jews in Christ, by likening their rebirth to a spiritual circumcision (2:11). Paul is addressing fundamental spiritual realities at the core of the Jewish and Christian faiths. In referring to festivals, new moons, and Sabbaths, he is clearly itemizing holy days that occurred every year (the calendar of Jewish festivals) and every month (the Jewish new moons). The final element in the triad must be something celebrated every week in Judaism. Nothing in the text limits Paul's focus to just some aspect of the ritual any more than with circumcision.

---

89. For perhaps the most convincing reconstruction of the heresy, see C. E. Arnold, *The Colossian Syncretism: The Interface Between Christianity and Folk Belief at Colossae* (Grand Rapids: Baker, 1996). For the most recent book-length study, complete with a succinct history of the debate, see I. K. Smith, *Heavenly Perspective: A Study of the Apostle Paul's Response to a Jewish Mystical Movement at Colossae* (London: T & T Clark, 2006).

90. K. Wood's argument to the contrary ("The 'Sabbath Days' of Colossians 2:16, 17," in *The Sabbath in Scripture and History*, ed. Strand, 342) is completely circular: the context is one of ceremonial or ritual laws, Sabbath observance cannot be merely a ceremonial or ritual law; therefore, only some ceremonial or ritual parts of the Sabbath can be in view. But this simply presupposes precisely what Wood has not demonstrated—that the Sabbath is a central moral law.

91. See, e.g., P. Giem, "Sabbatōn in Col 2:16," *AUSS* 19 (1981): 195–210.

The most natural antecedents for Paul to have in mind are the identical biblically mandated holidays, already linked together in this identical order in Ezek 45:17 and Hos 2:11 and in a different order in 1 Chron 23:31; 2 Chron 2:4; 31:3, Neh 10:33, and Isa 1:13–14.[92]

In other words, no Colossian Christian of any ethnicity, knowing of Christianity's Jewish roots, having just had his or her attention drawn to a distinctively Jewish ritual, could hear Paul's words in verse 16 and reasonably deduce that he was thinking *only* of pagan holidays or special Jewish Sabbaths or certain parts of regular Jewish Sabbaths and not also of what Jews universally meant the overwhelming majority of the time when they used the word *Sabbath* without qualification.[93] Could anyone be expected to conclude from this verse that Paul was in fact simultaneously implying the exact opposite of the straightforward language he used, something like "but of course you must still observe the *Jewish* Sabbath or the *biblical parts* of the Sabbath or the *non-ceremonial* elements of the Sabbath"? It would be as if an evangelical Christian were addressing a twenty-first century American Greek Orthodox congregation and reassuring them, "let no one judge you as to your celebration of Easter" (because the Orthodox typically observe this festival on a different day than the rest of the Christian world), and yet expecting them to understand that, while they were free to have their own Easter service on a different day of the spring, they were

---

92. R. McL. Wilson, *A Critical and Exegetical Commentary on Colossians and Philemon* (London: T & T Clark, 2005), 216. R. du Preez, *Judging the Sabbath: Discovering What Can't Be Found in Colossians 2:16* (Berrien Springs, MI: Andrews University Press, 2008), 55–81, disputes this by pointing out that the OT sequence is typically in the reverse order, refers to the times for sacrifice, and also usually begins with daily sacrifices, before moving to weekly, monthly, and annual ones. He correctly observes that none of the contextual indicators *proving* the weekly Sabbaths to be in view elsewhere in Scripture appears here, but this is a unique context. Nothing in du Preez's otherwise very thorough treatment of this one verse and its relevance to Sabbath-keeping overthrows the probability that a series of three elements, all dealing with holy days, beginning with annual ones and proceeding to monthly ones, should not next move to weekly ones, when the term that appears next does in the vast majority of cases mean precisely that. It would be as if someone today spoke, in the context of an unspecified sporting event, about the center, guard, and tackle. Granted a complete list of offensive linemen would usually start from the outside and move inward, thus yielding "end, tackle, guard, and center," granted that "guard and center" by themselves could suggest basketball and granted these are players and not the sport itself; nevertheless few familiar with American sports would argue for anything but football from the original triad.

93. See J. D. G. Dunn, *The Epistles to the Colossians and to Philemon* (Carlisle: Paternoster, 1996), 174–75.

still required to join the rest of Christendom and celebrate Easter on the same date as everybody else.

Far more likely, as acknowledged by the vast majority of interpreters, is the approach that understands verse 16 as applying broadly both to the Jewish dietary laws and to various pagan religious rituals involving the consumption or nonconsumption of different kinds of food and drink. Annual religious festivals characterized both Jewish and Gentile traditions as well. New moon celebrations would have referred to the festival days on the first of each month referred to in texts like Num 10:10; 2 Kings 4:23; and Ps 81:3. Sabbaths then complete the triad of annual, monthly, and weekly holidays, which Paul goes on in verse 17 to identify as the mere shadow of a reality (older translations often used the word *substance*), which is found in Christ (literally "of Christ").[94] Unless one is prepared to insist that *all* of these rituals remain incumbent on Christians, there is no warrant for maintaining that the Sabbath law, as cessation from work, must be practiced by believers, whether on Saturday, Sunday, or any other day of the week.[95] And if one did insist on mandating all of these, then those who acquiesced without a clear conscience confirming that they were the right practices for them, would be in violation of the first part of verse 16. They would be allowing others to judge them on these matters.

Verses 20–23 return to a sampling of these same issues. Paul asks why believers who have died to their past, whether Jewish or pagan, and have experienced freedom in Christ, would now submit to the rules of their past lives. As examples he again alludes to things declared "off limits" in those religious traditions, things which make people say, "Do not handle! Do not taste! Do not touch!" (v. 21). Turning from a rhetorical question to a blunt assertion, Paul

---

94. "That Paul without any qualification can relegate Sabbaths to shadows certainly indicates that he does not see them as binding and makes it extremely unlikely that he could have seen the Christian first day as a continuation of the Sabbath. When Sabbath observance was not being imposed on Gentiles as necessary for full salvation and did not form part of any syncretistic teaching, Paul evidently tolerated it but regarded those who practiced it as adolescent and not yet mature in Christ." A. T. Lincoln, "From Sabbath to Lord's Day: A Biblical and Theological Perspective," in *From Sabbath to Lord's Day*, ed. Carson, 368.

95. See D. J. Moo, *The Letters to the Colossians and to Philemon* (Grand Rapids: Eerdmans, 2008), 222: "But there is still reason to think that Paul calls into question here Sabbath observance per se. The language and logic of v. 17 suggest that the primary problem with Sabbath observance was a failure to reckon with the 'fulfillment' of such institutions in the new era of salvation."

continues, "These rules, which have to do with things that are all destined to perish with use, are based on merely human commands and teachings. Such regulations indeed have an appearance of wisdom, with their self-imposed worship, their false humility and their harsh treatment of the body, but they lack any value in restraining sensual indulgence" (vv. 22–23). Ouch![96]

Painful as it may be to hear it, we can scarcely avoid Paul's point. He is stressing that mandating practices like the dietary laws, Sabbath-keeping, and numerous other religious rituals in the salvation-historical era of Christian freedom inaugurated by Jesus' life, death, and resurrection reinstate rules that no longer have divine authorization and thus remain merely human tradition.[97] Worse still, while having the outward appearance of fostering piety and Christian maturity, they really have no bearing on the inward state of a person's mind and heart. As centuries of experience have demonstrated, godly, mature believers may or may not practice Sabbath-keeping, while Sabbath keepers may or may not be mature or godly. Indeed, the latter run the serious risk of taking pride in the fact that they do something they think other Christians should but don't or, more subtly, of appearing pious and humble on the outside as they rest and worship even as their inward judgments against those who disagree with them contradicts their external demeanor.[98]

Two other passages in Paul bolster our reflections on Colossians 2, even though they do not mention the Sabbath specifically. First Corinthians 8–10 deals with the problem of food sacrificed to idols in Corinth, to which Paul applies the same kind of principles he hints at in Colossians 2—only here he waxes eloquent in considerable

---

96. For excellent extrapolation of the components producing these results, along with insightful contemporary application, see D. E. Garland, *Colossians, Philemon*, NIV Application Commentary (Grand Rapids: Zondervan, 1998), 186–99.

97. B. B. Thurston, *Reading Colossians, Ephesians and 2 Thessalonians* (New York: Crossroad, 1995), 47, notes that 2:6–23 thus combats any "imposed spirituality" that judges others who do not practice spiritual disciplines in exactly our preferred fashions.

98. "The observances spoken of here—festivals, new moons, and Sabbaths—when coupled with other practices such as fasting and self-denial, suggest that the false teachers were urging these practices not as means of initiation into the body of Christ but as practices to be followed after such initiation, practices designed to initiate one into another realm of spiritual experience." M. M. Thompson, *Colossians and Philemon* (Grand Rapids: Eerdmans, 2005), 62. Sabbatarianism likewise insists that the truly mature Christian will not only worship on the day designated as the Sabbath but refrain from all kinds of activities, precisely what ascetics do. And Paul says that at best it doesn't work and at worst it creates greater immaturity!

detail. While there are a variety of exegetical questions surrounding just what he does and does not include as the food that is inherently acceptable to eat, even if sometimes one should refrain for the sake of the fellow believer who might be led into sin by our behavior,[99] there is broad agreement on his overall conclusions. First, believers are inherently free in the area of morally neutral matters to do as their consciences dictate (10:25–27,29b–30). Second, there are times when others will be harmed that we should voluntarily refrain from certain otherwise acceptable practices (vv. 28–29a). Third, Paul is more concerned to win the lost than to please the saved (9:19–23). Finally, "whatever you eat or drink or whatever you do, do it all for the glory of God" (v. 31).[100]

Because Colossians 2 includes Sabbath observance with the question of whether certain foods are inherently unclean, it is appropriate to apply Paul's principles concerning food sacrificed to idols to the Sabbath debate. The results then become: (1) Believers are free to rest from work one day in seven, including on Saturday or Sunday. Believers are similarly free not to rest according to any predictable pattern. (2) There may be times, if we are in the presence of fellow believers who believe in Sabbath-keeping and who might be tempted to violate the Sabbath according to the way their consciences understand it, when we should voluntarily refrain from what they deem to be work on the day they deem we should refrain from it. (3) A more important context in which Sabbatarian practices could commend themselves to us is for the sake of making Christianity as winsome as possible to non-Christians. Not unnecessarily offending Jews or Muslims by flaunting their "day of rest" traditions if we live in areas that are predominantly made up of adherents of those religions would form the most obvious twenty-first-century example. (4) Whatever choices we make in our activity on days that some around us consider to be Sabbaths should be for God's glory—engaging in work that is wholesome, beneficial, and/or kingdom

---

99. The most convincing reconstructions appear in B. N. Fisk, "Eating Meat Offered to Idols: Corinthian Behavior and Pauline Response in 1 Corinthians 8–10," *TrinJ* 10 (1989): 49–70; and E. C. Still, "The Meaning and Uses of *EIDOLUQUTWN* in First-Century Non-Pauline Literature and 1 Cor. 8:1–11:1: Toward Resolution of the Debate," *TrinJ* 23 (2002): 225–34.

100. See R. A. Ramsaran, *Liberating Words: Paul's Use of Rhetorical Maxims in 1 Corinthians 1–10* (Valley Forge: Trinity Press International, 1995), 71; R. L. Plummer, "Imitation of Paul and the Church's Missionary Role in 1 Corinthians," *JETS* 44 (2001): 225.

related rather than self-centered, destructive, or immoral. But, then, that should be true of our behavior seven days a week. Similarly, Christians who refrain from certain activities on days they call Sabbaths should do so not because they want to impress others, conform to their subgroup's standards or earn "brownie points" with God, others, or even themselves but because they truly believe that God will be magnified in the process and they desire His glory to be enhanced.

Similar conclusions follow from Romans 14:1–15:13.[101] Because it is likely that the Roman church had a larger minority of Jews than did the church in Corinth and because there are no references to distinctively Gentile customs like meat sacrificed to idols, it is possible that Paul has simply or primarily the Jewish dietary laws in view here. But most commentators suspect that we again have a combination of Jewish and Gentile scruples in view.[102] Again, no specific reference to Sabbaths occurs, but most likely they are included among the various sacred days of the Jewish calendar (along with Greco-Roman religious holy days) when Paul observes that "some [believers] consider one day more sacred than another," while "others consider every day alike" (14:5a).[103] Once more, his instruction proves clear. Where the one group highlights certain days as uniquely holy, with different behavioral codes linked to them, they do so in order to honor God with a special reverence for him on those days. Meanwhile, the other group continues in their devotion to the Lord, just as on other days, and thanks him for their opportunities to serve him through all the regular activities of those days (v. 6).[104] The key is that everyone must decide for themselves which approach fits best for them (v. 5b).

Thus, it becomes singularly inappropriate for fellow Christians to censure, criticize, or even mildly look down their noses on other Christians who voluntarily practice a Sabbath, just as it is equally

---

101. On this whole passage, see esp. R. Jewett, *Christian Tolerance: Paul's Message to the Modern Church* (Philadelphia: Westminster, 1982).

102. E.g., Moo, *Romans*, 837. For a full study of the issue, see M. Reasoner, *The Strong and the Weak: Romans 14.1–15.13 in Context* (Cambridge: Cambridge University Press, 1997).

103. The evidence is succinctly summarized in T. R. Schreiner, *Romans* (Grand Rapids: Baker, 1998), 714–16.

104. H. Weiss, "Paul and the Judging of Days," *ZNW* 86 [(1995): 137–53, plausibly suggests that this group viewed all days as manifestations of the eschatological Sabbath, so that there was a sabbatical quality to the entire week for believers now living under the new covenant.

wrong for Sabbatarian Christians to say anything negative or condescending toward their Christian sisters and brothers who do not do so (vv. 10–13). Again, Paul goes on to explain that "nothing is unclean in itself."[105] But for a person who regards something as unclean, it *is* unclean (v. 14). Thus neither group should do something that could cause the other to violate their conscience (vv. 15–23). As in 1 Corinthians 9, Paul here also generalizes not just to show concern for fellow Christians but for unsaved Jews and Gentiles as well (15:1–13).[106]

Galatians 4:10 likewise laments the observance of "special days and months and seasons and years" in the context of a book directly countering Jewish Christians who are claiming the observance of the law to be a practice incumbent on Christians for salvation (2:11–16; cf. Acts 15:1). While again various pagan festivals might well fall under Paul's purview, references to Jewish holy days must be primary in his mind. The special years must then refer to sabbatical or Jubilee years, the special seasons to the annual festivals like Passover, Pentecost, Purim, the Day of Atonement, Tabernacles, and so on. Months is probably shorthand for the new moon festivals,[107] and the special days can then only be special days of the week (the only category not covered under the other terms), namely, Sabbaths.[108]

Hebrews

If literal Sabbath-keeping is optional, then what does obedience to the Sabbath commandment look like for the Christian? We have already stressed that every commandment in the Old Testament does still apply in some way to Christians. We may not offer any of the identical sacrifices commanded in Leviticus, but every sacrificial commandment reminds us of our need to trust in Christ as our

---

105. In context, Paul is clearly talking about ceremonial or ritual practices, especially with respect to food and drink, not fundamentally immoral behavior! The language of this verse may well echo that of Mark 7:19 and allude to the episode of Peter and Cornelius in Acts 10. See R. Jewett, *Romans*, Hermeneia (Minneapolis; Fortress, 2007), 859–60.

106. See further J. C. Miller, *The Obedience of Faith, the Eschatological People of God, and the Purpose of Romans* (Atlanta: Society for Biblical Literature, 2000).

107. F. F. Bruce, *The Epistle to the Galatians*, NIGTC (Exeter: Paternoster, 1982), 206.

108. "While the language itself is not precise, as one finds for example in Col 2:16 . . . there can be little question that this is [Paul's] own language for the weekly, monthly, and annual feasts that gave rhythm to the Jewish way of life." G. D. Fee, *Galatians*, Pentecostal Commentary (Blandford Forum, Dorset: Deo, 2007), 160.

once-for-all sacrifice for sin. Various aspects of the sacrificial laws, moreover, can teach us principles that apply in other arenas of life—using the principle of less costly sacrifices for the very poor (Lev 5:7–13) to suggest charging sliding-scale prices for other goods depending on a person's income, for example.[109] Or we may observe how the NT applies the idea of sacrifice metaphorically to other activities in which Christians should still engage, for example, praising God (Heb 13:15), or dedicating body and spirit to Him (Rom 12:1–2).[110] How do we make comparable applicational transfers for the Sabbath commandments?

Hebrews 3:7–4:11 gives us a central answer to this question. The main, original purpose of the Sabbath, as outlined in the Pentateuch, was to enable God's people to rest from their labors and to do so in a way that focused their attention on Him by hallowing that day of rest. This identical kind of rest reappears in Hebrews' unfolding of the different stages of rest God has provided for His people throughout salvation history. That God rested on the seventh day of creation provided the basis for the original Sabbath legislation in the Torah. Hebrews 4:4 shows that the author of this epistle has that starting point in mind. But he points out that the Sabbath did not exhaust the "rest" that God wanted to provide for His people, because he observes how the psalmist, centuries after the giving of the Law, still warns God's people against failing to enter His rest. Indeed, he likens such failure to the Israelites' 40-year wanderings in the wilderness before they could enter and take possession of the promised land that would provide them rest in that era of history (3:7–19, citing Ps 95:7–11).[111] So we now have four stages of rest. In chronological order, they are: God's rest from creation, His people's rest every Saturday, the Israelites' rest in the land of Canaan when they occupied it under Joshua, and ongoing rest in the land over the centuries, contingent on their obedience to God.

As we have seen, elsewhere Hebrews can draw sharp contrasts between the eras of the old and new covenants. But the author of

---

109. The approach adopted by the Christian, not-for-profit Inner City Health Center in urban Denver, for example.

110. So even Seventh-day Adventist scholar R. Gane, in his "Contemporary Significance" Sections on Leviticus 1–9 in *Leviticus, Numbers*, NIV Application Commentary (Grand Rapids: Zondervan, 2004).

111. On the use of Psalm 95 throughout this portion of Hebrews, see esp. P. E. Enns, "Creation and Re-Creation: Psalm 95 and Its Interpretation in Hebrews 3:1–4:13," *WTJ* 55 (1993): 255–80.

this book perceives that the principle of resting 24–7 by staying close to God and faithful to the kind of life He wants His people to live is a principle that remains unchanged from Old to New Testaments. So the rest that David still wanted the Israelites to experience as he penned his psalms applies to first-century listeners who heard the gospel (4:1–3). It is still the same period of time designated as "today" in Ps 95:7 even after the coming of Jesus (4:6–8). The climax of this somewhat convoluted argument comes in Heb 4:9: "There remains, then, a Sabbath-rest for the people of God." This is the only appearance of the noun "Sabbath-rest" (Gk. *sabbatismos*) in the Bible. But Hebrews is not talking here about ceasing from work one day in seven; it is talking about remaining faithful to Jesus rather than committing the apostasy against which this letter so regularly warns (recall 3:16–4:3).[112]

To this end, Heb 4:10–11 continues, "For those who enter God's rest also rest from their own work, just as God did from his. Let us, therefore, make every effort to enter that rest, so that no one will perish by following their example of disobedience." Entering God's rest here cannot refer to literal Sabbath observance because it is contrasted with perishing through disobedience. In a book that judges people's salvation by the state in which they end their lives, regardless of any prior profession of faith,[113] Hebrews here has to be referring by "Sabbath rest" to a lifetime of perseverance in trusting in Christ, which will then eventuate in an eternity of rest from our labors.[114] Revelation 14:13 will reiterate this concept, as the apostle John hears a voice from heaven say, "Blessed are the dead who die in the Lord from now on," for "they will rest from their labor." Jesus Himself appears to have shared this perception when He describes coming to Him and following Him in discipleship as experiencing rest. What a marvelously compelling, attractive, and winsome invitation He sends out: "Come to me, all you who are weary and burdened, and I will give you rest. Take my yoke upon you and learn from me, for I am gentle and humble in heart, and you will find rest

---

112. See esp. H. Weiss, "*Sabbatismos* in the Epistle to the Hebrews," *CBQ* 58 (1996): 674–89; K. K. Yeo, "The Meaning and Usage of 'REST' (*Katapausis* and *sabbatismos*) in Hebrews 3:7–4:13," in *Asia Journal of Theology* 5 (April, 1991): 2–33..

113. See esp. throughout D. A. deSilva, *Perseverance in Gratitude: A Socio-Rhetorical Commentary on the Epistle "to the Hebrews"* (Grand Rapids: Eerdmans, 2000).

114. See further throughout Lincoln, "From Sabbath to Lord's Day," in *From Sabbath to Lord's Day*, ed. Carson, 343–412.

for your souls. For my yoke is easy and my burden is light" (Matt 11:28–30).

At last we can answer the question of how the Christian obeys God's Sabbath commands clearly and unequivocally. Because Jesus fulfilled the Law, and thus fulfilled the Sabbath commands, He, not some day of the week, is what offers the believers rest. *We obey the Sabbath commandment of the Decalogue as we spiritually rest in Christ, letting Him bear our heavy burdens, trusting Him for salvation, and committing our lives to Him in service, then remaining faithful in lifelong loyalty to Him rather than committing apostasy.*[115] No special day each week for rest or worship could ever come close to fulfilling this grander and far more enriching and exciting vision of life to the full![116]

Everett Ferguson's conclusion three decades ago, after reviewing key book-length defenses of both the Seventh-day Adventist and classic Reformed approaches, remains solid and forms a fitting summary of my position in this chapter:

> The view that the Sabbath is binding on Christians rests on no explicit text in the NT or early Christian literature. It is surpassingly strange that a supposedly central **Christian** religious duty depends on the interpretation of an OT text. Rather than seeing a continuing validity of the Sabbath, which was changed from Saturday to Sunday, whether legitimately by the apostles in the first century or illegitimately by the church in the second (or

---

115. See the excellent discussion in E. P. Clowney, *How Jesus Transforms the Ten Commandments*, ed. R. C. Jones (Phillipsburg, NJ: P&R, 2007), 51–65. S. H. Ringe, "'Holy, as the Lord Your God Commanded You': Sabbath in the New Testament," *Int* 59 (2005): 17–24, links this service with the good news for the poor at the core of the arrival of God's reign. Thus working for economic justice in our world is one key form of Sabbath fulfillment.

116. See Rordorf, *Sunday*, 296: "These [earliest] Christians said that it would be a misunderstanding of the sabbath commandment if we wanted to rest on a single day and to lull ourselves with the illusion that we were in this way fulfilling God's will: the duty of Sabbath observance did, in fact, include the whole span of our life, for to keep the Sabbath meant to lead day by day holy, sinless lives devoted to the loving service of our neighbour. These early Christians, of course, realized that they were not capable of this behaviour in this life: they, therefore, looked for the Sabbath at the end of the times, the blessed rest where sin would be entirely blotted out and sanctification would be complete. Christian thinking about the sabbath did, however, have its point of origin in the experience of the reality of salvation. Christ had brought to his own the true Sabbath rest, namely the forgiveness of sin and peace with God. They could now live in God's Sabbath which had already dawned. In the face of this fulfillment, the hard-and-fast commandment to rest on every seventh day was bound to lose its importance."

by Constantine in the fourth), it is better to see the Sabbath command as a part of the superseded Mosaic institution and the Lord's day as a different type of day, a day of assembly and worship.[117]

Clearing Up Some Misconceptions

Three common misunderstandings of this position may be addressed in this closing section by means of questions that others have often posed.

No Weekly Rest or Worship?

First, what prevents us as Christians from becoming workaholics and not getting the purely physical rest that our bodies regularly need, to say nothing of the consistent gathering together for worship and fellowship that the Bible likewise commands and models? It is easy to demonstrate a connection between the relaxing of laws requiring business closures on Sunday and the increasingly hectic pace of our world.[118] It would certainly be possible for someone to abuse our position grossly and infer that we were against good stewardship of our time, our work, our bodies, our families; but like gross abuses of all the other positions, those inferences would be unwarranted. We can theologically defend the need for all kinds of forms of rest by means of Scripture's teaching on humans as exercising godly dominion over creation and being temples of the Holy Spirit. But this does not require us to "keep Sunday [or Saturday] special."[119]

Put another way, declaring the Sabbath command to be fulfilled in Christ so that believers no longer have to cease from certain kinds of labor one day in every seven in no way reduces the need

---

117. E. F. Ferguson, "Sabbath: Saturday or Sunday? A Review Article," *ResQ* 23 (1980): 181. Ferguson was reviewing S. Bacchiocchi, *From Sabbath to Sunday: A Historical Investigation of the Rise of Sunday Observance in Early Christianity* (Rome: Pontifical Gregorian University Press, 1977); and R. T. Beckwith and W. Stott, *This Is the Day: The Biblical Doctrine of the Christian Sunday* (Greenwood, SC: Attic Press, 1978).

118. E.g., D. Klinghoffer, *Shattered Tablets: Why We Ignore the Ten Commandments at Our Peril* (New York: Doubleday, 2007), 81–100.

119. The title of a campaign in England in the mid-1980s to oppose longer business hours on Sundays. See C. Townsend and M. Schluter, *Why Keep Sunday Special?* (Cambridge: Jubilee Centre, 1985).

for regular physical rest and spiritual renewal. Those who find that the rhythm of one special day each week, in which they both rest from regular work and worship alone and/or with God's people, best provides their bodies and spirits the nurture and rejuvenation they need, as already seen, are more than free to adopt such a routine. But those who are prevented from adopting such a pattern or who find that other rhythms of rest, worship, and retreat work equally well or better are free to pursue those schedules as well. Neither group of individuals is exempted from being good stewards of the physical and spiritual dimensions of their lives; they are merely given the freedom to pursue that stewardship in whatever format works best for them under the circumstances in which they find themselves.[120]

Recall, too, that the Sabbath command in its OT form has nothing necessarily to do with worship, per se, so even those views that believe that one day in seven continues to be the only correct Christian model for rest still cannot justify biblically, from any prescriptive passage, that corporate worship must follow that same rhythm. Hebrews 10:25 commands us not to forsake the assembling of ourselves together as the church, but it does not prescribe the frequency of that assembly. Just as the early church met in small groups sometimes daily (Acts 2:46), we probably need to think about how to fellowship with other Christians and worship the Lord in various contexts *more* than once a week whenever possible. But no specific regimen is ever required in Scripture.

The Key to Spiritual Renewal?

What do we say, then, to fellow believers who have experienced marvelous spiritual and physical refreshment and renewal by beginning to observe a Sabbath, one day in seven, when previously they had no comparable experience?[121] Or perhaps their enjoyable Sabbath experiences have been lifelong because of the ecclesiastical tradition in which they were raised.[122] In either case, we praise

---

120. N. Wirzba, *Living the Sabbath: Discovering the Rhythms of Rest and Delight* (Grand Rapids: Brazos, 2006), offers choice reflections on the whole myriad of possibilities of incorporating Sabbath rest into everyday life, any day of the week, whether or not one formally observes a day off work every seven days.

121. E.g., L. M. Baab, *Sabbath Keeping: Finding Freedom in the Rhythms of Rest* (Downers Grove, IL: InterVarsity, 2005).

122. E.g., T. Edwards, *Sabbath Time: Understanding and Practice for Contemporary Christians* (New York: Seabury, 1982).

354 — PERSPECTIVES ON THE SABBATH

God for their experiences, old or new! We might even try to adopt similar habits and see if they have similar effects for us. We can understand why these people's enthusiasm for their own experiences can sometimes lead them to insist that others follow suit. But there is a difference between enthusiastically encouraging someone to try something one has found of great help in one's own life and telling them they *must* practice something because Scripture requires them to do so.[123] And there is no justification for any Christian or group of Christians censoring or censuring those who do not practice the Sabbath as they do, as in any way inferior or disobedient. In fact, it is precisely that kind of censure, as we have seen, that is itself excluded by the Bible as improper.

Agreeing to Disagree?

What, finally, do we say to believers who disagree with us on our understanding of Sabbath-keeping? It depends on what their specific position is. We may certainly commend those who say in good faith after considering the options and studying the Scriptures that their view is one of the others represented in this volume but that they recognize the complexity of the issue. They acknowledge that mature, Bible-believing Christians differ on the matter; and they agree that nothing is necessarily at stake with respect to the salvation or sanctification of believers who hold to a different option. We should be able to join hands with such Christians in fellowship, worship, and service in countless areas of Christian life and ministry. We all acknowledge our finitude and fallenness and realize that any one of us might be wrong in our views. Indeed, there will never likely be complete agreement among believers on this topic, as on many others, prior to Christ's return.

On the other hand, it is harder to respond as graciously to those who take the view that their position is the only one correct and viable approach to the topic. For, whether they ever say it in so many words, the implication necessarily follows that those who fall into the other "camps" are living in sin and disobedience to God.[124] If the view adopted in this chapter is correct, then anyone who takes that

---

123. For an apparent example of this harder line, see R. Sherman, "Reclaimed by Sabbath Rest," *Int* 59 (2005): 38–50.

124. This is the impression I come away with, e.g., after reading R. Lewis, *The Protestant Dilemma: How to Achieve Unity in a Completed Reformation* (Mountain View, CA: Pacific Press, 1961).

approach with us replicates the error of the Judaizers in the New Testament age and merits the harsh rebuke that Paul meted out to them, especially throughout Galatians 1–4 (see esp. 1:6–10; 2:11–21; and 4:8–5:12; cf. also 2 Cor 10–13 and Phil 3).[125] On the other hand, if Sabbatarians are right and we are wrong, then we are not replicating the sin of the legalists but of the libertines, with whom Paul, like Jesus before him, was consistently more generous. In the section of Galatians dealing with those who, perhaps unwittingly, turned freedom in Christ into antinomianism (chaps. 5–6), Paul writes, "Brothers and sisters, if someone is caught in a sin, you who live by the spirit should restore that person gently" (6:1a). The last part of the verse explains Paul's rationale: "But watch yourselves, or you also may be tempted." In other words, using severe censure may lead people to believe they are in some way superior to those whom they are correcting or to go beyond appropriate levels of correction into inappropriate anger or hostility.[126] Not to mention, as we have already seen, the summary of the Law and Prophets for Jesus is the Golden Rule. So let us treat those who err in a libertine direction no more harshly than we ourselves would want to be treated, at least when we were being honest about what would be best for us in the long run.

A Concluding Personalized Postscript

Although I did not come to a clear, personal knowledge of Jesus as my Lord through my (fairly liberal) Lutheran upbringing. I am grateful for many aspects of that Lutheran nurture. One of those was consistent, weekly church attendance without subsequent restrictions on Sunday activities that my parents modeled. There was seldom any doubt that we would go as a family to Sunday school and worship service on Sunday mornings. The rhythm of regular participation in corporate Christian gatherings was inculcated in me from early on. But on the rare occasions that illness, vacation, or a huge exam on Monday morning not yet adequately studied for suggested staying home, no one was uptight about that option. My father, who was a high-school Spanish teacher, almost always managed to get his class preparation and grading done during the rest

---

125. See further C. L. Blomberg, "The New Testament Definition of Heresy (or When Do Jesus and the Apostles Really Get Mad?)" *JETS* 45 (2002): 59–72.

126. See R. N. Longenecker, *Galatians* (Dallas: Word, 1990), 273–74.

of the week, including Sunday afternoons and evenings. Once or twice a year, however, usually when report cards were due the next day, he would take his papers still to be graded with him, sit in the back of the choir loft, and multitask during the service—long before anyone had invented the expression "multitasking"!

My true conversion to evangelical Christianity came through my high school's Campus Life/Youth for Christ club when I was 15. Campus Life and, in college, Campus Crusade for Christ, became my most cherished and influential sources of Christian nurture, instruction, worship, and fellowship for the next seven years, even though I attended a variety of churches on Sunday mornings and sometimes even on Sunday evenings. The leaders of the chapters of those two organizations to which I belonged struck a good balance between encouraging us not to settle for just the parachurch experience but neither to dismiss it, if we didn't make it to church as often as we might have, as somehow "not counting." Certainly, no one ever suggested that our worship was in any way less pleasing to God for not occurring on the weekend.

My seminary studies at Trinity Evangelical Divinity School introduced me to the perspective on the Sabbath I have fleshed out in this chapter. Even before his marvelous edited volume, *From Sabbath to Lord's Day*, to which we have frequently referred in the footnotes, was released in printed form in 1982, D. A. Carson was teaching the NT's understanding of the Sabbath as fulfilled in Christ in his classes. Gaining this understanding proved particularly timely for me because I proceeded immediately after seminary to doctoral studies in Scotland, which in the early 1980s was still permeated by a fair amount of Sabbatarianism, especially among evangelical Christians. My study in church history helped me understand why the otherwise fun-loving, balanced, godly Baptists in the church my wife and I joined for our three years in Aberdeen could sometimes behave so seemingly oddly to us—like preparing all their food to be eaten on Sundays the previous night or not permit their children to watch TV or kick a soccer ball around their yard on Sunday afternoon. I was doubtless too young and immature to challenge their views adequately when they began to generalize them and transfer their prohibitions to what they thought I was not allowed to do, but for the most part they were content to let us "foreigners" practice our own customs and treat us at worst as somewhat untutored in this area!

Today, of course, many Americans, especially younger ones, can scarcely conceive of such cultures. Today, businesses and sports have made it increasingly difficult for many Christians to join with the rest of their church members every Sunday morning. One of my suburban pastors periodically "rails" against parents who allow their children to participate in Sunday *morning* sports, not because he is against sports on Sunday but because of the message it sends to the children, that sports are more important than worship. I applaud those churches that have Sunday night, Saturday night, and even midweek evening services as their major (or one of their major) worship services of the week so that people forced by their employers to work on Sunday mornings have other options. I also admire those who give up certain jobs without having new ones lined up because they are unwilling to miss Sunday morning worship on a regular basis, though I could wish that there were enough alternative options for them that they didn't have to choose between the two.

As a nation, Americans are finally starting to take the unique needs of the physically challenged a little more seriously than they used to, but there is still much progress that needs to be made, especially with the more hidden disabilities. Both my wife and I contracted repetitive stress injuries a number of years ago that appear to have put permanent limitations on us as to how long we can do certain activities, including keyboarding, in one sitting. We can do a lot, so that no one would call us disabled in this respect, but we do have physical challenges. I am profoundly grateful that, just as I have to take short "sabbaths" every day from the work I might like to be doing, I can continue to do some of that work every day of the week. Working six full days (prior to resting one full day) is not an option for me, so if I believed I could not do any of my professional work one day each week, I would be restricted in ways most of my colleagues, presumably including the other contributors to this book, would not be. For all the literature extolling the value and even the felt need to preserve or reinstate one full 24-hour period in seven away from work, I have never once seen a contemporary author insist on the need to mandate six 12-hour days *of* work (the average length of time from sunup to sundown that the ancient Israelites worked). Yet that is the first half of the same commandment in the Decalogue they find so timeless in its second half! And there is no difference in the imperative forms of the two halves in the original Hebrew.

I see no reason to imagine that our modern, secular societies will ever turn back the clock to Sabbath-keeping, and some of us might even live long enough to see Sunday business hours everywhere match those of Monday through Saturday. I confess it would be nice not to worry, if my car broke down on the way to a rural church a number of miles from Denver early on a Sunday morning, whether I would find a service station with a mechanic open and available to help, or whether a local store would be open for the supplies I needed for a Sunday morning activity that I forgot. But such a society would require our churches having numerous opportunities for worship and more employers than now do recognizing the need for flex hours and schedules and limits on the amount of time people can work each week and still remain healthy. But these trends do already seem to be slowly developing. Rather than decrying the disappearance of an era that will never return, as conservative Christians seem to do on so many issues, let's see how creative we can become in helping people celebrate multiple mini-Sabbaths every week, and recognize their entire Christian lives as Sabbaths in the NT sense, in ways appropriate to the twenty-first century!

CHAPTER 8

Responses to
Craig L. Blomberg

Response by Skip MacCarty

Professor Blomberg's comprehensive, well-organized, easy-to-follow essay, meaningfully integrated with his personal testimony, offers a coherent theory of the NT's treatment of the Sabbath. Sabbatarians can benefit from his essay in multiple ways, including his warning against judgmentalism and his call for Christians to glorify God in every choice and action, including their relation to the Sabbath. With a scholar's mind and a pastor's heart, he attempts to strike a balance recognizing the place of Mosaic law and the offer of Christian freedom in the NT era. The extent to which his suggested balance is faithful to Scripture is a primary issue in this debate. It seems to us a radical paradigm shift from scriptural teachings on the Sabbath. I begin with some brief bulleted comments, then move to more substantive evaluation.

- The suggestion that the Sabbath was not connected to worship either in the OT or for the first three centuries of Christianity (pp. 307–12) is disputed both by Scripture (e.g., Lev 23:3)[1] and by many scholars. In addition to the supporting

---

1. C. F. Keil and F. Delitzsch, *Commentary on the Old Testament* (Grand Rapids: Eerdmans, 1973), 2:20, 438–39, commenting on Lev 23:3, "The seventh day is a Sabbath of rest, a day of sacred assembly" (Lev 23:3): "A meeting of the people for the worship of Jehovah." "Holy meetings for edification were held on the Sabbath in every place in the land, and it was out of this that the Synagogue arose."

comments in my original essay (pp. 16–18), H. Dressler contends that God's original "intention" with the Sabbath commandment was to provide one weekly day "in which they could worship and refresh their bodies."[2] My essay (p. 40) provides historical evidence that many Christians "celebrated the sacred mysteries [the Lord's Supper] on the Sabbath [Saturday] of every week" into the fourth and fifth centuries.

- The phrase "Jewish Sabbath" frequently used by Blomberg and others is misleading, as it never occurs in Scripture. Rather, Scripture calls it "a Sabbath to the Lord your God" (Exod 20:10), "my [God's] Sabbaths" (Lev 19:3) and "my [God's] holy day" (Isa 58:13). Jesus said, "The Sabbath was made for man" (not just the Jews), proclaiming it the day over which He is Lord (Mark 2:27–28), thus claiming it as His day. While God indeed called the Sabbath a sign between Him and Israel (Exod 31:17), He also gave the new covenant specifically to Israel (Heb 8:8–10); so if the Sabbath is exclusively "Jewish," so is the new covenant.
- For our view of the Ignatius quote (pp. 309–10), see my essay (p. 36–37). The phrase "Lord's Day" does not occur in the Greek manuscript of that document. The word *day* has been added by translators.
- Acts 16:13–15 reports that when there was no synagogue in town, the apostles sought out a place where prayer was being made on the Sabbath. Blomberg suggests that it was *Jewish* women (p. 341) who had established that place, but the text does not identify them as Jewish.
- The claim that the Sabbath commandment "mandate[s] six 12-hour days *of* work" (p. 357) is unsupported. It provides six days to accomplish our work and sanctifies the seventh for rest and worship.

Hermeneutics

Blomberg's treatment (pp. 317–23) of the hermeneutic that guides the Christian in determining which OT laws apply in the

---

2. H. H. P. Dressler, "The Sabbath in the Old Testament," in *From Sabbath to Lord's Day: A Biblical, Historical, and Theological Investigation*, ed. D. A. Carson (Eugene, OR: Wipf and Stock, 1982), 27, 35. Cf. C. Koester, *Hebrews*, AB (New York: Doubleday, 2001), 272: "Israel was not to do any work on the Sabbath 'except to praise the Lord in the assembly of the elders.'"

NT age is enlightening. He discusses four methods: (1) dispensational; (2) covenant theology; (3) recognizing moral, ceremonial, and civil functions of law, with the moral automatically transferring to the NT; and (4) "Privileging the Big Ten" (i.e., the Ten Commandments). His choice is a fifth method, identified as filtering all OT laws through Jesus and the love commandment, "the grid of fulfillment in Christ" (p. 327), which I will respectfully call the "fulfillment in Christ" filter. We see merit in this method, rightly applied.

However, while the third method (moral-ceremonial-civil law, with moral taking precedence) has the complexities he discusses, we should not abandon it altogether; systematic theologians have discerned and usefully applied it for centuries. And the great Christian creeds have recognized the Ten Commandments as having a unique role among biblical law, second only to the Great Commandment of love, and especially as a practical expression of the love commandment. More likely, we could properly apply a combination of Blomberg's last three methods of interpretation. Even then, however, the NT apostles commended believers who tested their own teachings by the OT Scriptures "to see if these things be true," a point often overlooked—almost like, "filter the NT through the OT!" (Acts 17:11).

Upon close investigation, Blomberg's "fulfillment in Christ" filter yields results remarkably similar in significant ways to the dispensational hermeneutic (method 1 above) that he rejects, especially regarding the Sabbath. Both refer to the old and new covenants in strictly dispensational, historical points of reference (OT and NT eras), and both appear to stress the discontinuities between them more than the continuities, especially with regard to law and grace.

Blomberg states: "John 1:17 contrasts the 'law . . . given through Moses' with 'grace and truth [that] came through Jesus Christ.' . . . The grace of the new far outstrips the grace of the old" (p. 329). The term *contrast* is Blomberg's, not John's. Though practically every translation inserts the conjunction *but* between the clauses about law and grace in John 1:17, John did not use it or any other conjunction. This suggests that he did not see a contrast but a development of grace. Notice how he develops this theme. John 1:16 states, "From the fullness of his grace we have all received one blessing after another [*charin anti charitos,* 'grace upon grace,' NRSV]." Though the first mention in the Bible of "grace" ("favor") occurs in Gen 6:8, the first scriptural revelation of God as a God of grace occurs in the Mosaic covenant, "the law" (Exod 34:6)—hence John's statement, "The law [revealing God as a God of grace] was given [*edothē*] through Moses." Jesus came among us as the very *source* and *originator* of that grace—hence John's statement, "Grace and truth came [*egeneto*] through Jesus Christ" (*egeneto* is used 20 times in the Septuagint in the Genesis 1 creation story). "From his fullness we have all received grace [first revealed through the law Jesus gave through Moses] upon grace [as revealed in Jesus, the originator of grace, when He was among us]" (1:16). John is not contrasting the old and new covenants, but emphasizing the continuity of God's progressive revelation of His grace, the same grace, through the Mosaic covenant and in Jesus.

Blomberg cites 2 Cor 3:1–4:6 as "the most detailed, sustained treatment in Paul of the role of the law in the age of the gospel and of the need to recognize a clean break between the two . . . from the old [Testament] age to the new [Testament] age. . . . One Ministry (the Mosaic covenant) brought death . . . ; the other (the age of the Spirit) brings life" (p. 328). It is true that 2 Corinthians 3 characterizes Moses' ministry to Israel as one that "brought death," "condemns," "kills," and is "engraved in letters on stone" and a "glory" that "was fading away," in contrast to Paul's "new covenant" ministry in Corinth that "gives life," "brings righteousness," is "freedom," "written . . . with the Spirit of the living God," "on tablets of human hearts," and an "ever-increasing glory" "which lasts." However, the 2 Corinthians 3 description of Moses' ministry *cannot* and *does not* describe the Mosaic covenant, or else Israel had no hope. Instructively, Paul characterized *his own* new covenant ministry as the "smell of death" to those who rejected his gospel and were thus "perishing" (2 Cor 2:15–16). Moses' "ministry that brought death" signified the *faulty response* of many of the people *to the gospel* of the Mosaic covenant (Heb 4:2), a gospel that was "the aroma of Christ," but one that became "the smell of death" to them because of their faithless, legalistic ("engraved in letters on stone") response, just as it became "the smell of death" for those who rejected Paul's gospel (2 Cor 2:14–16; 3:7). "The god of this age" had "blinded the minds" and "veiled" the hearts of those who rejected Moses' gospel—and Paul's—resulting in a lost condition that could be reversed only "whenever anyone turns to the Lord" (4:3–4; 3:16). Hebrews 11 presents a representative list of new covenant believers living in the OT era who had indeed turned to the Lord, accepted the gospel, and were saved. There is still a "glory" in the presentation of the gospel to those who end up rejecting it and "perishing," but it is a fading glory compared to a gospel presentation to those who accept it in faith and "are being saved." Moses' ministry and audience fit the former, while Paul's ministry to those who became believers in Corinth was a "surpassing glory . . . which lasts." *Second Corinthians 3 presents timeless and universal gospel principles, not dispensationally specific characterizations.*

Blomberg cites Heb 8:13—"By calling this covenant 'new,' [God] has made the first one obsolete, and what is obsolete and outdated will soon disappear"—as "the strongest statement in all of Scripture of the contrast between old and new covenants" (p. 330). While Hebrews 7–10 is generally historical in orientation, its discussion makes clear that what God declared obsolete (8:13) for the NT era, based on Jesus' sacrifice and subsequent high priestly ministry, were the sacrifices and priesthood related to the temple services in Jerusalem, not the moral law that God promised to write on the hearts of new covenant believers (Heb 8:10) in all ages.[3] Blomberg's suggestion, based on Hebrews 8:10, that "God's legislation will be internalized" only by NT believers (p. 330) is disputed by the psalmist: "Your law is within my heart" (Ps 40:8; cf. Isa 51:7; Deut 30:6,11–14).

Blomberg's interpretation of Rom 10:4—"Christ is the end of the Law"—includes the idea that He "terminated" the Law (p. 329). But better and more consistent with the rest of Scripture is the interpretation that Christ is the *goal* of the Law, not its termination.[4] Faith in Messiah Jesus was God's goal for every member of His covenants of every historical era. If Jesus truly "terminated" the Ten Commandments, they would not receive the positive attention they do in His own teachings and throughout the NT (see below).

Blomberg interprets Rom 7:1–6 to mean that "Christians are freed from the law as the covenant to which they are obligated" (ibid.). Romans 7:1–6 does indeed speak of believers "[dying] to the law . . . [to] belong to another [i.e., to be married to Christ]," that they might live in "the new way of the Spirit." Before people come to faith in God/Jesus, they are married to the law (dependent on their own works for

3. See chart on p. 49 of my essay that provides scriptural evidence that this new covenant promise applies to believers in all historical eras.
4. See R. Badenas, *Christ the End of the Law: Romans 10:4 in Pauline Perspective*, JSNTSup 10 (Sheffield, England: JSOT Press, 1985).

any hope of clemency in the judgment), and thus bound in guilt and religious slavery, living in "the old way of the written code [a purely externalized, legalistic, religious experience]" (Rom 7:6). This does not describe the OT believer or the covenant God made with Israel but a rebellious, perverted, legalistic attitude toward that covenant and its gospel message. The Mosaic covenant was a divine marriage covenant: "I was a husband to them" (Jer 31:32). After conversion all believers in every historical age experience marriage to God/Christ, freedom from guilt and from reliance on their own works, and begin to experience life in "the new way of the Spirit." Romans 7:1–6 is not oriented dispensationally but experientially.

Blomberg interprets Jas 2:8–13 to mean, "The Mosaic law . . . condemns," but "this liberating [new covenant] law ['love,' the 'royal law'] focuses on mercy rather than judgment" (p. 331). This false, dispensational dichotomy characterizing a Mosaic covenant emphasis on law, condemnation, and judgment in contrast to a NT emphasis on love and mercy not only seriously misinterprets James but also runs up against Jesus' teaching in Matt 5:21–22 (cf. Heb 6:4–8; 10:26–31). God exercised no less love in the OT era than in the NT era, as will be addressed below.

The polemical Pauline passages on the old and new covenants and the Mosaic law do not pit little grace, much law, and judgment in the OT era against little law, much grace, and mercy in the NT era but describe the age-old, universal war between belief and unbelief, flesh and spirit, and present both law and grace in perfect gospel harmony and balance in every historical era.

The Ten Commandments and the Love Commandment

Blomberg acknowledges (p. 322) the "unique role [of the Ten Commandments] as transcribed by the finger of God, preserved in the ark of the covenant and forming the heart of God's covenantal stipulations for Israel (Exod 24:8; Deut 4:13; and 10:4)," and that nine of the Ten Commandments "are taken up and endorsed in the New Testament." Yet he finds no scriptural evidence that the Ten Commandments are "set apart as uniquely timeless or cross cultural in application" (ibid.). As evidence, he observes that the Ten Commandments are referred to as a group only three times in Scripture, and only in the Pentateuch, "the Mosaic law." What is ignored is that the great commandments to "love God with all your heart" and "love your neighbor as yourself" also occur verbatim in Scripture only in the Pentateuch, "the Mosaic law," prior to Jesus' teaching (Deut 6:5; Lev 19:18).

Even though the term "Ten Commandments" does not recur beyond the Pentateuch, specific commandments of the Decalogue are often mentioned, including the Sabbath commandment. And the OT's frequent references to "the covenant" most often have the Ten Commandments in mind as the covenant's divinely established moral code and symbol (e.g., Deut 4:13; 1 Kings 8:21).

The phrase "Love God and keep His commandments" was the discipleship formula of the OT[5]—the precursor to Jesus' own discipleship formula: "If you love me, you will obey what I command [*entolas tas emas tērēsete,* 'obey my commandments']"; "whoever has my commands [*entolas,* 'commandments'] and obeys them, he is the one who loves me" (John 14:15,21). The NT statement, "Love fulfills the law," simply restated and reemphasized this previously established OT formula. In both testaments love for God was the priority, the underlying, motivating, and empowering principle of all true obedience to God and compassion to others.

After the exile the Jews daily recited[6] the Shema, which included, "Love the Lord your God with all your heart"—the first great commandment, and the Decalogue, to which the Shema itself refers when it says, "These commandments . . . are to be in your hearts." This statement of the Shema is itself a new covenant formulation: "I will put my laws in their minds and write them on their hearts" (Deut 6:5–6; 5:4–22; Matt 22:35–40; Heb 8:10). The love command and the Decalogue together held a unique place both in the divine covenant and in the hearts of God's faithful people. Paul wrote, "Circumcision is nothing and uncircumcision is nothing. Keeping God's commands [*entolas,* 'commandments'] is what counts" (1 Cor 7:19). Any Jewish Christian reading those words would have understood them as an affirmation of the permanency of the Shema and the Decalogue.

References and allusions to the Ten Commandments occur frequently in Jesus' teaching ministry[7] and in the rest of the NT.[8] Blomberg links the Ten Commandments with circumcision (pp. 342–44),

---

5. Deut 6:5; 7:9; 10:12–22; 11:1–24; 13:3–4; 19:8–9; 30:6,19–20; cf. MacCarty, *In Granite or Ingrained,* 143–67.

6. M. *Tamid* 5:1.

7. E.g., Matt 5:21–22,27–28; Mark 2:27–28; 7:9–13,20–23; 10:17–22; John 1:10.

8. E.g., Luke 23:56; Rom 1:29–31; 2:21–22; 7:7; 1 Cor 6:9–11; Eph 6:1–3; 1 Tim 1:8–11.

and yet Paul does the opposite (1 Cor 7:19). When Jesus proclaimed that He was Lord of the Sabbath (Mark 2:28), the spiritual Rock that attended Israel on their journeys (1 Cor 10:4), He revealed that it was He who had blessed and sanctified the seventh day at creation and had enshrined the Sabbath commandment in the heart of the Decalogue. James quotes the sixth and seventh Commandments as part of "the law that gives freedom" (Jas 2:10–12).[9] Lochman calls the Decalogue "a *charter of freedom*. . . . The Ten Commandments are the 'Ten Great Freedoms.'"[10]

The book of Revelation is permeated with direct and indirect allusions to the Ten Commandments (Lutheran numbering in brackets):

- 2nd[1st] Commandment—"worshiping . . . Idols" (Rev 9:20)
- 3rd [2nd]—"have not denied my name" (Rev 3:8; cf. 21:8)
- 4th [3rd]—"the Lord's Day" (Rev 1:10)
- 6th [5th]—"murders" (Rev 9:21; 21:8)
- 7th [6th]—"sexual immorality" (Rev 2:14,20; 9:21; 21:8)
- 8th [7th]—"thefts" (Rev 9:21)
- 9th [8th]—"liars" (Rev 21:8)

John sees a vision of "God's temple in heaven" containing "the ark of his covenant" (which contained the Ten Commandments in the OT period—Deut 10:4–5), and accompanying celestial signs reminiscent of the giving of the Ten Commandments at Sinai (Rev 11:19).[11] In the next several chapters John identifies God's people as "those who obey God's commandments and hold to the testimony of Jesus" (12:17), "the saints who obey God's commandments and remain faithful to Jesus" (14:12). In context these references to "God's commandments" clearly include the Ten Commandments that He gave His people and ordered be kept inside "the ark of the covenant." The scriptural evidence appears to us clear and convincing that the Ten Commandments are permanent and universal, "uniquely timeless and cross-cultural in application."

---

9. Blomberg's interpretation (p. 331) that James sets "mercy" (2:13) and "the royal law found in Scripture [the OT], 'Love your neighbor as yourself'" (2:8) in opposition to the Ten Commandments is in our view without foundation and seriously misunderstands the symbiotic relationship of love and the Decalogue throughout both testaments.

10. J. M. Lochman, *Signposts to Freedom: The Ten Commandments and Christian Ethics*, trans. D. Lewis (Minneapolis: Augsburg, 1982), 19.

11. See n. 66 on p. 38 of my essay.

Blomberg acknowledges that nine of the Ten Commandments are "endorsed" in the NT (p. 322). Only the Sabbath, He claims, is treated otherwise. We find no basis for this. Such a differential treatment of the Commandments was never spelled out by Jesus or any of His disciples, explicitly or implicitly.

The Fulfillment-in-Christ Filtered Sabbath

Running the Sabbath commandment through the fulfillment-in-Christ filter yields different results for Blomberg than it does for us, as it depends entirely on one's interpretation of Jesus' and the apostles' Sabbath practice and teachings. Blomberg sees Jesus laying the groundwork for a sweeping change, the withdrawal of God's blessing and sanctification of the seventh day, in preparation for a rest and worship practice that involves unspecified times depending on what one deems most convenient and meets one's immediate need (pp. 347, 351, 353). We find Jesus, the Lord of the Sabbath, restoring His original intent and purpose for the Sabbath as He had blessed and sanctified it in creation and later spoke and wrote it in His Ten Commandments.

Blomberg's fulfillment-in-Christ filter that leads him to conclude that the literal observance of the Sabbath commandment no longer applies to Christians (pp. 325, 352–53) is based on Jesus' statement: "Do not think that I have come to abolish the Law or the Prophets; I have not come to abolish them but to fulfill them" (Matt 5:17). This needs to be examined.

After His statement in Matt 5:17, Jesus immediately explained what He meant. He brought up two of the Ten Commandments and "fulfilled" them, which Blomberg says means "to give the true or complete meaning to something" (p. 323). Jesus explained that murder transcends the taking of someone's life, and reaches to the motivation: hating someone, or even being angry with them (Matt 5:21–22)! Adultery includes lusting (5:27–28). By providing "the true or complete meaning" to these commandments Jesus did not set aside their literal application, as if to say, as long as you are not angry with someone or do not hate them, murder is no longer a sin or forbidden. (For some, hating or being angry are not prerequisites for murder. Murder is their business; they are simply fulfilling a contract.) To say that God's literal commands prohibiting murder and adultery no longer apply because Jesus provided their "true and complete meaning" would be to "abolish" them, the very thing Jesus said He did not come to do. Yet that is exactly what Blomberg does with the Sabbath. He claims that in Heb 4:9 and Matt 11:28–30 Jesus provides the true and complete meaning of the Sabbath and "fulfills the Sabbath law by becoming our rest," and therefore "there is no reason for [Christ's followers] literally to observe the weekly holiday known as the Sabbath" (p. 339), rendering the literal application of the Sabbath commandment null and void in the NT era.

In his brief comments on Heb 3:7–4:11 Blomberg writes (pp. 349–50): "The climax of this somewhat convoluted argument comes in Hebrews 4:9: 'There remains, then, a Sabbath-rest for the people of God.' This is the only appearance of the noun 'Sabbath-rest' (Gk. *sabbatismos*) in the Bible. But Hebrews is not talking here about ceasing from work one day in seven; it is talking about remaining faithful to Jesus rather than committing the apostasy against which this letter so regularly warns (recall 3:16–4:3)." This reinterpretation of *sabbatismos* demonstrates the subjective character of Blomberg's fulfillment-in-Christ filter. The meaning of *sabbatismos* in extrabiblical literature and its cognate usage as a verb (*sabbatizō*) in the OT Greek means exactly "ceasing from work" in connection with Sabbath (either the seventh-day Sabbath or other Sabbaths of the Lord). In extrabiblical literature *sabbatismos* is most often used in connection with the seventh-day Sabbath, though pejoratively— those who do not work on the seventh day must be legalistic, lazy, or both.[12] Leaping over the clear meaning established everywhere else for this word and its cognates in Scripture and early Christian literature, Blomberg reinterprets and spiritualizes it to mean "remaining faithful to Jesus rather than committing apostasy." His expanded definition, toward which his entire essay builds, is: "We obey the Sabbath commandment of the Decalogue as we spiritually rest in Christ, letting Him bear our heavy burdens, trusting Him for salvation and committing our lives to Him in service, then

---

12. See H. Attridge, *The Epistle to the Hebrews*, Hermeneia (Philadelphia: Fortress, 1989), 131: "The word ['*sabbatismos*,' 'Sabbath observance'] appears in Plutarch [AD 46–120] *Superst.* 3(166A) in a list of superstitious practices. . . . Plutarch knows of and castigates the superstitious Jewish observance of the Sabbath. Cf. *Superst.* 8 (196C). Dependence of Plutarch on Hebrews is unlikely. Hence the contention . . . that the word [*sabbatismos*] is a neologism coined by [the author of Hebrews] may be ruled out." This supports the idea that the term *sabbatismos* was known and used to refer to seventh-day Sabbath observance in very early extrabiblical sources. Cf. p. 26, n. 39 in my essay, and p. 178, n. 6 of my critique of Dr. Pipa's "Christian Sabbath View" for further discussion of *sabbatismos*.

remaining faithful in lifelong loyalty to Him rather than committing apostasy" (p. 351). We are in full agreement with this sentiment, but neither Heb 4:9 nor 3:7–4:11 nor Rev 14:11 nor Matt 11:28–30 teach this as a replacement for the literal observance of the Sabbath commandment, any more than Jesus intended His teaching on the deeper meaning of the commandments prohibiting murder and adultery to be interpreted as repealing a literal observance of those commandments. The reference to God resting on the seventh day of creation (Heb 4:4), which Blomberg acknowledges was the basis for the Sabbath commandment (p. 349), coupled with the clear statement that "there remains, therefore, a Sabbath rest (*sabbatismos*, literal Sabbath observance) for the people of God" (Heb 4:9), should leave no doubt that a literal observance of the seventh-day Sabbath remains for God's people in the NT era. Blomberg's interpretation completely reverses the meaning of Heb 4:9, essentially rendering it as, "There *does not remain*, therefore, a Sabbath rest (*sabbatismos*, literal Sabbath observance) for the people of God." This should sound an alarm to anyone attracted to the "Sabbath fulfilled in Christ" position.

But what about Rom 14:4–5; Gal 4:10–11 and Col 2:16, which Blomberg uses as further proof of his position (pp. 341–48)?[13] Blomberg fails to note that Rom 14:4–5 is discussing "disputable matters," which none of the Ten Commandments ever were in Scripture, and that the word *sacred* does not occur in the Greek text. Romans 14 does not address "sacred" days, the Sabbath, or the Ten Commandments in general.

Galatians 4:10–11 is addressed to those who "formerly . . . did not know God" (4:8), "pagans,"[14] not to those who grew up practicing the Jewish faith. The calendar Paul refers to in Gal 4:10 is a pagan calendar, not Jewish.[15] Galatians 4:10–11 has nothing to do with the seventh-day Sabbath.

Blomberg says Col 2:16 is "the most important [passage] in all of the NT for confirming" his case (p. 341). But in-depth research seriously challenges his conclusion. Previously (p. 30) I referenced a sampling of commentaries that do not teach as Blomberg does that Col 2:16 abrogates the Sabbath commandment's appointed sacred

13. For my original discussion of these texts, see my essay, pp. 29–32 .
14. T. Martin, "Pagan and Judeo-Christian Time-Keeping Schemes in Gal. 4:10 and Col. 2:16," *NTS* 42 (1996): 110–12; cf. *NIV Study Bible* scholarly note.
15. Ibid.

time for rest and worship, among them R. du Preez's *Judging the Sabbath: Discovering What Can't Be Found in Colossians 2:16.* Blomberg responded to du Preez (p. 343, n. 81) but failed to address his major points.

Colossians 2:16–17 (RSV) reads: "Therefore let no one pass judgment on you in questions of food and drink or with regard to a festival (*heortēs*) or a new moon (*neomēnias*) or a sabbath (*sabbatōn*)."[16] In the context of ancient Israel's religious seasons, the Greek term *heortē* was used in the Greek translation of the OT and in the NT to identify most of the annual pilgrim festivals people had to travel to Jerusalem to attend (Passover, Pentecost, and Tabernacles). *Neomēnia* always refers to the new moon celebrations that marked when the ceremonial seasons began. The Hebrew *shabbat* and the Greek *sabbata* and *sabbaton* referred to the seventh-day Sabbath, or the other ceremonial sabbath periods (Day of Atonement, Trumpets, sabbatical years) that were not included in the pilgrim festivals. To determine how *shabbat* and *sabbata/sabbaton* were to be understood, the biblical authors used lucid "linguistic markers" and context to distinguish which *sabbath* they meant. The terms *keep, day, holy, my,* etc., associated with *sabbath* were used to designate the weekly Sabbath, never ceremonial sabbaths. Correspondingly, together with the context, the terms *afflict, weeks, of the land, her/its/she,* and *your* always designated the ceremonial sabbaths, never the weekly Sabbath. All biblically literate Jews were aware of this, Paul foremost among them. When he used *sabbatōn* in Col 2:16, he purposely did not include any of the linguistic indicators so frequently used throughout the Bible to identify the seventh-day Sabbath.

Furthermore, of the several OT passages Paul might have been alluding to with the specific string he used in Col 2:16—"a festival [*heortēs*] or a new moon [*neomēnias*] or a sabbath [*sabbatōn*]"— the only true match is Hos 2:11.[17] Paul quotes from Hosea several times[18] and never directly from the other references where rough

---

16. The RSV was selected since, of the more popular formal translations, it most accurately captures the meaning of the three key terms under discussion. Many translations add the word *day* to Sabbath, but this has no Greek manuscript support.

17. E. Schweizer, *The Letter to the Colossians: A Commentary*, trans. A. Chester (Minneapolis: Augsburg, 1982), 155: In Col 2:16 the sequence of festival-new moon-sabbath corresponds precisely to that of Hos 2:11.

18. E.g., Rom 9:25–26 quotes Hos 2:23 and 1:10, and 1 Cor 15:55 quotes Hos 13:14.

but mismatched approximations of this string occur—Numbers, 1 and 2 Chronicles, Nehemiah, and Ezekiel, which commentators have mistakenly associated with Col 2:16. In addition, Hos 2:11 is the only OT text that matches Col 2:16 in that its three-term string occurs in the singular, does not focus on sacrifices, and occurs in the exact order as in Col 2:16—"a festival (*heortēs*) or a new moon (*neomēnias*) or a sabbath (*sabbatōn*)." It is also the only text among them that prophesies the end of all these ceremonial seasons, while Colossians 2 announces its fulfillment! And in Hos 2:11, the Hebrew begins the string with the term *ag* (Gk., *heortēs*) for the three pilgrim festivals (rather than *mo'edim*, which included all of the religious seasons) and ends with *shabbatth*, "her sabbaths"—"sabbath" linked with the linguistic marker, "her," which signaled ceremonial sabbath periods and was never used for the weekly Sabbath. So when Paul in Col 2:16 used the particular string of terms that he did, a knowledgeable Jew or Gentile convert would have associated it with Hos 2:11 and would have known exactly what Paul was referring to: the pilgrim feasts (*heortēs*), new moon celebrations (*neomēnias*), and the remaining ceremonial sabbath periods (*sabbatōn*).[19] This illustrates the Acts 17:11 hermeneutic principle mentioned earlier: some NT texts, Col 2:16 among them, can be understood only through an accurate understanding of their OT counterparts. Even less-knowledgeable Jewish Christians would still most likely have known that the meaning of "sabbath" could only be ascertained by whatever linguistic markers were attached, and would have noticed immediately that all linguistic indicators for the weekly Sabbath were missing.

While all this may seem technical to modern readers and not easy to follow, it was commonplace parlance to an ancient Jew, especially to Paul who intentionally adopted the Hosea string sequence, using Hosea's very terms in his own Colossian message. Furthermore, in light of Col 2:17 (RSV), "These are only a shadow of what is to come; but the substance belongs to Christ," these early Christian believers would have thought of nothing else than the ceremonial sabbaths since they were all symbols and types of Christ who had indeed come.

---

19. The NKJV, NEB, HCSB (Holman Christian Standard Bible, 2004) translations that have "sabbaths," "sabbath days" and "sabbath day," respectively, rather than Sabbaths (upper case) in apparent recognition of this distinction.

To use Blomberg's football illustration (p. 343, n. 81): speak of "center, guard, tackle" in reference to an unspecified sporting event to someone familiar with American sports, and they think "football" and not some other sport. Similarly, if one were to speak of *heortē, neomēnia, sabbata/sabbatōn* to Jewish Christians or Gentile converts, they would immediately think "cultic times" of pilgrim festivals (i.e., Passover/Unleavened Bread, Pentecost, Tabernacles), new moon celebrations, and ceremonial sabbaths (i.e., Trumpets, Atonement, sabbatical years). Thus Col 2:16, rather than proving the abrogation of the Decalogue's weekly seventh-day Sabbath, actually does the opposite: it shows that the *ceremonial* sabbaths were abrogated.

In the context of Col 2:16, Blomberg associates the Decalogue's Sabbath with "morally neutral matters" (p. 346) and labels attempts to "mandate . . . Sabbath-keeping . . . in the salvation-historical era of Christian freedom . . . [as] merely human tradition" (p. 345). To us, nothing in the Ten Commandments has ever been or will be morally neutral. Rather, the "human tradition" is the attempt to redefine the Sabbath into a spiritual sentiment that abrogates the literal observance of the Sabbath commandment, thus nullifying the word of God (Matt 15:6).

Closing Questions

In addition to the issues discussed above, Professor Blomberg's essay raises several questions for me:

- If the seventh-day Sabbath was exclusively "Jewish," why should not the new covenant, which God said He made specifically "with the house of Israel," be an exclusively Jewish covenant (Jer 31:31–32; Heb 8:8,10)?
- Blomberg reports that some early church leaders postdating the NT wrote "that attempts to enforce Sabbath rest one day a week were . . . a danger to the gospel of salvation and spiritual living by grace through faith" (p. 309). Does Blomberg agree with this assessment? How would observing the Decalogue's seventh-day Sabbath commandment threaten spiritual living by grace in a way that observing any of its other nine commandments would not? Did God design the seventh-day Sabbath commandment to *threaten* or to *pro-*

mote "the gospel of salvation and spiritual living by grace through faith" among His people?

- If the Ten Commandments are not "uniquely timeless or cross-cultural in application" (p. 322), does that mean having no other God before the God of Scripture; children honoring parents; prohibition of murder, adultery, stealing and coveting are not "timeless or cross-cultural in application"? Or does this apply only to the Sabbath?

- Blomberg notes that immediately following the Heb 8:10–12 list of new covenant promises, Heb 8:13 states that the first covenant is "obsolete" (p. 330). What is the first covenant that is "obsolete," and what is its relation to the new covenant promises listed in Heb 8:10–12?

- In his essay he suggests that the complexity of determining what constitutes "work" makes a literal observance of the Sabbath inapplicable from a practical standpoint in today's era (p. 335). Is war murder? Is it murder on just one side, both, or neither? Who determines that? Is abortion in cases of rape and incest murder? Do such complexities make the prohibition of murder inapplicable from a practical standpoint in today's era? Or does the "complexity" argument against the applicability of a particular commandment apply only to the seventh-day Sabbath?

- The essay reports that "most forms of Sabbatarianism throughout history have themselves actually fostered the kind of externalism that Jesus eschews" (p. 338). Does the Sabbath commandment itself promote such "externalism?"

- Is it possible, even likely, that the OT believers represented in Hebrews 11's "Hall of Faith"—most if not all of whom observed the seventh-day Sabbath—"spiritually rested in [Yahweh], letting Him bear [their] heavy burdens, trusting Him for salvation and committing [their] lives to Him in service, and then remaining faithful in lifelong loyalty to Him rather than committing apostasy" (p. 351)? If so, why would one need to abandon the literal observance of the Sabbath commandment in order to have such an experience with Jesus?

- The essay notes that "today business and sports have made it increasingly difficult for many Christians to join with the rest of their church members every Sunday morning," implying that this is one benefit of being freed from a literal observance of the Sabbath commandment (p. 357). How does this balance out with Jesus' call to take up one's cross and follow Him (Luke 9:23) and the essay's reference to the Christian's "cruciform lifestyle" (p. 327)?

I look forward someday to meeting Professor Blomberg, a possibility made more likely by the fact that one of my sons lives in Denver, not far from his seminary. In the meantime, not adversarially but respectfully, I invite Professor Blomberg to experiment with a literal observance of the seventh-day Sabbath for one month, to see if God does not bless his production equal to, or greater than, months when he worked seven days a week.

Response by Joseph A. Pipa

Dr. Blomberg has written a scholarly and thoughtful exposition of the Sabbath commandment. He concludes: "Because Jesus fulfilled the Law, and thus fulfilled the Sabbath commands, He, not some day of the week, is what offers the believers rest. *We obey the Sabbath commandment of the Decalogue as we spiritually rest in Christ, letting Him bear our heavy burdens, trusting Him for salvation and committing our lives to Him in service, and then remaining faithful in lifelong loyalty to Him rather than committing apostasy.* No special day each week for rest or worship could ever come close to fulfilling this grander and far more enriching and exciting vision of life to the full" (p. 351).

In order to reach his conclusion, Blomberg develops a hermeneutic that interprets the Ten Commandments through the lenses of the NT. First, he surveys the historical perspective on the Sabbath. Unfortunately, he begins with Exod 16:23–29 and omits the Sabbath creation ordinance found in Gen 2:1–3. He says that Exodus 16 is "the first reference to a Sabbath in the Scriptures" (p. 305). He is correct about the term *Sabbath*, but obviously the concept is revealed in Gen 2:1–3, as seen in the Holy Spirit's interpretation in Exod 20:11: "For in six days the Lord made the heavens and the earth, the sea and all that is in them and rested on the seventh day, therefore the Lord blessed the Sabbath day and made it holy." As Dr. MacCarty and I point out, it is essential to any understanding of the Sabbath commandment and its perpetual requirements to interpret it in light of this creation ordinance (see Pipa, pp. 119–123; MacCarty, pp. 11–14).

His second error in his survey is to limit the Sabbath commandment to physical rest: "Indeed, if all we had were the Hebrew Scriptures, we might never guess that a day of rest eventually also became a day for worship" (p. 307). God, however, teaches in the Sabbath commandment that the purpose of rest is to sanctify the day. Moreover, Lev 23:3 makes clear that the Sabbath rest was for the purpose of corporate worship: "For six days work may be done; but on the seventh day there is a Sabbath of complete rest, a holy convocation. You shall not do any work; it is a Sabbath to the Lord in your dwellings." God commands the old covenant people to gather for corporate worship on the Sabbath. This commandment would have entailed their meeting in their cities and villages weekly for worship. Whether they used the synagogue system or simply had a place to meet for corporate worship, clearly they gathered for worship on the Sabbath. In Psalm 74, the psalmist laments not only the destruction of the temple, but also the destruction of the "meeting places of God in the land."

That God expected the old covenant people to use the Sabbath for worship is further proven by Psalm 92, which is titled "A Psalm, a Song for the Sabbath day." This psalm lays out the responsibility and blessings of Sabbath worship and was used by the old covenant church on the Sabbath.

With respect to the church in the NT, Dr. Blomberg says that "some Christians transferred their day of worship from Saturday to Sunday" (p. 307). In fact there is no biblical evidence of their worshipping on any other days. All Christians transferred their day of worship from Saturday to Sunday; their gathering at the synagogues was for evangelistic purposes and not to fulfill the responsibilities of corporate worship. Contrary to his own argument, he seems to concede that 1 Cor 16:1–2 is a reference to Sunday worship and that by the time of the apostle John, the church referred to the first day of the week as the Lord's Day.

However, Dr. Blomberg wants to separate first-day worship from a day of rest. His assertion, however, is a bit gratuitous because in the early centuries many Gentiles would not have had "regular opportunity to refrain from their occupations on that day, the concepts of rest and worship obviously became separated" (p. 309). We really do not know the number who would not have been able to keep a whole Sabbath, but the difficulty does not prove the concept wrong.

He seeks to buttress his separation of a day set aside for rest and a time for worship from the early church fathers: "A variety of quotations from patristic writers from the first four centuries shows that attempts to enforce Sabbath rest one day a week were frequently labeled as Judaizing and viewed as a danger to the gospel of salvation and spiritual living through faith alone" (p. 309).

It is true that the early church rejected the Jewish Sabbath, but they replaced it with the Lord's Day. This seems to be the point of the quotation by Ignatius (used by Blomberg on pp. 309–10). And it is true that the term *Sabbath* would not be regularly used for the Lord's Day until after Constantine. There are, however, early references to the Lord's Day being the Sabbath. Eusebius (ca. 260–339), in his commentary on Psalm 92, showed the relation of the seventh-day Sabbath to the Lord's Day: "The Word, through the New Covenant, has changed and transferred the feast of the sabbath to the rising of the light and handed to us the image (*eikōn*) of a true rest, the Lord's Day, that brings salvation, the first, and the day of light."[20] Stott wrote:

> It is clear that there are mystical elements in it, but the references to 'intervals of six days,' 'gatherings throughout the world,' the allusions to the Eucharist, including the bread and 'the blood of the Lamb which taketh away the sin of the world,' the emphasis on 'each Lord's day' several times, all suggest that it is a literal Sunday which Eusebius has in mind.[21]

Earlier, Origen (ca. 185–254) referred to the Lord's Day as the Sabbath. In the *Homilies on Numbers*, quoting Heb 4:9, he said, "Leaving the Jewish observance of the sabbath, let us see how the sabbath ought to be observed by a Christian."[22] He continued to discuss how the Sabbath should be spent. Stott wrote that "while elsewhere Origen clearly saw the sabbath as a type of the rest from sin and

---

20. Eusebius, *Commentary on the Psalms* 91 (92), quoted in R. T. Beckwith and W. Stott, *This Is the Day: The Biblical Doctrine of the Christian Sunday in Its Jewish and Early Church Setting* (London: Marshall, Morgan & Scott, 1978), 76.
21. Beckwith and Stott, *This Is the Day*, 77.
22. Ibid., 70.

evil works of all kinds, here he is dealing in a practical way with the observance of the Christian festal day."[23]

Origen taught that the Christian Sabbath was to be kept by abstaining from work and recreation:

> Leaving the Jewish observance of the sabbath, let us see how the sabbath ought to be observed by a Christian. . . . On the sabbath day all worldly pleasures ought to be abstained from. If therefore you cease from all secular works (*saecularia*) and execute nothing worldly, but give yourself up to spiritual exercises, repairing to the church (*ad ecclesiam*), attending to sacred reading and instruction, thinking of celestial things, solicitous for the future, placing the judgment to come before your eyes, not looking to things present and visible, but to those which are future and invisible, this is the observance of the Christian sabbath.[24]

For Origen, the highlight of the day was corporate worship, which Stott demonstrates would have required a number of hours. But, furthermore, there was an emphasis (as indicated in the preceding quotation from Origen) on devoting the whole day to holy exercises. Origen's mentor, Clement of Alexandria (ca. 150–215) wrote:

> Woman and man [probably "wife and husband"] are to go to church, decently attired, with natural step, embracing silence, possessing unfeigned love, pure in body, pure in heart, fit to pray to God. . . . But now I know not how people change their fashions and manners with the place. . . . So, laying aside the inspiration of the assembly, after their departure from it, they become like others with whom they associate . . . after having paid reverence to the discourse about God they leave within [the church] what they heard. And outside they foolishly amuse themselves with impious playing and amatory quavering, occupied with flute-playing and dancing and intoxication and all kinds of trash.[25]

---

23. Ibid., 72. Earlier Stott deals with a difficult passage in Clement of Alexandria in which Scott believes Clement refers to the eight day as the fulfillment of the fourth commandment and calls it the Sabbath, "And it (the eighth day) properly the sabbath, the rest, and the seventh (day of the week) a day of work," p. 68.

24. Ibid., 70.

25. Clement of Alexandria, *The Instructor* III.xi.

Even though they did not often use the term *Sabbath*, many in the early church were committed to keeping the whole day holy. The writer of the *Second Epistle of Clement* (AD 120–140) called his readers to a faithful observance of the day:

> "And let us not merely seem to believe and pay attention now, while we are being exhorted by the Elders, but also when we have gone home let us remember the commandments of the Lord, and let us not be dragged aside by worldly lusts, but let us try to come here more frequently, and to make progress in the commands of the Lord."[26]

The importance of spending the whole day remained an emphasis throughout the remainder of this period. For example, Chrysostom, in discussing the dangers of losing the spiritual benefits of the day, said in a homily on Matthew:

> For we ought not, as soon as we retire from the Communion, to plunge into affairs . . . unsuitable to the Communion, but as soon as ever we get home to take our Bible into our hands and call our wife and children to join us in putting together what we have heard and then, not before, engage in the business of life. . . . When you retire from the Communion, you must account nothing more necessary, than that you should put together the things that have been said to you. Yes, for it were the utmost folly, while we give up five or six days to the business of life, not to bestow on spiritual things so much as one day or rather not so much as a small part of one day. . . . Therefore let us write it down as an unalterable law for ourselves, for our wives and for our children, to give up this one day of the week entire to hearing and to the recollection of the things which we have heard.[27]

Commenting on 1 Cor 16:2, he called for the separation of the whole day:

> [O]n the first day of the week . . . the separation from all work; the soul becomes more joyful from this laying of it aside. . . . Because of this . . . it is fitting that we honour it with a spiritual

---

26. *Second Clement*, XVII. Dated c. AD 120–140.
27. Chrysostom, *Commentary on Matthew*, Homily 5:1. By "business of life" he is not referring to worldly occupations but the necessary work of the household.

honour . . . and every Lord's Day let the affairs connected with us as masters be laid aside at home.[28]

The term *Sunday*, although not used widely before Constantine, was already in use in the early church. Justin Martyr said the church met for worship on Sunday, the first day of the week,

> and on the day called Sunday, all who live in cities or in the country gather together to one place, and the memoirs of the apostles or the writings of the prophets are read. . . . But Sunday is the day on which we all hold our common assembly, because it is the first day on which God, having wrought a change in the darkness and matter, made the world; and Jesus Christ our Saviour on the same day rose from the dead.[29]

After Constantine the heathen term *Sunday* and the term *Sabbath* were used for the first day, and in an edict of Gratian in AD 386, the terms *Lord's Day* and *Sunday* are combined.[30]

Philip Schaff concluded:

> We see then that the ante-Nicene church clearly distinguished the Christian Sunday from the Jewish Sabbath, and put it on independent Christian ground. She did not fully appreciate the perpetual obligation of the fourth [Sabbath] commandment in its substance as a weekly day of rest, rooted in the physical and moral necessities of man. This is independent of those ceremonial enactments which were intended only for the Jews and abolished by the gospel. But, on the other hand, the church took no secular liberties with the day. She regarded Sunday as a sacred day, as the Day of the Lord, as the weekly commemoration of his resurrection and the Pentecostal effusion of the Spirit, and therefore as a day of holy joy and thanksgiving to be celebrated even before the rising sun by prayer, praise, and communion with the risen Lord and Saviour.[31]

---

28. Quoted in Beckwith and Stott, *This Is the Day*, 135. For references to other Fathers such as Augustine see Stott and Lee.

29. Justin Martyr, *Apology* I.67.

30. P. Schaff, *History of the Christian Church* (Grand Rapids: Eerdmans, 1985), 2:201–3.

31. Ibid., 205.

Therefore, contrary to Dr. Blomberg's assertion (p. 309), it appears that a Sabbath for rest and the first day for worship were interchangeable. It seems clear from some of the testimonies that the early church saw a close relation between the cessation of labor and a day for worship; the cessation from labor was for the purpose of worship.

Dr. Blomberg is correct in stating that Luther and Calvin along with other early reformers did not see a direct continuity between the Sabbath commandment and the church's worship on the first day of the week. Yet as he says, "The mingling of a day of worship and a day of rest continues for this period . . . but neither may we speak of this as Sabbatarianism—the mandated cessation of certain activities and practice of others on one specific day each week based on the Ten Commandments" (pp. 313–14). But at least in Calvin's case, he ended up at the same place as the later Puritans:

> The Sabbath should be to us a tower whereon we should mount aloft to contemplate afar the works of God, when we are not occupied nor hindered by any thing besides, from stretching forth all our faculties in considering the gifts and graces which He has bestowed on us. And if we properly apply ourselves to do this on the Sabbath, it is certain that we shall be no strangers to it during the rest of our time and that this meditation shall have formed our minds, that on Monday, and the other days of the week, we shall abide in the grateful remembrance of our God. . . . It is for us to dedicate ourselves wholly to God, renouncing ourselves, our feelings, and all our affections; and then, since we have this external ordinance, to act as becomes us, that is *to lay aside our earthly affairs and occupations, so that we may be entirely free* to meditate on the works of God, may exercise ourselves in considering the gifts which He has afforded us, and, above all, may apply ourselves to apprehend the grace which He daily offers us in His Gospel, and may be more and more conformed to it. And when we shall have employed the Sabbath in praising and magnifying the name of God, and meditating on His works, we must, through the rest of the week, show how we have profited thereby.[32]

---

32. J. Calvin, *Sermons on Deuteronomy* (Edinburgh: Banner of Truth Trust, 1987), 205, emphasis added.

We can certainly agree with Dr. Blomberg's assessment of the church in the twenty-first century: "By their actual practices, including sporadic attendance at worship and little sense that anything is 'off limits' during the portion of Sundays they are not in church, possibly the majority of American Christians today behave as if the OT Sabbath legislation did not apply to Christians at all" (p. 316). But such was not the case 50 years ago, and surely the teaching of men like Dr. Blomberg has contributed to the demise of the practice of the Christian Sabbath in almost every Protestant denomination.

In Dr. Blomberg's next section, he deals with the hermeneutical question of how one applies the OT laws in the NT age. He begins by surveying four various approaches: Dispensationalism; Covenant Theology; Moral, Civil, and Ceremonial Laws; and Privileging the "Big Ten." The problem is his confusion with respect to covenant theology. Covenant theology actually incorporates Blomberg's last three approaches. His opening statement with respect to covenant theology is partially correct: "The opposite approach therefore argues that everything in the OT carries over to the NT age unless the NT explicitly rescinds it" (p. 318). The problem lies in the term "explicitly." For example, covenant theology does not teach that every ceremonial law must be rescinded explicitly; they are all rescinded, because Christ fulfilled them.

Covenant theology also recognizes the distinction between ceremonial, civil, and moral laws. The Westminster Confession of Faith states:

> Beside this law, commonly called moral, God was pleased to give to the people of Israel, as a church under age, ceremonial laws, containing several typical ordinances, partly of worship, prefiguring Christ, his graces, actions, sufferings, and benefits; and partly, holding forth divers instructions of moral duties. All which ceremonial laws are now abrogated, under the New Testament. To them also, as a body politic, he gave sundry judicial laws, which expired together with the State of that people; not obliging any other now, further than the general equity thereof may require.[33]

---

33. WCF 19.3–4.

As to the mingling of these laws in the OT (for example, Leviticus 19), the answer lies in the fact that all the ceremonial and civil laws are applications of the various commandments of the moral law. Moreover, there are no such things as *a*moral laws (as Blomberg calls them). Any law given by God is morally binding on His people. Perhaps a more useful distinction to help understand the moral requirements of the ceremonial and civil laws is that of moral and positive law, as I develop it on pages 144–46 of my chapter. A positive law is an application of the moral law to a specific situation or time in covenant history. It is morally binding during its time. So, for example, it is a sin in the current age for a man to marry his sister, but such a relationship was not a sin in the Adamic age.

Covenant theology also emphasizes what Blomberg calls "Privileging the 'Big Ten.'" Covenant theology teaches that the Ten Commandments are a summary of God's moral law, first written on the heart of Adam and Eve and reinforced in creation ordinances (Sabbath, work, marriage) and further revelation to Adam and Eve. This was the law that God promised to write on the hearts of His people in the new covenant (Jer 31:33); not a new law or some NT abridgement of this law.

Blomberg fails to understand that the NT treats the Ten Commandments as a summary of God's moral law. For example, when asked what the greatest commandment is, Christ responded:

> You shall love the Lord your God with all your heart, and with all your soul, and with all your mind. This is the great and foremost commandment. The second is like it, You shall love your neighbor as yourself. On these two commandments depend the whole Law and the Prophets. (Matt 22:37–40)

Jesus was not offering an alternative summary of the moral law. He based his answer on two OT passages that summarize the Ten Commandments (Deut 6:5 and Lev 19:18). In Matt 19:18–19, Jesus taught the clear relationship of the second summary ("Love your neighbor as yourself") to the Ten Commandments. In answering the rich young ruler's question about which commandments he should keep, Jesus said, "You shall not commit murder; You shall not commit adultery; You shall not steal; You shall not bear false witness; Honor your father and mother; and You shall love your neighbor as yourself" (Matt 19:18–19; cf. Jas 2:8–11). Here we see that Jesus considered the second greatest commandment to be a summary of the last six commandments. Should we not reason that if the summary is morally binding, that which it summarizes is morally binding as well?

Some respond that the last six commandments still have moral standing because they are repeated in the NT. Jesus, however, in quoting the last six commandments, recognizes the Ten Commandments as a summary of God's moral law. And while none of the first four commandments is quoted in the NT, all four are alluded to and applied in the NT.[34]

Dr. Blomberg states his hermeneutical principle on page 326: "On the other hand, there is no commandment of Torah, even from the Ten Commandments, that Paul promotes *simply* because it appears in the Hebrew Scriptures. He filters each piece of legislation through its fulfillment in the law of love—the teaching and ministry of Jesus—to see how it applies in the Christian era." We noted above that Christ's law of love is the summary of the Ten Commandments. Moreover, Paul asserts the continuing role of the Ten Commandments. In 1 Cor 9:20–21, Paul clearly distinguishes between being under the law (obligated to keep old covenant ceremonies) and his obligation to keep God's moral law, which he calls the law of God (the Ten Commandments) and the law of Christ, demonstrating there is no difference between Christ's law and the Ten Commandments. The same principle is true in Jas 2:8–13, where James makes the royal law synonymous with the summary of the last six commandments.

The apostles did not change the moral principles of the Ten Commandments, but the positive laws attached to or derived from the moral principles. For example, the apostle Paul changes the promise attached to the commandment to honor one's father and mother. Initially God promised "that your days may be long in the land that the Lord your God is giving you." In the new covenant context, Paul writes that "it may be well with you, and that you may

---

34. Some claim that an OT commandment must be repeated in the NT in order to have a binding moral character on the Christian. They say the other nine commandments are repeated in the NT while it remains silent on the fourth. As we shall show, the NT is not silent about the Sabbath commandment. But even if it were, since the Decalogue is a summary of the moral law; its moral principles are binding, whether or not repeated, since each commandment is an unchangeable expression of God's moral will for mankind.

live long on the earth." The original promise related to the promised land. Paul applies it universally.

When Dr. Blomberg applies his hermeneutical principle to the Sabbath, he does not do justice to Christ's interpretation of the Sabbath commandment. He rightly points out that Christ frees the law from the accretions of Jewish tradition. But why does He do so? He frees the law from its man-made additions that it might be properly used as a blessing for His people. Christ is the divine lawgiver, who asserts His authority over the law as Lord of the Sabbath. The reference to Sabbath made for man takes us back to the creation ordinance, where God declared the Sabbath to be a means of blessing. If this is the case, then Blomberg's assertion, "a wholesale application of the first declaration [Sabbath made for man] fits poorly with any list, however short, of proscribed activities on whatever day is deemed to be today's equivalent of the Jewish Sabbath" (p. 334). What is strange about this assertion is that the Sabbath commandment's proscriptions are based on the creation ordinance. God evidently sees no tension between the Sabbath as a blessing and certain prohibitions. On this line of reasoning, one might as well say since God made marriage as a blessing for man, there ought to be no proscriptions attached to the adultery commandment. Moreover, with respect to the Sabbath, Jesus establishes the categories of work that do not break the Sabbath (necessity and mercy).

Dr. Blomberg also betrays an ignorance of Sabbatarianism when he says, "Ironically, most forms of Sabbatarianism throughout history have themselves actually fostered the kind of externalism Jesus eschews. Observant participants tend to focus on what they have successfully refrained from doing and at times obsess over determining precisely what those things should be, and miss the real purpose behind rest—physical and spiritual refreshment and renewal" (p. 338). In response I would point to the exposition of the Sabbath in the Westminster Confession of Faith; it focuses on the positive use of the day:

> This Sabbath is then kept holy unto the Lord, when men, after a due preparing of their hearts, and ordering of their common affairs beforehand, do not only observe an holy rest, all the day, from their own works, words, and thoughts about their worldly employments and recreations, but also are taken up, the whole

time, in the public and private exercises of his worship, and in the duties of necessity and mercy.[35]

In his interpretation of Col 2:16–17, Blomberg fails to distinguish between Sabbath observance and the Sabbath day. Paul clearly abrogates the seventh day but does not abrogate the principle of one day in seven being kept as a holy day to the Lord. The same would hold true for Paul's other references to days in Romans 14 and Galatians 4.

Dr. Blomberg also fails to note that when Paul says that certain laws were of no value against fleshly indulgence (Col 2:23), he is dealing with man-made laws and not biblical laws. This is evident by his use of the phrase "self-made religion." Paul is not saying that biblical law-keeping is of no value against fleshly indulgence.

The final passage I will deal with is his discussion of Heb 3:7–4:11. Here he fails to note the change of terminology in verse 9. The word translated "Sabbath rest" (*sabbatismos*) is a unique word used only this one time in the Bible. One of the few occurrences of the word outside the Bible is in Plutarch's *Moralia* in which, according to some versions, he uses *sabbatismos* to describe superstitious religious rest.[36] Hence, the word suggests religious observances. See my discussion on pages 156–58.

Why then does the writer select the unique word *sabbatismos* in verse 9? As I write in my main essay, he used *sabbatismos* to make a play on words. He emphasized that the spiritual, eternal rest promised by God has not been fulfilled; the promise of eternal rest remains, and they must enter it by persevering faith. That is, one enters this spiritual rest by faith in the Lord Jesus Christ, but it will be fully realized only when one enters the eternal rest of glory. Consequently, he emphasized the ongoing need to persevere.

But if this were all he wanted to say, he could have used the word *katapausis*. In fact, he used *katapausis* this way in verse 11: "Let us therefore be diligent to enter that rest (*katapausis*)." Neither does it make sense to say he chose *sabbatismos* for stylistic variety, as a synonym for *katapausis*. Such use does not make sense this late in the discourse. The uniqueness of the word suggests a deliberate, theological purpose. He selected or coined the term *sabbatismos* because, in addition to referring to spiritual rest, it suggested as

---

35. WCF 21.8. Cf. Westminster Larger Catechism 117.
36. BDAG, 909.

well an observance of that rest by a "Sabbath-keeping." Because the promised rest lies ahead for the new covenant people, they are to strive to enter the future rest. Yet as they do so, they anticipate it by continuing to keep the Sabbath.

Hence, the theology of redemption accomplished does not annul a continued Sabbath-keeping but requires it. And although we do not need a reinforcement or repetition of an OT moral command, yet since the Sabbath did have ceremonial and typical significance, God gives clear new covenant instruction. What better book to reiterate Sabbath observance than the book of Hebrews, which teaches most clearly how all OT ceremonial worship practices were fulfilled in Christ and therefore repealed. So, as the old covenant people of God had the promise of future rest portrayed in its day of rest, the new covenant people of God, the church, also has the promise of future rest portrayed in its day of religious rest.

As I point out, verse 10 then explains the change of day. Dr. Blomberg makes two exegetical mistakes on verse 10. First, he fails to notice the exegetical connections. Verse 10 is related to verse 9 by the preposition *for*. In other words, verse 10 relates to the ongoing responsibility of Sabbath-keeping. Verse 11 draws an inference then from the whole argument by starting out with "therefore." The Christian has the responsibility to persevere in entering God's rest, lest he fall away by disobedience.

The second error is in translating the verb in verse 10 as a plural: "for those who enter." The verb is singular ("the one who has entered") and not plural. Therefore it seems to me that because of these two exegetical errors his conclusion is not valid: "Entering God's rest here cannot refer to literal Sabbath observance because it is contrasted with perishing through disobedience" (p. 350). As I hope I have demonstrated, the "rest" of verse 11 does not refer to the Sabbath-keeping but to the eternal rest to which we are pressing on. The observance of the Christian Sabbath is a picture and means of persevering.

Therefore, I maintain that Dr. Blomberg's conclusion is not proven by Scripture when he writes, *"We obey the Sabbath commandment of the Decalogue as we spiritually rest in Christ, letting Him bear our heavy burdens, trusting Him for salvation and committing our lives to him in service, and then remaining faithful in lifelong loyalty to Him rather than committing apostasy.* No special day each week for rest and/or worship could ever come close to fulfilling this grander and far more enriching vision of life to the full" (p. 351).

In the cleavage between resting in Christ and observing a day of holy rest, he creates a false alternative. I wholeheartedly agree that the Sabbath commandment teaches us to rest in Christ alone for salvation. But that does not mean a one-day-in-seven observance of a Sabbath may not picture that rest for us. In Gen 2:1–3, one of the purposes of the Sabbath ordinance was to confirm the promise of eternal life to the people of God. The Heidelberg Catechism combines the practice of the day with the lifelong obligation to rest in Christ:

> In the first place, God wills that the ministry of the Gospel and schools be maintained, and that I, especially on the day of rest, diligently attend church to learn the Word of God, to use the holy sacraments, to call publicly upon the Lord, and to give Christian alms. In the second place, that all the days of my life I rest from my evil works, allow the Lord to work in me by his Spirit, and thus begin in this life the everlasting Sabbath.[37]

Furthermore, at the end of the day, Dr. Blomberg has so spiritualized the Sabbath commandment that he leaves no biblical warrant for weekly worship and basically is antinomian when it comes to the regulation of public worship or its requirement for the saints of God.

Response by Charles P. Arand

The papers by Drs. MacCarty and Pipa appeared to share a common understanding that Christians should observe one specific day out of seven, observe it entirely, and observe it correctly. They simply disagreed on whether that day must be Saturday or Sunday. It seems to me that my essay and Dr. Blomberg's share the view that we Christians are not obligated to set aside one specific day for rest and dedication to God's Word. However, we develop this with different nuances and emphases.

There was much in this paper that I agreed with and liked. I thought it was clear, cogent, and well argued. The way in which

---

37. Heidelberg Catechism 103.

Blomberg organized the NT data was quite helpful and demonstrated how conversant he is with NT scholarship in this area. Because I find few disagreements with Blomberg's essay, I will organize my comments first around themes that deserve to be highlighted and then around a few themes that merit further conversation and that may bring to light some different emphases, if not disagreements.

Agreements and Affirmations

Blomberg laid his hermeneutical cards on the table from the outset and outlined the larger theological framework within which he would discuss the issue of the Sabbath commandment, the Ten Commandments, and all of the Old Testament laws. The promise-fulfillment framework (as I'll call it) served the additional purpose of keeping the incarnation, death, and resurrection of Christ central to the discussion. I liked the way he spoke about filtering it all through the "grid of fulfillment in Christ."

I liked Blomberg's way of characterizing the Ten Commandments as "The Big Ten." I would add to his observation about the prominence of the Ten Commandments as a textual unit and the role that they play within the Scriptures by making a similar observation regarding how they rose to prominence within the Christian tradition. The Ten Commandments generally did not come to dominate Christian moral teaching and catechesis until the fourteenth and fifteenth centuries. Prior to that time, other summaries of proper godly living were used. Because of conflicts between the church and the synagogue, Christians often used the "two-ways" teaching from the book of Acts. During much of the Middle Ages, a collection of virtues and vices provided the basis for teaching godly living as they fit well with Paul's treatment of the fruits of the Spirit. Interestingly, virtues and vices tended to focus more on the character of the Christian than on specific commands and actions. With the outbreak of the plague and general social unrest, the Ten Commandments acquired a more prominent role, in part because the Sabbath commandment required obedience to the authorities. Certainly, by the time of the Reformation, the Decalogue had become the most widely used summary of Scripture's teaching on morality.[38]

---

38. See C. P. Arand, *That I May Be His Own: An Overview of Luther's Catechisms* (St. Louis: Concordia Academic Press, 2000).

I also found Blomberg's discussion of the relationship of the Decalogue to the whole of the 613 commands of the Torah to be helpful and essentially on target. He raised some good questions about them as well—for example, about the lack of any logical sequence among them, and so on. I also agree with him that the distinction between moral, civil, and ceremonial law is not always as clear-cut as it is made out to be. The categories are still useful at times, but I would agree that if the text itself does not identify them or distinguish between them, then that should give us some pause about relying too heavily on those distinctions.

With regard to the apostolic use of the Torah (pp. 323–31), I found myself wishing Blomberg had gone into a little more detail about the ways in which Paul uses the different kinds of laws found in the OT to make more precise his case. As Blomberg continued his discussion with Hebrews and James (pp. 329–31), I found it surprising that the longest quote from the OT in the New is the Jeremiah passage that speaks of a break from the old covenant to the new. It is also significant that the writer to the Hebrews emphasizes the faithfulness of God's people and the internalization of God's will, not ritualistic observance.

The fundamental point that Blomberg makes throughout these sections, however, is well taken. It is also the point Martin Luther saw very clearly: that first of all, the Sabbath is about hearing the Lord's voice and attending to His Word. In his comments on John 7:24 (p. 338), Blomberg reinforces the distinction between "externalism" and "motives." It makes the point that rules concerned with ensuring piety never work because, in contrast, piety centers on and is motivated by fearing, loving, and trusting the Lord above all else. I agreed with him that Colossians 2 is probably the most important passage in the NT for this topic (p. 341). His thorough discussion of the text makes pretty good sense to me. When he concludes his discussion of Colossians 2 shortly thereafter, he again makes a key point that ritual law may have the intention of fostering piety and Christian maturity, but it often fails inasmuch as it cannot touch the person's heart.

For Further Conversation

There are several topics in Blomberg's essay that I found intriguing and would merit further discussion. While Lutherans would probably agree with many of his conclusions, we might arrive at them through some additional ways. The three areas include: (1) the hermeneutics for understanding the relevance of the OT injunctions for the NT people; (2) the freedom we as Christians have to rest and/or worship on any day of the week; and (3) the nature of our Sabbath rest in Christ.

The first area worth pursuing concerns the appropriation of OT law by Christians. Several times Blomberg makes the point that being Christians does not mean "that we adhere to any OT law simply because it is in the Hebrew Scriptures" (p. 327). He says this about the Ten Commandments as well as the Torah and other instructions that we find in the OT. Instead, we must run everything through the "grid of fulfillment in Christ" to see if the application has changed in the era of the new covenant. This is where Blomberg's promise-fulfillment framework comes into play. At the same time he makes the point on several occasions that "every commandment in the OT does still apply in some way to Christians" (p. 348).

But I might also say that Christians don't adhere to all the instructions in the NT simply because they appear in the NT, as well. Now, there is a sense in which this is true in that we are followers of Jesus. But in another sense, I would also suggest that commands to love our neighbor are part of God's design for life with respect to all people, Christian or non-Christian. These commands are, in a certain sense, woven into the fabric of creation and into our creaturely life. The same applies to the appropriation of other OT laws or instructions by Christians. Why do we appropriate them? In part, we appropriate them because salvation must be understood in terms of the restoration and renewal of God's creation, including His design for human life in this age.

A creation/new-creation context allows us to find ways to speak about God's design for creation and human life within it. The commands and instructions in Scripture are not arbitrary, capricious, or heteronymous impositions from God. The rationale for them is not simply "because God says so" (although that would be sufficient). There is a theological rationale behind them that is rooted in creation. It is like a parent telling a young child "it's time for bed." The child may pout and stomp his feet demanding, "Why do I have to go to bed now?" The parent could simply respond, "Because I said so." But there is a reason behind the parent's command that goes to the needs and nature of the child. If the child does not get ten hours of sleep, he'll be cranky and irritable the next day. Similarly, *that* we rest (or the need for rest) is written into our very bodies. Similarly, *that* we devote time to God (or our idols) is a given, since no one can live without something or someone from whom they seek their good.

A creation/renewal-of-creation context allows us to embrace our humanity as coworkers of God. It enables us to receive wisdom and imagination as good gifts from God. God has made known His design for human life, and He lets us figure out how we can apply it to the specific needs and personalities of our neighbors. For example, I have the responsibility as a parent to discipline my children. But how do I do it? Time-out? Removing privileges? Grounding? Is there one God-given way? No. Try different things. See what works. Each child is different. The same principle applies when expressing our love for a spouse. Each of us will do so in a slightly different manner, but in a way that best communicates our love and is received as such by our beloved. This also applies to figuring out when we can best take time out for rest and how best to carry out God's will that we come together for worship.

In thinking through how we can best carry out God's will in our lives, the creation/new-creation context allows us to use the OT as it pertains to creation. Blomberg's understanding of "The Big Ten" suggests that we not limit ourselves to them. But, for example, were that to happen, it might be difficult to articulate any reason as to why Christians ought to care for God's living earth. After all, the Ten Commandments focus on our relationship to God and to neighbor. To be sure, creation undergirds the Commandments, as we cannot deal with God or neighbor except through the things of creation. But they do not speak directly to our responsibility for taking care of the earth along with all the creatures that dwell within it. The gospel allows us to consider the instructions that were given to Israel concerning its treatment of land and animals.[39] Finally, the creation/new-creation framework allows us to see how the first Great Commission (Gen 1:28; 2:15) connects with the second Great Commission (Matt 28:28–30).

---

39. See E. F. Davis, *Scripture, Culture, and Agriculture: An Agrarian Reading of the Bible* (Cambridge: Cambridge University Press, 2009).

The second area that deserves further discussion has to do with the freedom of the Christian with respect to observing the particularities of the old covenant law and how we might appropriate the instructions found in the OT for our lives today. In this regard, I was a bit surprised by how sharply Blomberg separates the Sabbath from worship. Can we take time to rest on any day of the week as Blomberg suggests? Can we choose to worship as a community on any day or time of the week? In principle, I agree with him, at least with regard to any Scripture texts that explicitly link the two in terms of a command. But it raises the interesting point as to how Christians best exercise their freedom in the gospel. The sixteenth-century Reformers gave this considerable thought and sought to have their freedom informed by a theology moderated by love.

Luther and the subsequent Lutheran confessional writings in the sixteenth century did not insist that Sunday must be the day on which one gathers for worship or that Sunday is the new Sabbath. (Only in the nineteenth century did an American Lutheran, Samuel Simon Schmucker, propose a revision of the Augsburg Confession in which the rejection of Sabbatarianism would be rescinded. But his proposal gained no traction.) The Lutheran reformation insists that there is freedom in matters that lack a specific command of God (e.g., on which day to worship). But Luther and his colleagues argued that the exercise of that freedom should be informed by an understanding of the purpose of practices that were neither commanded nor forbidden in Scripture (i.e., adiaphora). One of the clearest places where the Lutheran reformers laid out their thinking on these matters was in Article XV of the Apology of the Augsburg Confession on "Human Traditions."

In the first half of Article XV, Luther's colleague Philip Melanchthon takes up the topic of "human traditions" as a response to his opponents who insisted that one must observe such human traditions in order to be a member within the church and thus to be justified. Melanchthon explicitly rejects such views as belonging to the kingdom of the antichrist, for they seek to set up practices by which we seek justification, and they do so without any command or word from God. In fact, in this section, one of the passages he cites several times is the critical text of Colossians 2. He argues that when people see certain practices as having an "appearance of wisdom," they often conclude wrongly that those practices must therefore justify us in the eyes of God.

In the second half of the article, Melanchthon makes the point that while we are free to use or not use certain practices, some practices may be deemed better than others. And so he contends that Lutherans observe time-honored practices depending on the purpose they serve. The practices and traditions of the church should above all else teach the gospel. Here Melanchthon shows how Lutherans sing hymns, chant psalms, use drama, preach, and so on, all in order to teach the gospel. Second, practices should express the catholicity or unity of the church. Thus Melanchthon makes the point that Lutherans continue to use many traditional practices (vestments, liturgy, etc). Third, our practices should be contextualized for the sake of the church's mission. Here the Lutherans insisted on services in the vernacular, and Luther provided a cultural translation for his catechism.[40] Finally, the church should seek to do things together. At the end of the article, Melanchthon notes that the Lutherans are willing to observe many adiaphoristic practices with their opponents, even if it is somewhat burdensome for them to do so. These principles would likewise serve as guides when making a decision about identifying a day and a time for worship.

In light of these principles, the Lutheran reformers found no compelling reason to insist that worship should be on any other day than Sunday. This was probably due to the reality that Sunday, as the day of worship, was so deeply ingrained into the culture. The Lutheran reformation did not seek to "throw the baby out with the bathwater," by rejecting everything it had inherited. It sought to be both catholic and evangelical. The Lutheran reformers were generally conservative in their approach to such practices, keeping that which had proven its value and rejecting those practices that undermined or contradicted the gospel.

Blomberg may be right that the command to rest is rarely accompanied by a command to participate in corporate worship. And yet he notes that the original purpose of the Sabbath was "to enable God's people to rest from their labors, and do so in a way that focused their attention on Him by hallowing that day of rest" (p. 349). The day of rest and the day of worship are often brought together

---

40. See J. Nestingen, "Luther's Cultural Translation of the Catechism," *LQ* 15 (2001): 440–52.

not by a divine command but by means of an underlying theological rationale.

The theological rationale in the OT for the day of rest was rooted in either creation (Exodus 20) or the rescue of the Israelites from Egypt (Deuteronomy 5). I suppose it would be natural to identify those days for corporate worship and celebration (even as we observe the Independence of the United States on July 4). Blomberg's treatment of the OT was necessarily brief, as his goal was to focus on the NT data. But I wonder if his contention that the Sabbath command to rest was not connected to corporate worship on that day was a bit overstated. When were sacrifices offered at the temple? When did the community sing psalms? I suspect on the Sabbath. Certainly at festival times. This does not mean that Sabbath command entailed such things. But it was natural for people to rest and give an expression of their dependence on God for His gifts of creation and redemption.

In the NT the celebration of Christ's resurrection on Sunday provided the theological basis for gathering to worship. But the NT appears not to make it a major issue. The language that Blomberg uses when he speaks of a "second probable reference" in 1 Cor 16 (p. 308), with regard to the NT practice of Sunday worship, does raise the critical question: Why does the NT give so little attention to this vital element in Christian practice? Blomberg speaks about this again on page 339, when he observes how practices changed slowly and gradually among the followers of Jesus with regard to Christian worship.

The third area worth pursuing further pertains to Blomberg's statement, *"We obey the Sabbath commandment of the Decalogue as we spiritually rest in Christ, letting Him bear our burdens, trusting for salvation and committing our lives to Him in service, and then remaining faithful in lifelong loyalty to Him rather than committing apostasy"* (p. 351; emphasis original). But how does one rest in Christ by faith? And how do people "focus their attention on Him by hallowing that day of rest" (p. 349).

Here the nature of the Word stands front and center for Luther. When it comes to worship, what stands out as most important had to do with the place and promotion of the Word in our lives and practices. Why? Luther understood the Word of God to be an active, performative, creative, and re-creative Word. For Luther, the Word of the gospel was never merely a descriptive word. Instead, the Word did what it said. It created that of which it spoke. God said, "Sun," and the sun came into existence. God exclaims, "You are forgiven!" and it happens. God declares, "You are righteous," and we are righteous despite how many times we look at the instant replays of our lives and see the contrary. And when it came to the Sabbath, or the day of rest, Luther maintained God's Word of blessing made the day holy, however we might use the day. So, for Luther, the Word occupied a far more important place in his thinking of worship than did a specific day or any particular human observance of the day.

Now, Luther's practice, and the practices of Lutherans in the sixteenth century—as well as subsequent centuries—was to remain with Sunday as the day of rest and worship. By his day it had become too deeply ingrained in the culture to consider changing it. And there was really no good reason to do so. Therefore, it would probably be true to say that the Lutheran reformers did not really give any sustained or serious thought to worshipping corporately on any other day than Sunday. On that day the congregation celebrated the main service of the week, where one had the Word in all three forms: baptism, absolution/preaching, and the Lord's Supper.

As the mainspring of the Sunday observance, the Word then reverberated throughout the week. Here, it is worth noting that the practice of the church in Wittenberg was such that it continued the tradition of holding services throughout the week (at least on Wednesdays and Saturdays), services that were primarily preaching services. In addition, Luther established the practice of holding catechetical preaching services on Monday through Thursday (out of which grew his Large Catechism), four times a year over a two-week period. Some of Luther's special sermon series on books such as Matthew and John also came from preaching on other days of the week. One must keep in mind also that upwards of 90 percent of the people were illiterate, and so their primary access to the Word came from such preaching. But Luther envisioned that the Word would be taught in homes as well (ergo, his Small Catechism). In any event, it is the Word of God that blesses and sanctifies every day of the week.

The importance of the Word of God for Luther further comes to the fore in his understanding of the Christian life. The fulfillment of the Sabbath points toward Luther's eschatological perception that the entire Christian life is involved in a life-and-death struggle between God and Satan, between the truthful Word and lies of all kinds. In fact, for Luther, the struggles that one encounters in life do not occur in coming to faith; they commence with the awakening of faith. From the moment faith is ignited in a person who then prays "Our Father," that person has turned his or her back on Satan—a virtual declaration of war. And so Luther's interpretation of the Lord's Prayer in the Large Catechism is framed within the context of this struggle, and it could be appropriately titled, "The Battle Cry of Faith." The entire Christian life takes on the character of clinging to the Word of God against all of Satan's attempts to deprive us of that Word. In this context, Sabbath rest becomes an eschatological hope to be fulfilled when Christ finally "delivers us from the evil one."

In sum, Blomberg has provided the church a good service by laying out the NT data on the Sabbath in a clear and logical manner. He has also done so within a framework that centers on the decisive entry of Jesus Christ into the world. And finally, I appreciated his gracious attitude toward those with whom he disagreed.

Final Remarks
Craig L. Blomberg

I am grateful that this book breaks fresh ground among "multiple views" volumes on topics of theological debate by allowing each author a final opportunity to respond to the replies of the other contributors and thus to answer their questions, respond to their charges, and offer a final synthesis of one's own position. I will do as much of all of that as I can in the comparatively short space allotted to each of us for those tasks. I will proceed sequentially through each of the three responses to my chapter and then make some final, concluding remarks.

Response to MacCarty

Skip MacCarty thinks I argued that the Sabbath was not connected to worship until about the fourth century AD, whereas I acknowledged that by the time of the origins of the synagogue it clearly was so connected. This may have begun as far back as the

Babylonian exile. My only point was how little the *OT itself* actually tells us about what, if any, worship occurred on the Sabbath. Leviticus 23:3 may well refer to an assembly for worship, but it is at least interesting that the text never actually says that. And if worship took place, we have no hints here as to what specifically it involved.[41] My point in referring to Saturday rest as "Jewish Sabbath" was merely to make the contrast clear as to when I was not referring to Sunday rest—what especially the Reformed tradition has come to call the "Christian Sabbath." The vast majority of Acts commentators takes the women in Philippi to be Jewish for two reasons. First, it was Paul's regular pattern to look for a Jewish synagogue in which to begin his ministry in each new city he evangelized. Second, it was a Jewish (not Greek or Roman) tradition to have an outside place of prayer by a flowing stream in lieu of a synagogue when there was no quorum of Jewish males to constitute one (see p. 341).

Hermeneutically, MacCarty appears to support an approach that filters the NT through an OT grid (thus reversing my approach), based on his understanding of what was going on in Acts 17:11. Of course, such an approach would do away with the notion of preserving the moral law while jettisoning the civil and ceremonial laws, which he wants to preserve, because for the OT Jew all three categories were immutable. Israelite civil and ceremonial laws would then have to be reinstated for Christians. There *are* some parallels between my "fulfillment-in-Christ" hermeneutic and dispensationalism, it is true, because even the most thoroughgoing covenant theologian allows for at least three dispensations—the OT era, the NT era, and the eternal state (classic dispensationalism argues for seven). But overall my view occupies a fairly middle ground between the dispensationalist and covenantal ends of the theological spectrum.

MacCarty finds no law-gospel contrast in John 1:17. But it is the *anti* (lit., "instead of") in verse 16 that creates it, not some elliptically inserted adversative conjunction.[42] As the TNIV best captures it, "Grace in place of grace already given." Or, as D. A. Carson

---

41. See D. W. Baker, "Leviticus," in *Cornerstone Biblical Commentary*, ed. P. W. Comfort, vol. 2 (Carol Stream, IL: Tyndale, 2008), 167: "The exact nature of these Sabbath gatherings is unclear, since they are not mentioned elsewhere."

42. The asyndeton—the lack of *any* Greek conjunction—in the middle of verse 17, however, means a "but" is as appropriate as an "and" in translation, and overall context must determine which fits best.

summarizes his discussion of this issue: "The flow of the passage and the burden of the book as a whole magnify the fresh 'grace' that has come in Jesus Christ. That grace is necessarily greater than the 'grace' of the law whose function, in John's view, was primarily to anticipate the coming of the Word."[43] With respect to 2 Cor 3–4, MacCarty fears that my approach means no one could ever have been saved in OT times. No, my point is not that there weren't ways of using the Mosaic covenant rightly *while it was in force* but that with the coming of Jesus the Messiah, it was *now* a cul-de-sac. The sacrifices that had once allowed Israelites to be in right standing with God were fulfilled in Christ, so that only through belief in Him could people now be forgiven. To understand Paul aright, we must see much more than just the termination of a wrong way of following the Mosaic covenant. It is the end of the period of time in which God's people are bound to observe any of the precepts of that covenant *until they understand how they have been fulfilled in Christ* and their resulting significance for Christ's followers.[44] Romans 10:4 does indeed speak of the "goal" (*telos*) of the law, but when the goal of the law has been accomplished, it also comes to an "end" (see p. 329). When MacCarty limits the obsolescence of the old covenant in Hebrews 8 to the sacrifices, priesthood, and temple ministry, it is *he* who is introducing terms, distinctions, and limitations into the text that are simply not there.

MacCarty is correct that not all Jews experienced the law negatively, and Paul in Rom 7:1–6 is not maintaining that they did, though some did. But neither is he immediately *generalizing to whatever orientation to works-righteousness binds any person anywhere prior to their conversion,* valid as that may be *as a later application.* The analogy of marriage would be singularly inappropriate for making MacCarty's point. Some marriages are wonderful and couples want them never to end; others can't wait to get out of them. But either way, marriage laws normally bind people together for life. When a spouse dies, however, no matter how good or bad the marriage, the surviving spouse is free to remarry should that person choose to do so. So also, no matter how good or bad one's

43. D. A. Carson, *The Gospel According to John* (Leicester: Apollos; Grand Rapids: Eerdmans, 1991), 133.

44. For detailed unpacking, see W. W. Klein, C. L. Blomberg, and R. L. Hubbard Jr., *Introduction to Biblical Interpretation*, rev. ed. (Nashville: Nelson, 2004), 341–51, and the literature there cited.

experience was as a Jew under the Law, now that the age of the Law has passed (the Law has died, so to speak), people are freed from its requirements, free to choose allegiance to Christ. *Contra* MacCarty, the passage is oriented very much more dispensationally than experientially.[45] The same clarifications are required for James 2:8–13.

Turning to the relationship between the Ten Commandments and the double-love commandment, MacCarty notes that both occur only rarely in the OT "prior to Jesus' teaching" (p. 365), Fair enough. But my main point is that the double love commands prove *central* to Jesus' teaching and several other NT corpora, whereas the NT *never* refers to the Ten Commandments *as a package*. Individual commandments appear, as do small groups of them, and MacCarty helpfully lists these in several places, but not one of these texts enables us to affirm with any confidence that NT writers saw all ten in force or that they elevated them to a level above all other Mosaic commands. MacCarty's statement that the frequent OT references to "the covenant" have primarily the Ten Commandments in mind is sheer affirmation, without substantiation. When exegesis does allow us to determine what this covenant means, in contexts that refer to OT laws, it is almost always to the entire Mosaic legislation and arrangement with Israel, not just to one small part of it.[46]

MacCarty finds it unimaginable that Jesus or the first Christians, especially Jewish ones, could have ever reinterpreted any of the Ten Commandments in nonliteral fashion, but that is precisely what they did with circumcision, as in the very text MacCarty quotes—from 1 Cor 7:19. Little wonder that many Jews rejected the gospel message. A typical Jewish reaction to Paul's claim that what matters is neither circumcision nor uncircumcision but keeping God's commands would have been to protest, "But circumcision *is* God's command. It is the central, defining, and mandatory initiation rite for males into God's covenant with humanity. Paul, you are talking nonsense."[47] What, then did Paul mean by keeping God's

---

45. See F. F. Bruce, *The Epistle to the Galatians* (Exeter: Paternoster; Grand Rapids: Eerdmans, 1982), 160–61, commenting on the similarly oriented Gal 3:10–14.

46. For the full range of uses, see D. Patrick, "Covenant, OT and NT," in *The New Interpreter's Dictionary of the Bible*, ed. K. D. Sakenfeld (Nashville: Abingdon, 2006), 1:767–78.

47. See G. D. Fee, *The First Epistle to the Corinthians*, NICNT (Grand Rapids: Eerdmans, 1987), 313: "Paul's fellow Jew would have been . . . quite mystified by this [statement]. From his perspective these sentences would be totally non sequitur, indeed contradictory. To be circumcised *is* to keep the commandment of God. But Paul obviously

commandments? Not the Ten, as if they were somehow even more basic than circumcision. Here we do not have to guess. Galatians 5:6 answers the question for us when Paul again insists that circumcision and uncircumcision are matters of indifference, but adds that "the only thing that counts is faith expressing itself through love."[48]

To understand Matt 5:17, we must turn not only to the two antitheses MacCarty does (vv. 21–28) but to verses 18–19 and to the other four antitheses (see pp. 323–24). As for Heb 4:9, immediate context always trumps linguistic usage in other contexts by other writers at other times, especially later Christian ones who had not yet written. And *sabbatismos* is a "hapax," appearing nowhere else in the Greek Bible, so I am hardly "leaping over the clear meaning established everywhere else for this word" (p. 368)! The meaning of cognates may or may not be significant. Inasmuch as Sabbath (*sabbaton*) is the word used in all 198 other occurrences of the word group (including 177 in the OT and NT combined and 21 in the Apocrypha), then it is likely that the lone exception to the pattern appears because it means something at least a little different.[49] "God's resting on the seventh day of creation" (p. 179) or, more accurately, His resting after His six days of creation in 4:4 does begin the string of Sabbath references in Hebrews 4 and confirms that the author is speaking of rest in all of them. But God scarcely rested in the sense of cessation from work, since He providentially continued to uphold and preserve His creation and His Spirit worked in people's lives (and still does) in the same ways seven days a week.

In dealing with Rom 14:4–5 and Gal 4:10–11, MacCarty begins by assuming what in fact he has to demonstrate. Believing that no biblical author could ever have put one of the Ten Commandments into a category in which some believers were free to practice literal observance and others a more metaphorical (or what MacCarty calls "spiritualized") observance, he therefore concludes that these Pauline passages are talking only about ceremonial sabbaths or ceremo-

thinks otherwise. . . . Almost certainly, ['the command of God'] refers to the ethical imperatives of the Christian faith."

48. E. D. Burton, *A Critical and Exegetical Commentary on the Epistle to the Galatians* (Edinburgh: T & T Clark, 1921), 279, declares of this verse that "for the disclosure of the apostle's fundamental idea of the nature of religion, there is no more important sentence in the whole epistle, if, indeed, in any of Paul's epistles."

49. BDAG recognizes this, rendering *sabbatōn* as "the seventh day of the week in Israel's calendar, marked by rest fr. work and by special religious ceremonies," whereas for *sabbatismos* in Heb 4:9, it says, "a special period of rest for God's people modeled after the traditional Sabbath" (909).

nial aspects of the abiding moral Sabbath. But that is just circular reasoning. As for Col 2:16, he relies heavily on du Preez's distinctions between *shabbat*, in conjunction with one cluster of words, and *shabbat*, in conjunction with a different cluster. Du Preez believes that when this Hebrew word for Sabbath appeared with the words *afflict, weeks, of the land, her/its/she*, and *your*, it always referred to "ceremonial sabbaths, never the weekly Sabbath" (p. 370). With the words *keep, day, holy*, and *my*, OT writers referred to the weekly Sabbath. Whether this proves true in every instance, it is irrelevant for interpreting Col 2:16, since *none* of these key words appears with *sabbaton* here! And if partial OT parallels to Paul's triad of festival, new moon, and Sabbath be ruled off limits for comparison, then so must Hos 2:11, because it refers to "her Sabbaths," whereas Paul introduces no possessive pronoun. But it is highly unlikely that the Sabbaths in Hos 2:11 *are* limited to ceremonial ones, because the prophet sandwiches his triad of "her yearly festivals, her New Moons, her Sabbath days" inside references to stopping "all her celebrations" and "all her appointed festivals." One can scarcely exclude the weekly Sabbath from these expressions.[50]

I will conclude my response to MacCarty for now by answering *ad seriatim* his list of closing questions for me. The reason the seventh-day Sabbath was exclusively Jewish but Jeremiah's new covenant was not is because of the differing ways the NT understands each. What might uniquely threaten grace if the seventh-day Sabbath were preserved, which is not present in the rest of the Decalogue, are certain features of ritual in Israelite worship not present in the other commandments. MacCarty asks if the commandment was designed to promote or to threaten grace. It was designed to promote it, but in reality it often (not always) threatened it, and therefore Paul, especially in Gal 3:19–4:7, explains that the entire Mosaic law was a provisional arrangement until the greater grace of the gospel (as in John 1:16–17) would come.[51] If the Ten Commandments are not automatically timeless until we understand how they are fulfilled in Christ, does this place any of the other nine in the same category as the Sabbath? No, because the New Testament treats each of them differently.

---

50. See D. A. Hubbard, *Hosea* (Leicester, UK, and Downers Grove, IL: InterVarsity, 1989), 78.

51. On which, see esp. R. N. Longenecker, *Galatians* (Dallas: Word, 1990), 135–78.

What is the first covenant that Heb 8:13 declares obsolete? That which is obsolete is the practice of any or all of OT legislation apart from understanding how its fulfillment in Christ has or has not changed its application for believers. The new covenant is the covenant inaugurated by Jesus through His death, resurrection, exaltation, and sending of the Spirit at Pentecost, which takes up the OT and teaches Jesus' followers how it applies in this new age. The new covenant also includes all of the promises, commands, instructions, and arrangements inaugurated by Jesus and the apostles, as recorded in the NT.[52]

I did not intend to suggest that complexity of application had anything to do with whether a commandment was timeless. On re-reading my relevant sections, I don't see how MacCarty thinks I said that, but if it sounded that way, then I need to clarify. Those in the hall of faith in Hebrews 11, like many other ancient Israelites, were no doubt saved. What is inappropriate is trying to follow the Mosaic law once its time has expired, not while it was still in force. First Corinthians 9:19–23 makes Paul's understanding of various stumbling blocks to the gospel clear. If the crucifixion causes people to "stumble" and reject the gospel, that can't be helped (1 Cor 1:18–25). But wherever Paul can avoid unnecessary stumbling blocks, he does so. Keeping a seventh-day Sabbath for the sake of winning Jews to Christ is perfectly appropriate; so is resting and worshipping in countless other ways instead for the sake of winning Gentiles.[53]

MacCarty concludes, not by directly addressing my comments on my wife's and my physical limitations, but by challenging me to try keeping the seventh-day Sabbath for one month to see if I am not at least as productive in six (partial) days of work as I now am in seven such (partial) days. It would be interesting to know exactly what he thought would qualify as keeping Sabbath. Given my profession, presumably each Saturday I could not preach, teach, research, write, or study the Bible academically, though perhaps devotionally (yet in my own practice the two are fairly inextricably intertwined). I'm not sure if I would be prohibited from yard work or housework or television or recreation or sports or attendance at

52. See esp. B. C. Joslin, *Hebrews, Christ, and the Law: The Theology of the Mosaic Law in Hebrews 7:1–10:18* (Milton Keynes, UK, and Colorado Springs: Paternoster, 2008). On Hebrews 8 in particular, see pp. 173–223.

53. See M. Prior, *The Message of 1 Corinthians* (Leicester, UK, and Downers Grove, IL: InterVarsity, 1985). 162.

sporting events; we'd have to have that kind of conversation. Presumably, I'd want to worship in a local church, but would it have to be with a congregation of Seventh-day Adventists or Seventh Day Baptists? Or would attendance at one of a number of local congregations that outgrew two or three Sunday morning services and so began one on Saturday night be sufficient? Or if the arrangements of the OT Sabbath are still in place, then I imagine Saturday night shouldn't count, since the Sabbath ran from Friday sundown to Saturday sundown. May I then worship with one of our local Messianic congregations on Friday night or Saturday morning?

At any rate, during our three years in Scotland from 1979 to 1982 for graduate study, we did worship in a church that was fairly Sabbatarian, at least about *Sunday* behavior, and, for the sake of fitting in and not causing unnecessary offense, we often did "keep Sabbath," and for much longer than a month of Sundays. So I already know what happens to my productivity—it goes down! I'm scarcely saying productivity is that important, but it was MacCarty who phrased his challenge that way, so I'm replying in keeping with his wording. I suppose MacCarty could argue that, if I just transferred all those identical do's and don'ts to Saturdays instead, then God would miraculously increase my productivity the rest of the week in ways he didn't when I kept Sabbath on Sunday, but I confess that I seriously doubt that would happen.

Rejoinder to Pipa

Joseph Pipa's reply relies much more on historical theology than on biblical exegesis, so I can be a little briefer, both because I am not primarily a historical theologian and because I do not exalt the creeds and confessions of the church to quite the same level he does. If I do not see a doctrine taught by Scripture, I use Scripture to judge any creed that might teach otherwise, rather than vice versa.

Pipa takes me to task for not beginning my study with Genesis 1. Because I understood my mandate to deal with the practice of Sabbath-keeping *per se*, and not an entire biblical theology of rest, that choice was deliberate. As I mentioned above in reply to MacCarty, it is hard to get much more out of God's resting after His six days of creation than the foundation and precedent for *some kind of weekly rest for humanity*, since the nature of God's cessation of work is so different from all forms of human rest. And once worship becomes integrally tied up with this rest, appealing to what God did on the original seventh day offers no help at all, since presumably He wasn't worshipping Himself at that time! Psalm 74 does indeed lament the destruction of meeting places for worship. I certainly wouldn't want to be misinterpreted as saying I don't think the Israelites worshipped God before the era of the synagogue. But since there is nothing about the timing or composition of any of this worship in this psalm, I don't see how it is relevant to our discussion. That much of it probably took place on the Sabbath (thus the superscription to Psalm 92) is a very natural assumption. But if this is the most Pipa can add to our earlier treatment of the Old Testament, it merely reinforces my point about how little we know of Israelite worship and Sabbath practices for much of the period of the Mosaic covenant.[54]

As Pipa turns to the NT and beyond, he confuses absence of evidence with evidence of absence. It is simply not demonstrable, and it is historically highly implausible, that "all Christians transferred their day of worship from Saturday to Sunday" (p. 375). Three NT references to Christians doing something involved with worship on the first day of the week, one of which speaks only of an offering (1 Cor 16:1–4) and one of which involves only a solitary believer (Rev 1:10), hardly support so sweeping a claim. All of the other crucial issues of Jewish practice were debated with only gradual consensus coming about, sometimes not even until after NT times—topics like circumcision, dietary laws, temple sacrifices, the role of the Holy Land, tithes and offerings, baptism, church order, participation in the government, just war, sexual ethics, and on and on. Can we then seriously imagine *all Christians early on at the same time* migrating from Saturday to Sunday rest and worship? It is unlikely that they made *any* changes from old covenant practices on any widespread scale all at the same time on any issue.[55]

What we *do* know about early Christian worship in primarily pagan parts of the Roman Empire is that workers employed by others were required to work every day of the week but got to rest on

---

54. Indeed, we know far more about the *theology* of worship in the OT than about its *practice*, at least apart from the sacrificial cultus. See esp. Y. Hattori, "Theology of Worship in the Old Testament," in *Worship: Adoration and Action*, ed. D. A. Carson (Carlisle: Paternoster; Grand Rapids: Baker, 1993), 21–50.

55. See esp. J. D. G. Dunn, *The Parting of the Ways: Between Christianity and Judaism and Their Significance for the Character of Christianity* (London: SCM, rev. 2006).

the various holidays that occurred on fixed days every month in the Roman calendar. But these days of rest did not occur with uniform intervals of time between each of them.[56] That the believers in Troas were gathered at night time on the first day of the week (Acts 20:7–11) fits this model. They would have been worshipping either on Saturday or Sunday evening after already putting in a full day's work and having to work again the next day, except when either of those days was a pagan holiday (recall above).

Nevertheless, my main point with regard to the three NT texts that suggest Sunday worship is much more basic: none of them is *prescriptive*. All merely *describe* what took place. Given the ways in which narrative material often highlights exemplary behavior,[57] Luke may well have included these texts at least in part to commend Sunday worship. But they still lack any actual commands to do so. And the rest of the NT, overflowing as it is with imperatives, never once gives any command about the Sabbath except to *proscribe* the Jewish leaders' abuse of it and to *prescribe tolerance of diversity* of practice among Christians.

My point in quoting various patristic authors was not to deny the general transition in post-NT Christian circles from celebrating the Sabbath on Saturday to Sunday. Rather, my intent was merely to point out those instances in which different writers recognized that a fully literal form of Sabbath-keeping (i.e., on Saturday), such as MacCarty and Seventh-day Adventists require, was no longer mandatory, and that therefore to insist on it left one, like the Judaizer, self-condemned. Neither do I dispute that rest and worship were regularly linked together on the same day, as this transition from Saturday to Sunday gathered momentum; I merely point out that there are no biblical mandates that they *must* always be so linked.

By the time we get to John Calvin, I acknowledge that he sends mixed signals (p. 313, n. 9). I also document the sources that note it was not until the rise of Puritanism that a thoroughgoing theology of cessation of all play on top of the existing cessation of work predominated (pp. 314–15). Nothing in the quotation from Calvin that Pipa cites (p. 176, n. 4) calls this into question. When Pipa jumps to the last half century and declares that "surely the teaching of men like Dr. Blomberg has contributed to the demise of the practice of the

---

56. See esp. H. H. Scullard, *Festivals and Ceremonies of the Roman Republic* (Ithaca, NY: Cornell University Press, 1981).

57. See esp. W. L. Liefeld, *Interpreting the Book of Acts* (Grand Rapids: Baker, 1995).

Christian Sabbath in almost every Protestant denomination" (ibid.), I'm not sure whether to be flattered that he thinks my view has been so influential or offended that he views it as so destructive. Given how little known the fulfillment-in-Christ position is, and given the countless sermons lamenting the demise of Sabbath-keeping from Sabbatarian perspectives, it is far more likely that the combination of secularizing forces and the lack of a truly convincing case for Sabbatarianism are the two main forces contributing to its demise.[58] As for calling certain laws "*amoral*" as Pipa charges (p. 382), I don't. My two uses of that word are in contexts that *deny* the possibility of such a category (pp. 321, 327)!

Pipa next accuses me of failing "to understand that the NT treats the Ten Commandments as a summary of God's moral law" (p. 382). This time I am guilty as charged. The NT never once refers to the Ten Commandments *as a unit* by any terminology; no more than five of its commandments are ever listed in any one context; and Sabbath-keeping is never linked once with any of the other nine commandments in any NT context. For these reasons, I do indeed fail to understand how anyone can insist that Jesus or the apostolic writers viewed these ten mandates as a summary of God's moral law. Pipa's way around these observations is to argue that what the NT *does* use as a summary of the law—the double love commands—already in the OT were understood as summaries of the Decalogue. But nothing in the contexts of Deut 6:5 or Lev 19:18 suggests this, nor does any other OT passage.[59] Here Pipa has resorted to mere assertion rather than to actual argumentation.

In fact, the NT passage that contains the largest grouping of instructions from the Decalogue (Matt 19:18–19) lists the command to "love your neighbor as yourself" as the sixth and last of the sample commandments that the rich young ruler should be keeping. Pipa concludes that "here we see that Jesus considered the

---

58. W. M. Swartley, in *Slavery, Sabbath, War and Women* (Scottdale, PA, and Kitchener, ON: Herald, 1983), demonstrates striking parallels among the arguments for Sabbatarianism (whether of the seventh- or first-day variety) to those for slavery, warfare, and women's subordination, all of which have diminished in persuasive force over time, though to noticeably varying degrees, due both to hermeneutical and to secularizing factors.

59. Deuteronomy 6:5 comes *after* the restatement of the Decalogue in 5:6–21 but is not directly linked to it. Indeed, if the reference in 6:6 to "these commands" goes back to the Decalogue, then the command to love God in verse 5 is separated from them. Leviticus 19:18 is tucked into a chapter that contains what appear to be moral, civil, and ceremonial laws somewhat indiscriminately juxtaposed.

second greatest commandment to be a summary of the last six commandments" (p. 383). No, that's not at all what we see.[60] What we see is that the command to love your neighbor is simply the last on a list of six. If Jesus intended the last commandment as a summary of the previous five, He never said anything to indicate that, and the rhetorical form of a virtue list that He employed suggests otherwise. NT virtue lists nowhere else conclude with a commandment that summarizes all the others, though they sometimes conclude with the climactic or most important command. Otherwise, if there is any structure at all, it is indicated by small groupings rather than overarching patterns.[61] As for the other five of the Ten Commandments not mentioned here—the first four and the tenth in their original sequence—Pipa is correct that they all are "alluded to and applied in the NT" (p. 383). But all the contributors to this volume agree on that much. The question is *how* they are applied, and specifically how the Sabbath command is applied.

In 1 Cor 9:20, when Paul explains in the context of becoming like Jews to win Jews (those "under the law") that he is nevertheless not under the law (*nomos*), he would have to be referring to the entire Hebrew Scriptures because that is the *Torah* under which faithful Jews placed themselves. When Paul therefore qualifies his becoming like those not having the law in verse 21 with the caveat that he is not free from "God's law" but under "Christ's law," he cannot be referring to the OT or any part of it, *by itself*. Had Paul spoken *only* of "Christ's law," we might have imagined him thinking only of Jesus' teaching. However, by also referring to "God's law," he shows that he probably has in mind *Jesus' teaching as the fulfillment of the OT along with the rest of new covenant instruction* as the filter through which to pour OT law in order to determine its applicability in the new age Christ instituted.[62]

Pipa further worries that my "spiritualization" of the Sabbath command leaves the door open for rejecting literal portions of other commandments like the prohibition against adultery. But, as I have

---

60. By the way, Jesus lists only five of the Ten Commandments, not six, as Pipa alleges (ibid.).

61. J. D. Charles, "Vice and Virtue Lists," in *Dictionary of New Testament Background*, ed. C. A. Evans and S. E. Porter (Downers Grove, IL, and Leicester, UK: InterVarsity, 2000), 1252–57.

62. See A. C. Thiselton, *The First Epistle to the Corinthians: A Commentary on the Greek Text*, NIGTC (Carlisle: Paternoster; Grand Rapids: Eerdmans, 2000), 704; with D. E. Garland, *1 Corinthians*, BECNT (Grand Rapids: Baker, 2003), 432.

already noted in response to MacCarty, the NT treats the remaining commandments of the Decalogue as more timeless, and, therefore, so must I. When Pipa charges I fail to distinguish between Sabbath observance and the Sabbath day in Col 2:16–17, he is again correct. I do so because Paul introduces no such distinction into his text. When Pipa observes that one of the few known (non-Christian) usages of *sabbatismos* outside of Heb 4:9 is one in which the word means "superstitious religious rest," he concludes that therefore the word for Paul must include "religious observances" (p. 385). But why not on the same grounds conclude that it refers to "superstitious observances"? At any rate, one use from a later Greek writer is hardly an adequate sample space from which to draw valid linguistic generalizations. Again, one must pay attention to the author's flow of thought in the immediate context (see p. 350).

Pipa's concluding paragraph is inaccurate, unnecessary, offensive, and inappropriately polemical. I explicitly refer in my essay to prescriptive warrant for regular Christian gatherings for worship (Heb 10:25; see p. 353), and I could have added many other prescriptive and descriptive but exemplary texts. I find warrant for regular worship simply in *different* texts than those that explicitly mention the Sabbath.[63] Thus, for Pipa to allege that I leave no biblical warrant for weekly worship and am basically antinomian with respect to the practice flatly misrepresents my position.

Affirmation of Arand

At this point I can scarcely compose a "rejoinder" to Charles Arand, as I did to MacCarty and Pipa, because I find virtually nothing in his position with which to disagree. This could suggest several things. Maybe I am still more Lutheran than I realize, and maybe I imbibed more classic Lutheranism in my early years than I realized, since it is the liberal challenges to some of the fundamentals of the faith that I most remember from my teenage years in the old Lutheran Church in America. It could suggest, alternately, that what I have learned of classic Lutheran orthodoxy, both from Lutheran and non-Lutheran sources, in my more formal years of theological training, especially with its common, strong disjunction between law and gospel, was not as dominant an influence, at least for

---

63. Many of which appear throughout A. P. Ross, *Recalling the Hope of Glory: Biblical Worship from the Garden to the New Creation* (Grand Rapids: Kregel, 2006).

Martin Luther himself, as I have been led to believe. Or it could mean that Arand is just a much more sensitive and nuanced exponent of Lutheran beliefs than many have been.

At any rate, in my limited experience, conversations with hermeneutically trained classical Lutherans about issues of the role of the law in NT times have typically reminded me of similar conversations with thoughtful classic dispensationalists.[64] While I have strongly affirmed my sense of the salvation-historical distinctions between OT and NT ages, I actually lean a little more toward the Reformed view of more continuity between Testaments overall than the dispensationalist emphasis on discontinuity.[65] It's just that on certain issues, as I try to deal with each exegetically one at a time without presupposing some established theological grid, I find more discontinuity on some than on others. On the Sabbath issue I find much more discontinuity, so perhaps that is why I line up so closely with Arand's exposition of Lutheran thought on this topic.

I even agree with Arand in his three additional areas for exploration. Creation/new creation is an even better salvation-historical distinction to make than law/gospel, and maybe I just don't know enough of Luther to recognize classic Lutheranism in that schema. I also agree that we shouldn't gratuitously change the day of worship in a given culture or even the principle of one day in seven without good reason. If it sounded like I was arguing otherwise, then I need to clarify that point. I thought I was suggesting that sometimes there *were* good reasons for doing something different, but short of this I am not someone who is inclined to "fix" what is not "broken." Finally, I heartily agree with Arand and Luther on the centrality of the Word in worship. I am grateful that Arand and I see eye to eye in so many ways, lest my views otherwise have appeared as the odd one out in this volume!

Conclusion

One way in which MacCarty, Pipa, and Arand differ from me, if I have read them correctly, is that each of them expounds the

---

64. See, e.g., the similarities between the relevant chapters in *The Law, the Gospel, and the Modern Christian: Five Views*, ed. W. G. Strickland (Grand Rapids: Zondervan, 1993), even when the Lutheran viewpoint depicted is described merely as "modified," and modified specifically in a slightly Reformed direction.

65. On both of which, see further *Continuity and Discontinuity: Perspectives on the Relationship Between the Old and New Testaments*, ed. J. S. Feinberg (Wheaton: Crossway, 1988).

Scriptures out of a definable theological and hermeneutical tradition with venerable pedigree. At the risk of oversimplifying, MacCarty starts with the "functional nonnegotiable"[66] that the Ten Commandments are absolute moral laws for all time and that nothing in Scripture is more central than they are. Therefore, no matter what text anywhere may seem to teach something different, it cannot. We must therefore keep wrestling with the text until we come up with the next most likely interpretation that preserves the "big ten" inviolable. Pipa, on the other hand, starts with the teaching of Calvin and the Westminster divines as embodying the most inviolable theological and hermeneutical principles and therefore is quite happy, indeed, even insists on transferring Sabbath theology to Sunday without remainder. Any arguments, even biblical ones, which suggest otherwise, must be resisted and their proponents vilified. Sadly, in my experience, of all the different theological subdivisions of evangelicalism, it seems that Reformed theologians more than anyone else (for some reason) feel the need for heightened polemics in their rhetoric. I refer readers to my discussion above about the grave dangers inherent in such polemics (p. 408).[67] Arand, too, sees his task as expounding a preexisting system, that is, a Lutheran approach to the Bible, even if with more latitude for creativity and nuance of that position than MacCarty and Pipa insert into theirs.

Of course, most all theological traditions within evangelical Christianity arose and have been preserved because at least some and often many of their tenets best reflect what Scripture actually teaches. But, as the centuries go by, the danger is always that followers of a given theological tradition may not rethink the biblical data for themselves, or rethink it as rigorously as its founders did, or even feel they have the freedom to rethink it as rigorously. What once were seemingly radical ideas diverging from the mainstream and returning to Scripture then become the encrusted dogmatism *of* that tradition from which adherents may diverge only at their peril.[68]

---

66. That is, "preunderstandings" that are theoretically open to change but would require massive amounts of data and almost an entire worldview shift to precipitate such change.

67. See further C. L. Blomberg, "The New Testament Definition of Heresy (or When Do Jesus and the Apostles Really Get Mad?)" *JETS* 45 (2002): 59–72.

68. As has happened at times in all three traditions represented by the other authors of this book.

As a professional biblical scholar, I always try hard to resist falling into such "ruts," though I am much aware of my fallibility in this respect. My goal, at least, is always to let scriptural exegesis more than presuppositions, "functional nonnegotiables," or theological traditions determine my conclusions. And if that leaves me with a disparate conglomeration of beliefs on a variety of topics that don't easily fit one well-known and existing label or branch of historical theology, then so be it.[69] Indeed, I almost feel reassured when that happens that I was able to preserve some measure of objectivity. When I subsequently discover that others have created a similar synthesis, and perhaps even given it a label, my reassurance grows. That is largely how my views of biblical teaching on the Sabbath have developed. Whether that makes my case more persuasive than any other must of course be for readers to judge. I remain grateful for the opportunity to participate in this dialogue and hope that a wide swath of readership finds the format of multiple-views books like this one as helpful in their own quests for theological convictions and understanding as I have found them over the years.

---

69. I am not hereby opposing systematic theology, merely its abuse. For an excellent example of how they should properly interact, see D. A. Carson, "Unity and Diversity in the New Testament: The Possibility of Systematic Theology," in *Scripture and Truth*, ed. D. A. Carson and J. D. Woodbridge (Grand Rapids: Zondervan, 1983), 65–95.

Name Index

Scripture Index